Demystifying Theories in Tourism Research

Demystifying Theories in Tourism Research

Edited by

Kelly S. Bricker
Professor, Department of Parks, Recreation, and Tourism, College of Health, University of Utah, USA

and

Holly Donohoe
Assistant Professor, Department of Tourism, Recreation and Sport Management; Associate Director, Eric Friedheim Tourism Institute; Associate Director, Tourism Crisis Management, University of Florida, USA

www.cabi.org

CABI is a trading name of CAB International

CABI
Nosworthy Way
Wallingford
Oxfordshire OX10 8DE
UK

Tel: +44 (0)1491 832111
Fax: +44 (0)1491 833508
E-mail: info@cabi.org
Website: www.cabi.org

CABI
745 Atlantic Avenue
8th Floor
Boston, MA 02111
USA

Tel: +1 617 682 9015
E-mail: cabi-nao@cabi.org

A catalogue record for this book is available from the British Library, London, UK.

Library of Congress Cataloging-in-Publication Data

Demystifying theories in tourism research / edited by Kelly S. Bricker, Professor, Department of Parks, Recreation, and Tourism, College of Health, University of Utah, USA and Holly Donohoe, Assistant Professor, Department of Tourism, Recreation & Sport Management; Associate Director, Eric Friedheim Tourism Institute; Associate Director, Tourism Crisis Management, University of Florida, USA.
    pages cm
  Includes bibliographical references and index.
  ISBN 978-1-78064-691-6 (pbk. : alk. paper) -- ISBN 978-1-78064-722-7 (hardback : alk. paper) 1. Tourism--Research. I. Bricker, Kelly S., editor. II. Donohoe, Holly, editor.

  G155.A1D459 2015
  910'.01--dc23

                                        2015020192

ISBN-13: 978 1 78064 722 7 (hbk)
         978 1 78064 691 6 (pbk)

Commissioning editor: Claire Parfitt
Associate editor: Alexandra Lainsbury
Production editor: Tim Kapp

Typeset by SPi, Pondicherry, India.
Printed and bound by Gutenberg Press Ltd, Tarxien, Malta.

Contents

Editor Biographies

Kelly S. Bricker is Chair and Professor in the Department of Parks, Recreation, and Tourism, College of Health, University of Utah. Dr. Bricker's academic interests center on the impact of outdoor recreation on quality of life, sustainable management of natural resources and outdoor experiences, and social, cultural, and ecological impacts of nature-based tourism and recreation. Prior to pursuing her PhD, she worked for more than 20 years in the outdoors as guide, manager, and ecotourism business owner of diverse outdoor adventure programs. Her PhD research with the Pennsylvania State University focused on the value of natural resources, sustainability, and management of natural areas. Dr. Bricker has completed research on the impacts of outdoor recreation and tourism on quality of life and well-being, social and environmental impacts of tourism, and sustainable management of parks and protected areas. She has authored and edited books on sustainability, which highlight sustainable development goals in *Sustainable Tourism & the Millennium Development Goals: Effecting Positive Change;* educational texts focused on adventure education in *Adventure Programming and Travel for the 21st Century* and graduate education in *Demystifying Theories in Tourism Research.* Most recently, relevant to current projects, she has co-edited *This Land Is Your Land: Toward a Better Understanding of Nature's Resiliency-Building and Restorative Power for Armed Forces Personnel, Veterans, and Their Families.* Dr. Bricker serves on the boards of the Global Sustainable Tourism Council, The International Ecotourism Society, The Multi-Stakeholder Advisory Committee of the United Nations World Tourism Organization 10YFP for sustainable development, and the Tourism and Protected Area Specialist Group of the IUCN. Mailing address: Department of Parks, Recreation, and Tourism, College of Health, University of Utah, 1901 E. So. Campus Drive, Salt Lake City, UT 84112-0920, USA. E-mail address: kelly.bricker@health.utah.edu

Holly Donohoe is an assistant professor in the Department of Tourism, Recreation and Sport Management at the University of Florida. Central to her research are critical examinations of tourism planning, management and marketing while evaluation science and its use of select methods and techniques for risk, impact, and policy analysis are considered her realm of expertise. Current research includes projects related to vector-borne diseases and their impact on the tourism industry. Studies range from baseline studies of public awareness, the analysis of public health and tourism crisis management policy frameworks, to the assessment of occupational risk for tourism and recreation professionals in at-risk environments. Mailing address: Eric Friedheim Tourism Institute, Department of Tourism, Recreation and Sport Management, University of Florida, PO Box 118208, Gainesville, FL 32611-8208 USA. E-mail address: hdonohoe@hhp.ufl.edu

Author Biographies

Alisha Ali is a senior lecturer at Sheffield Hallam University, UK, where she teaches in the areas of ICT, innovation, and sustainable tourism and focuses on the specific applications of these concepts to the tourism and hospitality industry. Her research focuses on computer-mediated sustainability, tourism innovation and destination management. She completed a BSc in Tourism Management and a Masters in Management and her PhD, which concentrated on investigating the uses and applications of ICT for sustainable tourism for destinations. She is also the Academic Support Officer for the PhD students in the Sheffield Business School and course leader for the MSc in International Hospitality Design and Management Consultancy. Alisha has delivered guest lectures at Cesar Ritz Colleges, Switzerland, HAAGA-HELIA University of Applied Sciences and teaches Hotel Benchmarking to students of the Ecole Hoteliere de Lausanne and The Emirates Academy of Hospitality Management. She has recently published a textbook on ICT for sustainable tourism. Mailing address: Sheffield Business School, Sheffield Hallam University, City Campus, Howard Street, Sheffield, S1 1WB, UK. E-mail address: Alisha.Ali@shu.ac.uk

Kathleen Andereck is the Director of the School of Community Resources and Development at Arizona State University where she holds the rank of professor. Dr Andereck is also a Senior Sustainability Scientist with ASU's Global Institute for Sustainability. Her research focuses on the tourism experience from the perspective of both visitors and residents particularly as it applies to sustainable community tourism development. Some of her specific areas of interest include tourism and quality of life, residents' attitudes toward tourism, volunteer tourism, and tourist behavior in recreation settings. Dr Andereck has done research work with a diversity of organizations and agencies at the federal and state level including the Bureau of Land Management, the USDA Forest Service, the Arizona Office of Tourism and the Arizona Department of Transportation. Mailing address: School of Community Resources and Development, Arizona State University, 411 N. Central Avenue, Ste. 550, Phoenix, AZ 85004, USA. E-mail address: kandereck@asu.edu

Laura Becerra is a pursuing a PhD in Forestry and Conservation Sciences at the University of Montana. Her work has focused on understanding the link between conservation and economic development through nature-based tourism (NBT). Her PhD dissertation in Zambia examined issues of equity, governance, and power in relation to NBT. Laura completed an MS in Environmental Studies from the University of Montana, with an emphasis on sustainable tourism development in Patagonia, Chile. Laura has worked on a variety of conservation projects in rural areas of Western USA, South America, and Southern Africa. She has been involved with the International Seminar on Protected Area Management, an intensive 3-week course for conservation leaders from the global south for the last 6 years. She currently resides in Kenya. E-mail address: becerra.lb@gmail.com

Rosemary Black is an Associate Professor in the School of Environmental Sciences at Charles Sturt University where she teaches and undertakes research in the fields of tour guiding, ecotourism, heritage interpretation, sustainable behaviors, and adventure tourism. She is one of the world's leading experts in tour guiding research and has published extensively in this field. Rosemary began her career working in the tourism and conservation industries and later became an academic. She has produced six books and over 50 publications. Rosemary holds a Ministerial appointment with the New South Wales National Parks and Wildlife Service and is an active member of the Guiding Organisations of Australia National Committee. She is an Associate Editor with the *Journal of Ecotourism* and the *Journal of Interpretation Research*. She undertakes applied research with industry partners including protected area management agencies, and tourism and community-based organizations. Rosemary is a qualified diver, cross-country ski instructor, and adventure travel leader, enjoys travelling, and is passionate about life. Mailing address: School of Environmental Sciences, Charles Sturt University, PO Box 789, Albury, NSW 2640, Australia. E-mail address: rblack@csu.edu.au

Doris A. Carson is a human/economic geographer interested in the socioeconomic development of communities in sparsely populated areas. She completed her PhD at James Cook University (Australia) in 2011, looking at the dynamics of tourism innovation systems in remote resource peripheries and the complex relationships between tourism and the "staples trap." In 2014, Doris completed a post-doctoral research fellowship at the University of South Australia (Centre for Rural Health and Community Development), where she conducted research on rural community resilience, the concept of Indigenous itinerants as tourists, and the value of using a local systems perspective in rural innovation studies. She is now a researcher and lecturer within the Department of Geography & Economic History at Umeå University in northern Sweden. Her current research focuses on understanding how different types of mobile populations—such as tourists, lifestyle migrants, seasonal workers, and other temporary populations—impact on innovation capacity in small rural communities. Mailing address: Department of Geography & Economic History, Umeå University, Sweden. E-mail address: doris.carson@umu.se

Deepak Chhabra is an associate professor at Arizona State University. She also holds the title of Senior Sustainability Scientist at the Global Institute of Sustainability, Arizona State University. Three broad themes underline her research: (i) sustainable and smart marketing of tourism. This includes a critical examination of the commoditization of authenticity as a marketing tool to draw visitors and revenue for the associated heritage institutions; (ii) determination of visitor expenditures and economic benefits of different forms of heritage tourism for the host communities and the local and state governments. This includes calculating direct and indirect (multiplier) impacts; and (iii) application of social science theories to real life situations and persons and examining their dynamism among diverse constituencies on the supply as well as the demand side. She has presented research papers at global, national, and regional conferences. She has also published in leading refereed journals. These include the *Annals of Tourism Research*, *Journal of Travel Research*, *Tourism Analysis*, *Event Management*, *Loisir*, *Journal of Heritage Tourism*, and *Journal of Vacation Marketing*. Moreover, she has served as a project director and principal investigating officer on several statewide projects associated with socioeconomic impacts of tourism. In addition to the nationwide, statewide, and local newspaper coverage, some of her results have been broadcast on radio and television across several states in the USA. Mailing address: Arizona State University, School of Community Resources and Development, 411 N Central Avenue, Phoenix, AZ 85004, USA. E-mail address: deepak.chhabra@asu.edu

Statia Elliot is the Director of the University of Guelph's School of Hospitality and Tourism Management with a combination of academic study in business and over 10 years' work experience in tourism. From Consultant with Tourism Ontario, to Director of Marketing for Travel Manitoba, Statia's career spans the fields of marketing, research, policy, and management. A graduate of Carleton University in Ottawa, she has published in top journals, such as the *Journal of Travel Research*, *Cornell Hospitality Quarterly*, and the *Journal of Business Research*. Statia is the 2015 Chair of the Travel and Tourism Research Association Canada Chapter, and actively participates in hospitality, food and tourism conferences and committees internationally. She researches destination marketing, place image, and e-marketing. Statia has traveled extensively, lived and studied in South Korea, and now makes Guelph, Ontario her home. Mailing address: School of Hospitality and Tourism Management, University of Guelph, Guelph, Ontario, Canada. E-mail address: statia@uoguelph.ca

Laurlyn K. Harmon is an assistant professor in Recreation Management at the University of Wisconsin—La Crosse. She received her doctorate in Leisure Studies at The Pennsylvania State University and her bachelor's and master's degrees from Michigan State University. As an educator, she emphasizes the role of "self as learner" and encourages students to engage in collaborative and empowered learning by using authentic and locally relevant projects. She uses a social-psychological approach in her research, focusing on the person–place relationship and the transformative nature of outdoor environments with a particular interest in the role technology plays in facilitating interactions with nature. Her scholarly contributions build on her Landscape Architect practitioner work by paying tribute to and valuing the role places play in our leisure experiences. Laurie has recently published in *Children, Youth and Environments*, *Environmental Ethics*, and *International Journal of Culture, Tourism & Hospitality Research* and presented at NRPA, George Wright Society, and NAAEE. Mailing address: Department of Recreation Management & Therapeutic Recreation, University of Wisconsin—La Crosse, 2044 Health Science Center, 1725 State Street, La Crosse, WI 54601, USA. E-mail address: lharmon@uwlax.edu

Mercedes M. Hunt is in the final year of her doctoral program at the University of Utah in the Department of Parks, Recreation and Tourism. She is currently studying the sustainability of US convention centers using systems theory. She has spent the last 3 years actively involved in The International Ecotourism Society (TIES) first as the Events Director, then as the Managing Director, and finally as a voluntary consultant, where she has overseen and worked various TIES events, including four Ecotourism and Sustainable Tourism Conferences in the USA, Kenya, Brazil, and Ecuador. She received her bachelor's degree in Leisure Studies and Recreation at Cal State Northridge and master's degree in Recreation, Parks and Tourism at San Francisco State University, focused on Ecotourism and Sustainable Tourism. She maintains an active membership with PCMA, GMIC, ESPA, IAVM, and TIES. Mailing address: Department of Parks, Recreation, and Tourism, College of Health, University of Utah, 1901 E So. Campus Drive, Salt Lake City, UT 84112–0920, USA. E-mail address: mercedes.hunt@utah.edu

Claudia Jurowski is currently a professor in the School of Hotel and Restaurant Management in the W.A. Franke College of Business at Northern Arizona University, and has been teaching and working with the travel and tourism industry for more than 35 years. Her career in the industry began as a resort owner/operator where she doubled the worth of her business in the first 3 years of operation and worked as executive director of the Fort Gibson Lake Association. Academically, she earned a PhD degree from Virginia Polytechnic Institute and State University, an MBA from Oklahoma City University, an MA in French from Miami University, and a BSEd from Bowling Green State University. She has served her professional community as board member and president of the Greater Western Chapter of the Travel and Tourism Research Association and Chair of the Module Development Committee of Business Enterprises for Sustainable Travel Education Network. Her academic research interests focus on tourism development issues including sustainable tourism development, environmental management, quality service, human resource management, and marketing. Her work has won awards from the International Travel and Tourism Research Association and from the hospitality educators' organization, CHRIE. Mailing address: School of Hotel and Restaurant Management, W.A. Franke College of Business, Northern Arizona University, Box 5638 NAU, Flagstaff, AZ 86011-5638, USA. E-mail address: claudia.jurowski@nau.edu

Rhonda Koster's research interests focus on working with and for rural communities in examining the contribution of various forms of tourism towards rural sustainability. A specific research interest is the role of and capacity for community-based tourism in First Nations communities in Canada. As a result of an ongoing, multi-year project with the Red Rock Indian Band, her research collaboration was recognized with an Aboriginal Partnership Research Award in 2010, from Lakehead University. In these areas she has conducted research and published on: determinants of success in rural tourism planning; experiential tourism development as a niche for rural communities; the role of Appreciative Inquiry in tourism development; the opportunities for gateway communities in relationship to protected areas; the role of rural tourism in the Canadian urban fringe; and frameworks for evaluating tourism as a community economic development endeavor. Dr Koster has been the recipient of two Social Sciences and Humanities Research Council funded research projects. One project examined the inter-community and governance level networks with an aim to determine how these interactions can contribute to and impede a regional approach to tourism development in rural resourced-based regions. She has several publications related to this research including an examination of the hindrances and opportunities for tourism development in various peripheral regions of Canada, and theoretical modeling of regionalism as an approach to tourism development. Dr Koster was also part of a team examining aging-in-place in a remote, former mining community; several publications have also resulted from this work including the role of the local hospital and volunteerism in supporting the health and well-being of a community. Mailing address: School of Outdoor Recreation, Parks and Tourism, Lakehead University, Thunder Bay, Ontario, Canada. E-mail address: rkoster@lakeheadu.ca

Norma Polovitz Nickerson is interested in the impacts of tourism to the environment and surrounding communities. She focuses her work on maintaining a viable tourism industry throughout the state, while sustaining the quality of life and natural resources that Montana has to offer. As research professor and Director of the Institute for Tourism and Recreation Research, Norma and her team conduct research to provide information that will help the tourism industry make informed decisions about planning, promotion, and management to entities that provide services to visitors. She is very much interested in finding the balance between the tourism industry and sustaining our environmental resources, along with the social and environmental impacts of tourism.

Ara Pachmayer is currently an instructor at Arizona State University. She earned her PhD in Community Resources and Development focusing on the relationship between participation in study abroad programs, cross-cultural understanding and intercultural competence among university students, considering the study-abroad student as a tourist. Her primary research interests include the impact of tourism development on perception of community life, sustainable and community based tourism development and qualitative research methods, the common thread in the research being how hosts and travelers experience tourism and the resulting impacts on communities and individuals. Mailing address: School of Community Resources and Development, Arizona State University, 411 N. Central Avenue, Ste. 550, Phoenix, AZ 85004, USA. E-mail address: ara@asu.edu

Rhonda Phillips' research and outreach activities are focused on community and economic development and planning along with well-being. She is Dean of the Honors College and professor in Purdue's Agricultural Economics Department, and has held certifications in economic and community development (CEcD, International Economic Development Council) and urban and regional planning (AICP, American Institute of Certified Planners). Honors include serving twice as a Fulbright Scholar—UK Ulster Policy Fellow Fulbright Scholar and a Senior Specialist to Panama. Rhonda is author or editor of 18 books, including *Growing Livelihoods: Local Food Systems and Community Development*; *Sustainable Communities, Creating a Durable Local Economy*; *Community Development Indicators Measuring Systems*; and *Introduction to Community Development*. She formerly served as a Senior Sustainability Scientist, Global Institute of Sustainability for Arizona State University's School of Sustainability and Professor, School of Community Resources and Development, and Director, Center for Building Better Communities at the University of Florida. Mailing address: AICP, Purdue University, Agricultural Economics and Honors College, 205 N Russell Street, West Lafayette, IN 47906, USA. E-mail address: rphillips@purdue.edu

Yvette Reisinger is a Professor of Marketing in the College of Business Administration, Gulf University for Science and Technology (GUST), Kuwait. Prior to joining GUST she taught in the USA and Australia. She has a long-standing research interest in tourism, culture, and communication, particularly in the area of cultural influences on tourist behavior and destination marketing. Her other research interests include acculturation and human transformation through tourism. She is the author or editor of several books and more than 150 academic papers. Her books *Cross-Cultural Behaviour in Tourism: Concepts and Analysis* (2003), *International Tourism: Cultures and Behaviour* (2009), and *Transformational Tourism* (2013, 2015) provide a path to very important fields of tourism study in a global world and the first account of tourism research in these areas. She is now focusing on the multicultural aspects of tourism and its influence on quality of life. Mailing address: College of Business Administration, Gulf University for Sciences and Technology, Mishref, Kuwait. E-mail address: reisinger.y@gust.edu.kw

Bianca Reyes attended the University of Florida where she earned a BSc in recreation, parks, and tourism with a specialization in hospitality management. She interned in hotels in Brazil, where she learned hotel management skills, but became disenchanted by the commercial aspects of tourism. Upon return to the USA she pursued the deeper qualities of tourism and recreation by earning an MSc in the same field but this time with a different specialization in ecotourism, tropical conservation, and development. In July 2012 she participated as a student peace ambassador in a project geared towards stimulating peace through tourism on the Turkish-Armenian border and formulated a 5-year tourism plan for a conservation site in Belize. She now works for Holbrook Travel, a well-known travel wholesaler that wholeheartedly supports conservation through individual and group travel, specializing in environmental education and natural history programs in Central and South America, Africa, and the Pacific and Polar regions. Mailing address: Department of Tourism, Recreation and Sport Management, University of Florida, PO Box 118208, Gainesville, FL 32611-8208, USA. E-mail address: bianx61@ufl.edu

Nicole Vaugeois is the British Columbia (BC) Regional Innovation Chair in Tourism (BCRIC) and Sustainable Rural Development at Vancouver Island University and the co-director of the World Leisure Center (WLC) of Excellence in Sustainability and Innovation. In her role as BCRIC, she supports people in rural BC communities to diversify through amenity-based opportunities like recreation and tourism by providing insights, innovation, and ideas. She collaborates with academics from other institutions and maintains strong ties with policy makers in the provincial and federal government to ensure that her research informs decision making. As co-director for the WLC, Nicole is seeking to gather academics interested in the concepts of sustainability and innovation in leisure around shared research, teaching, and practice. Nicole's research interests include amenity-based development, innovation in tourism, sustainability models, and population mobility into and out of rural areas. Outside of her discipline, Nicole maintains an active research portfolio in understanding how academics can best share their work to create impact using different forms of knowledge mobilization. She is also a teaching scholar who studies the uptake of knowledge by learners, particularly in the area of research methods. Her blog is available at: http://sustainableruraltourism.ca/. Mailing address: BC Regional Innovation Chair in Tourism and Sustainable Rural Development, Vancouver Island University, 900 Fifth Street, Nanaimo, BC, Canada V9R 5H5. E-mail address: nicole.vaugeois@ viu.ca

Betty Weiler is Research Professor in the School of Business and Tourism at Southern Cross University (Australia) and has been researching and teaching tourism in Australian universities for the past 25 years. She has published 90 papers and book chapters. Much of Betty's research has focused on nature-based and heritage tourism, communication with tourists via interpretation, and tour guiding, including guide roles, competencies, training, accreditation, perceptions of quality, and contributions to sustainability. She has undertaken research with domestic and international visitors and research on tour guides in several locations, including North America, Latin America, South-east Asia, and Australia including in national parks, zoos, and heritage attractions. More recently her work has focused on the use of persuasive communication to influence tourist behavior and on visitor planning and management, particularly in protected areas, heritage and nature-based attractions. Betty is known for her collaborations with a range of industry partners particularly managers of protected areas, heritage, and wildlife attractions. Mailing address: School of Business and Tourism, Southern Cross University, Locked Mail Bag 4, Coolangatta, QLD 4225, Australia. E-mail address: betty.weiler@ scu.edu.au

Shengnan (Nancy) Zhao is an Assistant Professor at California State University, Long Beach. She earned her PhD in Community Resources and Development with a focus on Tourism Management from Arizona State University. She has a Master's degree in Tourism Management from Zhejiang University, China, and a Bachelor's degree in Public Administration from Fuzhou University, China. Her research interests are primarily in the fields of human-environment interaction in tourism systems, sustainable tourism, community-based tourism development, heritage tourism, and the politics of tourism. Mailing address: 1250 Bellflower Blvd., ET-101C, Long Beach, CA 90840, USA. E-mail address: shengnan.zhao@csulb.edu

Acknowledgements

From idea to fruition, the development of this book has been a long journey! The idea for this text originated from a writing retreat held in southern Utah hosted through the University of Utah at Zion Ponderosa Ranch in February of 2011. While the contributors since the book's origins have changed somewhat, the original thought and outline was developed by: Cathy Hsu, Christine Oschell, Claudia Jurowski, Deborah Kerstetter, Holly Donohoe, Kathy Andereck, Kelly Bricker, Laurlyn K. Harmon, Lori Pennington-Gray, Norma Nickerson, Rosemary Black, Samantha Rich, and Callie Spencer (now Shultz)—we thank this group for their contributions, creativity, and knowledge! We also appreciate the support of Zion Ponderosa Ranch and Dr Michael Kane and his team for hosting this retreat.

We also acknowledge the support we received from many individuals and organizations without whom this book would not have been completed. First and foremost we would like to thank all the contributors for writing, revising, and submitting their chapters for inclusion in this text—it has been a very long journey, and we appreciate their patience and unwavering support. The support of the University of Utah and University of Florida where Kelly and Holly respectively work as academics is also greatly appreciated. We would like to express our sincere thanks for the support of Claire Parfitt and Alexandra Lainsbury and all the staff at CABI. They have been a delight to work with and helped make the text a reality of which we are very proud. Finally, we would also like to thank our respective partners, Nate and Jan for their support and acknowledge the lost time together on weekends and evenings. And to all of those along the journey, who provided us with academic curiosity and critical review, we thank you for your contributions to the quality and enrichment of our academic lives. And last, but certainly not least, our sincerest thanks go to the reviewers, who generously gave their time and expertise to provide feedback and comments for the authors and who have enhanced the quality of the chapters: Kathy Andereck, Laura Becerra, Zac Cole, Rich Harrill, Mette Hjalager, Marion Joppe, Claudia Jurowksi, George Karlis, Rhonda Phillips, Laura Prazeres, Chris Ryan, Svetlana Stepchenkova, Brijesh Thapa, and Jane Widfeldt.

Dedications

This book is dedicated to the many people who have helped me pursue a career in academe and learn the value of research. From my early mentors at Lincoln Land Community College who demonstrated a deep-seated passion for knowledge and sharing their knowledge in interesting and experiential ways, to Dr Frank Lupton who inspired me to pursue dreams, work hard, and always expand my comfort zone; and, Dr Nick DiGrino who unlocked doors for me to higher education. Pursuing the PhD at Penn State was indeed a highlight in my academic journey. My committee members supported a range of intellectual pursuits and provided guidance along the way, for which I am forever grateful. A heartfelt *vinaka vaka levu* to Dr Kerstetter, Dr Graefe, Dr Caldwell, and Dr Wright. As I continue my academic career, I am also grateful to those colleagues who continue to inspire, educate—a heartfelt thank you to the Zuni's, Dr Dustin, and my colleagues on this text, and co-editor, Dr Holly Donohoe—whose youth and enthusiasm inspired its completion. Family is an important support system and provides a place of comfort and love through all the trials and tribulations of an academic career, and for this I am truly grateful to my loving husband Nate, my parents for all their support over many years, and my sister Kim and brother Ken and their families—without everyone, this text or much else of what I do in life would not be possible.

Kelly S. Bricker

This book is dedicated to the many individuals that have encouraged me to pursue my passions for academic work and to those that have inspired me along the way. First and foremost, I must thank my family for their unconditional and lasting support and encouragement. I must specifically thank my new husband, Jan, who is unwavering in his support of my academic pursuits regardless of their timing, location, or requirements. I would like to thank Dr Lori Pennington-Gray who, in addition to being a great friend, has been an incredible mentor as I fumble my way towards tenure. I would like to thank my co-editor Dr Kelly Bricker who, through catalyzing and facilitating the creative musings of a group of incredible women and scholars, made this book possible.

Holly Donohoe

1 Theoretical Perspectives on Tourism—An Introduction

KELLY S. BRICKER,[1]* HOLLY DONOHOE,[2]
LAURA BECERRA, AND NORMA NICKERSON[3]

[1]Department of Parks, Recreation, and Tourism, College of Health, University of Utah, Salt Lake City, Utah; [2]Eric Friedheim Tourism Institute, Department of Tourism, Recreation and Sport Management, University of Florida, Gainesville, Florida; [3]Institute for Tourism & Recreation Research, College of Forestry and Conservation, University of Montana, Missoula, Montana

Why this Book?

During October of 2010, a researcher in tourism posted to a list serve of tourism researchers and posed various questions within his post:

> I'm currently trying to find major theories in tourism. I have been doing some readings but somehow I could not find any major tourism theories (the ones that were developed within tourism studies). To my knowledge, we always borrow, adopt and adapt theories from other traditional fields (e.g. psychology, sociology, etc.) to suit our need (research?). We do have several major models or conceptual frameworks such as the Butler's destination life cycle, Doxey Irridex and the like. However, based on the definition of a theory in social science, I would not call those as theories (they do not have an interrelated set of constructs to predict a certain phenomenon (behavior?). I have asked several tourism scholars about this stuff, and somehow they could not name major theories in tourism either. So I was wondering if any of you could help me with this stuff. Do we really have theories that were developed within tourism studies? If so what are those? Or do we simply assume that we have theories while in reality we don't
>
> (Trinet Discussion Post, 18 October 2010)

This post produced several reactions and responses, including more questions and perhaps a bit more confusion than any kind of consensus or clarity on the subject. Selected examples of the list serve responses (names of respondents purposefully not referenced here) relevant to the question posed included:

> I do not understand why theory is necessary for a discipline or why you need theories in order to substantiate an argument. Among the social sciences, even economics (considered the queen of the social sciences) does not have a substantial theory.
>
> (Trinet Post, 19 October 2010)

> A theory seeks to explain how and why a phenomenon occurs, with reference to: abstract concepts, the relationships between those concepts, and reasons for those relationships.

*Corresponding author, e-mail: kelly.bricker@health.utah.edu

I am still not aware if there is a universally accepted definition of theory. In my mind I think in social sciences context theory is somewhat a "gut feeling" and hypothesis is an educated guess with regard to that gut feeling.

(Trinet Post, 19 October 2010)

A theory is an interrelated set of concepts (sometimes conceptions, that is, concepts-in-the-making) which explain a phenomenon, either abstract or concrete, through their logicality. The logicality may not necessarily be philosophical, but may be ordinary socio-logic (the kind that goes into the understanding of social phenomena, like marriage and permissible sex, or, the opposite, incest, and religion, magic and so on) and linguistic logic. In our everyday lives we also have theories or, more often, working theories, such as how a car functions, how to drive a car, how to use a computer, etc. The logic of science is not the logic of religion. However, science can be partly understood through religion and vice versa. A theory, then, is essentially a way of understanding the world, but the types of explanations may differ: science is a mode of explanation (as different from philosopher Carl G. Hempel's term "model of explanation"), so is religion, and literature and paintings are also modes (albeit artistic modes) of explanation

(Trinet Post, 19 October 2010)

And as a somewhat closing post, after all of the banter to and fro:

After all this elucidating discussion and some rough and tumble banter on "terms of the trade" from various academic corners, I think the ring is now free again for your question, which was:

"So I was wondering if any of you could help me with this stuff. Do we really have theories that were developed within tourism studies? If so what are those? or we simply assume that we have th [sic]"

(Trinet Post, 18 October 2010)

As the previous exchange shows, and funny enough, we really only have managed to spell out the "th" in "theory." I think that all contributions are truly helpful in a) answering your question and b) showing up the dilemma tourism scholars find themselves in. A theory can be comprised of a set of cohesive thoughts, concepts or even constructs that attempt to describe all or essential components of a phenomenon, considered sufficient to distinguish it from other phenomena whereby it is important to note that the other phenomena must be contiguous or somehow surrounding the phenomenon under scrutiny. This creates the context within which the theory resides. As the discussion has shown however … theories can be anywhere on a continuum from being vague right through to being as substantive as laws are made out to be. Unfortunately, even these laws may also become vague again in turn not only because new paradigms emerge but far less dramatic, by changing focus, context or relevance…

As we are all battling our way to publications through the gauntlet of reviewers who may or may not have their own agendas, and may or may not have the insight that their own stance may be blinkered, the task of constructively working towards a cohesive theory of tourism has been lost for many amongst us. Some researchers have become consultants, milking tourism for what it is worth, others have redirected their energy back towards their home-discipline or wandered off into new imaginations and to substantiate new theories such as "mobility." You have found yourself right in the middle of it … The problem why you do not find a well-structured theory in tourism as comprehensive as the periodic table, for one reason, is because of the above. Another reason is, of course, nobody (apart from people like Leiper, Kaspar or maybe Moutinho, Macintosh and Goeldner to finger a few, … but they do exist) has tried to create something like a periodic table of the tourism phenomenon as yet, probably because only few of us

K.S. Bricker, H. Donohoe, L. Becerra, and N. Nickerson

are willing to listen carefully enough to what others are saying, and honest enough to consider and firmly state our own limited point of view (of course, the flip-side is that we do the same as critics). To answer your question then, all of the theories you mentioned (Doxey's or Butler's or even my own, for that matter, on motivation and expectation formation) are all tourism theories albeit begged, stolen or borrowed from different disciplines and applied to comprehend (aspects of) the phenomenon of tourism. That all of these and other theories of tourism do not appear yet in our own "periodic table" is just a reflection of the state tourism research is in. These theories may, one day, become part of the tourism research domain, if we keep on working towards that end (and I believe that there is such an end but that requires more time and space).

(Trinet Post, 19 October 2010)

As students entering higher education with an interest in studying tourism, many are confronted with a sea of confusion with respect to understanding theories, conceptual frameworks, and how to apply these ideas to a research endeavor. The more one delves into the literature, the more one can become overwhelmed by the process of identifying a problem, identifying a lens from which to view the problem, and then ultimately testing the problem or ideas we have about a problem.

So What is a Theory?

Our intent is not to provide a lesson on theory or theory development, however it may be helpful to review a few ideas surrounding theory and terms. Given the discussion above, you may already realize that the term "theory" is one of the most elusive and misunderstood terms in science and as a result there are many working definitions. McCool (1995: 11) defined theory as "a formulation of apparent relationships or underlying principles of certain observed phenomena which has been verified to some degree." Theory has also been defined as "a closed system from which are generated predictions about the nature of the world, predictions that must be open to some empirical test" (Dubin, 1969: 8). Others including Deutsch (1972: 19) describe theory as "a coding scheme for the storage and retrieval of information." Babbie (2010: 44) describes theory as "systematic sets of interrelated statements intended to explain some aspect of social life."

Babbie (2010: 58) sees theory as serving as a tool, which guides inquiry and analysis. Theory guides inquiry, for example, in shaping the development of a hypothesis. A hypothesis is a specified testable expectation about empirical reality that follows an expectation about the nature of things derived from a theory. Theory also shapes research analysis by aiming to explain observations through concepts. Concepts are abstract elements representing classes of phenomena within the field of study (McCool, 1995).

Briefly, there are two models or ways of understanding how theories are developed, the deductive and the inductive models. In the deductive model, research is used to test theory (i.e. scientific method). In the inductive model, theories are developed from the analysis of research data (i.e. observation, then theoretical application, e.g. grounded theory) (Strauss and Corbin, 2007).

Theories function in research in several ways. Theories, for example, prevent research errors. They assist in making sense of observed patterns and they shape and direct research efforts. Theories also guide and specify paradigms. Paradigms are the various vantage points, frames or perspectives on an issue or concept, and theories aim to explain the issue and the perspective under which it was observed. A paradigm is also defined as a "fundamental frame of reference used to organize observations and reasoning" (Babbie, 2010: 33). Theoretical underpinnings are often reinforced and operationalized through models. According to Frankfort-Nachmias and Nachmias (1992: 44), models are:

> representations of reality, delineating certain aspects of the real world as being relevant to the problem under investigation, exposing complex relationships and enabling the formulation of empirically testable propositions regarding the relationships.

Hence, models are used in research to simplify theory, and demonstrate its relevance and applicability in real life.

Specifically with graduate students of tourism studies in mind, we have developed this text to attempt to "demystify" this process somewhat through the provision of a range of topics relative to tourism studies that have applied various theories or conceptual frameworks to address problems and issues in tourism. We do not claim to be comprehensive in this endeavor, but instead have selected from a range of topic areas we felt were relative to a broad-brush approach to tourism research.

The Structure of the Book

Demystifying Theories in Tourism Research is organized into five sections, and also includes an introductory chapter and a conclusion chapter. We purposefully included two types of chapters: the first providing an in-depth look into one theory (for example, see Chapter 7 on Tourism Systems) and the second providing an in-depth look at the theories relevant to a specific tourism topic area (for example, see Chapter 4 on Tour Guiding). Each chapter begins with a real life scenario in the form of a *vignette*. The vignette outlines some of the issues, challenges, or ideas that can and do provide context for developing a research question or idea in the tourism domain. Following the vignette, the context or research setting is explained, based on the theory or theories discussed. From this point, each author moves on to explain the theory or theories of their focused chapter. Finally, each chapter concludes with a look at the future with respect to the theory or theories discussed in the chapter.

Part 1, Theoretical Perspectives on Tourism Planning and Management, is comprised of six chapters (Chapters 2–7). Chapter 2 addresses tourism's role in community development, specifically how planning and policies are addressed in the literature, considering community participation in these processes, as well as the social, economic, and environmental aspects of a destination. Chapter 3 is dedicated to stakeholder theory and its application within sustainability in tourism and highlights the need for inter-organizational cooperation; it concludes with a case study on ecotourism. Chapter 4 addresses the specific role of tour guiding and Cohen's tour guiding conceptual framework. It also explores the application of relevant theories from psychology, sociology, labor, and communications studies that have contributed to the development of tour guiding research. Chapter 5 explores theories relative to rural tourism development. This chapter explores several theories appropriate to the examination of tourism in remote resource peripheries. Chapter 6 examines the evolution of innovation theory and its application to tourism research. The chapter addresses

K.S. Bricker, H. Donohoe, L. Becerra, and N. Nickerson

questions related to understanding how innovative new products emerge, who is involved, and what motivates innovation to occur in tourism. Chapter 7 is focused on systems theory and related concepts. After explaining elements of systems theory, it describes how the theory has been applied in tourism and its relationship to understanding complex ideas such as sustainable tourism development and management.

Part 2, Theoretical Perspectives on Tourism Marketing and Communications, is comprised of two chapters. Chapter 8 explores the broad field of marketing tourism products and the multitude of theories used in the application of tourism marketing research. Complementing the broad suite of theories in tourism marketing, Chapter 9 examines three theoretical approaches to understanding destination image research.

Part 3, Theoretical Perspectives on Host Communities and Guests, is comprised of three chapters. Chapter 10 discusses select theories commonly used to understand residents and how they perceive tourism within their communities. Chapter 11 explores theories that have been applied to the study of tourism and sustainable community development, as well as theories from other fields that might be adapted to the examination of the role tourism can play in achieving sustainable communities. Chapter 12 examines selected cultural theories in the context of increasing cultural diversity around the world. It explores culture from a touristic perspective, including difficulties in encountering new cultures, and strategies used to minimize these difficulties.

Part 4, Theoretical Perspectives on Tourism Consumers, is comprised of two chapters. Chapter 13 explores how place perceptions are developed and how place connections are formed relative to tourism destinations and experiences. This chapter examines several theoretical applications to understanding sense of place and place identity development of individuals and groups. Chapter 14 presents a number of theories and conceptual models relative to understanding how environmentalism influences consumer travel choices.

Part 5, Conclusion, contains the final chapter on 'Theory and the Future of Tourism Research'. Here, the editors summarize the book's key themes and findings with a view to the future and new opportunities for research as we continue to "demystify" the use and application of theory in tourism studies.

This text provides an overview and analysis of the way in which we utilize theory in tourism research. While not meant to be a comprehensive and complete use of theory applied to tourism problems and issues, it is meant to provide guidance to researchers, either beginning their journey or for those that have been researching for some time and would like to creatively consider new theories or application of theories in their own line of work. We hope this book will assist scholars at all stages of their careers to gain an understanding of past and contemporary uses of theory within the vast and complex field of tourism studies.

References

Babbie, E. (2010) *The Practice of Social Research*, 12th edn. Wadsworth, Belmont, California.

Deutsch, K. (1972) The contribution of experiments within the framework of political theory. In: Laponce, J.A. and Smoker, P. (eds) *Experimentation and Simulation in Political Science*. Toronto University Press, Toronto, Canada.

Dubin, R. (1969) *Theory Building*. The Free Press, New York.

Frankfort-Nachmias, C. and Nachmias, D. (1992) *Research Methods in Social Sciences*, 4th edn. St. Martin's Press, New York.

McCool, D. (1995) *Public Policy, Theories, Models and Concepts: An Anthology*. Prentice-Hall, Englewood Cliffs, New Jersey.

Strauss, A. and Corbin, J. (2007) *Basics of Qualitative Research: Techniques and Procedures for Developing Grounded Theory*, 3rd edn. Sage, Newbury Park, California.

K.S. Bricker, H. Donohoe, L. Becerra, and N. Nickerson

2 Theoretical Perspectives on Tourism Planning and Development

RHONDA PHILLIPS[1]* AND DEEPAK CHHABRA[2]

[1]*Purdue University, Agricultural Economics and Honors College, West Lafayette, Indiana; [2]Arizona State University, School of Community Resources and Development, Phoenix, Arizona*

The Objectives

1. Learn about planning and development theories that help explain influences on communities.
2. Explore planning and development in the context of community development as a process and an outcome.
3. Understand ways to integrate tourism into community planning and development.

The Vignette

Marly, an artist, recently relocated to Sedona, Arizona seeking a community characterized by free spirits and deep connection to nature, surrounded by breath-taking and unique surroundings. This would be the place for inspired art! Famous for its red rocks (Fig. 2.1), Sedona draws tourists from around the world, fostering a festive, aesthetically rich social environment (Fig. 2.2). Plus, it did not hurt that Sedona is located just two hours north of the fifth largest metropolitan area in the USA—Phoenix, home to many art buyers and galleries. One of the first things she noticed was a commitment to place by the residents and a fierce need to protect the land and its special resources from overdevelopment. This resonated with her, and as a self-described environmentalist, Marly quickly volunteered with community-based ecology efforts in Sedona.

Tourism is the largest industry in Sedona and while it is crucial to the success of her own arts-based business, residents recognize the dangers of overstressing a system with too many visitors. Marly and others in her community are rather vocal about their strong desire to protect Sedona, while recognizing the need to balance ecological with economic needs. After all, tourists are needed to fuel the local economy that specializes in offering one-of-a-kind shopping opportunities and who would want to keep tourists from sharing in the magical environment Sedona offers? With its fragile high-altitude desert environment, Sedona also needs strong advocates to ensure

*Corresponding author, e-mail: rphillips@purdue.edu

Fig. 2.1. Summit of Bell Rock—reputed to be the site of an energy vortex! Thousands of tourists visit this area each year to enjoy the famous red rocks (photo courtesy of R. Phillips).

Fig. 2.2. Downtown Sedona. Sedona's quaint downtown offers venues for both citizens and tourists to gather (photo courtesy of R. Phillips).

its preservation. How could Sedona's residents balance seemingly conflicting needs? Instead of fighting with local and regional government, a more effective approach can be found by participating in decision making and influencing the governance process via the community planning process. Can tourism really be part of a planning process, and if so, what is the best way to include it? Are there land use and policy tools that can be used to enable tourism to have a voice in decision-making processes impacting communities? And can a citizen, such as Marly, who wants to help achieve balance in the community be included in meaningful ways?

The Context

Communities face challenges within and across all dimensions of well-being, not the least of which are economic considerations. Because tourism is often a major player

R. Phillips and D. Chhabra

in a local economy (with investments, policies, and projects) the need to have good governance around its interface in a community is vital. And as already well recognized in the sustainability related literature and research, it is about more than economic considerations as social and environmental aspects of communities are impacted too. As a result, there has been a shift in thinking about tourism, one that reflects more inclusion of citizens and stakeholders—those directly impacted by tourism. Participation and inclusion in decision-making processes is a hallmark of community planning and development practice, so this brings the two fields much closer. As noted:

> within the context of transformations in governance structures, strident demands from civil society for equity and fairness, the growth of international tourism, and the ubiquity of social media, among other noticeable trends, the need to explore this interplay between tourism development planning and communities become[s] even more urgent.
>
> (Phillips and Roberts, 2013: 1)

This underscores reasons to explore further the role that tourism plays in community planning and development particularly as related to inclusion and participation, and having tourism adequately reflected within policies. Before these concerns are addressed, applicable theories are presented, followed by discussion of foundational concepts of community development and planning.

Theory guiding planning emanates from four traditions—policy analysis, social learning, social reform, and social mobilization. There are numerous theories embedded within each of these traditions, such as systems, organizational development, sociological, and utopian theories (Friedmann, 1987). One of the best known theories in planning is rational choice theory, grounded in utilitarian assessment of consequences, and serving as the general theory of planning for many decades (Alexander, 1995). The typical stages of the rational choice method are as follows:

1. Formulation of goals and objectives.
2. Identification and design of major alternatives for reaching the goals identified within the given decision-making situation.
3. Prediction of major sets of consequences that would be expected to follow upon adoption of each alternative.
4. Evaluation of consequences in relation to desired objectives and other important values.
5. Decision based on information provided in the preceding steps.
6. Implementation of this decision through appropriate institutions.
7. Feedback of actual program results and their assessment in light of the new decision-situation (Friedmann, 1987; Alexander, 1995).

This is the process used by most planning agencies although there are variations and improvements, guided by the need to include more normative thinking in decision making, for example. It should be noted that the rational choice model has been criticized for many years, on the basis that systems are too complex to reduce to a set of values on which to form policy and action. One counter to this problem is that of successive limited comparison in which decision makers rely on incremental methods to arrive at an understanding of problems and issues, and potential solutions (Lindblom, 1995).

This is referred to as disjointed incrementalism theory, or fondly as, "the science of muddling through," which in reality is often what happens in community planning and development processes.

The Theory

Community development draws on several theories that can provide guidance for building a sense of community, with members actively participating. As mentioned, social capital is a key ingredient in the community development process; theory points to the need to focus on bridging social capital where new connections, ideas, and wealth can be generated by forming new social ties and relationships to expand networks (Hustedde, 2015). Stakeholder theory is allied with social capital theory, as it helps foster understanding of having voice for community members, and being able to participate meaningfully in community processes. By encouraging participation, social capital is strengthened within communities. In addition to fostering trust in relationships, there is another theory providing guidance for community development, conflict theory. Power differences and conflict in social life exist in communities, and can be especially apparent during development processes. Power resides in who controls or has access to resources (land, labor, capital, and knowledge, for example), and since community development is about building capacity (social capital), it has to be considered (Hustedde, 2015: 24). Recognizing that conflict exists as an integral part of social life, as the theory states, then the community can respond by analyzing sources of power and craft appropriate responses. Conflict is not always negative, sometimes it references community interests and can serve as a catalyst to bring diverse groups together for finding potential solutions to issues.

What additional guidance can be sought from theory? There are several theories beyond the typical set that can be used to better incorporate tourism with community development and planning, including sustainable development and complex systems theories. Sustainable development does not have a unifying, underlying theory or set of theories; rather, it draws on numerous constructs and models, and related theories. These include sociological, political, and ecological constructs such as the sustainable livelihoods approach, as well as economic and sociological understandings including Rostow's stages of growth model and world systems theory. Despite the ambiguity, sustainable development concepts and approaches can provide guidance for tourism to achieve objectives such as: developing multiple use infrastructure and recreational facilities for both citizens and tourists; formulating a framework to enhance local resident quality of life, ensuring that development is both reflective and sensitive to the resources of the area; and considering social, cultural, and economic values of the community (Inskeep, 1998; Mason, 2003; Goeldner and Ritchie, 2006). As related to tourism, integrating with community planning can allow for "future flexibility of new development and revitalization of older tourism areas" (Inskeep, 1998: 17). Complex systems theory offers exciting areas of thought, with scientific and mathematical approaches holding promise for greater understanding of relationships between systems. Many approaches use a reductionist viewpoint, which may help break down components within systems. This is an evolving area, and one that will help push forward understanding of sustainability, with application to community planning and development.

Community Development

Often defined as both a process and an outcome, community development can be thought of as:

> A process: developing and enhancing the ability to act collectively, and an outcome: (1) taking collection action and (2) the result of that action for improvement in a community in any or all realms: physical, environmental, cultural, social, political, economic, etc.
>
> (Phillips and Pittman, 2009: 6)

Social capacity (developing the ability to take action) of a community facilitates community development. One way to help increase capacity is to include those impacted by planning and development in meaningful ways. Citizen or stakeholder participation is a central tenet of community development principles. The "promise of combining the broader goals of community development with less traditional approaches to planning tourism" offers enrichment to tourism development approaches (Mair and Reid, 2007: 407). Social capital is the extent to which stakeholders and citizens can work together effectively for problem solving and decision making. Figure 2.3 illustrates the connection between capacity building, social capital, and achieving community development outcomes.

Community development is important to consider for tourism because it is the arena in which issues and opportunities can be addressed. Crouch and Ritchie (1999: 189) point out that tourism development can become an important engine for achieving broader social goals. Achieving broader social goals is a major focus of community development, this helps understanding of the relationship between tourism and community development.

Planning

A simple definition of planning is that it provides the opportunity to envision what a community or region wants, and the best way to achieve that. As its basis, it implies that what people value in their communities will be represented. Planning is "a process and a movement; not merely an outcome or product," and helps expand ways community members can express themselves and also have more control over what

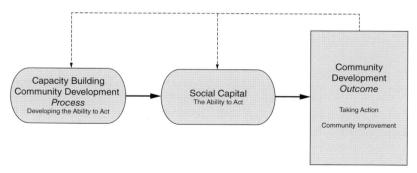

Fig. 2.3. Community development chain (from Phillips and Pittman, 2009: 6).

happens in the area (Mair and Reid, 2007: 407). Further, planning can be thought of as a guide to action—assessing, identifying, and laying out the steps needed to accomplish community goals and objectives. In technical terms, community and regional planners develop plans and programs for the public sector for the use of land and related policies impacting ecological, economic, and social dimensions of the areas they serve. Planning tools and policies are used to create communities, guide growth and development, or help revitalize facilities and supporting infrastructure.

There are numerous tools and assessment techniques used in the planning process. These include regulations such as land use zoning, the most well-known of planning tools. Zoning is the practice of designating permitted uses, reflected on a map of the area, that separates uses or groups uses together based on compatibility and protecting public safety and health, for example. Many tools such as geographic information systems (GIS) are applied to assess situations in communities as well as help predict future needs and demands. GIS has soared in popularity as it is both useful and accessible, allowing community stakeholders and others to gauge development activities and opportunities. There are tools and assessment approaches as well for processes focusing on dialogue, inclusion, and participation. Since planning is an important component of public sector governance at the local and regional levels, it is essential to include participation and democratic representation in the process. Most US states specifically direct local governments to include citizen participation in their planning activities. While there is variation in approaches, most have state-enabling legislation addressing how zoning and other dimensions of land use planning are to be enacted.

Zoning and other regulations and policies are typically reflected in a comprehensive plan—a local government's guide to physical, social, environmental, and economic development. Comprehensive plans provide the platform for making good choices for the community and serve as a long-term vision for future planning and community decisions. Most are 15 or 20 years in scope, some are longer. It also mandates that citizen participation has to be included in crafting the vision for the community's future. Each comprehensive plan is unique and will reflect the community's desires, needs, and goals. Comprehensive plans include elements that specifically address dimensions of the community, such as public facilities, transportation, housing, natural resources, current and future land uses, economic development, and intergovernmental cooperation. Some states will specify which of these elements have to be included in local government plans.

The planning process can be quite long for comprehensive planning, and in some respects, it never ends as needs and situations change in communities. For smaller plans or specifically focused areas (such as neighborhood, coastal zone management, or downtown revitalization plans), the process may not be as long. Planning processes traditionally begin with an inventory or research phase, construction of actions or policies needed, followed by assessment, evaluation or monitoring of the outcomes phase.

Inclusion and Participation: The Importance of Voice

Citizen or stakeholder participation is essential in both planning and community development. Mechanisms for making concerns and desires known in development processes must be included. Planning and community development have a rich history of including citizen and stakeholder participation in processes as a means to reflect the voices of those most impacted (Phillips and Roberts, 2013). Being able to voice concerns is vitally important to those living in tourism-dependent areas as they may have multiple perspectives on tourism development's impacts and how their quality of life is affected (Budruk and Phillips, 2011). Stakeholder theory, growing out of the organizational development tradition, is used in planning and community development as a guide to understanding interactional and relational effects. It is especially useful in the context of establishing the importance of relationships and benefits.

These ideas are not unknown to tourism planning as stakeholder engagement has been encouraged for quite a while, with earlier studies advocating for citizen representation within the process. The influence of sustainable development theory is evident in process too, with the notion of sustainable tourism development prompting more inclusive approaches. Chase *et al.* (2012: 488–489) provide considerations for those seeking to engage stakeholders:

1. Identify important stakes.
2. Be inclusive.
3. Consider using multiple techniques for incorporating stakeholder input.
4. Encourage constructive deliberation and understanding.
5. Find ways to balance competing interests.

There are also challenges to engaging stakeholders, which include:

1. Resistance from some stakeholders.
2. Ensuring equity and fairness.
3. Problematic relationships among institutions.
4. Communication issues.
5. Lack of time and money.
6. Difficulty defining and measuring quality of life.

Even faced with these challenges, it is important for the community planning process to ensure that all voices are heard, especially those most impacted by tourism. Typically, community planning processes focus on citizen stakeholders and it should be noted that tourism planning should include all impacted by its development (for example, organizations and the tourists themselves).

Who is a "stakeholder?" Essentially it implies anyone who has direct interest or involvement in a particular issue (Decker *et al.*, 1996). Chase *et al.* (2012: 488) provides examples of stakeholders in tourism planning and development to include:

> residents of host communities, businesses that cater to tourism (hotels, restaurants, attractions, gas stations, and souvenir and specialty stores), chambers of commerce, local government officials, environmentalists, farmers, and landowners. Some of these stakeholders, such as chambers of commerce and environmental groups, may be well organized. Others, such as residents frustrated by tourism traffic during their daily commute, may not be organized at all.

Stakeholders reside in communities where their quality of life can be gauged by various indicators. Quality of life can be thought of as being reflective of the values existing in a community (Budruk and Phillips, 2011). One method to gauge a host community's quality of life is by measuring and aggregating the quality-of-life indicators of various stakeholders. Understanding the relationships and values inherent in indicators, tourism planning and development can then influence quality-of-life outcomes. Indicators could then be utilized for promoting a particular set of values by making clear that residents' qualify of life is of vital importance as reflected in the indicators chosen (Budruk and Phillips, 2011). It should be noted that quality of life is different for various stakeholders. Chase *et al.* (2012) provide the following illustration (Fig. 2.4) to demonstrate how tourism development can impact stakeholders. As seen, there are numerous impacts in a community system that can influence quality of life; tourism planning and development can integrate these quality-of-life considerations into their processes.

Reflecting Tourism in Development Policy

A scan of planning activity in the US a few years ago revealed that less than one-third of city or regional comprehensive land use plans include a tourism element. Of those that did include it, slightly less than half of those elements were directly linked or embedded within economic development planning elements. Tourism is often a vital component of a local economy, and having adequate representation of it within land use and community planning policy and regulation is essential. By integrating tourism, development processes and outcomes can be guided to ensure more compatible and desirable results. While tourism is not necessarily a required element, it may be found within an economic development element. One of the best ways a community can integrate tourism into overall planning and development is to support including

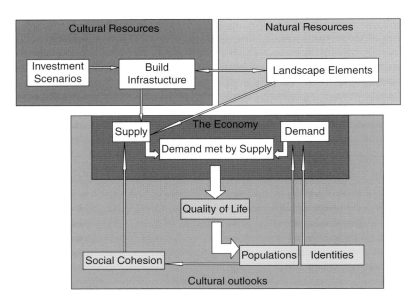

Fig. 2.4. Quality of life as a centerpiece of community development (from Chase *et al.*, 2012: 483).

R. Phillips and D. Chhabra

it as an element (or dimension of another element such as economic development) in the comprehensive land use plan for the area. Another way to ensure its reflection is to encourage tourism to be included in specific plans, such as for revitalization or strategic planning for the community. There are numerous examples of communities incorporating tourism into specific plans. Some states provide tools and suggestions for their local governments and organizations to embark on tourism planning, often via their cooperative extension program, for example, see Ohio's "Tourism Toolbox" (Ohio Tourism, 2013) or Minnesota's "Tourism Assessment Program" (University of Minnesota, 2013).

The Future

Theory provides a guide to action within planning and development. The most commonly encountered is the rational choice model, although in reality it is more of an incremental decision-making process. Social capital theory, as well as stakeholder theory, provides guidance for inclusion and strengthening community, typically via incorporating participation by those in the community. Applications from sustainable development and complex systems theory can also help provide guidance, even if these theories are more ambiguous in nature (see Chapter 6).

Moving to applications, there are two areas that are important to consider in planning and development policy as applied to tourism. First, citizen and stakeholder participation is a crucial factor for the long-term viability of a community. It is vital to consider voices in the community, as well as address points of conflict. The following considerations illustrate briefly a planning process incorporating community development elements such as participation and decision making (Chhabra and Phillips, 2009: 241).

1. *What do we have?* Inventory assets (people; organizations; cultural/heritage; natural, financial and built resources) and contexts (political, economic, social, environmental) of the community. This is the research phase and can include a variety of sources and tools such as surveys, focus groups, asset mapping, etc. It includes considering the social capacity and capital of the community.
2. *What do we want?* At this point, the all-important vision as a guide to seeing what *could happen* is crafted by stakeholders—those in the community that have an interest in helping achieve a more desirable future. Belief is a powerful tool and can inspire a community to achieve remarkable outcomes. The vision should be bold enough to inspire and realistic enough to attain.
3. *How do we get there?* This stage is about developing the plan so it is a guide with specifics for achieving the vision and includes goal statements and actions. Most importantly, it selects the strategies or approaches desired. It also identifies which organizations or groups of collaborators will be responsible for the tasks and action items. Collaborative efforts typically work best, but in some cases, it takes a "champion" to start the efforts and others will join in later.
4. *What have we done, and what do we need to do now?* Monitoring is critical to see if the above steps are working; if not, then adjustments and revisions are needed. Because the nature of this process is continuous, it provides feedback for refining ongoing activities as well as starting new initiatives until desirable change is elicited (and adjusted and maintained).

Second, it is crucial that tourism be included in overall community planning efforts. One encouraging sign is that more places have begun to incorporate community indicators into their planning processes to gauge and monitor progress towards goals. Some include tourism and cultural indicators, which are quite helpful in helping integrate further with planning processes. For example, Seattle, Washington, via a non-profit organization Sustainable Seattle, with its community partners identified indicators for gauging its status (progressing, regressing, or staying static), calling attention to issues that need further policy response. Indicators are a reflection of the values in a community, which in turn reflects quality-of-life considerations.

Tourism planning and development recognizes the need for coordination and collaboration among all sectors involved, which leads to the need for planning. It works both ways—tourism needs to be "at the table" to discuss what is valued and needed to make it feasible and communities need to incorporate tourism into their overall comprehensive planning processes and community development efforts. Theory can help provide guidance for understanding issues and systems, while at the same time providing guidance for action.

Questions

1. What are shared concerns of community development, planning, and tourism?
2. How can these shared concerns be better understood by theory?
3. What are some examples of communities that are reflecting tourism in their development policies?
4. How is stakeholder participation important to planning?

References

Alexander, E. (1995) *Approaches to Planning: Introducing Current Planning Theories, Concepts, and Issues*. Gordon and Breach Science Publishers, Luxembourg.

Budruk, M. and Phillips, R. (eds) (2011) *Quality of Life and Community Indicators for Parks, Recreation and Tourism Management*. Springer, The Netherlands.

Chase, L.C., Amsden, B. and Phillips, R.G. (2012) Stakeholder engagement in tourism planning and development. In: Uysal, M., *et al*. (eds) *Handbook of Tourism and Quality-of-Life Research: Enhancing the Lives of Tourists and Residents of Host Communities*. International Handbooks of Quality-of-Life. Springer, New York.

Chhabra, D. and Phillips, R. (2009) Tourism-based development. In: Phillips, R. and Pittman, R. (eds) *Introduction to Community Development*. Routledge, London, pp. 236–248.

Crouch, G. and Ritchie, J.B. (1999) Tourism, competitiveness, and social prosperity. *Journal of Business Research* 44(3), 137–152.

Decker, D., Krueger, C., Baer, R., Knuth, B. and Richmond, M. (1996) From clients to stakeholders: A philosophical shift for fish and wildlife management. *Human Dimensions of Wildlife* 1(1), 70–82.

Friedmann, J. (1987) *Planning in the Public Domain: From Knowledge to Action*. Princeton University Press, New Jersey.

Goeldner, C. and Ritchie, J. (2006) *Tourism Principles, Practices, Philosophies*. Wiley, New Jersey.

Hustedde, R. (2015) Seven theories for seven community developers. In: Phillips, R. and Pittman, R. (eds) *Introduction to Community Development*. Routledge, London, pp. 22–44.

R. Phillips and D. Chhabra

Inskeep, E. (1991) *Tourism Planning, An Integrated and Sustainable Approach.* Wiley, New York.

Inskeep, E. (1998) *Tourism Planning. An Integrated and Sustainable Development Approach*, 2nd edn. Wiley, New York.

Lindblom, C. (1995) The science of "muddling through." In: Stein, J. (ed.) *Classic Readings in Urban Planning.* McGraw-Hill, New York, pp. 35–48.

Mair, H. and Reid, D.G. (2007) Tourism and community development vs tourism for community development: Conceptualizing planning as power, knowledge, and control. *Leisure/Loisir* 31(2), 403–426.

Mason, P. (2003) *Tourism Impacts, Planning and Management.* Butterworth-Heinemann, Amsterdam.

Ohio Tourism (2013) Ohio Tourism Toolbox. Available at: http://ohiotourism.osu.edu/content/community.htm (accessed 29 April 2013).

Phillips, R. and Pittman, R. (2009) *Introduction to Community Development.* Routledge, London.

Phillips, R. and Roberts, S. (2013) *Tourism and Community Development.* Routledge, London.

University of Minnesota (2013) Tourism Assessment Program. Available at: http://www1.extension.umn.edu/community/tourism-development (accessed 27 April 2013).

3 Theoretical Perspectives on Stakeholders in Tourism Management

HOLLY DONOHOE,[1]* BIANCA REYES,[1] AND LAURA BECERRA[2]

[1]Department of Tourism, Recreation and Sport Management, University of Florida, Gainesville, Florida; [2]College of Forestry and Conservation, University of Montana, Missoula, Montana

The Objectives

The purpose of this chapter is to examine the stakeholder theory approach to tourism planning and development. The objectives are to:

1. Provide a definition and brief historical synopsis on stakeholder theory.
2. Provide a critical review of stakeholder theory applications in tourism.
3. Illustrate the practical application of stakeholder theory with a tourism case study.

The Vignette

In their own words, small ecotourism operators Ray and Jody Hetchka (personal communication, 24 January 2012) describe the importance of stakeholders in the development and management of their small ecotourism enterprise near Jacksonville, Florida:

> Partnership and collaboration are the "glue" that binds relationships both in business and in life. From the business perspective, they can help an enterprise (especially a small business) stretch limited resources and accomplish far more than their size would seem to allow. Kayak Amelia has thrived because of our close working relationships with Florida State Parks, National Park Service, VisitFlorida, The Amelia Island CVB/VisitJacksonville and dozens of environmental/kayaking businesses and organizations. At the risk of overusing an old truism, there really are benefits to "learning to play together nicely"!

The Theory

Stakeholder theory is concerned with organizational management and ethics (Phillips *et al.*, 2003). The theory builds on key antecedents such as Smith (1759), Berle and Means (1932), and Barnard (1938), who argued that an organization or business is a

---

*Corresponding author, e-mail: hdonohoe@hhp.ufl.edu

social institution that depends on cooperative systems and their effectiveness for the achievement of a common purpose. The term "stakeholder" is described as those groups or individuals who can affect, or are affected by the activities of an organization (Freeman, 1984). In his seminal book *Stakeholder Management: A Stakeholder Approach*, Freeman (1984) drew from the aforementioned and the literature on corporate planning, systems theory, corporate social responsibility, and organization theory to introduce "Stakeholder Theory." The theory began as an alternative way to understand organizations, in contrast to traditional models which depicted managers in simplistic terms (dealing only with employees, customers, suppliers) or which claimed organizations existed only to make profits (serve the interests of one group) (Jones *et al.*, 2001). Freeman argued that organizational realities had become more complex and that groups that are vital to the success of an organization's initiatives are overlooked or excluded. He proposed a strategic paradigm shift in business management and ethics whereby organizations configure with the external environment (i.e. stakeholders) in order to enhance and then achieve organizational goals and objectives. This stakeholder approach could conceivably enable organizations and their managers better to understand complex realities so that they can plan and manage accordingly.

While there is disagreement among stakeholder theorists about the scope and precise meaning of both "stakeholder" and "theory," the body of literature that has emerged in the last 25 years suggests two basic or common principles: (i) to perform well, managers need to be sensitive to a wide array of stakeholders (including but extending beyond shareholders); and (ii) that managers have an obligation to these stakeholders (Jones *et al.*, 2001; Phillips *et al.*, 2003). Phillips *et al.* (2003: 481) concede that "stakeholder theory is distinct because it addresses morals and values explicitly as a central feature of managing organizations" and fair attention to the interests, well-being, and representative power of stakeholders is the theory's central doctrine. While it has been said that stakeholder theory stands virtually unopposed (Jones, 1995; Donaldson and Preston, 1995), at its current stage of theoretical development, it is not without critics. Phillips *et al.* (2003) argue that the breadth of interpretation is one of stakeholder theory's greatest strengths and is its central liability. In their widely cited critique, Donaldson and Preston (1995) argue that stakeholder research is "managerial" and in this context, stakeholder theory and the legs upon which it stands—equality, morality, and ethics—can be ambiguous. Both critiques point to the misinterpretations and distortions that can manifest when stakeholder theory is applied. However, Phillips *et al.* (2003) argue that this critical discourse is evidence of theoretical maturity and this has made stakeholder theory more resilient to attack.

Donaldson and Preston's (1995) "hub and spoke" model is commonly used to represent the theory's stakeholder relationships. However, it neglects the broader socio-cultural, ecological, and economic environments (i.e. peripheral stakeholders) in which organizations operate. They have been integrated into the model (Fig. 3.1) to reflect the sustainable development paradigm that is shaping contemporary management theory and research in a diversity of fields (e.g. Gladwin *et al.*, 1995; Byrd, 2007).

The Context

Stakeholder theory has been applied in a variety of fields that include but are not limited to environmental management (e.g. Buysse and Verbeke, 2003; Steurer, 2006),

Fig. 3.1. Stakeholder theory model.

marketing (e.g. Miles and Covin, 2000; De Bussy *et al.*, 2003; Mellahi and Wood, 2003; Munilla and Miles, 2005; Knox and Gruar, 2007), information systems (e.g. Vidgen, 1997; Chua *et al.*, 2005), healthcare (e.g. Werhane, 2000; Elms *et al.*, 2002; Kelner *et al.*, 2004; Murdoch, 2004), and public and private governance (e.g. Starik, 1995; Rowley, 1997; Phillips and Reichart, 2000; Doh, 2003; Buchholz and Rosenthal, 2004; Flak and Rose, 2005; Zhang *et al.*, 2005). In the tourism context, Getz and Timur (2005) and Nicholas *et al.* (2009) concede that the application of stakeholder theory has been relatively recent and limited but there is evidence that the theory is informing research and management. For example, it is being used to explore the normative values, attitudes, and behaviors of tourism stakeholders thereby providing a deeper understanding of their needs, motivations, perceptions, and their abilities to influence tourism organizations or enterprises (e.g. Sheehan and Ritchie, 2005; Byrd, 2007; Stokes, 2008; Byrd *et al.*, 2009). It is guiding research concerned with power dynamics, ethics, gender, and outcomes in the tourism domain (Ryan, 2002; Jamal *et al.*, 2006; Bornhorst *et al.*, 2010; UNWTO and UN Women, 2011). It is being used to identify and map the role of stakeholders in tourism planning and development processes (e.g. Medeiros de Araujo and Bramwell, 1999; Sautter and Leisen, 1999) and specifically sustainable tourism development (e.g. Berno and Bricker, 2001; Hardy and Beeton, 2001; Byrd, 2007; Timur and Getz, 2007). It is being used to enhance understanding of the role and contribution of governments to the tourism exchange and it is guiding tourism marketing research and strategy (e.g. Robson and Robson, 1996; Caffyn and Jobbins, 2003; Fyall and Garrod, 2004; D'Angella and Go, 2009). Stakeholder theory is guiding the development of pedagogical models and policies in the tourism domain (Lewis, 2006) and it is being used to enhance understanding of conflict and resolution in the management of tourism in ecologically and culturally sensitive areas (e.g. Burns and Howard, 2003; Lester and Weeden, 2004; Aas *et al.*, 2005; Moswete, 2009).

H. Donohoe, B. Reyes, and L. Becerra

Stakeholder theory has also been used to inform research concerned with ecotourism development and management. The International Ecotourism Society (TIES) defines ecotourism as "responsible travel to natural areas that conserves the environment, sustains the well-being of the local people, and involves interpretation and education" (TIES, 2015). Ecotourism is, therefore, sensitive to and dependent on the socio-cultural, ecological, and economic environments in which ecotourism activities take place (Donohoe and Needham, 2006). Concomitantly, the literature—both academic and professional—indicates that stakeholder involvement is essential for the success and sustainability of tourism attractions and destinations (Getzner, 2002; Wood, 2002; Getz and Timur, 2005; Nicholas *et al.*, 2009; Moswete *et al.*, 2011). "Increasingly, planners and developers are realizing that policy must involve the many stakeholders who stand to be impacted by ecotourism development" (Fennell, 2002: 107). Therefore, the utility of stakeholder theory is that it provides a management framework that is congruent with the values and ethics of the sustainable development paradigm (Getz and Timur, 2005), and by extension, the tenets of ecotourism (Donohoe and Needham, 2006). The utility of stakeholder theory-driven analysis is that the perspectives of all stakeholder groups are included with respect to decision making and the general management of natural and cultural resources (Moswete *et al.*, 2011).

According to Ceballos-Lascuráin (1996), ecotourism stakeholder groups may include local communities, protected area personnel, the tourism industry, non-governmental organizations, financial institutions, consumers, and national ecotourism associations. Fennell and Dowling (2003) argue that government is often the cog in stakeholder interactions as it is charged with the responsibility of balancing the demands of all while driving a dual tourism development and conservation mandate. A commonly cited best-practice of participatory policy development is the Australian *National Ecotourism Strategy*. The intent of the strategy is "to provide broad direction for the future of ecotourism by identifying priority issues for its sustainable development and recommending approaches for addressing these issues" (Commonwealth Department of Tourism, 1994: 6). This policy was informed by the collective opinions of Australians gathered at a series of public consultation workshops involving community groups, educational institutions, environmental and non-governmental organizations, industry, and government. This policy was instrumental in establishing the leadership and innovation of Australian ecotourism and it has since become a model that other governments are using to develop national ecotourism strategies and destination policies (Fennell, 2002). Like Australia, Fiji has developed an ecotourism governance framework through a collaborative participatory model (Bricker, 2003). Following a government coup in 2000 and an election in 2001, the recovery of the tourism industry and the ecotourism industry specifically has been the result of the coordinated and collaborative effort of stakeholders (Bricker, 2002). These examples speak to the successful outcomes that may result from stakeholder theory-informed managerial action.

While stakeholder input is an essential aspect of policy development from the perspective of inclusion, Fennell *et al.* (2001) caution that achieving consensus or compromise between a diversity of stakeholders is challenging. This is particularly true of ecotourism, which must balance the use and preservation of the natural and cultural resources upon which the visitor experience and the host community depends (Donohoe and Needham, 2006). Ideally, ecotourism projects should involve local people as equal stakeholders but effective participation of local communities in the planning and management of ecotourism is rarely a feature of ecotourism projects (Garrod, 2003). The misinterpretation of "involvement" and/or the involvement inequalities may very well undermine the development of the social capital required for sustainable development (Hall, 1999) and it is congruent with the aforementioned critiques of stakeholder theory.

A representative example of this misinterpretation includes Moswete *et al.*'s (2011) study of community-based ecotourism in Botswana. Interviews with local and national representatives (living or working in the region) revealed conflicting opinions regarding the management of the Kgalagadi Transfrontier Park. It was evident that the power over resource management remains predominantly with the primary stakeholder—the government—and there is an absence of cooperation and collaboration between public sector officials, the park authority, and the local community. The devolution of authority and responsibility and the evolution of collaborative and integrated management has not occurred (except on paper). Fennell and Dowling (2003: 334) remind us that the Kgalagadi case is not unique: "Recognizing the need to relinquish control is one thing; doing it is quite another." In Kgalagadi, the conflicts are putting at risk the sustainability of the destination, the legitimacy of the institutional arrangements and policy frameworks, and the benefits of ecotourism for the environment and the local community. This example is reflective of the challenging reality of stakeholder theory-driven management.

Ecotourism in Florida: A Case Study

Although Florida may be known for its sun, sand, and surf reputation as well as its amusement parks, nature-based tourism is expanding beyond the world-famous Florida Everglades National Park and World Heritage Site. Ecotourism is a comparatively new industry in Florida and it is rich in potential benefits for businesses, landowners, communities, residents, and visitors (Best and Stein, 2010). In the 1990s, state tourism officials took interest in this potential growth area and initiated a plan to protect and promote Florida's natural tourism assets so as to deliver sustainable economic benefits, conserve the state's resources, and to improve the quality of life for Floridians. The involvement of a wide array of stakeholders was perceived necessary for goal achievement. Public sector representatives from state, regional, local government agencies, private-sector associations, community associations, and research institutions have come together to plan and manage ecotourism for the benefit of Florida's residents and visitors.

The policy formulation process has been confounded by the differing priorities of relevant stakeholder groups. Stein *et al.* (2003) report that public sector tourism professionals regard ecotourism as a way to use protected areas to generate revenue, while public land agency managers are more focused on the role of ecotourism in promoting conservation. Best and Stein's (2010) assessment of ecotourism businesses in north Florida found that business owners identify the absence of a centralized network, resource portal, or governmental agency through which to access or share expertise and information on ecotourism planning and management as a major challenge. They also identify the importance of networking with other ecotourism businesses and the tourism industry in general, but found that the support and resources offered

H. Donohoe, B. Reyes, and L. Becerra

through traditional institutions such as the state tourism association, the local visitor and convention bureau, and the tourism development council was inaccessible (due to membership and marketing fees). Both studies confirm that an understanding of stakeholder values is necessary to develop a visionary and sustainable platform for effective ecotourism planning and management in Florida and that a stronger stakeholder network is required to capture and share expertise between and among stakeholder groups. While the priorities of ecotourism stakeholders may be in conflict and while others may have been overlooked, it is certainly possible to deliver economic, socio-cultural, and environmental benefits to a range of stakeholders if collaboration is embedded in planning and management processes (Stein *et al.*, 2003).

An emergent best-practice is resulting from public–private partnerships in the state of Florida. These arrangements are often sought by public agencies lacking financial or other resources to offer visitor experiences as directed in public agency legislation (Bustam and Stein, 2010). These partnerships feature profit sharing between the private business owner and public land agency and they often result in a better distribution of benefits across stakeholder groups (e.g. local community, land owners, business, government agencies). These partnership-driven ecotourism businesses are increasing and they are contributing to a growing diversity of ecotourism offerings in Florida (Bustam and Stein, 2010). Kayak Amelia (KA; http://www.kayakamelia.com) is a representative example of a local business that has partnered with a public agency—Florida State Parks. KA is the official service provider for Big Talbot Island and Little Talbot Island State Parks (approximately 27 miles north-east of Jacksonville). Offering a selection of guided tours and canoe/kayak rentals, KA's mission statement is:

> To create a wake, whose ripples provide our guests with a sense of wonder about the natural world, while minimizing our impact on the daily lives of the nonhuman neighbors whose home we share.

To this end, KA has been a steward of the state parks in which it operates and a leader in the local community and state-wide ecotourism movement. They donate approximately 2% of their gross sales to conservation initiatives such as The Nature Conservancy, The League of Environmental Educators in Florida, and the North Florida Land Trust. KA was involved with the development of the first EcoHeritage Tourism Provider Certification Course created in 1998 and they help to coordinate the annual Wild Amelia Nature Festival—an event whose mission is to help local residents and visitors gain a deeper appreciation of the bioregion (Fig. 3.2).

After moving to Amelia Island in 1996, owners Ray and Jody Hetchka realized that "What you see with your eyes, you will treasure with your heart" and they committed to contributing to the protection of the local environment through their ecotourism operation (Kayak Amelia, 2011; Fig. 3.3). According to the Hetchkas, the benefits of ecotourism operations include the ability to make a living and grow the business, help protect the natural environment, and encourage locals and visitors alike better to understand and protect the environment (Best and Stein, 2010). However, the journey for KA has not been without challenges and developing a network through which to share information and resources is perhaps the most significant. On a basic level, not knowing what agency(ies) to contact for business start-up, marketing or other operational support was a challenge for them as new operators and this was magnified by a lack of institutional knowledge regarding ecotourism. Among the lessons they have

Fig. 3.2. Kayak Amelia Ecotour, Florida.

H. Donohoe, B. Reyes, and L. Becerra

Fig 3.3. Ray Hetchka, Kayak Amelia.

learned, partnering with agencies such as Florida Parks to develop products and VISITFLORIDA™ and other trade associations for marketing and information gathering has proven to be an advantage and one of the keys to their success.

The KA story is echoed in Best and Stein's (2010) analysis of private ecotourism operators in Florida. The study reports that operators commonly report that access to information and expertise regarding ecotourism planning and management is limited and that marketing is a significant challenge. The operators also agree that collaboration between stakeholders is essential for success. Coming together to pool resources—whether they be best-practices, marketing strategies, capital for shared marketing campaigns, expertise or other—operators report that a participatory stakeholder network is the essential "hub and spokes" of success and sustainability.

The Future

Stakeholder theory is congruent with the principles of sustainability and contemporary tourism management paradigms. The literature concedes that tourism's economic, socio-cultural, and environmental benefits are conditional on inter-organizational cooperation that brings together diverse groups of stakeholders, identifies their commonalities and differences, and integrates them into planning and management frameworks. "Perhaps more importantly, this means that the content and direction of policy is as much a result of the local political discourse as it is a product of the various stakeholder groups involved in its production" (Fennell and Dowling, 2003: 334).

Ecotourism is a representative example of the complexity that defines the tourism industry. The unpredictability of the economic, socio-cultural, and natural environments and their interrelationships with tourism industry stakeholders creates a complex planning and management laboratory. The economic crisis of the late 2000s, the tsunami in South-east Asia in 2006, and the current political chaos in Egypt have had and are having a significant impact on the tourism industry. Add to this yet another layer of complexity—the diverse needs, perspectives, and agendas of key stakeholder groups that ideally, should be integrated into destination planning and management. While this complexity of interrelationships may help us better to understand the context in which tourism occurs, there is certainly recognition that traditional "top-down" decision-making models are no longer appropriate. Innovative, integrated, and sustainable governance strategies are providing the structural basis for present and future collaborative tourism-related decision making.

Looking forward, there is still much to learn and to improve upon if the tourism industry is to continue to benefit from the tendrils of stakeholder theory. There continues to be inequality between stakeholders with communities and local business owners struggling to maintain a voice in the decision-making process. By extension, there remains limited understanding of the mechanisms, processes, and prerequisites for a successful collaborative process in the tourism industry. The tools and techniques for measuring success and/or the economic, socio-cultural, and environmental benefits are limited and have not been subject to testing and critical review (Stein *et al.*, 2003). Therefore, future research is needed to obtain a better understanding of the relationship(s) between stakeholder theory, tourism success, and sustainability.

For students and researchers, stakeholder theory serves as a lens through which to examine tourism issues and problems. It is an established theoretical framework that has proven to be useful for identifying tourism stakeholders, understanding the complex relationship and power dynamics that may or may not exist between them, identifying their commonalities and differences, examining conflict and consensus processes, and understanding the process and outcomes of planning and management activities. Stakeholder theory contributes to the development of new insights and innovative solutions—both of which are essential to the long-term success and sustainability of the tourism industry.

Questions

1. How can stakeholder theory-driven research help us to understand the role of partnerships and collaboration in tourism management?

2. In your opinion, how do stakeholder relations impact the success of a small or medium tourism enterprise?

3. How can researchers advance theoretical developments in the area of tourism stakeholder research?

4. Are there theories from other disciplines that may apply to the study of tourism stakeholders that have yet to be applied or are not covered in this chapter?

References

Aas, C., Ladkin, A. and Fletcher, J. (2005) Stakeholder collaboration and heritage management. *Annals of Tourism Research* 32(1), 28–48.

Barnard, C. (1938) *The Function of the Executive*. Harvard University Press, Cambridge.

Berle, A. and Means, G. (1932) *The Modern Corporation and Private Property*. Commerce Clearing House, New York.

Berno, T. and Bricker, K. (2001) Sustainable tourism development: the long road from theory to practice. *International Journal of Economic Development* 3(3), 1–18.

Best, M. and Stein, T. (2010) *Ecotourism in Florida: Letting Nature Work for You. Publication #CIR 1517*. School of Forest Resources and Conservation, Florida Cooperative Extension Service, Institute of Food and Agricultural Sciences, University of Florida, Gainesville, Florida. Available at: http://edis.ifas.ufl.edu/pdffiles/fr/fr17800.pdf (accessed 30 June 2015).

Bornhorst, T., Ritchie, T.R.B. and Sheehan, L. (2010) Determinants of tourism success for DMOs and destinations: an empirical examination of stakeholders' perspectives. *Tourism Management* 31(5), 572–589.

Bricker, K. (2002) Planning for ecotourism amidst political unrest: Fiji navigates a way forward. In: Honey, M. (ed.) *Setting Standards: The Greening of the Tourism Industry*. Island Press, Washington, DC.

Bricker, K. (2003) Ecotourism development in Fiji: policy, practice and political instability. In: Fennell, D. and Dowling, R. (eds) *Ecotourism Policy and Planning*. CAB International, Wallingford, UK, pp. 187–203.

Buchholz, R. and Rosenthal, S. (2004) Stakeholder theory and public policy: how governments matter. *Journal of Business Ethics* 51(2), 143–153.

Burns, G. and Howard, P. (2003) When wildlife tourism goes wrong: a case study of stakeholder and management issues regarding Dingoes on Fraser Island, Australia. *Tourism Management* 24(6), 699–712.

Bustam, T. and Stein, T. (2010) *Principles for Developing Your Ecotourism Business Plan*, *Publication #FOR237*. School of Forest Resources and Conservation, Florida Cooperative Extension Service, Institute of Food and Agricultural Sciences, University of Florida, Gainesville, Florida. Available at: http://edis.ifas.ufl.edu/pdffiles/FR/FR29900.pdf (accessed 30 June 2015).

Buysse, K. and Verbeke, A. (2003) Proactive environmental strategies: a stakeholder management perspective. *Strategic Management Journal* 24(5), 453–470.

Byrd, E. (2007) Stakeholders in sustainable tourism development and their roles: applying stakeholder theory to sustainable tourism development. *Tourism Review* 62(2), 6–13.

Byrd, E., Bosley, H. and Dronberger, M. (2009) Comparisons of stakeholder perceptions of tourism impacts in rural eastern North Carolina. *Tourism Management* 30(5), 693–703.

Caffyn, A. and Jobbins, G. (2003) Governance capacity and stakeholder interactions in the development and management of coastal tourism: examples from Morocco and Tunisia. *Journal of Sustainable Tourism* 11(2–3), 224–245.

Ceballos-Lascuráin, H. (1996) *Tourism, Ecotourism, and Protected Areas*. International Union for the Conservation of Nature and Natural Resources, Gland, Switzerland.

Chua, C.E.H., Straub, D.W., Khoo, H.M., Kadiyala, S. and Kuechler, D. (2005) The evolution of e-commerce research: a stakeholder perspective. *Journal of Electronic Commerce Research* 6(4), 262–279.

Commonwealth Department of Tourism (1994) *National Ecotourism Strategy*. Commonwealth of Australia, Canberra, Australia.

D'Angella, F. and Go, F. (2009) Tale of two cities' collaborative tourism marketing: towards a theory of destination stakeholder assessment. *Tourism Management* 30(3), 429–440.

De Bussy, N., Ewing, M. and Pitt, L. (2003) Stakeholder theory and internal marketing communications: a framework for analyzing the influence of new media. *Journal of Marketing Communications* 9(3), 147–161.

Doh, J.P. (2003) Nongovernmental organizations, corporate strategy, and public policy: NGOs as agents of change. In: Doh, J.P. and Teegen, H.J. (eds) *Globalization and NGOs: Transforming Business, Governments, and Society*. Praeger Books, Westport, Connecticut.

Donaldson, T. and Preston, L. (1995) The stakeholder theory of the corporation: concepts, evidence, and implications. *Academy of Management Review* 20(1), 65–91.

Donohoe, H.M. and Needham, R.D. (2006) Ecotourism: the evolving contemporary definition. *Journal of Ecotourism* 5(3), 192–210.

Elms, H., Berman, S. and Wisks, A. (2002) Ethics and incentives: an evaluation and development of stakeholder theory in the health care industry. *Business Ethics Quarterly* 12(4), 413–432.

Fennell, D. (2002) *Ecotourism*, 2nd edn. Routledge, New York.

Fennell, D. and Dowling, R. (2003) Ecotourism policy and planning: stakeholders, management and governance. In: Fennell, D. and Dowling, R. (eds) *Ecotourism Policy and Planning*. CAB International, Wallingford, UK, pp. 331–345.

Fennell, D., Buckley, R. and Weaver, D. (2001) Policy and planning. In: Weaver, D. (ed.) *The Encyclopedia of Ecotourism*. CAB International, Wallingford, UK.

Flak, L.S. and Rose, J. (2005) Stakeholder governance: adapting stakeholder theory to e-government. *Communications of the Association for Information Systems* 16(31), 1–46.

Freeman, E. (1984) *Strategic Management: A Stakeholder Approach*. Pitman Press, Boston.

Fyall, A. and Garrod, B. (2004) *Tourism Marketing: A Collaborative Approach*. Channel View Publications, UK.

Garrod, B. (2003) Local participation in the planning and management of ecotourism: a revised model approach. *Journal of Ecotourism* 2(1), 33–53.

Getz, D. and Timur, S. (2005) Stakeholder involvement in sustainable tourism: balancing the voices. In: Theobald, W. (ed.) *Global Tourism*, 3rd edn. Butterworth Heinemann, Oxford, UK, pp. 230–247.

H. Donohoe, B. Reyes, and L. Becerra

Getzner, M. (2002) Ecotourism, stakeholders and regional sustainable development. In: Hagedorn, K. (ed.) *Environmental Cooperation and Institutional Change: Theories and Policies for European Agriculture*. Edward Elgar Publishing Limited, Northampton, Massachusetts, pp. 315–341.

Gladwin, T., Kennelly, J. and Krause, T. (1995) Shifting paradigms for sustainable development. *The Academy of Management Review* 20(4), 874–907.

Hall, M. (1999) Rethinking collaboration and partnership: a public policy perspective. *Journal of Sustainable Tourism* 7(3-4), 274–289.

Hardy, A. and Beeton, R. (2001) Sustainable tourism or maintainable tourism: managing resources for more than average outcomes. *Journal of Sustainable Tourism* 9(3), 168–192.

Jamal, T., Borgesa, M. and Stronza, A. (2006) The institutionalization of ecotourism: certification, cultural equity and praxis. *Journal of Ecotourism* 5(3), 145–175.

Jones, M. (1995) Instrumental stakeholder theory: a synthesis of ethics and economics. *Academy of Management Review* 20(2), 404–437.

Jones, T., Wicks, A. and Freeman, R.E. (2001) Stakeholder theory: the state of the art. In: Bowie, N.E. (ed.) *Blackwell Guide to Business Ethics*. Blackwell Publishers, Oxford, UK, pp. 19–37.

Kayak Amelia (2011) Our Team. Available at: http://www.kayakamelia.com/about.htm (accessed 30 June 2015).

Kelner, M., Wellman, B., Boon, H. and Welsh, S. (2004) Responses of established healthcare to the professionalization of complementary and alternative medicine in Ontario. *Social Science and Medicine* 59, 915–930.

Knox, S. and Gruar, C. (2007) The application of stakeholder theory to relationship marketing strategy development in a non-profit organization. *Journal of Business Ethics* 75(2), 115–135.

Lester, J. and Weeden, C. (2004) Stakeholders, the natural environment and the future of Caribbean cruise tourism. *International Journal of Tourism Research* 6(1), 39–50.

Lewis, A. (2006) Stakeholder informed tourism education: voices from the Caribbean. *Journal of Hospitality, Leisure, Sport and Tourism Education* 5(2), 14–24.

Medeiros de Araujo, L. and Bramwell, B. (1999) Stakeholder assessment and collaborative tourism planning: the case of Brazil's Costa Dourada project. *Journal of Sustainable Tourism* 7(3–4), 356–378.

Mellahi, K. and Wood, G. (2003) The role and potential of stakeholders in "Hollow Participation": conventional stakeholder theory and institutionalist alternatives. *Business and Society Review* 108(2), 183–202.

Miles, M.P. and Covin, J.G. (2000) Environmental marketing: a source of reputational, competitive, and financial advantage. *Journal of Business Ethics* 23(3), 299–311.

Moswete, N.N. (2009) Stakeholder perspectives on the potential for community-based ecotourism development and support for the Kgalagadi Transfrontier Park in Botswana. PhD dissertation in Recreation, Parks and Tourism. University of Florida.

Moswete, N., Thapa, B. and Child, B. (2011) Attitudes and opinions of local and national public sector stakeholders towards Kgalagadi Transfrontier Park, Botswana. *International Journal of Sustainable Development & World Ecology*. DOI:10.1080/13504509.2011.592551 Online First (19 July).

Munilla, L. and Miles, P. (2005) The corporate social responsibility continuum as a component of stakeholder theory. *Business and Society Review* 110(4), 371–387.

Murdoch, A. (2004) Stakeholder theory, partnerships and alliances in the health care sector of the UK and Scotland. *International Public Management Review* 5(1), 21–40.

Nicholas, N., Thapa, B. and Ko, Y. (2009) Residents' perspective of a World Heritage Site: the Pitons Management Area, St. Lucia. *Annals of Tourism Research* 36(3), 390–412.

Phillips, R. and Reichart, J. (2000) The environment as a stakeholder? A fairness-based approach. *Journal of Business Ethics* 23(2), 185–197.

Phillips, R., Freeman, R.E. and Wicks, A. (2003) What stakeholder theory is not. *Business Ethics Quarterly* 13(4), 479–502.

Robson, J. and Robson, I. (1996) From shareholders to stakeholders: critical issues for tourism marketers. *Tourism Management* 17(7), 533–540.

Rowley, T. (1997) Moving beyond dyadic ties: a network theory of stakeholder influences. *Academy of Management Review* 22(4), 887–910.

Ryan, C. (2002) Equity, management, power sharing and sustainability—issues of the 'New Tourism'. *Tourism Management* 23(1), 17–26.

Sautter, E. and Leisen, B. (1999) Managing stakeholders: a tourism planning model. *Annals of Tourism Research* 26(2), 312–328.

Sheehan, L. and Ritchie, J.R.B. (2005) Destination stakeholders exploring identity and salience. *Annals of Tourism Research* 32(3), 711–734.

Smith, A. (1759) *The Theory of Moral Sentiments*. Liberty Fund Inc., Indianapolis, Indiana.

Starik, M. (1995) Should trees have managerial standing? Toward stakeholder status for non-human nature. *Journal of Business Ethics* 14(3), 207–217.

Stein, T., Clark, J. and Rickards, J. (2003) Assessing nature's role in ecotourism development in Florida: perspectives of tourism professionals and government decision-makers. *Journal of Ecotourism* 2(3), 155–172.

Steurer, R. (2006) Mapping stakeholder theory anew: from the stakeholder theory of the firm to three perspectives on business-society relations. *Business Strategy and the Environment* 15(1), 55–69.

Stokes, R. (2008) Tourism strategy making: insights to the events tourism domain. *Tourism Management* 29(2), 252–262.

The International Ecotourism Society (TIES) (2015) Definition revised. Retrieved from http://www.ecotourism.org/what-is-ecotourism (accessed 30 June 2015).

Timur, S. and Getz, D. (2007) A network perspective on managing stakeholders for sustainable urban tourism. *International Journal of Contemporary Hospitality Management* 20(4), 445–461.

Vidgen, R. (1997) Stakeholders, soft systems and technology: separation and mediation in the analysis of information system requirements. *Information Systems Journal* 7(1), 21–46.

Werhane, P.H. (2000) Business ethics, stakeholder theory, and the ethics of healthcare organizations. *Cambridge Quarterly of Healthcare Ethics* 9(2), 169–181.

Wood, M. (2002) Ecotourism: principles, practices and policies for sustainability. *UNEP Publication*, in collaboration with The International Ecotourism Society.

World Tourism Organization (UNWTO) and United Nations Entity for Gender Equality and The Empowerment of Women (UN Women) (2011) *Global Report on Women in Tourism 2010*. UNWTO and UN Women, Madrid, Spain.

Zhang, J., Dawes, S.S. and Sarkis, J. (2005) Exploring stakeholders' expectations of the benefits and barriers of e-government knowledge sharing. *Journal of Enterprise Information Management* 18(5/6), 548–567.

H. Donohoe, B. Reyes, and L. Becerra

4 Theoretical Perspectives on Tour Guiding

Rosemary Black[1]* and Betty Weiler[2]

[1]School of Environmental Sciences, Charles Sturt University, Albury, New South Wales; [2]School of Business and Tourism, Southern Cross University, Coolangatta, Queensland, Australia

The Objectives

1. To explore the theories, conceptual frameworks, and models that have been proposed and developed to describe the roles played by guides and how well they perform them, and to foster quality tour guiding.
2. To examine the application of emotional labor theory to the tour guiding context.
3. To introduce theories from a range of disciplines that can be applied in future studies to progress research on tour guiding.

The Vignette

"We want to take guiding to a new level" says Gary Muir of Wild on Walpole Tours based in Western Australia. He leaps up on to a plastic chair and launches into a spirited geological history of the planet, from the breakup of Pangea to the breakup of Gondwana and beyond, using a bunch of stuffed cuddly toys to represent continents and plates. Each toy is humorously tossed aside as it is torn off; leaving the Australian continent as the central and key remaining land mass. Gary Muir is not your average tour guide,…having won awards for his dedication to environmental causes and his company's educational programs based in Walpole-Nornnalup National Park in Western Australia. He was the inaugural Australian National EcoGuide in 2002 and was awarded the Western Australian Golden Guide Award in 2003. One suspects that if one were to test the liquid in Gary's blood, it might show up as pure caffeine. But more likely, pure enthusiasm. Gary shows us the best that Western Australia tourism has to offer. He is passionate, energetic and totally committed to the Walpole area, the tourism industry and to his educational and environmental roles. Leaving on a WOW (Wild on Walpole) Wilderness eco-cruise on the *Naughty Lass*, we embark on a true little journey—a performance, an entertainment, an education, an inspiration. …When not leading tours, [Gary and other] WOW staff are working on [environmental] research and fundraising projects around the area. "We want to take guiding to a new level," says Gary, "We want to set a new standard in ecotourism, which is one of the fastest growing industries in the world."

(From Western Australian Newspaper)

*Corresponding author, e-mail: rblack@csu.edu.au

The Context

In a special issue on tour guides in *Annals of Tourism Research*, Jafari described tour guiding as a subject that had "received little attention in tourism research" (Jafari, 1985: 1). Moreover, many of the early papers on tour guiding emanated from sociologists and anthropologists and were primarily non-empirical in nature (Smith, 1961; Holloway, 1981; Cohen, 1985). For at least another 15 years following the special issue, the paucity of published studies on tour guides continued to be lamented by various authors (Pond, 1993; Ap and Wong, 2001). None the less, tour guiding gained some prominence in the literature from the early 1990s, including empirical studies on the relationship of guiding practice to tourist satisfaction and consumer behavior (Geva and Goldman, 1991; Hughes, 1991). This was followed soon after by a burgeoning of research discussing and examining the roles of tour guides (Weiler *et al.*, 1992; Weiler and Crabtree, 1998; Ballantyne and Hughes, 2001; Howard *et al.*, 2001; Weiler and Ham, 2001; Haig and McIntyre, 2002; Black and Ham, 2005) and more recently on the performance of guiding (Jonasson and Scherle, 2012; Overend, 2012).

However, more than 50 years after tour guiding first made its debut in the academic literature, there is a lack of theoretical engagement in much of the tour guiding literature. As will be shown in this chapter, there has been some effort given to proposing and developing theories, conceptual frameworks, and models to describe what guides do (their roles), how well they perform and how to foster quality tour guiding. One area of study where theory-building is evident relates to tour guiding roles, including the underpinnings, performance, and outcomes of particular roles. The first part of this chapter presents Cohen's (1985) seminal tour guide role framework and its application and refinement by later authors. In addition to theory-building, some attention has been paid to drawing on theory from other mainstream and applied disciplines such as psychology, sociology, labor studies, and communications studies, and applying, adapting, and testing these in a tour guiding context. The second part of the chapter focuses on a relatively recent area of tour guiding research, the application of the theory of emotional labor to the tour guiding context. The final part of the chapter identifies areas where theories from a range of disciplines can be applied in future studies to progress research on tour guiding beyond what has been primarily a descriptive focus. The ecotour and adventure guide flavor of this chapter reflects the contexts of the majority of research undertaken to date in these two areas of tour guiding research.

The Theories

Role theory

An early seminal work in the field of tour guiding is Cohen's (Cohen, 1985) sociological perspective on the interrelationships between the guide and tour participants. His paper, entitled "The tourist guide: the origins, structure and dynamics of a role," presents a conceptual framework of the various roles and functions of the tour guide as a basis for comparative studies of guiding in a range of environments. This section of the chapter provides a brief overview of, and subsequent extensions to, Cohen's framework.

According to Cohen, guides play both pathfinding and mentoring roles, the former being the geographic way-finding role associated with traditional guiding, and the latter being a more modern, complex, and heterogeneous role, which can range from spiritual advice to educational tutelage. He labels these as the *leadership* and *mediatory* spheres (respectively) of guiding. Each of these has an outer- and an inner-directed aspect, i.e. each has tasks directed outside the tour group and tasks directed within the group, creating four major components or roles played by guides. These are the *instrumental*, *social*, *interactional*, and *communicative* roles of the guide, as illustrated in Table 4.1. The outer-directed component of the leadership sphere, which Cohen labels as the instrumental role of the guide (cell 1), includes tasks such as navigating, providing special access, and shepherding the group. The social role of the guide (cell 2), which is inner-directed but still part of the leadership sphere, includes tension management, managing the group, maintaining good humor and morale within the group, and entertaining group members. Thus, the tasks associated with both the outer and the inner aspects of Cohen's leadership sphere are largely oriented toward managing the group.

Within the mediatory sphere, Cohen also identifies outer- and inner-directed aspects. According to Cohen, the inner-directed aspect of mediation is the communicative role of guiding (cell 4), which he describes as being "the kernel of the professional guide." This can range from information provision to mentoring, and Cohen identifies interpretation as "the distinguishing communicative function of the trained tour guide" (Cohen, 1985: 15). Others, however, have focused on the outer-directed mediatory aspect of guiding, for example, providing opportunities for engagement with locals, which Cohen labels as the interactionary role of the guide (cell 3) (de Kadt, 1979; Holloway, 1981; Cohen, 1985; Gurung *et al.*, 1996; Pearce *et al.*, 1998). The tasks associated with both the outer and inner aspects of the mediatory sphere seem to be oriented toward enhancing the experience of individual group members.

There has been some confusion as to what constitutes inner-directed versus outer-directed mediation in Cohen's framework. For example, interpretation, as understood in the tourism literature and practiced in the industry, involves more than delivering commentary to the group—it includes the provision of information but also education and engagement. Interpretation seeks to enrich and enhance the visitor experience by involving visitors, deepening their understanding of people, places, events, and objects from the past and present and developing a sense of connection with these. Thus, a guide's interpretation can be both inner- and outer-directed.

Cohen's (1985) framework is based on applying sociological concepts and dimensions to tour guiding, with limited empirical testing, which may be regarded as a limitation of

Table 4.1. The dynamics of the tourist guide's role (from Cohen, 1985: 17).

	Outer-directed	Inner-directed
Leadership sphere (group-focused)	(1) Original guide (Instrumental role)	(2) Animator (Social role)
Mediatory sphere (individual-focused)	(3) Tour-leader (Interactionary role)	(4) Professional guide (Communicative role)

the framework. However, the framework has served as an important and useful launching pad for further discussion and exploration of the roles of the tour guide and the dimensions associated with these roles.

A few authors preceding Cohen also drew on sociological theories to describe the guide's roles, such as Holloway (1981), who in fact drew on Cohen's (1979) earlier work on the relationship between tourists and hosts, to suggest that a guide can be a mediator between hosts and tourists. Holloway identified other important roles such as that of "cultural broker," a focus that has been pursued by a number of other researchers (de Kadt, 1979; Cohen, 1985; Gurung *et al.*, 1996; Pearce *et al.*, 1998). Holloway (1981) also noted that the role of the guide is multifaceted and has not been institutionalized or ritualized, but is subject to the interpretation of the clients participating in a tour. Thirty years later, this situation has remained unchanged, whereby the role of a guide can be defined not only by tourists' expectations, but also by stakeholders such as tour operators and protected area managers (Weiler and Ham, 2001).

While there have been many authors since the early 1980s who have referred to Cohen's work, most of these have undertaken to inventory or otherwise try to capture the diverse roles played by tour guides and have been largely atheoretical and unempirical in their approach. It is neither possible nor particularly useful to list all of the roles identified by these various authors. Perhaps of more use is Black and Weiler's (2005) review of 12 of these studies over a period of 22 years (1979–2001), which identified ten key roles that are expected of guides. In descending order of frequency of mention, these were: (i) interpreter/educator; (ii) information giver; (iii) leader; (iv) motivator of conservation values/role model; (v) social role/catalyst; (vi) cultural broker/mediator; (vii) navigator/protector; (viii) tour and group manager/organizer; (ix) public relations/company representative; and (x) facilitator of access to non-public areas. Most of the authors of these studies acknowledge, however, that "the number [and relative importance] of roles vary depending on…the tour setting, the type of group and their needs and interests, and the employer's and industry's expectations of the guide" (Black and Weiler, 2005: 26–27).

Comprehensive lists and inventories of roles can be cumbersome to work with and to build on for both research and practical outcomes such as training, quality assurance, and assessment of guide performance. It is partly for this reason that Cohen's (1985) conceptual framework of the roles of the tour guide continues to be widely cited. One notable limitation, however, is that Cohen's framework focuses entirely on the perspective of the tourist and does not explicitly consider the goals or needs of other stakeholders such as those associated with the destination, industry, individual business/organization, host population, or natural environment. Thus, his framework provides limited insight into the positive (or negative) contributions of tour guiding to host communities, environments, and destinations. Since Cohen published his paper in 1985, there has been a growth in niche tourism including ecotourism and nature-based tourism, tourism genres which are particularly dependent on the natural and cultural environment. Cohen's model has thus come under scrutiny as failing to acknowledge the role of the guide in ensuring an environmentally and culturally responsible tourist experience.

In an effort to make theoretical sense of tour guiding roles, particularly in the growing field of ecotourism and nature-based tourism, Weiler and Davis (1993) developed a model depicting the roles of the nature-based/ecotour leader/guide. Informed by a survey of tour operators and a content analysis of tour brochures, they proposed

R. Black and B. Weiler

that an ecotour guide's multiple roles could be collapsed into three meaningful dimensions, each of which included two distinct roles. The first and second dimensions—tour management and experience management—are adaptations of Cohen's (1985) original theoretical framework (dimension 1, leadership sphere and dimension 2, mediatory sphere; see Table 4.2). As in Cohen's framework, the first dimension focuses on pathfinding, leading and managing the group, while the second dimension focuses on the mediation, communication, and experiential needs of individuals within the group. Weiler and Davis (1993) added a third dimension—resource management—which focuses on the needs of host communities and environments. In this dimension, the guide plays a key role in motivating and managing tourists' on-site behavior to minimize adverse effects on the natural and cultural environment, as well as fostering longer-term understanding, appreciation, and conservation of those environments, mainly through interpretation and persuasive communication.

Although informed by a fairly limited analysis of guides and guided tours in Australia, Weiler and Davis's (1993) six-cell model became a point of departure for subsequent papers (e.g. Gurung *et al.*, 1996; Ballantyne and Hughes, 2001) and also served as a theoretical framework for at least four empirical studies (Howard *et al.*, 2001; Haig and McIntyre, 2002; Randall and Rollins, 2009; Pereira and Mykletun, 2012). For example, Gurung *et al.*'s (1996) survey of 117 Nepalese tour and trekking guides revealed that interpretation of bio-geography and culture is, according to these guides, their most important role. Howard *et al.* (2001), on the basis of interviews with Australian Indigenous guides and observations of selected tours, confirmed the relevance of all six of Weiler and Davis's (1993) tour guiding roles to Indigenous tours and identified specific and multiple examples of guides performing all of these roles.

Haig and McIntyre (2002) and Randall and Rollins (2009) undertook to operationalize Weiler and Davis's (1993) model and assess tourists' perceptions of the relative importance and/or performance of each guiding role. In Haig and McIntyre's (2002) study, tourists rated all the six roles identified by Weiler and Davis (1993) as important, however, the role of entertainer was viewed as notably less important by ecotour clients (in comparison to the ratings by tourists staying at an ecotourism resort). Using 12 rating items, Randall and Rollins (2009) obtained tourists' perceptions of both role importance and guides' performance of the six roles. Communication was rated as somewhat less important, although this could be a result of the particular items that Randall and Rollins used to measure this dimension. Guides were rated by

Table 4.2. Roles played by the tour guide/leader in nature-based tourism (from Weiler and Davis, 1993).

	Outer-directed (Resourced from outside the group)	Inner-directed (Resourced from inside the group)
Tour management (Focus on group)	"Organizer"	"Entertainer"
Experience management (Focus on individual)	"Group leader"	"Teacher"
Resource management (Focus on environment)	"Motivator"	"Environmental interpreter"

tour clients as performing well on all six roles. Given that guides often perform multiple roles simultaneously and sometimes these roles conflict (Arnould and Price, 1993), this was a somewhat unexpected result.

On the other hand, the results of other studies indicate that some destination and protected area managers, operators, and guides underestimate the importance of the mediating and brokering roles of the guide, and judge the provision of information as more important than roles such as good interpretation, the delivery of minimal impact messages, and influencing tourist attitudes and behavior (Weiler, 1999; Ballantyne and Hughes, 2001). Overall, results of these studies are mixed, not widely generalizable and largely inconclusive, other than to confirm that all six roles identified by Weiler and Davis (1993) are seen as important by most operators, guides, and tourists. Most of these studies have called for wider investigation of and further refinement in measuring both role importance and guide performance.

Weiler and Davis (1993) developed their model as a heuristic rather than a testable theoretical model. While some (e.g. Randall and Rollins, 2009; Pereira and Mykletun, 2012) have used it as a basis to develop indicators for measuring role performance, further theoretical development, operationalization, and testing have been limited. None the less, both Cohen's (1985) and Weiler and Davis's (1993) conceptual frameworks have stood the test of time in drawing attention to both the many mainstream guiding roles and the specialist roles that ecotour guides are required to perform. In the ensuing years, the widespread adoption of sustainable tourism as an ideology has shone even more light on the importance of the tour guide, particularly the performance of roles associated with the resource management dimension of Weiler and Davis's model (Weiler and Kim, 2011).

In a recent operationalization of Weiler and Davis's (1993) three spheres/dimensions of leadership, mediation and resource management, Pereira and Mykletun (2012) argue for the addition of a fourth sphere: the economy. This goes a step further in incorporating the roles of the guide vis-à-vis other stakeholders, acknowledged earlier in this chapter as a shortcoming of Cohen's original model. Further examination and testing of their expanded version of the framework is called for, particularly in relation to sustainability and in defining with more precision exactly what roles guides should be and are performing in order to foster sustainability.

A number of case studies have explored both the "eco" and the more generic roles of guides, particularly in developing countries, including Botswana (Almagor, 1985), Nepal (Gurung *et al.*, 1996), several Latin American countries (Weiler and Ham, 1999; Ham and Weiler, 2000), and Madagascar (Ormsby and Mannle, 2006). The findings from these studies have revealed important subthemes about the roles of guides that seem particularly relevant to developing countries, notably that guiding in these countries is a means of livelihood that may help to reduce poverty (Shephard and Royston-Airey, 2000). McGrath (2007) also suggests that the role of the guide in developing countries needs to mature to being a facilitator and broker of multiple meanings rather than the more traditional "show and tell" role currently played by guides in many of these countries.

In summary, the documentation and analysis of tour guide roles has served a number of purposes (Black, 2002; Black and Weiler, 2005) including the development of competencies required by a guide to undertake these roles such as group management, communication, presentation, and leadership skills. These identified guiding roles have formed the building blocks of training programs and other quality

R. Black and B. Weiler

assurance schemes such as guide certification programs and tools developed within these programs for assessing and improving performance (Ballantyne and Hughes, 2001; Black, 2002; Black and Ham, 2005). On the other hand, Hillman (2006) and others are critical of the applications and extensions of Cohen's model in the literature as being largely descriptive representations of a guide's roles, functioning, and performance. The next section of this chapter presents the application of emotional labor theory as one avenue of research that provides a deeper and more critical examination of the role performance of guides, including its antecedents and consequences for both guides and tourists.

Emotional labor theory

An important research subtheme within tour guiding roles has been the normative role expectations and performance of guides with respect to their emotions, which, in the context of the workplace, is referred to as emotional labor (Hochschild, 1983). As discussed in the first part of this chapter, the guide is expected to perform a wide range of roles. As such, guides engage in emotional labor when, for example, presenting interpretation, creating rapport and group cohesion, responding to tourists' feelings and emotions, dealing with problems and complaints, ensuring group satisfaction and role modeling appropriate environmental and cultural behavior.

Drawing on the work of Goffman (1959) who was the first to theorize about performance and interaction between individuals using the concepts of "frontstage-backstage," Hochschild (1983) coined the term "emotional labor" in her book *The Managed Heart: Commercialization of Human Feeling*. She described it as "labor that requires one to induce or suppress feeling in order to sustain the outward countenance that produces the proper state of mind in others" (p. 7) and defined it as the "management of feeling to create a publicly observable facial and bodily display" (1983: 7). According to Hochschild (1983), emotional laborers are those who enter into face-to-face or voice-to-voice contact with the public, such as airline and hospitality workers.

Emotional labor is, in effect, the commodification of feeling where workers act out an expected feeling in line with organizational requirements. As such, Hochschild suggested that emotional labor can have a negative impact on employees. Hochshild (1983) found in her study that, when employees act out feelings that are not indicative of their real feelings, they can suffer from feelings of estrangement and alienation from self, which can in turn translate into a loss of job satisfaction, cynicism, withdrawal, and feelings of moral failure.

Hochschild (1983) found with airline workers that when they experienced a misfit of emotion, they actively worked to realign their felt emotions with those prescribed by the job. She found they engaged in two strategies: surface acting and deep acting. Surface acting occurs when employees make an effort to maintain an outward appearance of the expected emotion while keeping their "real" emotions hidden. With deep acting, individuals make an active effort to genuinely feel the emotions prescribed in their job.

Although research on emotional labor is extensive in a wide range of occupational groups such as nurses (Dahling, 2007), teachers (Jenkins and Conley, 2005), and hotel workers (Johanson and Woods, 2008), there has been limited research on tour guides and leaders. This is surprising, given that some guides such as adventure guides operate in high risk environments and many guides are required to be in close proximity with clients, often over extended periods of time with few opportunities to retreat to "backstage" areas where they can relax and step out of their leader persona. Tour guides are at the frontline, acting as the organization's representative, as role models through displaying their emotions, and as facilitators of appropriate emotional reactions from tourists. As found by Carnicelli-Filho (2010) and others in the adventure tourism context, the guide embodies the product being sold such as "adventure," "excitement," or "fantasy" and is expected to maintain this image irrespective of the mundaneness they themselves may experience when performing their role. In other words, according to Van Dijk *et al.* (2011), the performance of emotional labor is inextricably linked to the tourism product.

Until quite recently the particular emotional demands of tour guides have been all but neglected in the literature (Torland, 2011b). However, since the early 1990s there have been a number of papers focusing on tour guiding and emotions, most of them drawing from the original theory of Hochschild's (1983) emotional labor, with the majority of studies contextualized in adventure guiding. Adventure guiding usually involves seasonal work across many different natural and cultural environments and often requires specific technical skills, specialized qualifications and training. These types of guides often work for small companies and may be expected to perform multiple roles within a company, take personal responsibility (e.g. for clients, safety, logistics), and cope with extended exposure to clients and other guides. These aspects, together with heightened levels of risk and uncertainty, suggest that the work of adventure guides may involve a unique combination of stress and emotions.

At the same time, many have argued that emotion is a fundamental aspect of what tourists expect of a guided adventure experience (Arnould and Price, 1993) and is a key attraction of adventure activities (Holyfield, 1999), which has implications for adventure guides. The adventure guide plays an important role in socializing tour participants into the world of adventure, acting as an expressive role model orienting and providing cues to how the experience "feels," and generating emotions among participants.

Sharpe (2005) was one of the first to focus on emotional labor in the context of adventure guiding. Using a descriptive ethnographic approach she studied adventure guides employed by an outdoor adventure company. Her study revealed three key findings: (i) that the guides were required to fulfill a demanding set of emotional expectations, mostly prescribed by the adventure company; (ii) that the guides regularly engaged in strategies to help them manage these expectations, carving out backstage areas and self-talk; and (iii) that the guides recognized they were being called upon to enact a persona, yet they resisted the notion that they were acting. Thus the descriptions the guides provided in relation to locating their "real self" were conflicting and incongruous. Sharpe (2005) explained this using the discourse in authenticity that surrounds outdoor adventure. For example, the guides describe outdoor adventure experiences as "more real" than everyday life. A second explanation is that these guides may have a different understanding of self than has been traditionally assumed. Hochschild's (1983) work on emotional labor assumes that we have a core self, a fixed and stable essence or character that guides our actions and outlook irrespective of the context. Any impacts on the core self can, according to Hochschild (1983), lead to confusion, frustration, and exhaustion. However, the guides in Sharpe's (2005) study did not feel any anxiety of self-estrangement as described by Hochschild (1983), suggesting they have little commitment to the idea of core self and that the trip persona was just one of many versions of self they held to be true.

R. Black and B. Weiler

A more recent study on adventure guides (Carnicelli-Filho, 2010) looked at the emotional role and lifestyle of rafting guides. This qualitative study found that the rafting guides' responsibilities are related to emotional relationships established with the tour participants and that participants' expectations of these are often highly demanding. Carnicelli-Filho (2010) described rafting guides as "emotional facilitators" who use deep acting as well as emotional contagion (Mann, 1997) to increase empathy. However, according to Carnicelli-Filho (2010) such work can create negative emotions, impair performance, and extend work beyond the activity and the river to permeate their lifestyle.

Torland's (2011a, b) study of adventure guides sought to critically examine the relationships between emotional labor and job satisfaction among Australian adventure tour leaders and in particular the relationships between surface acting and deep acting. She found that deep acting had a positive impact on their job satisfaction, in contrast to surface acting that did not. These findings are consistent with Hochschild (1983) and Sharpe (2005), that deep acting can help convey a sense of authenticity and a feeling of achievement in employees and thus lead to higher levels of job satisfaction. This may be because adventure tour leaders often spend long periods of time with clients and will typically make "friends" and develop "boundary open" relationships with clients (Arnould and Price, 1993: 71). Torland (2011a) suggested that the feeling of achievement and a sense of authenticity are key reasons why deep acting has a positive effect on job satisfaction. According to the continuum of emotional labor (Brotheridge and Lee, 2002), because surface acting requires less competence than deep acting, those with less experience as guides are more likely to use surface acting. Moreover, even though surface acting was seen as a moral flaw by the adventure tour leaders, some guides still occasionally engaged in it, possibly reflecting the limited experience of some leaders in the profession.

A further aspect of Torland's (2011b) study considered the relationship between gender and emotional labor. She found there were no significant differences between males and females in relation to surface acting, deep acting, and their impact on job satisfaction. This finding contrasts with other studies that suggest that women in general are better at managing their emotions and are more emotionally intelligent than men. Torland (2011b) proposes that adventure tour leaders may behave as "shape-shifters," drawing on the best aspects of masculine and feminine traits to meet the job requirements, rather than conforming to mainstream gender stereotypes. Torland (2011a) does acknowledge that her study has some limitations such as the narrow scales used to measure deep and surface acting, the self-report nature of the questionnaires with associated risks of social desirability bias, and the purposive sample employed that may not be representative of the whole population.

While tourism research has applied many psychological theories and frameworks to examine tourists' experiences (Pearce, 1996, 2011), most have limited their investigations to studies covering only brief timespans (e.g. Arnould and Price, 1993; Mak *et al.*, 2011) and have applied Hochschild's (1983) emotional labor theory perspectives on these experiences. In contrast, Mackenzie and Kerr (2013) utilized psychological theories to investigate stress and emotion of one rafting guide and there have been a few sociological studies on mountaineering guides (Pomfret, 2006; Mackenzie and Kerr, 2013). Mackenzie and Kerr's study of a North American river guide's experiences in South America explored the emotional stress and emotions resulting from employer–guide interactions over a 16-week period in an intercultural context. They drew on reversal theory (Apter, 2001) that identifies key motivational states, sources of stress, and resulting emotions. Their findings confirmed those of some other studies (Ap and Wong, 2001; Sharpe, 2005), that adventure guiding requires high levels of emotional labor and can be associated with negative well-being outcomes related to both guide–client and guide–employer relations. However, the latter finding contrasts with Sharpe (2005) who found that guides in her study did not experience any feelings of estrangement. Brotheridge and Lee (2002) suggest more research is needed on the longitudinal nature of emotional labor to look in detail at how emotional labor develops over time.

A limited number of studies in the tour guiding literature have explored emotional labor in other tour guiding contexts. For example, Wong and Wang (2009) concluded from their study of Taiwanese tour leaders that the tour leaders were required to perform significant emotional labor resulting from a range of interpersonal interactions and that they adopted both surface and deep acting (Hochschild, 1983). Most of these emotional experiences are set by the tour participants' expectation that "the customer is always right," thus requiring the tour leader to perform the role of entertainer (Cohen, 1985) in order to deal with problems and complaints. Similar to Torland (2011a, b) and Mackenzie and Kerr (2013), Wong and Wang (2009) found that tour leaders displayed emotional labor in dealing both internally with the clients, as well as externally with other travel-related employees such as bus drivers and local guides.

In a study of interpretive guides at a heritage site, Van Dijk and Kirk (2007) examined the relationship between emotional labor and emotional dissonance using concepts derived from cognitive dissonance theory. They found that in contrast to other studies (Morris and Feldman, 1996), emotional labor and emotional dissonance are distinct constructs and that the negative outcomes of emotional labor are linked to conflicting cognitive appraisals. Van Dijk and Kirk (2007) suggest that additional proactive coping measures should be identified and included in models linking emotional labor and the provision of quality service and clearer conceptualization of the relationship between emotional labor and emotional dissonance.

In a more recent study of interpretive guides based at a zoo, Van Dijk et al. (2011) sought to assess the assumed positive relationship between deep acting and a range of organizationally desired visitor outcomes (e.g. word-of-mouth advertising, satisfaction) in comparison to surface acting. Torland (2011a) notes that the emotional performance of guides can impact tourists' experiences and satisfaction, as well as other outcomes important to tour operators such as profit, repeat visits, and image, but she does not measure these in her study. Using tourist surveys and self-reported emotional labor from guides, Van Dijk et al. (2011) found that there was no relationship between guide-reported acting and tourist perceptions of acting. In other words, tourists could not tell whether a guide was surface acting or deep acting (really "feeling") the emotion, and were satisfied with both, suggesting that the guides in this study were competent in displaying both deep and surface acting consistent with tourist expectations. A key management implication of this study is that rather than focusing on emotion management strategies to ensure an authentic display of emotion, the most effective way to ensure visitor outcomes may be to manage tourists' expectations and perceptions.

At some variance to these previous studies that support the work of Hochschild (1983) is a study by Guerrier and Adib (2003) on the emotional labor of tour representatives (reps) based in Mallorca, Spain. Their study was based on qualitative interviews with 15 tour reps at two resorts over 7 days with some potential limitations to the study. While they found that the reps experienced emotional labor, they managed the negative aspects of their work using their autonomy and discretion and developed strategies like making "friends" with the clients and gaining support from their colleagues. In contrast to Hochschild (1983), the researchers argue that it is emotional dissonance (i.e. behaving inauthentically) rather than emotional labor that affected the reps. They found the reps displayed deep authenticity where they can be "themselves," and surface authenticity where they are willing to manage the "dirty parts" of their job because it is part of that lifestyle.

These findings on the emotional experience of tour guiding in various contexts and over time, and the potential sources of stress, are important for guides as well as tour operators to help reduce issues such as burnout, staff turnover, and poor service quality. Many of these studies provide useful guidelines and recommendations for tour operators in relation to the recruitment, selection, training and education, and performance appraisal, and for guides themselves in terms of knowing about and using strategies to cope with the emotional labor.

The Future

Further opportunities exist to research both guide roles and emotions/emotional labor in the context of tour guiding. Overall, results of research on tour guiding roles have been mixed, not widely generalizable and largely inconclusive, other than to confirm that the various guiding roles identified by researchers are seen as important by most operators, guides, and tourists. The extent to which guides are recruited, trained, and empowered to deal with variations in role expectations and performance would be a fruitful avenue for further research, as would an examination of the impact of changing tourist expectations, industry trends (such as increased travel from new and emerging markets), and increased threats (such as litigation and terrorism) on tour guides' roles. Most studies have called for wider investigation of and further refinement in measuring both role importance and guide performance, but a deeper understanding of specific roles is also needed. For example, the role of the guide as mediator would benefit from greater research, to identify and describe the nature of the role, quantify and evaluate its contribution to the experience, and examine how to utilize the role as a tool for marketing what guided tours can offer tourists.

Until recently, most studies on the emotional dimension of tour guiding have adopted a qualitative research approach. There is a need for more quantitative studies that can generate reliable population-based and generalizable data and are well suited to establishing cause-and-effect relationships. In particular, more research is needed on the links between emotional labor and tourist and organizational outcomes. Many of the studies have focused on the negative effects of emotional labor but there may be opportunities to study the positive consequences for tour guides, tourists, and other stakeholders. Other avenues could include studies of tour guide emotions over time, comparative studies of tour guides in a range of tourism and intercultural contexts, and the response of tour guides to the experience of emotional dissonance. Finally, while most of the studies on emotional labor and tour guiding have applied Hochschild's (1983) theory, there are opportunities to apply other theories including reversal theory, consumptive emotion models, and tourist satisfaction theory.

A key finding of this review of two areas of tour guiding research is that many of the studies on tour guide roles and emotional labor have been undertaken in the adventure and ecotourism contexts that may or may not be applicable to other tour guiding contexts as well as the development of tour guiding theory. While tour guiding has been explored quite extensively in the literature, there is scope for broadening the context in which the research is undertaken, as well as drawing more explicitly on theory from other disciplines to progress this focus. Some authors have suggested the application of intercultural communication and linguistics theory, which has received limited attention, mainly in the context of Chinese tour guiding (Huang, 2004; Yu and Weiler, 2006; Scherle and Nonnenmann, 2008; Dioko *et al.*, 2013). Leadership theory in the tour guiding context has been discussed in the literature (Weiler, 1996; Howard, 1998) but has not been empirically tested. Both Weiler (1996) and Howard (1998) draw on Hersey and Blanchard's leadership model and identify the need for further work in this area, specifically to identify the extent to which tour guides play a role in influencing tourist behavior and attitudes, to explore appropriate leadership styles for tour guides and to develop a methodology for assessing tourists' level of readiness in relation to leadership.

While some guiding literature is theory-based, the development, testing, and refinement of tour guiding theory have been very limited. In some cases, theories have been suggested, for example, Weiler and Yu (2007) identify the brokering of physical access, understanding, and encounters with locals as three dimensions of cultural mediation, but these have not been explored, tested, or refined beyond the Chinese inbound guiding context. McGrath's (2007) highlighting of "emotional access" could well be a fourth dimension of guide mediation to add to Weiler and Yu's (2007) three dimensions. A recent new avenue of tour guiding research has been in the area of tour guide performance, largely utilizing constructivist-based approaches to researching tour guiding (Jonasson and Scherle, 2012; Overend, 2012). These studies are beginning to build a body of knowledge about what drives the content and style of individual guided tours and the consequences of these for tourists, their experiences and the site.

A review of the tour guiding literature undertaken by the authors for this book chapter indicates there has been some application of theories from other disciplines to tour guiding but that this has been ad hoc and in most cases isolated studies with limited building of knowledge from one study to another. There have been few instances where a theory has been proposed in relation to a tour guiding issue and then applied and empirically tested. Clearly there are many opportunities to draw on theories from other disciplines such as anthropology, history, psychology, geography, environmental science, economics, sociology, communications, linguistics, intercultural studies, political science, policy studies, planning, education, and business studies such as consumer behavior, marketing and management. We would recommend a more strategic and theoretical approach to tour guiding research, to further this important area of tourism study.

Questions

1. Can you think of any other roles that tour guides play that are not included in Cohen's model?
2. How well do you think that Cohen's model represents today's practice of tour guiding?
3. Are there other dimensions that could be added to Weiler and Davis's model?

4. What strategies can guides develop and use to address some of the negative consequences of deep and surface acting?

5. What strategies can employers implement to assist guides in addressing some of the negative emotional outcomes of emotional labor?

References

Almagor, U. (1985) A tourist's "Vision Quest" in an African game reserve. *Annals of Tourism Research* 12(1), 31–47.

Ap, J. and Wong, K.K.F. (2001) Case study on tour guiding: professionalism, issues and problems. *Tourism Management* 22(5), 551–563. DOI: 10.1016/s0261-5177(01)00013-9.

Apter, M.J. (2001) *Motivational Styles in Everyday Life: A Guide to Reversal Theory.* American Psychological Association, Washington, DC.

Arnould, E.J. and Price, L.L. (1993) River magic: extraordinary experience and the extended service encounter. *Journal of Consumer Research* 20(1), 24–45.

Ballantyne, R. and Hughes, K. (2001) Interpretation in ecotourism settings: investigating tour guides' perceptions of their role, responsibilities and training needs. *Journal of Tourism Studies* 12(2), 2–9.

Black, R. (2002) Towards a model for tour guide certification: an analysis of the Australian ecoguide program. PhD, Monash University, Melbourne, Australia.

Black, R. and Ham, S. (2005) Improving the quality of tour guiding: towards a model for tour guide certification. *Journal of Ecotourism* 4(3), 178–195.

Black, R. and Weiler, B. (2005) Quality assurance and regulatory mechanisms in the tour guiding industry: a systematic review. *Journal of Tourism Studies* 16(1), 24–37.

Brotheridge, C.M. and Lee, R.T. (2002) Testing a conservation of resources model of the dynamics of emotional labor. *Journal of Occupational Health Psychology* 7(1), 57–67.

Carnicelli-Filho, S. (2010) Rafting guides: leisure, work and lifestyle. *Annals of Leisure Research* 13(1/2), 282–297.

Cohen, E. (1979) Rethinking the sociology of tourism. *Annals of Tourism Research* 6(1), 18–35.

Cohen, E. (1985) The tourist guide: the origins, structure and dynamics of a role. *Annals of Tourism Research* 12(1), 5–29. DOI: 10.1016/0160-7383(85)90037-4.

Dahling, J.J. (2007) Suppressing positive emotional displays at work: an analysis of the individual and organizational consequences among nurses. PhD, University of Akron, Ohio.

de Kadt, E. (1979) *Tourism: Passport to Development?* Oxford University Press, New York.

Dioko, L.A.N., Harrill, R. and Cardon, P.W. (2013) The wit and wisdom of Chinese tour guides: a critical tourism perspective. *Journal of China Tourism Research* 9(1), 27–49.

Geva, A. and Goldman, A. (1991) Satisfaction measurements in guided tours. *Annals of Tourism Research* 18, 177–185.

Goffman, E. (1959) *The Presentation of Self in Everyday Life.* Doubleday, Garden City, New York.

Guerrier, Y. and Adib, A. (2003) Work at leisure and leisure at work: a study of the emotional labour of tour reps. *Human Relations* 56(11), 1399–1417.

Gurung, G., Simmons, D. and Devlin, P. (1996) The evolving role of tourist guides: the Nepali experience. In: Butler, R. and Hinch, T. (eds) *Tourism and Indigenous Peoples.* International Thomson Business Press, London, pp. 108–128.

Haig, I. and McIntyre, N. (2002) Viewing nature: the role of the guide and the advantages of participating in commercial ecotourism. *The Journal of Tourism Studies* 13(1), 39–49.

Ham, S.H. and Weiler, B. (2000) *Six Principles for Tour Guide Training and Sustainable Development in Developing Countries.* Paper Presented at the 9th Nordic Tourism Conference "Tourism in Peripheral Areas—Experiences for the 21st Century." Research Centre of Bornholm, Denmark.

Hillman, W. (2006) Tour Guides and Emotional Labour: An Overview of Links in the Literature. *TASA Conference Proceedings*.

Hochschild, A.E. (1983) *The Managed Heart: Commercialization of Human Feeling*. University of California Press, Berkeley, California.

Holloway, J.C. (1981) The guided tour a sociological approach. *Annals of Tourism Research* 8(3), 377–402.

Holyfield, L. (1999) Manufacturing adventure: the buying and selling of emotions. *Journal of Contemporary Ethnography* 28(1), 3–32.

Howard, J. (1998) Towards best practice in interpretive guided activities. *Australian Parks and Recreation* Summer, 28–31.

Howard, J., Thwaites, R. and Smith, B. (2001) Investigating the roles of the Indigenous tour guide. *Journal of Tourism Studies* 12(2), 32–39.

Huang, Y. (2004) A study of intercultural communication of professional tour guides in Yunnan. PhD, La Trobe University, Melbourne, Australia.

Hughes, K. (1991) Tourist satisfaction: a guided cultural tour in North Queensland. *Australian Psychologist* 26(3), 166–171.

Jafari, J. (1985) Editor's page. *Annals of Tourism Research* 12, 1–2.

Jenkins, S. and Conley, H. (2005) Emotional labour in the teaching profession. *Management Research News* 28(9), 67–68.

Johanson, M.M. and Woods, R.H. (2008) Recognizing the emotional element in service excellence. *Cornell Hospitality Quarterly* 49(3), 310–316.

Jonasson, M. and Scherle, N. (2012) Performing co-produced guided tours. *Scandinavian Journal of Hospitality and Tourism* 12(1), 55–73.

Mackenzie, S.H. and Kerr, J.H. (2013) Stress and emotions at work: an adventure tourism guide's experiences. *Tourism Management* 36, 3–14.

Mak, A.H.N., Wong, K.K.F. and Chang, R.C.Y. (2011) Critical issues affecting the service quality and professionalism of the tour guides in Hong Kong and Macau. *Tourism Management* 32(6), 1442–1452. DOI: 10.1016/j.tourman.2011.01.003.

Mann, S. (997) Emotional labor in organizations. *Leadership and Organization Development Journal* 18(1), 4–12.

McGrath, G. (2007) Towards developing tour guides as interpreters of cultural heritage: the case of Cusco, Peru. In: Black, R. and Crabtree, A. (eds) *Quality Assurance and Certification in Ecotourism*. CAB International, Wallingford, UK, pp. 364–394.

Morris, J.A. and Feldman, D.C. (1996) The dimensions, antecedents, and consequences of emotional labor. *Academy of Management Review* 21(4), 986–1010.

Ormsby, A. and Mannle, K. (2006) Ecotourism benefits and the role of local guides at Masoala National Park, Madagascar. *Journal of Sustainable Tourism* 14(3), 271–287.

Overend, D. (2012) Performing sites: illusion and authenticity in the spatial stories of the guided tour. *Scandinavian Journal of Hospitality and Tourism* 12(1), 44–54.

Pearce, P.L. (1996) Recent research in tourist behaviour. *Asia Pacific Journal of Tourism Research* 1(1), 7–17.

Pearce, P.L. (2011) *Tourist Behaviour and the Contemporary World*. Channel View Publications, Bristol, UK.

Pearce, P.L., Kim, E. and Syamsul, L. (1998) Facilitating tourist-host social interaction. In: Laws, E., Faulkner, B. and Moscardo, G. (eds) *Embracing and Managing Change in Tourism*. Routledge, London, pp. 347–364.

Pereira, E.M. and Mykletun, R.J. (2012) Guides as contributors to sustainable tourism? A case study from the Amazon. *Scandinavian Journal of Hospitality and Tourism* 12(1), 74–94.

Pomfret, G. (2006) Mountaineering adventure tourists: a conceptual framework for research. *Tourism Management* 27(1), 113–123.

Pond, K. (1993) *The Professional Guide: Dynamics of Tour Guiding*. Van Nostrand Reinhold, New York.

Randall, C. and Rollins, R.B. (2009) Visitor perceptions of the role of tour guides in natural areas. *Journal of Sustainable Tourism* 17(3), 357–374.

Scherle, N. and Nonnenmann, A. (2008) Swimming in cultural flows: conceptualising tour guides as intercultural mediators and cosmopolitans. *Journal of Tourism and Cultural Change* 6(2), 120–137.

Sharpe, E.K. (2005) "Going above and beyond": the emotional labor of adventure guides. *Journal of Leisure Research* 37(1), 29–50.

Shephard, K. and Royston-Airey, P. (2000) Exploring the role of part-time ecotourism guides in central Southern England. *Journal of Sustainable Tourism* 8(4), 324–332.

Smith, V.L. (1961) Needed: geographically-trained tourist guides. *The Professional Geographer* 13(6), 28–30.

Torland, M. (2011a) Effects of emotional labor on adventure tour leaders' job satisfaction. *Tourism Review International* 14, 129–142.

Torland, M. (2011b) Emotional labour and job satisfaction of adventure tour leaders: does gender matter? *Annals of Leisure Research* 14(4), 369–389.

Van Dijk, P.A. and Kirk, A. (2007) Being somebody else: emotional labour and emotional dissonance in the context of the service experience at a heritage tourism site. *Journal of Hospitality and Tourism Management* 14, 157–169.

Van Dijk, P., Smith, L.D.G. and Cooper, B.K. (2011) Are you for real? an evaluation of the relationship between emotional labour and visitor outcomes. *Tourism Management* 31(1), 39–45.

Weiler, B. (1996) Leading tours, greening tourists: applying leadership theory to guiding nature tours. *Australian Journal of Leisure and Recreation* 7(4), 43–47.

Weiler, B. (1999) Assessing the interpretation competencies of ecotour guides. *Journal of Interpretation Research* 4(1), 80–83.

Weiler, B. and Crabtree, A. (1998) *Developing Competent Ecotour Guides.* National Centre for Vocational Education Research, Adelaide, Australia.

Weiler, B. and Davis, D. (1993) An exploratory investigation into the roles of the nature-based tour leader. *Tourism Management* 14(2), 91–98.

Weiler, B. and Ham, S.H. (1999) *Training Ecotour Guides in Developing Countries: Lessons Learned from Panama's First Guide Course.* Paper Presented at the New Frontiers in Tourism Research. The International Society of Travel and Tourism Educators, Vancouver, Canada.

Weiler, B. and Ham, S.H. (2001) Tour guides and interpretation. In: Weaver, D. (ed.) *Encyclopedia of Ecotourism*. CAB International, Wallingford, UK.

Weiler, B. and Kim, A.K. (2011) Tour guides as agents of sustainability: rhetoric, reality and implications for research. *Tourism Recreation Research* 36(2), 113–125.

Weiler, B. and Yu, X. (2007) Dimensions of cultural mediation in guiding Chinese tour groups: implications for interpretation. *Tourism Recreation Research* 32(3), 13–22.

Weiler, B., Johnson, T. and Davis, D. (1992) *Roles of the Tour Leader in Environmentally Responsible Tourism*. Paper Presented at the Ecotourism Incorporating The Global Classroom, University of Queensland, Brisbane, Queensland.

Wong, J.Y. and Wang, C.H. (2009) Emotional labor of the tour leaders: an exploratory study. *Tourism Management* 30(2), 249–259.

Yu, X. and Weiler, B. (2006) Guiding Chinese tour groups in Australia: an analysis using role theory. In: Prideaux, B. and Moscardo, G. (eds) *Managing Tourism and Hospitality Services: Theory and International Application*. CAB International, Wallingford, UK, pp. 181–194.

5 Theoretical Perspectives on Rural Tourism Development

Doris A. Carson[1] and Rhonda Koster[2]*

[1]Department of Geography and Economic History, Umeå University, Umeå, Sweden and Centre for Rural Health & Community Development, University of South Australia, Whyalla, South Australia; [2]School of Outdoor Recreation, Parks and Tourism, Lakehead University, Thunder Bay, Ontario, Canada

The Objectives

The purpose of this chapter is to discuss several theories appropriate to the examination of tourism in remote resource peripheries. The objectives are to:

1. Discuss how remote resource peripheries are distinct from rural areas in the urban periphery, illustrating the challenges and opportunities this engenders for rural tourism development.
2. Provide a review of theories appropriate to the examination of tourism in remote resource peripheries, including new regionalism, network models, and the staples thesis of resource-dependent economic development.
3. Introduce a case study from Australia to illustrate the application of these theories in rural tourism research.

The Vignette

> One of our main challenges is to develop a brand that reflects the spirit of the whole region. I mean the region is huge, and the south is certainly quite different from the areas around Wilpena Pound and further north. Just different landscapes, different people… But trying to get everybody to the table and to understand that we need to be a region, and not a bunch of individual towns and stations, is just so difficult…And I think this is a real challenge for us, because "the region" is not part of a local identity, especially in the south…People have to learn how to become a region, and we need to keep working on this, it won't happen overnight.
>
> (Regional Tourism Development Officer in the Flinders Ranges, South Australia)

As the quote from a tourism industry representative in South Australia illustrates, tourism in remote resource peripheries is often plagued with unique sets of issues and

*Corresponding author, e-mail: rkoster@lakeheadu.ca

challenges. In this chapter we will discuss a number of theoretical approaches that help us better understand the dynamics of tourism in remote resource peripheries.

The Context

Rural tourism is difficult to define, illustrated by an ongoing debate among researchers.[1] In its simplest form, rural tourism includes activities (leisure and recreational) that occur in the countryside or rural spaces (Sharpley, 2004); the difficulty is that such a characterization relies on a common definition of rural, which is even more complex. Lane (1994) suggests there are three aspects of rural that are critical within the context of tourism: small population densities and settlement sizes; traditional economic activities (usually agricultural in focus); and traditional social structures. The nature of these criteria is problematic and as a result, many researchers have agreed to a rural–urban continuum as a way of defining different degrees of rurality—from the economically and often gentrified areas on the urban fringe through to more remote outer peripheries (Sharpley, 2004; Hall and Boyd, 2005; Schmallegger *et al.*, 2010). This chapter examines rural tourism in more remote peripheral areas, particularly remote resource-dependent peripheries as found within the Canadian and Australian context.

The literature suggests that there are no universal rules for defining rural, remote, or peripheral localities that can be applied across different jurisdictions (Carson *et al.*, 2011). Within the Canadian context, rural areas have been defined as comprising towns and municipalities outside the commuting zone of larger urban centers (i.e. those with a population of 10,000 or more) (Du Plessis *et al.*, 2001). In Australia, definitions have varied according to the purpose of different policy programs, but usually reflect a location's low population density and low levels of access to services (Carson *et al.*, 2011). Crudely put, the terms "rural" and "remote" are used to describe non-urban localities with small populations (less than 25,000 people for rural, and less than 5000 for remote) and increasingly restricted access to services because of distance or lack of transport infrastructure (Roufeil and Battye, 2008). Yet, understanding the context of rural requires more than demographic definitions. As Carson *et al.* (2011) suggest, remoteness and peripherality are subjective terms, defined at times by those outside and at times by those inside a particular region. They argue that "remoteness can be nested within a region, such that the region itself is remote from some core, and there is an internal organization within the region of central and peripheral locations" (p. 4).

A common feature of remote peripheral areas is that community economies are predominantly based on the extraction and export of natural resources, resulting in a further designation as being resource peripheries. Such communities are peripheral from an economic and political point of view, as they are dependent on external markets, capital flows and decision making based in distant urban core areas (Bradbury, 1987; Huskey and Morehouse, 1992; Markey *et al.*, 2000; Howlett and Brownsey, 2008). It is this context of remote resource peripheries which is the main focus of this chapter.

Rural tourism has become a significant element in economic and regional development strategies, especially in those areas struggling with changes to their resource-based economies. There are various reasons for tourism's perceived positive impact on rural economies, as identified by several researchers (Fleischer and Felsenstein, 2000; Briedenhann and Wickens, 2004; Hall and Boyd, 2005; Mitchell and Hall, 2005; Williams and Copus, 2005; Garrod *et al.*, 2006; Müller and Jansson, 2007; George *et al.*, 2009):

- Tourism offers opportunities for economic diversification from dependence on traditional rural (and natural resource-based) industries.
- Tourism is perceived as a relatively "easy" and "cheap" option to encourage economic development that can take advantage of existing infrastructure and resources and requires little in terms of new investment (compared to other primary or secondary industries).
- Due to increasingly urbanized lifestyles, there is a greater desire to reconnect with the rural idyll, providing opportunities for rural communities to commodify and sell "authentic" rural experiences as a tourism product.
- Improved infrastructure and transport technologies have facilitated greater tourist access to rural areas, even to those further away from major access corridors.

As Weaver and Lawton (2004) and Lane (1994) suggest, it is likely those communities located within the rural–urban fringe, or inner periphery, are able to benefit the most from tourism development due to their proximity to large urban populations. Yet, there is increasing interest in the prospects for tourism development in more remote areas, which have considerably fewer economic development options other than those offered by natural resource industries (Müller and Jansson, 2007; George *et al.*, 2009; Koster and Lemelin, 2009; Noakes and Johnston, 2010; Carson and Carson, 2011). Despite the perceived opportunities, the literature has identified a long list of challenges for tourism in these areas (Hohl and Tisdell, 1995; Wanhill, 1997; Hall and Boyd, 2005; Moscardo, 2005; Noakes and Johnston, 2010), including:

- geographic isolation from mass markets, suppliers, intermediaries, and political decision makers;
- extreme climatic conditions causing strong seasonality in tourism;
- relatively narrow market opportunities resulting in over-dependence on a limited number of key markets;
- lack of tourism infrastructure and product to generate a comprehensive destination experience;
- lack of critical mass and density of businesses resulting in a highly fragmented industry;
- dominance of small and micro businesses with limited knowledge and entrepreneurial capabilities;
- lack of community experience and knowledge in managing tourism impacts on fragile social and natural environments;
- dependence on external and/or government stakeholders for marketing, planning, and funding; and
- limited organizational structures and institutional "thinness" leading to poor representation of community interests.

To overcome these challenges, it has often been argued that individual tourism stakeholders and communities need to collaborate more effectively on a wider regional basis. Such collaboration is seen as vital to create a better "destination package" of products and experiences that can attract visitors and extend their length of stay

D.A. Carson and R. Koster

(Roberts and Hall, 2001; Gunn and Var, 2002; Reid, 2003; Meyer-Cech, 2005). Yet, the tourism literature also suggests that regional collaboration in these areas is missing, or at best limited, due to reasons such as: embedded competition between communities; a lack of regional identity; a lack of history of working together; and limited local capabilities and experience in managing collaborative initiatives (Reed, 2000; Wilson et al., 2001; Dredge and Jenkins, 2003; Freshwater, 2004; Petrzelka et al., 2006; Koster, 2008).

These issues are often exacerbated by externally driven regional tourism planning initiatives, which take regional cohesion and collaboration in tourism for granted, without questioning whether individual stakeholders and communities actually can (or want to) work together (Dredge, 2005; Carson et al., 2014). Developing more sustainable tourism industries in remote rural areas requires a better understanding of how tourism systems operate in such areas and what factors influence their capacities to interact and work together as a strong regional tourism destination. The following section reviews theoretical concepts drawn from the literature on new regionalism, network models in rural tourism, and the staples thesis of resource dependence to provide a more holistic understanding of tourism dynamics in remote resource peripheries.

The Theory

The following theories are identified to help researchers understand tourism in remote resource peripheries.

New regionalism (and its challenges in peripheral areas)

The idea of "New Regionalism" emerged during the 1990s as a theoretical approach towards economic development, recognizing "regions" as the key units for understanding socioeconomic activity (MacLeod, 2001; Rainnie and Grant, 2005). In the face of increasing pressures from globalization, it has been argued that localized institutions and networks of social relations determine the success of a regional socioeconomic system by differentiating themselves from one another, reasserting localized interests and strengths, and developing competitive advantage in a global marketplace (Webb and Collis, 2000; MacLeod, 2001). The new regionalism body of thought draws heavily on institutionalist conceptions of economic development, suggesting that embedded customs, accepted norms, conventions and routines determine how individuals and organizations interact and, thus, shape economic development (Morgan, 1997; Storper, 1997; Amin, 1999). From this perspective, the "region" is seen as the ideal level at which networks of interactions occur, as it is small enough to allow for regular contact that encourages reciprocal trust and cooperative relationships, yet at the same time big enough to include a critical mass of actors, organizations, and network relationships (Webb and Collis, 2000).

This "institutional turn" in economic analysis recognizes that institutions are highly place- and path-dependent, meaning that different forms and degrees of social interaction occur in different places, depending on the unique socio-political and cultural factors that continue to reshape a system's development path over time (Jones, 2001;

Martin and Sunley, 2006). This approach is used to explain why different regions with different histories develop different levels of capacity to assert their regional differences and achieve competitive advantage (Amin, 1999). It is also one of the fundamental tenets in the increasing body of work on Regional Innovation Systems (RIS) (Doloreux and Parto, 2005; Tödtling and Trippl, 2005; Asheim et al., 2011), which suggests that innovation capacity is contextualized and embedded within a particular socio-political and cultural environment, depending on the nature and extent of interactions and the diffusion of knowledge and ideas.

At what geographic scale the region should operate, and how its boundaries should be defined, has remained a contested issue in the literature (Doloreux and Parto, 2005; Shearmur, 2011). The designation, coordination, and governance of regions can be based on "top-down" regionalization approaches driven by centralized government bodies, or it can emerge from endogenous "bottom-up" processes of regionalism driven by local stakeholders who self-organize around a shared goal or identity into a coherent system (Webb and Collis, 2000; Jones and MacLeod, 2004; Hamin and Marcucci, 2008; Taylor, 2012). Other authors have argued that regions should be seen as open functional systems where processes of interaction and learning occur across space, irrespective of geo-spatial boundaries, allowing for optimal learning outcomes (Bunnell and Coe, 2001; Shearmur, 2011).

Questions of system coherence, appropriate boundaries, and regional self-organization are particularly important in the context of peripheral regions that, from an administrative point of view, usually cover vast geographical territories. These territories are likely to be internally heterogeneous, as they are patchworks of multiple dispersed and disconnected communities with different socioeconomic development paths (Carson et al., 2011). These communities may have completely different embedded perceptions of "their" region. Hence, the boundaries created by external regionalization processes and internal regionalism dynamics may not necessarily align (Hamin and Marcucci, 2008), leading to issues of local resistance to regional policy programs, competition between different embedded network constellations, and a lack of cross-regional collaborative interactions (Taylor, 2012).

In tourism, conflicts emerging from regional boundaries that are incompatible with locally embedded network dynamics and perceptions of the region are not uncommon (Dredge, 2005; Henriksen and Halkier, 2009; Carson et al., 2014; Koster and Lemelin, 2013). In many countries, including Canada and Australia, regional boundaries for tourism planning and destination marketing are drawn by centralized government agencies to create manageable sub-regions, usually delineated by grouping communities sharing similar natural and cultural features within a bounded geographical space to create distinctive regional destination brands (Reid, 1998; Dredge, 2005). Dredge's work in New South Wales, Australia, observed that such state-driven production of regional tourism destinations failed to encourage regional interaction and collaboration, because externally imposed destination boundaries and branding messages clashed with different local practices and priorities (Dredge and Jenkins, 2003; Dredge, 2005). High levels of embedded parochialism led to intra-regional competition for tourism resources, a lack of collaborative tourism initiatives within both local government and industry sectors, and resistance to state government-endorsed regional tourism organizations.

These issues are likely to become even more pronounced in more remote peripheral regions where communities are separated not only by distance but by different development

D.A. Carson and R. Koster

paths and local identities. Yet, even though the need for regional collaboration in rural tourism development has repeatedly been emphasized (Meyer-Cech, 2005; Jackson and Murphy, 2006; Novelli *et al.*, 2006), the relevance of regionalism and the impacts of regionalization on regional interactions have largely been neglected in tourism research (Dredge and Jenkins, 2003; Carson *et al.*, 2014). As argued by Koster (2007), much of the research on rural tourism appears to focus on those factors *within* communities that make tourism successful, not *between* communities in a region, assuming that communities already have a strong network in place that supports and encourages regional participation. Such assumptions may be appropriate if the regions already have a reasonable history in tourism development; they are less likely to apply in the context of remote resource peripheries, where distant communities (many of them with a history as a single-industry resource town) are turning to tourism as a way of diversifying their economy.

Koster's work (2007, 2010) on tourism development in some of Canada's resource peripheries found that community resistance to regional collaboration was rooted in a history of competition between communities and a commensurate interest in hoarding resources locally to maintain a sense of independence. Collaborative action was limited to temporary initiatives, usually required by higher level government agencies. Koster concluded that regional collaboration in those resource peripheries was a very delicate issue complicated by many different layers, including historic social, political, and cultural relationships between individuals, groups, and organizations, both within and between communities. Understanding the prospects for regionalism, and the development of strong collaborative regional tourism systems, in remote peripheral areas therefore requires a more critical examination of local community interactions within the region and how the evolution of local attitudes, network processes, and institutional structures impacts on regional system dynamics.

Network models in rural tourism

Several authors have examined rural tourism from various network-based approaches to understand the actors and relationships involved in localities where tourism takes place (Reed, 2000; Dredge, 2006; Jackson and Murphy, 2006; Novelli *et al.*, 2006; Saxena, 2006; Koster, 2007; Hall and Williams, 2008; Saxena and Ilbery, 2008). Networks in this context are the social relationships which actors form to achieve tourism-related goals, and several authors (Hall, 2000; Dredge, 2006; Saxena, 2006; Saxena and Ilbery, 2008) have determined the variety of characteristics that define networks, based on a continuum from:

- Formal (structured organizations with paid staff, for example a regional tourism association) to loose groupings of like-minded individuals (e.g. volunteers working on a community beautification project).
- Hard (economic and profit-oriented, forming to achieve shared objectives, and based on formal agreements) to soft (open membership, driven by need or crisis, likely to require continuing agency support, and based on cooperation and reciprocity).
- Horizontal (between different actors/organizations operating at the same level) and vertical (between actors/organizations operating at different levels).

- Open (made up of spatially dispersed participants, multiple actors, and complex power relationships) to closed (bonds between actors are more personal, there is a greater sense of place attachment, and knowledge is more easily shared and transferred).

Saxena and Ilbery (2008: 239) have developed the concept of Integrated Rural Tourism (IRT), defining it as "a mesh of networks of local and external actors, in which endogenous and embedded resources are mobilized in order to expand the assets and capabilities of rural communities and empower them to participate in, negotiate with, influence, and hold accountable the actors and institutions that affect their lives." The key theoretical strains in their conceptualization are embeddedness, endogenous development and community empowerment. Embeddedness suggests that the way people undertake economic development is tied to the social relationships that they belong to, and that those relationships are in turn tied to a particular place (for example, people living and working in a small agricultural community would be more likely to understand and support the construction of a new grain terminal instead of a theme park that is not related to the socioeconomic history of the community). Endogenous development refers to development strategies that are: (i) based on locally unique economic, environmental, and cultural resources; (ii) undertaken to retain the greatest benefits within the locality; (iii) structured to be complementary to existing resource use and values; and (iv) include local community members in decision making. Connected to and building on this idea, Saxena and Ilbery (2008: 239) conceive of community empowerment as a process that provides "a shared understanding and ownership of goals and objectives, helping members realize the 'network advantage' by aggregating and creating new knowledge and building capacity" for tourism development.

Similar ideas have been incorporated in studies analyzing tourism cluster dynamics, particularly in the context of rural areas where getting disconnected stakeholders to cooperate in order to build a strong destination experience is required (Hall, 2005; Jackson and Murphy, 2006; Novelli et al., 2006; Taylor et al., 2007; Weidenfeld et al., 2010). For example, Novelli et al. (2006) argue that business operators in particular often regard one another as competitors, so addressing issues of social ties and trust becomes instrumental in influencing willingness to cooperate for the sake of long-term benefits. Reed (2000) and Dredge (2006) echo the importance of cooperation in tourism planning, but propose that it is difficult to achieve because of the power differentials that exist within communities. In addition, Jackson and Murphy (2006) suggest that embedded levels of local leadership and institutional support determine the extent to which fragmented industry members can operate as a well-functioning destination that is both collaborative and competitive.

Extending the work on tourism clusters, an increasing number of authors have applied the concept of RIS to a tourism context (Hall and Williams, 2008; Prats et al., 2008; Hjalager, 2010; Romeiro and Costa, 2010; Weidenfeld, 2013). These approaches have included a more comprehensive institutional perspective on tourism network dynamics, including consideration of government interactions, public-private partnerships and the impacts of institutional infrastructures on stakeholder interactions and collective learning. Like Saxena and Ilbery's (2008) work on IRT, studies on RIS in tourism consider innovation capacity as embedded within particular geographical scales and contextualized through place-specific economic, political, and cultural determinants.

The RIS framework has recently been applied to the analysis of tourism development in remote resource peripheries (Schmallegger, 2010; Carson and Carson, 2011), focusing specifically on how the institutional legacies inherited from resource dependence impact on the behavior of emergent tourism systems. The following section summarizes this work, paying particular attention to the implications of the "staples thesis" and the role of resource-based path dependence in rural tourism analysis.

Staples thesis and resource-based path dependence

The staples thesis emerged in the early 20th century as a theoretical approach to explaining the processes of unbalanced economic development experienced in "countries of recent settlement" (such as Canada, Australia, New Zealand, South Africa, or Argentina). These countries had traditionally relied on exporting minimally processed natural bulk resources, such as minerals, grain, fish, lumber, or wool, to distant core markets (Altman, 2003; Howlett and Brownsey, 2008). It was argued that economies reliant on staples export can easily become trapped in fragile economic development paths where they become over-dependent on external markets and fail to convert export-driven growth into more diversified and self-sustaining economic activity (Watkins, 1963; Barnes *et al.*, 2001; Wellstead, 2008). This situation came to be known as the "staples trap," meaning that economies struggle to diversify and continue to focus on staples industries even when these industries no longer generate sufficient income (Watkins, 1963; Wellstead, 2008). While initially developed in the context of nation states, subsequent studies have applied the staples approach to the analysis of economic development paths at a regional level in order to explain why peripheral regions dependent on resource export continue to be at the economic and social margins of their states or provinces (Barnes *et al.*, 2001; Gunton, 2003; Halseth, 2010).

From an evolutionary institutional perspective, the staples trap is comparable to a situation of "lock-in" where the institutional environment has become politically, socially, and culturally embedded to the extent that the economy becomes addicted to and stuck in established practices, ideas, and networks, and unable to engage in processes of economic change, renewal, and innovation (Martin and Sunley, 2006). Carson and Carson (2011) have summarized the staples literature identifying a number of reasons why such lock-in occurs in economies dependent on resource export; long-term resource dependence can lead to a form of institutional lock-in that is characterized by an entrenched export mentality among governments, a strong culture of dependence on externally-based decision makers among local communities, a lack of local entrepreneurship and leadership capabilities, a lack of local skills and knowledge to manage economic transition, strong attachment to traditional industries limiting local aspirations for change, and a lack of local experience in mobilizing joint forces to develop and implement new ideas.

The work by Schmallegger and colleagues (Schmallegger, 2010; Schmallegger *et al.*, 2010; Carson and Carson, 2011) illustrated how examining peripheral tourism destinations through the lens of the staples thesis adds a more comprehensive perspective to tourism research in remote resource peripheries, thus contributing to a better understanding of "integrated rural tourism." Using an RIS framework, they determined how traditional approaches to economic development in remote resource peripheries have impacted on local abilities to diversify to new industries such as tourism, paying particular attention to:

- the characteristics of economic policy directions;
- the nature of public-private sector interactions;
- the climate for entrepreneurialism and leadership;
- the prevalent networking, cluster, and knowledge exchange dynamics;
- the existing level of skills and strategies for human capital development; and
- community attitudes towards supporting a new (non-resource-related) industry.

The following case study from Australia builds on these considerations and provides an example of how considerations drawn from the literature on resource dependence, new regionalism, and network models in tourism can be used as a theoretical lens to help us examine and explain the unique nature and dynamics of tourism development in remote resource peripheries.

Case Study: The Flinders Ranges in South Australia[2]

The Flinders Ranges (Fig. 5.1) is a sparsely populated mountain region in South Australia that stretches from Port Pirie (200 km north of Adelaide) to Arkaroola (650 km north of Adelaide). It is home to approximately 44,000 people, most of whom live in the two regional centers, Port Pirie and Port Augusta (Australian Bureau of Statistics, 2013). The region is very diverse in terms of demographic, economic, and topographic characteristics and can be divided into three sub-regions: the more densely populated Southern Flinders Ranges (characterized by semi-arid agricultural landscape and numerous small communities relying on broadacre agriculture and livestock grazing); the Central Flinders Ranges (characterized by rugged mountains, arid vegetation, and a number of dispersed settlements and pastoral stations); and the Northern Flinders Ranges (characterized by rugged mountains and dry desert plains, limited accessibility via unsealed roads, and very small and isolated mining communities, pastoral stations, and Indigenous communities).

Since the first European settlement in the mid-19th century, the region has been dependent on three of South Australia's most prominent staples industries: grain farming (wheat and barley), pastoralism (sheep and cattle), and mining (copper and coal). As a classic resource hinterland, it has been quite vulnerable to regular "boom and bust" cycles caused by either depletion of mineral resources, collapsing commodity prices, or prolonged periods of drought. Tourism as a form of economic diversification was first introduced in the late 1960s, when local stakeholders in the Central and Northern Flinders Ranges realized that increasing numbers of independent tourists offered potential for new income streams. Since then a couple of bigger resorts have been developed in the vicinity of Wilpena Pound and Arkaroola, and a number of small pastoral stations have started to offer station-based accommodation and activities. Tourism in the agriculture-dominated Southern Flinders Ranges did not start as a serious industry until the late 1990s when a record drought forced southern communities to consider options for economic diversification (until then the south had always been much less affected by extreme climatic conditions than the north). During the "millennium drought," government support programs for farmers were made

D.A. Carson and R. Koster

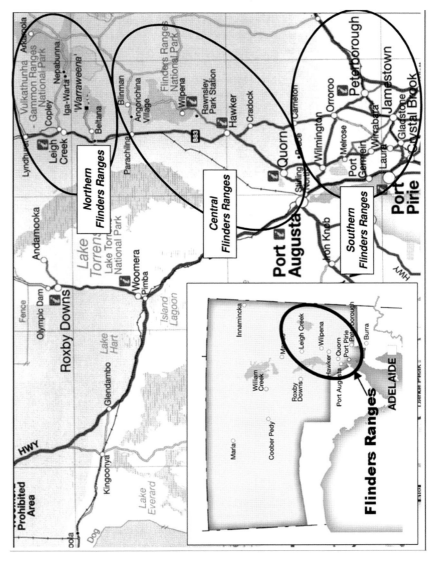

Fig. 5.1. Flinders Ranges, South Australia.

available to encourage tourism as an on-farm diversification option, and some of the southern local governments provided funding for a regional tourism development officer to stimulate tourism in their communities.

Creating a strong cohesive and collaborative regional tourism system in the Flinders Ranges has remained a very challenging task until today. Part of the reason for this is that past tourism "regionalization" approaches by the state government have not been well aligned with local perceptions of the region. While the Flinders Ranges destination during the 1970s and 1980s comprised only the central and northern parts (which share a common destination image based around rugged mountains, pastoral and mining heritage), the state tourism organization decided in the mid-1990s to merge some rural destinations for cost-saving reasons. During that period, the Flinders Ranges were officially joined by the former Far North region (also known as the South Australian Outback) and the northern parts of the former Mid North region (now known as the Southern Flinders Ranges). This new tourism region was called "Flinders Ranges and Outback South Australia"—a vast area comprising almost 800,000 km² or more than 80% of the state's landmass.

Encouraging regional collaboration across this vast territory was repeatedly identified as one of the biggest challenges in subsequent strategic tourism plans rolled out by the state tourism organization. Tourism stakeholders in the south, north, and the even more remote Outback had no aspirations or incentives to network and collaborate. The new tourism region was spanning across pre-existing boundaries that had previously been created for economic development and natural resource management in order to delineate different staples and land use forms. It "forced" the agricultural districts from the Mid North, the pastoral districts from the Flinders Ranges, and the desert-like Outback areas (including remote mining towns, cattle stations, and Indigenous communities) to act as one region, even though these sub-regions had no common history of working together. This "tourism amalgamation" resulted in some tensions around the definition of the region's tourism brand. Marketing collateral produced by the state and regional tourism organizations usually featured images of the Central and Northern Flinders Ranges, because the mountains were considered to be the most attractive features of the region, and that area was also more advanced in terms of product development. Not surprisingly, stakeholders in the south and in the Outback (where the landscape is less "exciting" and product development comparatively limited) felt neglected and demanded more support from destination marketing agencies.

In response to these tensions, several local governments in the south decided to form their own Southern Flinders regional tourism authority in the early 2000s to foster product development and marketing in the south. However, even within this southern form of tourism collaboration there were tensions between individual communities, as certain towns and places were perceived to be given priority over others in terms of marketing focus and infrastructure funding. Embedded competition for government services and funding was clearly an issue in the south, where agricultural communities had historically been quite independent from each other. Traditional competition and small-town jealousies were further exacerbated by local government amalgamations (which had been enforced during the 1990s), which saw some of the smaller communities losing their sense of independence and self-esteem.

Competition and parochialism were less of a problem in the north, where pastoral communities were used to having strong personal support networks to survive in the

D.A. Carson and R. Koster

harsh environment and unstable economic climate. The northern pastoralists had a much stronger regional, rather than local, sense of place, and felt socially and culturally connected to other pastoralists in the area who were facing similar challenges. However, this sense of togetherness did not really translate into collaboration on a business level for tourism purposes. Instead, pastoral families were used to operating their stations in isolation, focusing on the delivery of raw materials (i.e. wool) to large external wholesalers. As staples producers, they were not familiar with the various tasks involved in tourism product commercialization (packaging, promotion, distribution) and struggled to develop linkages with other tourism stakeholders to market their products and the broader destination. Opportunities for business collaboration were further compromised by a lack of product complementarity and limited knowledge of how to develop tourism synergies at a destination level. As they were used to producing homogeneous bulk commodities, they seemed to be unable to differentiate their tourism products from their neighbors' products. This led to a homogenized form of diversification, where pastoral communities in various locations ended up offering very similar experiences (station-based accommodation and four-wheel-drive tracks), thus limiting opportunities for business linkages and collaborative marketing.

A certain embedded dependency culture on government investment and leadership also constrained collaborative dynamics at the regional level. Not only did many farm-based tourism operators continuously expect grants for new product development and government investment in new tourism infrastructure, there was a clear "addiction" to public sector leadership for managing new regional tourism initiatives. Such new initiatives (e.g. cycle tourism development in the south or geotourism development in the north) always relied on: (i) generous government grants to raise industry interest in the first instance; and (ii) some sort of public leader or coordinator to maintain that interest over a longer period of time and deliver tangible outcomes. Even the formation of a strong viable regional tourism association (with paying members) initially required "incubators" from the government-funded regional development board, start-up grants, several years of cluster development workshops, and continuous support from the state tourism organization to attract more government grants.

The reliance on public sector leadership for tourism development has raised serious questions over the long-term sustainability of tourism in the Flinders Ranges, particularly as the various levels of government were themselves caught in an entrenched staples export mentality. The resurgence of traditional staples industries (mining and grain farming) during the late 2000s meant that tourism had to take a back seat again in state and local government priorities. The breaking of the drought in 2010 and the prospects of new "bumper crops" in the southern agricultural districts have since stalled tourism initiatives in the Southern Flinders Ranges. Most local governments, after recognizing that tourism could only ever generate a fraction of the income offered by agriculture, abandoned previous tourism strategies and withdrew their funding for the regional tourism development officer.

The northern pastoral communities, on the other hand, have felt the impacts of the mining boom since 2006, as government attention and resources were increasingly redirected to the mining hotspots in the Far North. Support funding schemes for on-farm tourism start-ups have largely disappeared from regional development agendas, and what used to be the regional *tourism* development officer in the Far North turned into a more general *economic* development officer (focusing on how to get local businesses and Indigenous people to work for the mining sector). As visitor nights and expenditure in South Australia dropped substantially between 2006 and 2011 (mainly as a result of the high Australian dollar), even the state tourism organization had to cut back support funding for regional tourism. In 2011, it closed its regional marketing offices and withdrew funding for regional marketing managers. What this means is that the Flinders Ranges region has now been left on its own to coordinate regional tourism planning and development, yet without the resources, leadership, and coordination that it used to rely on in the past.

The Future

The case study presented in this chapter has shown that tourism is faced with challenges that are somewhat unique to the particular socioeconomic and geopolitical context of remote resource peripheries. The legacies of entrenched staples dependence—exemplified by a culture of dependence on external decision makers, an embedded expectation of public sector leadership and patronage, lack of homegrown entrepreneurialism, and a lack of experience and appreciation of how to work together beyond individual community borders—have clearly had a negative impact on the viability of tourism in the region. In addition to problems caused by the inherent geographical characteristics of the region (vast terrains, sparse populations, isolated settlements), these issues have been exacerbated by centrally driven regionalization approaches that have sought to lump together the "boring leftover bits" of the state into administrative tourism "mega-regions." The regionalization approach ignored not only existing sub-regional boundaries and place-specific local identities (which subsequently fueled some degree of resistance to the imposed regional frameworks), but more importantly they ignored the inherited lack of local community capacities to connect and collaborate as part of a larger region. From this perspective, the combined insights drawn from the literature on staples dependence, new regionalism, and endogenous network dynamics in tourism offer some convincing explanations of the challenges for regional tourism development in remote resource peripheries.

The case study suggests that the provision of public funded leaders at the local level appears to be a vital step towards bridging the apparent industry fragmentation and encouraging regional collaboration in tourism. Yet, it is not clear if such public sector leadership will translate into increased regional industry or community collaboration, or if it will perpetuate dependence on external coordination. Similarly, incentives for collaborative participation in regional initiatives may be useful to encourage regional interaction in the short term, but it is unknown if such incentives will embed regional thinking (and acting).

Longevity of tourism systems in remote resource peripheries is in itself a very important area for further research. As the case study in this chapter has demonstrated, tourism has remained a very fragile industry despite several decades of concerted development efforts. The entrenched addiction to resource industries among governments and communities means that a recovery or resurgence of staples appears to jeopardize tourism and render previous diversification efforts obsolete. It seems that recurring boom and bust cycles in remote resource peripheries have become the expected norm, so that tourism will only ever play the role of a temporary gap-filler as communities desperately wait for "their" staple to return.

D.A. Carson and R. Koster

Questions

1. What is the importance of the staples thesis in sustainable tourism development?
2. What key characteristics define networks and what is their application to rural tourism?
3. How would you apply the idea of "new regionalism" in a study of tourism development?

Notes

[1] Readers are encouraged to read both Sharpley (2004) and Lane (1994) for a comprehensive discussion on the definition of rural tourism.

[2] For more detailed information on the Flinders Ranges case study refer to Schmallegger (2010).

References

Altman, M. (2003) Staple theory and export-led growth: constructing differential growth. *Australian Economic History Review* 43(3), 230–255.

Amin, A. (1999) An institutionalist perspective on regional economic development. *International Journal of Urban and Regional Research* 23(2), 365–378.

Asheim, B., Smith, H.L. and Oughton, C. (2011) Regional innovation systems: theory, empirics and policy. *Regional Studies* 45(7), 875–891.

Australian Bureau of Statistics (2013) Census for a brighter future. Census data quick stats. Available at: http://www.abs.gov.au/websitedbs/censushome.nsf/home/census?opendocument&navpos=10 (accessed 28 July 2013).

Barnes, T.J., Hayter, R. and Hay, E. (2001) Stormy weather: cyclones, Harold Innis and Port Alberni, BC. *Environment and Planning A* 33(12), 2127–2147.

Bradbury, J. (1987) British Columbia: metropolis and hinterland in microcosm. In: McCann, L.D. (ed.) *Heartland and Hinterland: A Geography of Canada*. Prentice-Hall, Scarborough, UK, pp. 400–441.

Briedenhann, J. and Wickens, E. (2004) Tourism routes as a tool for the economic development of rural areas: vibrant hope or impossible dream? *Tourism Management* 25(1), 71–79.

Bunnell, T.G. and Coe, N.M. (2001) Spaces and scales of innovation. *Progress in Human Geography* 25(4), 569–589.

Carson, D.A. and Carson, D.B. (2011) Why tourism may not be everybody's business: the challenge of tradition in resource peripheries. *The Rangeland Journal* 33, 373–383.

Carson, D., Ensign, P., Rasmussen, R. and Taylor, A. (2011) Perspectives on 'demography at the edge'. In: Carson, D., Rasmussen, R., Ensign, P., Huskey, L. and Taylor, A. (eds) *Demography at the Edge: Remote Human Populations in Developed Nations*. Ashgate, Farnham, UK, pp. 3–20.

Carson, D.A., Carson, D.B. and Hodge, H. (2014) Understanding local innovation systems in peripheral tourism destinations. *Tourism Geographies: An International Journal of Tourism Space, Place and Environment* 16(3), 457–473.

Doloreux, D. and Parto, S. (2005) Regional innovation systems: current discourse and unresolved issues. *Technology in Society* 27(2), 133–153.

Dredge, D. (2005) Local versus state-driven production of 'The Region': regional tourism policy in the Hunter, New South Wales, Australia. In: Rainnie, A. and Grobbelaar, M. (eds) *New Regionalism in Australia*. Ashgate, Aldershot, UK, pp. 299–319.

Dredge, D. (2006) Networks, conflict and collaborative communities. *Journal of Sustainable Tourism* 14, 562–581.

Dredge, D. and Jenkins, J. (2003) Destination place identity and regional tourism policy. *Tourism Geographies* 5(4), 383–407.

Du Plessis, V., Beshiri, R., Bollman, R. and Clemenson, H. (2001) *Definitions of Rural*. Rural and Small Town Analysis Bulletin. Statistics Canada, Ottawa.

Fleischer, A. and Felsenstein, D. (2000) Support for rural tourism: does it make a difference? *Annals of Tourism Research* 27(4), 1007–1024.

Freshwater, D. (2004) Delusions of grandeur: the search for a vibrant rural America. In: Halseth, G. and Halseth, R. (eds) *Building for Success: Explorations of Rural Community and Rural Development*. Rural Development Institute, Brandon, Manitoba, pp. 29–49.

Garrod, B., Wornell, R. and Youell, R. (2006) Re-conceptualising rural resources as countryside capital: the case of rural tourism. *Journal of Rural Studies* 22(1), 117–128.

George, E.W., Mair, H. and Reid, D.G. (2009) *Rural Tourism Development: Localism and Cultural Change*. Channel View Publications, Bristol, UK.

Gunn, C. and Var, T. (2002) *Tourism Planning*, 4th edn. Routledge, New York.

Gunton, T. (2003) Natural resources and regional development: an assessment of dependency and comparative advantage paradigms. *Economic Geography* 79(1), 67–94.

Hall, C.M. (2000) Rethinking collaboration and partnership: a public policy perspective. In: Bramwell, B. and Lane, B. (eds) *Tourism, Collaboration and Partnerships: Politics, Practice and Sustainability*. Channel View Publications, Bristol, UK, pp. 143–158.

Hall, C.M. (2005) Rural wine and food tourism cluster and network development. In: Hall, D., Kirkpatrick, I. and Mitchell, M. (eds) *Rural Tourism and Sustainable Business*. Channel View Publications, Clevedon, UK, pp. 149–164.

Hall, C.M. and Boyd, S. (2005) Nature-based tourism in peripheral areas: introduction. In: Hall, C.M. and Boyd, S. (eds) *Nature-Based Tourism in Peripheral Areas: Development or Disaster?* Channel View Publications, Clevedon, UK, pp. 3–17.

Hall, C.M. and Williams, A.M. (2008) *Tourism and Innovation*. Routledge, Abingdon, UK.

Halseth, G. (2010) Understanding and transforming a staples-based economy: place-based development in Northern British Columbia, Canada. In: Halseth, G., Markey, S. and Bruce, D. (eds) *The Next Rural Economies: Constructing Rural Place in a Global Economy*. CAB International, Wallingford, UK, pp. 251–262.

Hamin, E.M. and Marcucci, D.J. (2008) Ad hoc rural regionalism. *Journal of Rural Studies* 24(4), 467–477.

Henriksen, P.F. and Halkier, H. (2009) From local promotion towards regional tourism policies: knowledge processes and actor networks in North Jutland, Denmark. *European Planning Studies* 17(10), 1445–1462.

Hjalager, A.M. (2010) Regional innovation systems: the case of angling tourism. *Tourism Geographies* 12, 192–216.

Hohl, A.E. and Tisdell, C.A. (1995) Peripheral tourism: development and management. *Annals of Tourism Research* 22(3), 517–534.

Howlett, M. and Brownsey, K. (2008) Introduction: toward a post-staples state? In: Howlett, M. and Brownsey, K. (eds) *Canada's Resource Economy in Transition: The Past, Present, and Future of Canadian Staples Industries*. Emond Montgomery Publications, Toronto, pp. 3–15.

Huskey, L. and Morehouse, T.A. (1992) Development in remote regions: what do we know? *Arctic* 45(2), 128–137.

Jackson, J. and Murphy, P. (2006) Clusters in regional tourism: an Australian case. *Annals of Tourism Research* 33(4), 1018–1035.

Jones, M. (2001) The rise of the regional state in economic governance: 'partnerships for prosperity' or new scales of state power? *Environment and Planning A* 33(7), 1185–1211.

Jones, M. and MacLeod, G. (2004) Regional spaces, spaces of regionalism: territory, insurgent politics and the English question. *Transactions of the Institute of British Geographers* 29(4), 433–452.

D.A. Carson and R. Koster

Koster, R.L. (2007) A regional approach to rural tourism development: towards a conceptual framework for communities in transition. *Society and Leisure* 30(1), 133–156.

Koster, R.L. (2008) Rural based tourism as a strategy for rural community economic development. In: Woodside, A.G. (ed.) *Advances in Culture, Tourism and Hospitality Research*, Vol. 2. Emerald Group, Bingley, UK, pp. 153–292.

Koster, R.L. (2010) Local contexts for community economic development strategies: a comparison of rural Saskatchewan and Ontario communities. In: Winchell, D.G., Ramsey, D., Koster, R.L. and Robinson, G.M. (eds) *Geographical Perspectives on Sustainable Rural Change*. Rural Development Institute, Brandon, Manitoba, pp. 461–483.

Koster, R.L. and Lemelin, R.H. (2009) Appreciative inquiry and rural tourism: a case study from Canada. *Tourism Geographies* 11(2), 256–269.

Koster, R.L. and Lemelin, R.H. (2013) The forgotten industry in the forgotten north: tourism developments in northern Ontario. In: Conteh, C. and Segsworth, R. (eds) *Governance in Northern Ontario*. University of Toronto Press Inc., Toronto, Canada.

Lane, B. (1994) What is rural tourism? *Journal of Sustainable Tourism* 2(1–2), 7–21.

MacLeod, G. (2001) New regionalism reconsidered: globalization and the remaking of political economic space. *International Journal of Urban and Regional Research* 25(4), 804–829.

Markey, S., Pierce, J. and Vodden, K. (2000) Resources, people and the environment: a regional analysis of the evolution of resource policy in Canada. *Journal of Regional Science* XXIII(3), 427–454.

Martin, A. and Sunley, P. (2006) Path dependence and regional economic evolution. *Journal of Economic Geography* 6(4), 395–437.

Meyer-Cech, K. (2005) Regional cooperation in rural theme trails. In: Hall, D., Kirkpatrick, I. and Mitchell, M. (eds) *Rural Tourism and Sustainable Business*. Channel View Publications, Clevedon, UK, pp. 137–148.

Mitchell, M. and Hall, D. (2005) Rural tourism as sustainable business: key themes and issues. In: Hall, D., Kirkpatrick, I. and Mitchell, M. (eds) *Rural Tourism and Sustainable Business*. Channel View Publications, Clevedon, UK, pp. 3–14.

Morgan, K. (1997) The learning region: institutions, innovation and regional renewal. *Regional Studies* 31(5), 491–503.

Moscardo, G. (2005) Peripheral tourism development: challenges, issues and success factors. *Tourism Recreation Research* 30(1), 27–43.

Müller, D.K. and Jansson, B. (2007) The difficult business of making pleasure peripheries prosperous: perspectives on space, place and environment. In: Müller, D.K. and Jansson, B. (eds) *Tourism in Peripheries: Perspectives from the Far North and South*. CAB International, Wallingford, UK, pp. 3–18.

Noakes, J.L. and Johnston, M.E. (2010) Constraints and opportunities in the development of diamond tourism in Yellowknife, Northwest Territories. In: Hall, C.M. and Saarinen, J. (eds) *Tourism and Change in Polar Regions: Climate, Environments and Experiences*. Routledge, New York, pp. 165–179.

Novelli, M., Schmitz, B. and Spencer, T. (2006) Networks, clusters and innovation in tourism: a UK experience. *Tourism Management* 27(6), 1141–1152.

Petrzelka, P., Krannich, R. and Brehm, J. (2006) Identification with resource-based occupations and desire for tourism: are the two necessarily inconsistent? *Society and Natural Resources* 19(8), 693–707.

Prats, L., Guia, J. and Molina, F.X. (2008) How tourism destinations evolve: the notion of tourism local innovation system. *Tourism and Hospitality Research* 8(3), 178–191.

Rainnie, A. and Grant, J. (2005) The knowledge economy, new regionalism and the re-emergence of regions. In: Rainnie, A. and Grobbelaar, M. (eds) *New Regionalism in Australia*. Ashgate, Aldershot, UK, pp. 3–24.

Reed, M.G. (2000) Collaborative tourism planning as adaptive experiments in emergent tourism settings. In: Bramwell, B. and Lane, B. (eds) *Tourism Collaboration and Partnerships: Politics, Practice and Sustainability*. Channel View Publications, Clevedon, UK, pp. 247–270.

Reid, D. (1998) Rural tourism development: Canadian provincial issues. In: Butler, R., Hall, C.M. and Jenkins, J. (eds) *Tourism and Recreation in Rural Areas*. Wiley, Chichester, UK, pp. 69–80.

Reid, D. (2003) *Tourism, Globalization and Development: Responsible Tourism Planning*. Pluto Press, London.

Roberts, L. and Hall, D. (2001) *Rural Tourism and Recreation: Principles to Practice*. CAB International, Wallingford, UK.

Romeiro, P. and Costa, C. (2010) The potential of management networks in the innovation and competitiveness of rural tourism: a case study on the Valle del Jerte (Spain). *Current Issues in Tourism* 13(1), 75–91.

Roufeil, L. and Battye, K. (2008) Effective regional, rural and remote family and relationships service delivery. Australian Family Relationships Clearinghouse Briefing Paper No. 10. Australian Institute of Family Studies, Melbourne. Available at: http://www.aifs.gov.au/afrc/pubs/briefing/b10pdf/b10.pdf (accessed 27 July 2013).

Saxena, G. (2006) Beyond mistrust and competition—the role of social and personal bonding processes in sustaining livelihoods of rural tourism businesses: a case of the Peak District National Park. *International Journal of Tourism Research* 8, 263–277.

Saxena, G. and Ilbery, B. (2008) Integrated rural tourism: a border case study. *Annals of Tourism Research* 35(1), 233–254.

Schmallegger, D. (2010) Understanding the impact of the inherited institutional environment on tourism innovation systems in resource dependent peripheries: a case study of the Flinders Ranges in South Australia. Unpublished PhD thesis, James Cook University, Townsville, Australia. Available at: http://eprints.jcu.edu.au/19032 (accessed 21 March 2012).

Schmallegger, D., Carson, D. and Tremblay, P. (2010) The economic geography of remote tourism: the problem of connection seeking. *Tourism Analysis* 15, 127–139.

Sharpley, R. (2004) Tourism and the countryside. In: Lew, A., Hall, C.M. and Williams, A. (eds) *A Companion to Tourism*. Blackwell Publishing, Oxford, UK, pp. 374–386.

Shearmur, R. (2011) Innovation, regions and proximity: from neo-regionalism to spatial analysis. *Regional Studies* 45(9), 1225–1243.

Storper, M. (1997) *The Regional World: Territorial Development in a Global Economy*. Guilford Press, New York.

Taylor, B.M. (2012) Regionalism as resistance: governance and identity in Western Australia's Wheatbelt. *Geoforum* 43(3), 507–517.

Taylor, P., McRae-Williams, P. and Lowe, J. (2007) The determinants of cluster activities in the Australian wine and tourism industries. *Tourism Economics* 13(4), 639–656.

Tödtling, F. and Trippl, M. (2005) One size fits all? Towards a differentiated regional innovation policy approach. *Research Policy* 34(8), 1203–1219.

Wanhill, S. (1997) Peripheral area tourism: a European perspective. *Progress in Tourism and Hospitality Research* 3(1), 47–70.

Watkins, M.H. (1963) A staple theory of economic growth. *Canadian Journal of Economics and Political Science* 29(2), 141–158.

Weaver, D.B. and Lawton, L.J. (2004) Visitor attitudes toward tourism development and product integration in an Australian urban-rural fringe. *Journal of Travel Research* 42(3), 286–296.

Webb, D. and Collis, C. (2000) Regional development agencies and the 'New Regionalism' in England. *Regional Studies* 34(9), 857–873.

Weidenfeld, A. (2013) Tourism and cross border regional innovation systems. *Annals of Tourism Research* 42, 191–213.

D.A. Carson and R. Koster

Weidenfeld, A., Williams, A.M. and Butler, R.W. (2010) Knowledge transfer and innovation among attractions. *Annals of Tourism Research* 37(3), 604–626.

Wellstead, A. (2008) The (post)staples economy and the (post)staples state in historical perspective. In: Howlett, M. and Brownsey, K. (eds) *Canada's Resource Economy in Transition: The Past, Present, and Future of Canadian Staples Industries*. Emond Montgomery Publications, Toronto, pp. 19–37.

Williams, F. and Copus, A. (2005) Business development, rural tourism, and the implications of milieu. In: Hall, D., Kirkpatrick, I. and Mitchell, M. (eds) *Rural Tourism and Sustainable Business*. Channel View Publications, Clevedon, UK, pp. 305–322.

Wilson, S., Fesenmaier, D.R., Fesenmaier, J. and Van Es, J.C. (2001) Factors for success in rural tourism development. *Journal of Travel Research* 40(2), 132–138.

6 Theoretical Perspectives on Tourism Innovation

NICOLE L. VAUGEOIS*

Vancouver Island University, Nanaimo, British Columbia, Canada

The Objectives

The purpose of this chapter is to examine the evolution of innovation theory and its application in tourism research. The objectives are to:

1. Define and describe the tenets of innovation theory including its types, determinants, and actors.
2. Trace the evolution of innovation theory and its introduction to tourism research.
3. Synthesize the insights gained from the application of innovation theory in tourism research.
4. Identify the stage of theoretical development for innovation theory in tourism.
5. Provide a critical review of existing tourism innovation research and suggest topics and approaches for further inquiry.

The Vignette

Muriel was excited to start her new position as tourism development officer in the central region of the state. It would be her job to help the region diversify the economy through tourism and she was looking forward to bringing her knowledge on innovation into her new position. Tourism was not well established in the region and would require the introduction of new ways of thinking and acting among existing stakeholders. Before she started, Muriel decided to delve into her new book on "Innovative Case Studies in Tourism Development" (2020) to help her answer questions such as: (i) how does innovation occur? (ii) what drives innovation? and (iii) how could she support the adoption of innovation in her role?

The Context

Tourism research has been accused as being weak in theory and method and lagging behind other areas in terms of paradigm adoption (Feng *et al.*, 2012). By way of introducing the use of innovation theory in tourism research, this criticism is certainly supported. Innovation theory has been applied for a short time frame in tourism research, however

*Corresponding author, e-mail: nicole.vaugeois@viu.ca

interest among researchers is both rapid and growing (Aldebert *et al.*, 2011; Nagy, 2012). Researchers who are keen to understand how innovative new products emerge, who is involved and what motivates innovation to occur have all been contributing to innovation theory in tourism. And, while these new insights are growing, there is much work to be done to investigate innovation in the tourism context and to be able to translate this new knowledge to managers like Muriel who may benefit from its application.

Why is innovation theory relevant to tourism?

While travel has existed for centuries, the pursuit of tourism development at the destination level is perhaps a more modern phenomenon in many regions of the world. Embedding it into the economic, social, and environmental context of destinations is fraught with complexities and often requires a broad range of actors to imagine new possibilities and forge new working relationships. Like the case with Muriel, looking to innovation theory may provide insights for these actor groups to create conditions that are conducive to change.

Similarly, the ability for destinations and firms to innovate is essential in tourism due to the dynamic and competitive nature of the market. Consumers and their interests often change, so destinations and firms cannot rely on their current products to remain relevant for tomorrow's markets. And, in an era where more destination areas are contemplating tourism as an economic development strategy, customers are able to select from a wider array of choices in the competitive marketplace. Incorporating innovation theory into future studies may assist tourism researchers to gain new insights into the evolution and adaptations of the industry and at the same time, provide managers, like Muriel, advice on how to develop tourism in ways that support the economic, social, and environmental goals in destinations.

The Theory

So what is innovation theory?

Innovation theory, while only recently used in tourism, has been actively pursued by a range of disciplines such as economics, business, technology, anthropology, sociology, and engineering for decades. It was first introduced to the lexicon by Joseph Schumpeter in his book *Theory of Economic Development* in 1934. In this text, innovation was seen to be the introduction of a new good, a new method of production, the opening of a new market, the conquest of a new source of supply, or the reorganization of an industry. Later, in 1983, the most influential theorist in innovation theory, Everett Rogers, defined innovation as "an idea, practice, or object that is perceived as new by an individual or other unit of adoption" (Rogers, 1962: 11). The term innovation refers to both radical and incremental changes in thinking, in things, in process, or in services (McKeown, 2008). Creativity is central to the notion of innovation and, while an important basis for innovation, the two terms are not synonymous. Creativity refers to the process of coming up with new ideas; however, bringing new ideas to life is where innovation occurs.

Probably the most prominent researcher associated to the use of innovation theory in modern studies is Everett Rogers. In 1962, Rogers developed the diffusion of innovation theory (DOI theory; Rogers, 1962) when he combined findings from studies about information and ideas and the flow of information and the role of personal influence. DOI theory suggests that the adoption of innovation is a mental process that individuals pass through before adopting or rejecting an innovation. These stages include gaining exposure to new ideas or knowledge, receiving persuasion to influence adoption of the idea, making a decision to adopt or reject the idea, implementation or trial, and finally confirmation (if deemed successful) or rejection (if deemed unsuccessful). While this process was conceptualized at the individual level, Rogers also explored how the adoption of innovative ideas took place among members of social units. The rate of adoption is measured by the length of time a certain percentage or critical mass of individuals or units of a social system take to adopt an innovation. Rogers hypothesized that the life cycle of innovations followed an "s-curve" wherein at early stages, the adoption of a new idea is slow until it becomes more established. At this point, demand for the new idea increases incrementally if persuasive communications are used until the majority of the population has adopted the new idea.

Rogers classified individuals into five categories based on their predisposition toward innovation including, in order of innovativeness: Innovators, Early adopters, Early majority, Late majority and Laggards. In an effort to understand how to influence adoption rates for innovative ideas, Rogers identified five items that increase the likelihood of adoption.

1. The innovation must be viewed as having a relative advantage over existing options available to an individual.
2. The ideas central to the innovation must be compatible with the existing values, past experiences, and needs in the social system that it is being introduced into.
3. It must be simple to understand and any complexity associated to its introduction must be simplified to enable its implementation.
4. It must be something that can be experimented with or tried before full commitment.
5. Before full adoption, it must yield positive results. If any of these factors is not met in the social system, the likelihood of adoption of the innovation decreases.

Roger's work has been useful for those who are interested in introducing innovative ideas into new social systems. Since its introduction, the DOI theory has been utilized for 50 years in over 4000 research articles in disciplines including anthropology, sociology, agriculture, manufacturing, and health (Rogers, 2003). There is a vast amount of empirical research to support the theory and it has been utilized to inform practical applications in marketing, agriculture, health, and technology. Despite its many strengths, the theory is not without its critics or limitations. Some have accused the theory of being too linear in its explanation of social change where an innovation is suggested by an agent of change who then uses the communication process to exert an influence over adoption among a social group. Others have criticized the theory for under-exaggerating the role and influence of the media on social change, when, particularly in the era of social media, innovative ideas are often shared quickly in society, where they take root and spread.

Application in Tourism

With a basic understanding of innovation theory, how it has evolved, and some of its early observations, this section will now move on to cover how the concept of innovation has been studied within tourism research. To date, innovation has been explored in an effort to understand changes and adaptations "within" the tourism industry as well as changes as a "result" of tourism.

Innovation theory to explore "within industry" change

The primary emphasis of existing research that links tourism with innovation has been to understand "within" industry changes and adaptations. Researchers have made progress in understanding who is innovating, how, and why. Innovation theory to date has been applied to gain an understanding of the types of innovation (Brooker *et al.*, 2012; Grissemann *et al.*, 2013), the influencers or drivers of innovation (Daugėlienė and Brundza, 2009; Čavlek *et al.*, 2010; Grissemann *et al.*, 2013), actors (Hjalager, 2010a, b; Kokkranikal and Morrison, 2011), and the process of adoption (Sørensen, 2007; Prats *et al.*, 2008; Paget *et al.*, 2010; Smerecnik and Andersen, 2011; Lee, 2013).

Types of tourism innovation

What type of innovation occurs in tourism?

To date, researchers in tourism suggest that innovations can take place in what is produced (product), how it is produced (process), and how it is communicated (marketing) to external audiences (Hjalager, 2010a; Tejada and Moreno, 2013). In a review of innovation research in tourism, Hjalager (2010a) provides a thorough synthesis of the categories of innovation as well as the determinants of innovation. According to Hjalager, innovation can occur in five categories including tourism products, the processes used to create products, managerial processes, marketing, and within institutional domains. Many of these types of innovation have been further studied by Tejada and Moreno (2013), who studied types of tourism innovation in small businesses using the categories of product, process, marketing, and organizational innovations. Their work also explored to what extent distinctive innovation patterns were present in small tourism businesses suggesting that dependency on tour operators, geographic localization, and cooperation were all related to resulting levels of innovation.

Influencers or drivers of innovation

While understanding the types of innovation has been central to clarifying and defining the concept for researchers, others have sought to understand what influences the level of innovation in a firm or destination. This line of inquiry is particularly useful for those who seek to create the conditions that stimulate innovation to take place. To date, researchers have identified a number of determinants for innovation including influential entrepreneurs, product clusters, technology, engagement of actor groups, and knowledge exchange and networks.

What determines the level of innovation in a firm or business?

Hjalager (2010a) identified a number of determinants to innovation including the role of entrepreneurship, technology, and industry clusters. Having access to knowledge was also recognized as playing a critical role in the innovation process. In another study by Čavlek *et al.* (2010), innovations in tourism appeared in four areas including: (i) products and content; (ii) distribution channels and brands; (iii) business models and people; and (iv) growth and capital allocation. Grissemann *et al.* (2013) later sought to identify determinants of innovation and found that five dimensions influence innovative behavior in tourism firms, including: employee engagement, customer engagement, information technologies, innovation management, and innovation networks.

These studies appear to suggest a number of variables that determine the level or presence of innovation in tourism in different contexts, however a commonly adopted set has yet to emerge in the research literature. Further work to replicate work and establish a more definitive set of drivers will be helpful to those, like Muriel, who are interested in utilizing innovation theory.

Who is responsible for driving innovation?

Creating conditions where innovation can take place will also require individuals like Muriel to understand who or what is responsible for driving innovation. Čavlek *et al.* (2010) critically assessed the four major drivers of innovation in tourism, including tourists (users), tour operating companies, technology, and competition. Of these four, users and tour operating companies and entrepreneurs have received the most attention in tourism literature.

User-driven innovation

Visitors are recognized as co-creators in their travel experience. An emerging line of inquiry that utilizes innovation theory has been in the area of "user-driven innovation," which seeks to understand the influence and role that visitors have in the adoption of innovation practices at the firm or destination level. Hjalager and Nordin (2011) advance the potential application of user-driven innovation by offering a typology of 16 methods ranging from users being actively involved to those without user engagement. Nimrod and Rotem (2012) explored patterns of innovation in older adults' tourism. Their study identified three groups of older tourists ranging from non-innovators, external innovators, and absolute innovators who were differentiated with respect to travel patterns and destination activities. Beyond suggesting new ways to cluster sub-sectors of visitors, their findings also suggest that innovation theory may assist in understanding differences in visitor experience.

Producers

While there has been limited work on understanding the role of consumers or users in the innovation process, a larger body of work exists where the producers are the foci

N. Vaugeois

of studies. Of the potential actors involved in tourism, tour operators, small and medium size enterprises, and entrepreneurs have been well studied.

The role of tour operators in driving innovation in tourism has garnered attention in recent studies. Rønningen (2010) studied the role of the tour operator as a driver of innovation and found differing levels of the influence among entrepreneurs working with a tour operator based on the size of the company (where smaller businesses were more influenced and more professional firms were less influenced). The tourism operator has also been identified as a subset within the industry that is linked to the creation of new tourism products or business cooperation by others including Čavlek et al. (2010) and Tejada and Moreno (2013).

Entrepreneurial innovation has also been prioritized by researchers as a core actor group to understand based on their decision-making status in organizations and communities (Kokkranikal and Morrison, 2011). In an attempt to describe the main elements of an innovative tourism sector, Daugėlienė and Brundza (2009) analyzed the entrepreneurship characteristics of firms in Scotland and Slovenia. Their findings suggest that proactivity, dynamism, creativity, and social responsibility among entrepreneurs are elements that underlie innovative firms.

Where does innovation take place?

For Muriel and others interested in applying innovation theory to tourism, it is also important to understand where innovation can take place. Much of the broader literature on innovation has focused on studies at the firm or organizational level. This has enabled us to learn more about the types, determinants, and drivers of innovation as already discussed. While firm-level studies have aided in the understanding of individual and unit adoption behavior, some have advocated that tourism research needs to move beyond its preoccupation with firm-level analysis and focus more on innovation in wider geographic areas (Williams and Shaw, 2011).

Innovation theory has been utilized to understand tourism development beyond the firm level. For example, Paget et al. (2010) used actor-network theory to study innovation among French ski resorts. Their study found that entrepreneurs can interest and enroll other actors in a project to create innovative products and enhance overall competitiveness. Building on this notion, Prats et al. (2008) studied how tourism destinations evolve using systems of innovation and social network analysis. They introduced the Tourism Local Innovation System (TLIS) model as a way to design relational network structures that favor innovation and demonstrated its utility in a case study in Costa Brava Centre in Spain. Social networks have also been linked to tourism innovation by Sørensen (2007).

Process of innovation

How does innovation take place?

Probably most central to the potential application of innovation theory to tourism is the question about how it comes about. For example, Muriel will need to understand the process that is used to bring about innovation in a tourism context.

On this question, however, there have been few investigations that explore the innovation process used either at the firm, local, regional, or national level. Of those that do exist, there is mounting evidence to suggest that the DOI theory is helpful to explain the adoption process.

For example, in a study of small and medium sized operators throughout rural British Columbia, Thuot *et al.* (2010) found support for the DOI theory in the incorporation of sustainable tourism practices. Their study sought to understand the forces that influence the adoption of sustainable tourism practices (the innovation) including motivations and constraints and to identify ways to support entrepreneurial and collective efforts in sustainability. Findings suggest that three groups of entrepreneurs exist when clustered by level of adoption, including: (i) those committed to sustainability; (ii) those still in pilot stage; and (iii) uncommitted. Differences between these groups resulted in the authors suggesting that supports for operators should be designed to appeal to the differing motivations and barriers incurred by the different stages of adoption.

In another case study in Thailand, Dabphet *et al.* (2012) also applied DOI theory to destination stakeholder understanding of the concept of sustainable tourism. Their findings validated the use of the theory as a means to understand how stakeholders transfer knowledge and advance the adoption of sustainability in the destination. The authors argued that advancing the concept of sustainable tourism in destinations could be advanced by understanding the diffusion process, and in particular, by noting the importance of identification of actor groups and the role of knowledge transmission through interpersonal and media communication.

In another study focused on sustainable tourism, Smerecnik and Anderson (2011) also utilized DOI theory to explore environmental sustainability innovations in North American hotels and ski resorts. They found that the perceived simplicity of sustainability innovations and high levels of opinion leadership were associated with the adoption of sustainability practices.

While DOI theory was not the construct used by Brooker *et al.* (2012) in the study of innovation within the Australian outdoor hospitality parks industry, the findings appear to support the theoretical construct. For example, the grouping of "strategic innovators" was found to adopt ideas infused from outside of the Australian context. The changes resulting from the introduction of these innovations were observed at the firm level over a period of from 3 to 4-year cycles, which coincided with the length of time for competitors to incorporate similar practices.

These studies suggest to Muriel and others that innovation within different tourism contexts appears to be linked to DOI theory. Innovators appear to be gaining and sharing ideas with others and diffusing them through personal and informational networks. Even though these innovations appear to be happening around the notion of sustainable tourism, these studies may suggest that DOI is relevant to other types of innovation in tourism.

Muriel may also benefit from understanding how another emerging application of innovation theory has been used to understand system innovation. The "innovation systems or systems of innovation" approach has been utilized as a popular framework in microeconomic research and provides researchers with a tool to understand better the dynamic nature and role that context and actors exert on innovation. This approach has been used by Hjalager (2010b) in a case study on angling tourism, Sorrie (2014) in a study on regional tourism development along the Alaska Highway Corridor, and Huibin and Marzuki (2012) on community participation of cultural heritage tourism. Additional conceptual advancements have been offered by Prats *et al.* (2008), who introduced the Tourism Local Innovation System (TLIS) model, which can be used to assess the innovation capacity in tourism destinations and to explore the network structures in ways that favor innovation.

In essence, this emerging line of inquiry around systems of innovation suggests that tourism needs to be investigated at a broader regional or system level. At this level of analysis, the role of different actor groups, the networks and relationships that exist among them, and the processes used to bring about change all merit further research attention using systems of innovation theory.

Innovation as a result of tourism

Recent research has highlighted a new approach to understanding the link between tourism and innovation. Unlike the majority of studies that seek to explain how innovation occurs within tourism, these studies explore the extent to which tourism exerts an influence over innovation.

For example, Brouder (2012) explored the dynamics of local tourism innovation in the Arctic rural community of Jokkmokk to understand the tourism development process and its benefits to stakeholders. Findings suggest that tourism can assist in surfacing latent social capital in destinations and that it can act as a catalyst for innovation at the local level. Deemed "creative outposts," these destinations co-evolve through engagement in tourism resulting in Brouder stating that "tourism has a subtle yet palpable positive social role in the community."

Similarly, in a case study in the Indian State of Kerala, entrepreneurial innovation in tourism was found to assist in the formation of a community network offering sustainable livelihood diversification opportunities to stakeholders in the periphery of tourism (Kokkranikal and Morrison, 2011). In other words, innovation at the firm level created by entrepreneurs had further-reaching impacts for the broader community. At an even broader scale, Weidenfeld (2013) studied the potential role of tourism and its mobilities in facilitating innovative processes in cross-border regions in Europe. In this case, tourism was found to be the conduit for knowledge exchange and the diffusion of innovative ideas beyond the tourism industry. These studies suggest new opportunities for researchers to explore the role that tourism plays in diffusing innovative ideas.

Critical assessment of innovation theory applied to tourism

Several studies utilizing innovation theory were discussed in this chapter. Yet, "there is still only limited systematic and comparable evidence of the level of innovative activities and their impacts and wider implications for destinations and national economies" (Hjalager, 2010a). At this point in time, inquiry has largely been exploratory in nature with efforts to clarify the concept of innovation, determine its types and drivers, and understand what processes are used to bring about innovation. The use of innovation theory is still scantly noticed in tourism research, students of tourism programs have limited exposure to it in programs, and managers, like Muriel, are unaware of its potential utility. There is ample opportunity to expand on existing work to further test the theory within tourism. Applying a critical lens to the existing research that uses innovation theory provides us insights on where we should focus greater attention.

There is growing awareness in the innovation literature of the need to measure innovation and the impacts associated to the adoption of innovative management practices (Volo, 2005; Bloch and Bugge, 2013). According to Volo (2005), there are two problems limiting the innovation literature related to tourism: (i) problems in operational definitions; and (ii) measurement of innovation. These two problems limit standardization and aggregation of statistics on innovation in tourism products, providers, markets, and geographic regions. In response to the lack of conceptual clarity on innovation, a number of studies have produced models that may merit further attention in future research (Prats *et al.*, 2008; Daugėlienė and Brundza, 2009; Lee, 2013; Sorrie, 2014). Volo proposes a model that categorizes innovation along two dimensions: an "invention-adoption continuum" and an "impact on the tourism experience" dimension. The model is advocated as a potential enhancement to innovation measurement in tourism, which would allow for improved comparability of data from different sources.

Advancements in measurement may also produce enabling supports among policy makers. As Hall (2009) found in Australia, while innovation policy is recognized in national tourism policy and vice versa, there is yet little indication of how innovation will be encouraged by the state. Until this happens, those trying to use innovation theory in application, like Muriel in the Vignette, will be disadvantaged. Further studies that identify the enabling and constraining factors associated to systems of innovation at the regional and national levels may provide evidence to decision makers to inform future supports.

In terms of topics of inquiry, the literature on innovation in tourism has been somewhat preoccupied with the influence of information technology (Bougias, 2007; Aldebert *et al.*, 2011), entrepreneurs (Kokkranikal and Morrison, 2011; Tejada and Moreno, 2013), and the role of tour operators (Weiermair, 2005; Rønningen, 2010). While this begins to suggest that these determinants are perhaps central to innovation taking place within tourism, we need to question whether or not these determinants are available in all contexts (i.e. rural areas) and if other determinants such as competition, marketing, and knowledge sharing among others may play a more significant role than we are currently aware of due to limited research.

It is important to note that current studies using innovation theory in tourism has resulted in us learning more about some sub-sectors and contexts than others. For example, the level of innovation and types of innovation has been explored more in hospitality (Smerecnik and Andersen, 2011; Brooker *et al.*, 2012; Nagy, 2012; Grissemann *et al.*, 2013) than in other sectors. Geographic analysis of the existing research also indicates the application of the theory is more predominant in the Australian and European contexts (Bougias, 2007; Hall, 2009; Brooker *et al.*, 2012) and in understanding adaptations in rural areas (Brouder, 2012). Keeping an inventory of sub-sectors and regions that we are applying innovation theory to and those that we are not, will help identify potential areas for further investigation. At this time, expanding the use of innovation theory in other sectors and outside of western industrialized contexts is needed.

As discussed earlier in the drivers of innovation, further work is needed to expand on studies aimed at understanding the role of user-driven innovation. Firms and

N. Vaugeois

destination areas are driven to satisfy customer needs when creating tourism products. Understanding how they are evaluating customer needs and responding may identify other insights on user-driven innovation. In light of the current influence of social media on consumer decision-making, this line of inquiry is particularly timely and relevant. And, while studies to date on producer-driven innovation are bringing forward insights on a number of potential drivers (i.e. technology, marketing, distribution channels, tour operators), we have yet to develop a consistent set or to determine which drivers are more central to innovation at both the firm and destination level.

In summary, there has been no shortage of attention paid to innovation in tourism. While growing in popularity, the existing literature demonstrates limited consolidation of knowledge or use of promising theoretical developments on innovation theory from other disciplines (i.e. DOI theory and systems of innovation theory). The resulting literature appears to remain at the development of a conceptual understanding of the topic.

The Future

The recent use of innovation theory in tourism and the emerging evidence substantiating further application suggests that the theory holds much promise to advance knowledge development in tourism. To address the criticisms identified in the previous section, this chapter will close with suggestions on the future potential application of innovation theory.

In order to advance beyond the exploratory stage to a descriptive stage of knowledge development, future research should: (i) incorporate promising theoretical developments from outside of the tourism literature; and (ii) expand the scope of topics where innovation theory may be useful in tourism such as destinations, sustainability, product development, stakeholder or actor networks, and visitor behavior. Additionally, innovation theory may be helpful to apply to research design as a way to modernize the tools available to study tourism and to share findings with diverse audiences.

Incorporate promising theoretical developments from outside tourism

When comparing literature utilizing innovation theory from outside of tourism, a few worthwhile observations are made. First, while few tourism studies are utilizing diffusion of innovation theory, those that have, have found supporting evidence for wider application of the theory (Thuot *et al.*, 2010; Smerecnik and Andersen, 2011; Dabphet *et al.*, 2012). Rogers' DOI theory has been heavily utilized resulting in over 4000 published studies in disciplines ranging from agriculture, health, mass media, sociology, and communication (Smerecnik and Andersen, 2011). There is much to gain from building on existing evidence in these studies and integrating knowledge into the tourism domain. Efforts to do so would likely result in an expedited journey to knowledge development.

Similarly, studies that seek to understand innovation using a systems approach are becoming more widespread. Based on the geographic nature of tourism and the range of stakeholders involved in destination development, further application of systems of innovation theory is merited. This work would also address the criticism that the majority of studies to date have focused on innovation at the firm level and expand our understanding of the process involved in bringing about regional innovation.

Expand the scope of topics where innovation theory may be useful in tourism

If innovation theory becomes understood at a wider level by tourism researchers, it may also be used to inform, support, or test observations in a wide range of topics currently being explored. For example, the vignette of Muriel identifies the potential use of innovation theory in destination development. To date, innovation theory has been used to some extent in this realm but there is much room for further application. Innovation theory could assist in gaining a better understanding of the process or models used in developing or refining tourism in destination areas and the network and role of actors involved.

Another area where innovation theory is already providing valuable new insights is in sustainable tourism. As highlighted previously, sustainability can be viewed as a new idea for firms and destination areas. Early evidence suggests that DOI theory may help to explain how sustainability practices take root. Expanded application of innovation theory to understand how businesses and destinations bring about more sustainable tourism practices may provide much needed insight to further this work.

Apply innovation theory to research design and dissemination

Beyond using innovation as the topic of inquiry, some researchers are proposing that the concept be used to advance research practices in tourism. For example, Moscardo (2008) argues that the notion of innovation be expanded to "challenge existing assumptions and ways of thinking" about tourism. Using sustainable tourism as an example, Moscardo illustrates how questioning popular concepts may lead to innovative alternatives. Bramwell and Lane (2012) also reflect on the level of innovation in research on sustainable tourism. Their suggestions may provide useful guidance to emerging researchers to incorporate innovative research methods and dissemination practices into their career. Much of the research to date on innovation in tourism has been developed using in-depth and semi-structured interviews, surveys, and case study methodology. Expanding the use of methods employed as well as the number and types of contexts where innovation is studied may offer advancements to current understanding of the theory in tourism.

As the sharing of ideas is central to innovation theory, researchers should recognize the important role that they play to communicate the results of research with those who may be able to apply them. For example, individuals like Muriel would benefit from being able to access insights gained from researchers who have studied situations similar to hers. Ensuring access may require researchers to innovate and share in different forms, through new media, and with different audiences.

Questions

1. Discuss the realities of the current stage of knowledge on innovation in tourism. Are we at the exploratory, descriptive, or explanatory stage of knowledge development? What research is needed to advance us along this continuum?
2. Studying innovation presents challenges for researchers based on the complexities of actor groups involved, the number and types of contexts it occurs within, and the

pace of adaptation. Should our priority be to understand the innovation process or measure the impacts of innovation?

3. This chapter closes with some thoughts on how the concept of innovation can influence research practices. What assumptions do tourism researchers need to challenge in order to ensure we remain innovative in our research questions, design, and sharing practices?

4. The role of knowledge appears to be important to facilitate the adoption of innovation. Knowing this, discuss the importance of access to knowledge about tourism for managers or practitioners. How can researchers help to create or share knowledge in ways that are accessible for managers or practitioners?

References

Aldebert, B., Dang, R.J. and Longhi, C. (2011) Innovation in the tourism industry: the case of tourism@. *Tourism Management* 32(5), 1204–1213. DOI: 10.1016/j.tourman.2010.08.010.

Bloch, C. and Bugge, M.M. (2013) Public sector innovation—from theory to measurement. *Structural Change and Economic Dynamics* 27, 133–145.

Bougias, G. (2007) Innovation and tourism in the 21st century: rethinking Australian tourism in a global economy. *Australasian Parks & Leisure* 10(3), 8–11.

Bramwell, B. and Lane, B. (2012) Towards innovation in sustainable tourism research? *Journal of Sustainable Tourism* 20(1), 1–7. DOI: 10.1080/09669582.2011.641559.

Brooker, E., Joppe, M., Davidson, M.C.G. and Marles, K. (2012) Innovation within the Australian outdoor hospitality parks industry. *International Journal of Contemporary Hospitality Management* 24(5), 682–700. DOI: 10.1108/09596111211237246.

Brouder, P. (2012) Creative outposts: tourism's place in rural innovation. *Tourism Planning & Development* 9(4), 383–396. DOI: 10.1080/21568316.2012.726254.

Čavlek, N., Matečić, I. and Hodak, D.F. (2010) Drivers of innovations in tourism: some theoretical and practical aspects. *Acta Turistica* 22(2), 220–218.

Dabphet, S., Scott, N. and Ruhanen, L. (2012) Applying diffusion theory to destination stakeholder understanding of sustainable tourism development: a case from Thailand. *Journal of Sustainable Tourism* 20(8), 1107–1124. DOI: 10.1080/09669582.2012.673618.

Daugėliené, R. and Brundza, A. (2009) Theoretical possibilities of expression of innovation in tourism sector: the case of Scotland and Slovenia European Integration Studies. Research & Topicalities. Kaunas University, Lithuania. Retrieved from: http://search.ebscohost.com/login.aspx?direct=true&db=bth&AN=43973313&site=ehost-live (accessed March 2013).

Feng, Z., Bao, J. and Xiang, Y. (2012) Actor-network-theory (ANT) and paradigm innovation for tourism research (English). *Tourism Tribune/Lvyou Xuekan* 27(11), 24–31. DOI: 10.3969/j.issn.1002-5006.2012.11.003.

Grissemann, U.S., Pikkemaat, B. and Weger, C. (2013) Antecedents of innovation activities in tourism: an empirical investigation of the alpine hospitality industry. *Tourism (13327461)* 61(1), 7–27.

Hall, C.M. (2009) Innovation and tourism policy in Australia and New Zealand: never the twain shall meet? *Journal of Policy Research in Tourism, Leisure & Events* 1(1), 2–18. DOI: 10.1080/19407960802703466.

Hjalager, A. (2010a) Regional innovation systems: the case of angling tourism. *Tourism Geographies* 12(2), 192–216. DOI: 10.1080/14616681003725201.

Hjalager, A. (2010b) A review of innovation research in tourism. *Tourism Management* 31(1), 1–12. DOI: 10.1016/j.tourman.2009.08.012.

Hjalager, A. and Nordin, S. (2011) User-driven innovation in tourism—a review of methodologies. *Journal of Quality Assurance in Hospitality & Tourism* 12(4), 289–315. DOI: 10.1080/1528008X.2011.541837.

Huibin, X. and Marzuki, A. (2012) Community participation of cultural heritage tourism from innovation system perspective. *International Journal of Services Technology & Management* 18(3), 105–127.

Kokkranikal, J. and Morrison, A. (2011) Community networks and sustainable livelihoods in tourism: the role of entrepreneurial innovation. *Tourism Planning & Development* 8(2), 137–156. DOI: 10.1080/21568316.2011.573914.

Lee, G. (2013) Modeling consumers' co-creation in tourism innovation. ProQuest Information & Learning. *Dissertation Abstracts International Section A: Humanities and Social Sciences* 73(10).

McKeown, M. (2008) *The Truth about Innovation: A Small Book about Big Ideas*. Pearson/Prentice Hall, Harlow, UK.

Moscardo, G. (2008) Sustainable tourism innovation: challenging basic assumptions. *Tourism & Hospitality Research* 8(1), 4–13. DOI: 10.1057/thr.2008.7.

Nagy, A. (2012) A review of tourism and hospitality innovation research. Annals of the University of Oradea, Economic Science Series. Retrieved from http://search.ebscohost.com/login.aspx?direct=true&db=bth&AN=85948955&site=ehost-live (accessed March 2013).

Nimrod, G. and Rotem, A. (2012) An exploration of the innovation theory of successful ageing among older tourists. *Ageing & Society* 32(3), 379–404. DOI: 10.1017/S0144686X1100033X.

Paget, E., Dimanche, F. and Mounet, J. (2010) A tourism innovation case: an actor-network approach. *Annals of Tourism Research* 37(3), 828–847.

Prats, L., Guia, J. and Molina, F. (2008) How tourism destinations evolve: the notion of tourism local innovation system. *Tourism & Hospitality Research* 8(3), 178–191. DOI: 10.1057/thr.2008.24.

Rogers, E.M. (1962) *Diffusion of Innovations*. Free Press, New York.

Rogers, E.M. (2003) *Diffusion of Innovations*, 5th edn. Free Press, New York.

Rønningen, M. (2010) Innovative processes in a nature-based tourism case: the role of a tour-operator as the driver of innovation. *Scandinavian Journal of Hospitality & Tourism* 10(3), 190–206. DOI: 10.1080/15022250.2010.491255.

Schumpeter, J.A. (1934) *Theory of Economic Development: Inquiry into Profits, Capital, Credit, Interest of the Business Cycle*. Transaction Publishers, Cambridge, Massachusetts.

Smerecnik, K.R. and Andersen, P.A. (2011) The diffusion of environmental sustainability innovations in North American hotels and ski resorts. *Journal of Sustainable Tourism* 19(2), 171–196. DOI: 10.1080/09669582.2010.517316.

Sørensen, F. (2007) The geographies of social networks and innovation in tourism. *Tourism Geographies* 9(1), 22–48. DOI: 10.1080/14616680601092857.

Sorrie, M. (2014) Evaluating regional tourism innovation: exploring the system of innovation along the British Columbia portion of the Alaska highway driving route. Master's Thesis in Sustainable Leisure Management submitted to Vancouver Island University.

Tejada, P. and Moreno, P. (2013) Patterns of innovation in tourism 'small and medium-size enterprises'. *Service Industries Journal* 33(7), 749–758. DOI: 10.1080/02642069.2013.740469.

Thuot, L., Vaugeois, N. and Maher, P. (2010) Fostering the adoption of sustainable tourism. *Journal of Rural and Community Development* 5(1/2), 76–89.

Volo, S. (2005) A consumer-based measurement of tourism innovation. *Journal of Quality Assurance in Hospitality & Tourism* 6(3), 73–87. DOI: 10.1300/J162v06n03-05.

Weidenfeld, A. (2013) Tourism and cross border regional innovation systems. *Annals of Tourism Research* 42, 191–213.

Weiermair, K. (2005) Prospects for innovation in tourism: analyzing the innovation potential throughout the tourism value chain. *Journal of Quality Assurance in Hospitality & Tourism* 6(3), 59–72. DOI: 10.1300/J162v06n03-04.

Williams, A.M. and Shaw, G. (2011) Internationalization and innovation in tourism. *Annals of Tourism Research* 38(1), 27–51.

7 Theoretical Perspectives on Systems and Sustainability

MERCEDES M. HUNT* AND KELLY S. BRICKER

Department of Parks, Recreation, and Tourism, College of Health, University of Utah, Salt Lake City, Utah

The Objectives

1. Describe how theory helps our understanding of how resources are utilized in a tourism system.
2. Provide key terms and a background of systems theory and how those concepts can be applied.
3. Understand the relationship between systems, sustainability, and tourism.
4. Offer opportunities for future research utilizing systems theory as it pertains to tourism.

The Vignette

A small river company located in Fiji hosts approximately 5000 guests throughout a year. With the support of several landowners along the river corridor, the river company secured a lease for conservation, which allows for non-motorized use along the river, traditional use of the surrounding forests and river for subsistence living, and protects 200 m on both sides of the river from commercial extractive uses. The river operation runs year-round, employs guides from the landowning groups along the river, and employs office and technical staff from the community where it is based. The success of the river company depends on many things, including but not limited to: protection of the river corridor from extractive use which may cause pollution due to mining and unsustainable logging practices and development; cooperation from several local landowning communities that support the lease and provide employees; government, which allows for the lease to occur and supports the waterway as a protected wetland of international importance; the tourists, who purchase the product to support the river company and livelihoods; the suppliers, who supply safety equipment, rafts and kayaks, food, and transportation that enables the river trips to occur; the weather, which supplies rainfall and keeps the river drainage viable for rafting; the support of the company, which must earn a profit to benefit local communities through employment, and various philanthropic services; the training provided by the company, which supports a safe and interesting river trip; national and international marketing efforts; and the image of the destination globally, including a stable political environment. While this may

*Corresponding author, e-mail: mercedes.hunt@utah.edu

not be entirely exhaustive, it does demonstrate a wide range of factors that will either support the success or failure of the river company. This company works within a system, a system of governmental, managerial, or institutional guidelines (i.e. the lease), ecological processes (i.e. the river corridor, weather), and social-cultural processes (i.e. employees, training programs, cultural norms, etc.).

The Context

This chapter will address tourism operations and management, destination management, and destination management in the context of systems theory. The focus of this section of the chapter is on the elements of a system and how to understand system functions. Systems theory is relatively new to tourism, especially as it relates to sustainable tourism management (Miller and Twining-Ward, 2005; Liu, 2003).

First, it is important to understand the various elements of a system and how they interact. As briefly reflected in the Vignette, even a tourism operation (small or large) is a system of parts which deliver an experience to customers—the delivery of that experience is dependent upon several components that enable a tourism enterprise to deliver. Systems theory provides a holistic and conceptual approach to understanding tourism from macro- to micro-enterprises.

Within the context of this theory, a *system* is broadly defined as "a set of things—people, cells, molecules, or whatever—interconnected in such a way that they produce their own pattern of behavior over time" (Meadows, 2008: 2). These "things" can range from small interactions such as the purchase of food, to thoughts and actions of an individual, to larger interactions such as those within a group of individuals. A system includes parts that are identifiable; parts that affect each other; the parts together produce an effect that would otherwise be different from the effect of each part on its own; and potentially, this effect or behavior over time, persists in a variety of circumstances (Meadows, 2008). The complexity of a system ranges based on the defined limitations set by a researcher.

Information in Fig. 7.1 provides some examples of the different scales that one can use to assess systems relating to hotels. For example, a researcher could choose to

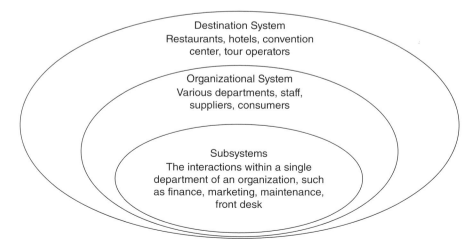

Fig. 7.1. Scale levels for tourism systems.

M. Hunt and K. Bricker

look at a destination and study how each of the components within the system interacts with each other: hotels, restaurants, convention centers, tour operators, public transportation, etc. A hotel may be part of a tourism destination system, providing for tourists who visit an area and closely tied to event venues, restaurants, adventure activities, the local community, governmental policies, and the health of the natural environment. On a smaller scale, systems thinking could also allow a researcher to assess the entirety of a hotel with interconnected relationships between staff members, subsystems of departments, outside organizations, visitors, and others or on an even smaller scale, the role of an individual person and their interconnection to the well-being of various components or departments within an organization. This concept can be applied to any "system" within the field of tourism, and as systems thinkers say, almost everything can be conceived of as a system.

A system is a complex set of inputs, regulation elements, and outputs (see Fig. 7.2). At the heart of each system is a *stock*. A stock can be a tangible or intangible part of a system. A tangible element is one that can be touched, viewed, calculated, or measured; it can be a mass, collection, store of information, a physical object, or collection of materials over time (Meadows, 2008). For example, with respect to the Vignette, these might be the physical river rafts, oars, direct economic benefits to the local community, the percent of those employed full-time, the amount of a specific resource reduction. Intangible "stock" elements or impalpable elements are those that cannot be easily seen, touched, or measured, such as information systems. For example, computer systems may play a role in automatically attributing to the buying and selling of financial transactions for rafting tours, with a computer network acting as an agent. In this example, the money and interactions exist intangibly because one cannot touch the virtual money. A computer system comprises tangible (physical parts) and intangible elements (virtual parts) that collectively work to buy and sell rafting tours. Other examples of intangible "stock" elements have included ideas such as intellectual property, relationships, employee competency, the efficiency of a department, an individual's trust in others, or the world's belief in climate change (Allee, 2008; Meadows, 2008). However, there remains some ambiguity regarding "intangible" elements of a system, as researchers work on ways to actually measure some of these concepts.

Reflecting on the Vignette, a stock could be the water in the river used by the rafting company, the number of guests going on a rafting trip, the conservation lease, the prevention of pollution from mining, or the profit from the company.

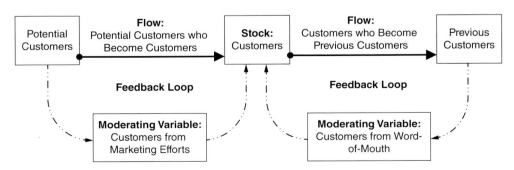

Fig. 7.2. Stocks, flows, feedback loops, and moderating variables.

As time passes by, stocks can change; this change is called a *flow*. Flows can be the creation and destruction of a stock such as turning on a faucet to fill a sink and then emptying the sink (Meadows, 2008). A job that is created and then terminated, seasonal employees hired by a resort may then leave when the season ends, a win then a loss, all of these things are part of the flow. A stock could be seen as the middle of a story between two flows. If the stock in the river company was a high quality guest experience, conserving the river and its biodiversity, clean water, etc. would be crucial to running a successful river business. A possible input flow would be the conservation of the river corridor. An output flow would be illegal logging operations that pollute the river and destroy the scenic qualities that guests enjoy. If illegal logging were to continue, the quality of the river and its surroundings could jeopardize the pristine river experience that guests seek. Therefore, ideally, the corridor will continue to be conserved, which is natural capital the system depends on for the guest experience, maintaining a balance of use, which accounts for possible inflows and outflows.

Continuing this example, if the river company is suddenly fully booked up or the opposite happens and there is absolutely no one booking rafting or kayaking, there is usually something at play. This positive or negative process affecting the system is usually caused by a *feedback loop* or a closed interlinked mechanism from a stock caused by choices, policies, physical laws, or events that are reliant on the quantity of a stock (Meadows, 2008). Revisiting the Vignette example, if the mechanism to protect the corridor is diminished in any way (i.e. the lease expires and is not renewed; regulations to monitor illegal logging are not enforced, etc.) and guests begin to notice results, such as water and noise pollution or increased landslides, this may upset equilibrium, and the business could decline. In the same way, if the river company is able to work with local communities to protect the river corridor, the business continues to grow, and the company provides increased income to local communities, reducing the desire to illegally log within the protected area. These feedback loops can take many forms depending on the stocks, inputs, and outputs of a given system. Not all systems have feedback loops. The systems without feedback loops tend to be simplistic in nature and do not have these types of interactions. Alternatively, other systems may have varying types of feedback loops (Meadows, 2008). A complex system such as a destination with hotels, event venues, restaurants, etc. not only contains many different systems, but also varying feedback loops. There may be different mechanisms and feedback loops associated with business tourists versus leisure tourists in the same destination system.

The system of any tourism entity is complex with many moderating variables such as time and quality, which can affect the stock (customer service at the reception, events running on time, etc.). For example, in regards to the Vignette, the rafting company may require snacks and beverages for passengers, fuel for trucks, and water running down the river bed; these concepts would be *inputs*. If all of the passengers were loaded on a raft and prior to leaving the river bank a safety check was conducted that found a leak in the raft, which required a patch or a back-up raft, this could be viewed as a *moderating variable*. The moderation could affect the eventual *output* or in this case, outcome of the service such as the rafting trip running late, customers feeling good about their experience using that particular tour operator or simply arriving safely at the final destination all affecting the stock of a pleasant customer experience. By looking at each individual as a smaller system within a larger organizational system, it is easier to understand the importance of each component and how each individual or department as a whole helps to run an organization.

The change, growth, and value of a stock usually transforms slowly over time. *Dynamic equilibrium* means that the state of a stock is constant, even if the inputs and outputs are not. For example, a lake will be in a state of dynamic equilibrium (staying at the same water level) when the amount of water flowing in is equal to the amount of water flowing out. The same concept can be applied to sustainability in tourism, especially with respect to emissions. For example, a hotel will always be producing a certain amount of greenhouse gas emissions, and must engage in some activities if it hopes to reach a net-zero effect. Three options are always possible to achieve a dynamic sustainable equilibrium, and could be pursued at the same time. The first is to reduce the amount of undesirable emission consumption, through changing light bulbs, and turning computers off when not in use, etc. Second, efforts should be taken to acquire energy from more sustainable sources such as solar or wind power use. Third, an organization could increase the amount of offsets, such as by engaging in more recycling efforts or trying to improve environmental ramifications elsewhere equal to the cost of the garbage, such as planting more trees.

As would be expected, systems have the possibility to grow and change. A cruise company may start utilizing Alaska as their primary destination. Yet, as they seek growth in their business, they may decide to expand to alternate seasons, using their stock or boats to operate in the southern hemisphere during other times of year. In the same way, a tour operator may change their activities due to various levels of rainfall throughout the year. This idea that a system has the ability to change and adapt is called *self-organization*. Self-organization can sometimes be surrendered to immediate or short-lived gains. Sometimes companies make business choices that have short-term gains and as a result cause instability in the system (Meadows, 2008). Self-organization has also resulted in creative opportunities viewed as either liberating or threatening to the status quo (Meadows, 2008). Regardless of how self-organization is viewed, it is a natural part of the ebb and flow within any system. Managers must constantly make decisions that can affect the long-term well-being of a company. This aspect of a system is one way in which systems express growth and change.

A system may contain sub-systems, for example a hotel can have many departments. The hotel itself can be viewed as a system and the departments within the hotel can be viewed as sub-systems. This is called a *hierarchy* of systems (Clayton and Radcliffe, 1996; Meadows, 2008). Bonds between attributes of a sub-system usually have stronger relationships within themselves than they do with other sub-systems (Meadows, 2008). Logically, the employees of a finance department, for example, would interact with each other more than the sales department. Because most of the information within a sub-system is shared internally, the bulk of information does not transfer far from the source. Conceptually, this allows the greater system to work more efficiently (Meadows, 2008).

Systems may be vulnerable to changes such as natural disasters, economic downturns, bad decisions, etc. and conceptually, these are identified as *shocks*. The shock disturbs the functioning of the system and therefore systems must explore ways to be prepared for shocks. The response by the system to various shocks depends on the *resilience* of the system, or "the capacity of a system to absorb disturbance and still retain its basic function and structure" (Walker and Salt, 2006: xiii). Resilience of a system typically refers to a system over a period of time. When planning for destination management, groups must look at the long-term picture. As a destination grows, changes, or declines, decisions must be made to help with the destination's viability. When a shock occurs within a destination (i.e. the recession in 2007), how resilient a destination is to that shock depends upon its ability to overcome the stress and challenges caused by the disturbance. Resilience literature is also connected to the field of sustainability as it relates to a system's ability to meet the needs of the present situation while also working to help future generations to also meet their own needs (World Commission on Environment and Development, 1987; Walker and Salt, 2006). Whether a destination survives shocks depends on its resilience, and most authors attribute resiliency to a long-range perspective, rather than short moments in time (Walker and Salt, 2006).

As we have learned so far, systems are rarely linear. Research has shown the dynamic, adaptable, interdependent, and non-linearity of many systems (Waldrop, 1992; Gunderson *et al.*, 1995; Prigogine, 1997; Levin, 1998; McKercher, 1999; NRC, 1999; Farrell and Twining-Ward, 2004). To understand systems thinking and systems theory, one must also acknowledge that systems are naturally complex, and very often chaotic. Complexity theory and chaos theory build on systems theory by recognizing that systems are unique, not machine-like, subtle, abstruse and variable (McKercher, 1999). "Chaos deals with situations such as turbulence that lead to disorganized and unmanageable systems. Complexity theory deals with systems that have many interacting agents and although hard to predict, these systems have structure and permit improvement" (Zahra and Ryan, 2007: 855). When initially assessing a system, relationships among components may seem jumbled and random, though at an inherent level identifiable designs appear that can aid in describing the operation of the system as a whole, leading to spontaneous order (Parry and Drost, 1995; Zahra and Ryan, 2007).

Hayles (1991) suggests that chaos is complete non-order. Waldrop (1992) defined complexity as a developing science that borders the line between order and chaos. Chaos theory stresses that to understand a complex and dynamic system or organization, one must assess the whole instead of the sum of its parts (Zahra and Ryan, 2007). For instance, while Butler's (1980) destination life-cycle model describes resort development, the model lacks a definite explanation for why certain destinations never completely advance, nor does it explain the variance in the time it takes each destination to reach the different stages (Zahra and Ryan, 2007). Additionally, Butler's model is not deterministic—destinations have the ability to become revitalized, they do not automatically degenerate (Zahra and Ryan, 2007).

The Theory

Systems theory was first developed by a biologist named Ludwig Von Bertalanffy in the 1940s (Haines, 2000). Since that time, other disciplines have embraced systems theory as a way to understand various complexities in the world, including urban planning, engineering, and management, among others. Systems theory allows for both a framework of theory while also allowing for flexibility and adaptability. Leiper (1979) was one of the first to utilize a systems theory approach to tourism exploring the "system" of tourist movement starting from the moment a person departs from their home, the travel to the destination, the experience of a destination, and then back again. Leiper (1979) described the tourism system from the perspective of the traveler and the systems they employed from start to finish. Butler (1980) developed

M. Hunt and K. Bricker

the destination life-cycle model, which recognized tourism as a living system with various stages in its life cycle. Murphy (1985) explored the tourism system through a destination-focused approach and identified life cycles within destinations which were similar to those natural systems that occur as seasons. Building on the ideas of Butler (1980) and Murphy (1985), Holling (1986) identified that tourism destinations as systems will ultimately work towards a constant, peak state. Other important works utilizing a systems approach to tourism were Mill and Morrison (1985, 1992), McIntosh and Goeldner (1986), Getz (1987), and Pearce (1989). After Murphy's (1985) research, tourism systems theory was focused on spatial factors, and not necessarily recognizing the multifaceted approach within systems theory and the various layers, flows, and functions (Farrell and Twining-Ward, 2005).

The literature of the 1990s connected tourism destination systems to chaos, complexity, and change concepts (Faulkner and Russell, 1997; Laws *et al.*, 1998; McKercher, 1999; Russell and Faulkner, 1999). Russell and Faulkner (1999, 2004) reviewed Butler's (1980) destination area life-cycle model and described how entrepreneurs overcame times of turbulence and chaos by applying creativity, which changed the course of destinations and influenced competitive advantage. McKercher (1999: 425) also argued that the nature of the tourism system is "chaotic, non-linear, non-deterministic" and as a result, the existing tourism life-cycle models at the time failed to describe the connected relationships among the various components of the system.

Integrating systems theory into tourism

There are several approaches to utilizing systems theory in tourism. These have included layers of the system itself, such as management, spatial relationships, markets, and geography. The approach or definition of the system explored ultimately delimits the results. Hence the researcher provides the ultimate context based upon the problem to be solved.

Senge (1992) stated that systems theory should be connected to management as it has the potential to improve upon organizational learning and operations. Aronsson (1994) focused on tourism through the relationship between supply and demand as related to sustainable rural tourism systems in Sweden. Other researchers, for example Walker *et al.* (1999), were more interested in the tourism destination and how systems theory can help understand the complex relationships between the tourism industry, and the quadruple bottom line of: economy, policy, the natural environment, and the local community. They argued that systems theory allowed for one to explain, simplify and offer alternatives for mechanisms influencing the industry. To aid in this understanding, the researchers used two different areas in Australia as case study samples to help them develop the "Tourism Futures Simulator" (Walker *et al.*, 1999: 59), a framework for assessing the advantages and influences of nature-based tourism and the opportunities for policies that may help with the management of tourism and growth.

With the dawn of the new millennium, the literature on tourism and systems theory has increased. The focus has moved in the direction of sustainability and tourism development. This may be because of the interrelationships and interdependencies between the environment, local community, economic well-being of an area and governmental policies that lend themselves to a systems approach. Miller and Twining-Ward (2005) explored sustainable tourism through the development of sustainability indicators using a systems theory approach. Lim and Cooper (2009) connected sustainable development, tourism, and systems theory to small island tourism, again using a geographical approach. Bonetti *et al.* (2006) developed a multi-level destination approach to sustainability and tourism systems. The conceptual model had four components: (i) they worked to develop a conceptual model that assessed the territory of a tourism system where the stakeholder relationships develop over time; (ii) the model would recognize that the various forms of tourism systems can create value for particular market sectors; (iii) the model acknowledges that an individuals' perception of a destination is affected by tourist interactions; and (iv) the model works to guide the evolutionary courses by dynamically connecting the different levels.

Bosch *et al.* (2007) discussed how issues can be better understood using the mechanism of systems theory. The paper provided an overview of three examples of systems theory tools that can help organizations to accomplish their sustainability goals. The end of the paper argued that there is a need for a paradigm shift towards the use of thinking in systems as systems allow for "sophisticated and unsophisticated modelling technologies, and associated collaborative learning environments" (Bosch *et al.*, 2007: 57).

Ropret *et al.* (2014) used a system dynamics methodology to evaluate a development and policy plan for Slovenian tourism, concluding that a qualitative tourism development model connecting the research results to systems theory was the next step forward. Peric and Djurkin (2014) addressed sustainability from a community perspective by recognizing the characteristics of a model for community-based organizational structure, reasons for socially sustainable practices, and a case study focusing on a community-based tourism business. They determined that a community-based tourism enterprise can benefit from a systems approach especially regarding the theory and practice of sustainable development and socially responsible tourism.

Liu (2003) argued that for a "sustainable" tourism industry to move forward, a systems perspective is required. Liu summarized that "research on tourism resources should recognize its complex and dynamic nature and advance beyond the state of pleading for conservation and preservation to a realm of retaining a balance between the consumption, transformation and creation of tourism resources" (Liu, 2003: 465). Farrell and Twining-Ward (2005) linked systems theory to tourism, and found that because the tourism system is ever changing and evolving, the ability to overcome disturbance and maintain resiliency should be the focus of tourism research. This approach discards somewhat ideas surrounding stability and/or optimization of a tourism system. Their seven steps included the following.

1. To understand complex adaptive systems.
2. To learn from natural ecosystems.
3. A call for human and natural systems to find a sustainable way to co-evolve.
4. To acknowledge tourism as a system.
5. Integration with reference to: the previous steps mentioned above; human and natural ecosystems within scholarship; development of sustainability science which would include: social, technological and biophysical science; and finally integration of information.
6. To add post-normal or post-linear science.
7. Facilitating a sustainability transition or the continual development of human and biophysical well-being.

M. Hunt and K. Bricker

Lu and Nepal (2009) have argued that researchers in sustainable tourism are beginning to recognize tourism as a dynamic complex system, and as such, the realization of more adaptive management approaches to sustainable management are necessary.

What research is demonstrating is that a systems theory approach is relevant to understanding sustainable tourism management. Whether it is a destination-level assessment or individual tourism enterprises, the intangible nature and interconnected dynamics of the tourism industry require a sophisticated and complex methodology to address sustainable development and management—and systems theory can be a framework and theoretical basis to address this.

Tourism marketing systems

Another theme relating tourism and systems is that of marketing and promotion of destinations. Batat and Prentovic (2014) used systems theory as a way of rethinking sustainable tourism promotion in France, Serbia, and the UK. They found that online videos in the UK and France tended to be more commercial and focused primarily on environmental responsibility. The Serbian online tourism videos were less commercial and stressed community and cultural heritage, in that they were more centered on social issues within sustainable tourism. Buhalis (2000) looked at strategic marketing and management strategies for destinations by providing an overview of each strategy and providing international examples, using a systems perspective. The paper argued that destination marketing strategies should incorporate all stakeholders and sustainability of community resources. Destinations must set themselves apart by cultivating public/private partnerships, utilizing new technology, and capitalizing on the internet as a way of becoming more competitive, increasing visibility, decreasing costs, and developing local collaboration. The paper closed by stating that marketing of destinations needs to steer towards optimization of tourism impacts and fulfillment of stakeholder objectives.

Operationalization of systems theory in tourism

Over the course of the last 15 years, numerous researchers have begun to try to operationalize systems theory to better conceptualize the tourism system. Walker *et al.* (1999) developed the Tourism Futures Simulator (see Integrating systems theory into tourism).

Maani and Cavana (2007) developed two different models. The first model provided the four levels of human interaction: events, patterns, systemic structures, and mental models. They argued that the tools of systems theory focus on all levels of thinking. Their next model, known as the Causal Loop Diagram or language of systems theory, offers insights into the causal relationships between a group of variables (labeled as factors) that impact the system.

Rocha *et al.* (2007: 83) developed an integrated management systems model to help understand prevailing management systems of "quality, environment, occupational health and safety, and corporate social responsibility" that have the potential to be more representative of sustainable development. The authors incorporated both a macro-level standpoint stressing systems theory for looking at the integrated management system and a micro-level outlook that incorporates the foundational seven elements of the model. Their research focused on how sustainable development cannot be seen as a separate concept and existing business infrastructure requires application of sustainable development practices. Some research has identified the need to move beyond the exploratory when it comes to systems theory and tourism and begin utilizing more experimental or quasi-experimental approaches (Lu and Nepal, 2009). Cabrera *et al.* (2008) have argued that there is very little agreement among researchers as to the components of the tourism system. Even with increased research on sustainable tourism and systems theory, researchers still acknowledge the lack of applied use of systems theory in tourism and the field is still in its infancy (Liu, 2003; Farrell and Twining-Ward, 2005). Therefore, while tourism research has gradually begun to use systems theory as a methodology, there is still much potential for systems to be used as a way of better understanding the industry.

The Future

Early research relating tourism to systems theory focused on the need for a holistic perspective, emphasizing the idea that chaos, complexity, and change are all an integral part of the tourism system and have the possibility of helping destinations and operations to use creative methods of overcoming disturbances and becoming more resilient. As we entered the new millennium, and saw the rise of global concerns surrounding poverty alleviation, production, and consumption of goods and services, and allocation and access to resources, biodiversity, etc., research in tourism and its contribution to effecting positive change has become even more relevant (Bricker *et al.*, 2012). The impact of this global industry lends itself to a complex systems approach to understanding. The tourism industry is moving towards defining what sustainability is through certification programs and relevant accreditation processes (see Global Sustainable Tourism Council, 2015). Within these processes and voluntary guidelines, research on their effectiveness and outcomes could be addressed. From destinations to operators, there are several tourism sectors engaging in sustainable tourism practices that can provide excellent evaluation opportunities to employ a systems theory approach. This can enhance contributions to understanding research relative to developing tourism products, community-based developments, and sector-specific management strategies such as hotels and tour operators. There is also evidence of a relationship between sector-related sustainability and systems research. To date, destination life cycles, operational resiliency of a business, and enhancing the well-being of local communities are relevant directions using a systems theory approach.

While the number of studies linking tourism with systems theory has increased with time (Miller and Twining-Ward, 2005; Testa and Sipe, 2006), the potential for innovative research is high, especially with considerable concerns surrounding issues connected to sustainable tourism development and management. This may partially be due to the idea that it is difficult to assess sustainability without looking at the interrelationships among variables (i.e. stakeholders, sectors, divisions) (Camus *et al.*, 2012; Miller and Twining-Ward, 2005; Weaver, 2006, 2009; Peric and Djurkin, 2014). Though some researchers have attempted to operationalize elements of systems theory as it pertains to tourism, it can be challenging because there are no universal concrete set of principles in tourism. Destination systems are different to organizational systems, management systems are different to ecological systems, and yet all of these systems are interrelated. Miller and Twining-Ward (2005: 46) identified stakeholder participation as critical to adaptive management strategies within a system, "for sustainable tourism to be place-based and promote the developmental needs of the destination with greater surety, tourism needs to be more stakeholder-driven." Stakeholder involvement is an area of tourism that systems theory has the potential to help better understand and yet is an area that has not been studied widely (see Chapters 1 and 3).

Areas of the tourism system that have not received much attention within systems research are tourism marketing, the role of stakeholder involvement, and the relationship between sustainable tourism indicators (such as global sustainable tourism criteria and indicators; GSTC, 2015) (i.e. destination, tour operations, and accommodation) and the sustainable functioning of a tourism system. There is also limited research connecting systems theory-specific sectors such as tour operations and events. A limited number of studies have emphasized the benefits of systems theory of smaller systems such as accommodation providers, cruise lines, resorts, etc. Though many researchers have used systems theory as a way of understanding transportation systems, few researchers have used systems theory to assess transportation systems utilized specifically for tourism (e.g. trains, planes, bus tours). Yet, access remains a critical aspect of the tourism system, impacting local communities, tour operators, accommodation sectors, and the traveler. Systems theory can also provide a framework for addressing complexity, adaptability, and resilience of the industry at the destination and community level. So much of what is studied is how to optimize a travel destination, rather than growth within a reasonable level allowing for the ebb and flow of markets, crisis management, and a destination's ability to recover, as these fields have not been widely explored.

With a theory that may appear somewhat nebulous, one might ask, "Where do I start using this theory to help understand a tourism system?" "How can I utilize systems theory as a way of better understanding the tourism industry?" Meadows (2008) argued that observations are one of the best ways to assess systems. Meadows (2008: 171) said that it is important to watch a system's behavior before disrupting the system in any respect:

> Watching what really happens, instead of listening to peoples' theories of what happens, can explode many careless causal hypotheses…Starting with the behavior of the system forces you to focus on facts, not theories. It keeps you from falling too quickly into your own beliefs or misconceptions, or those of others.

From watching a system's behavior, it is possible then to draw models, describe the system in words, or depict the system in pictures, collect quantitative and/or qualitative data regarding the system and to begin to understand its inter-workings—then actually test what happens when elements of the system are disrupted, or changed in some way.

Systems theory can be a useful tool for research and allows one to assess a system using deductive reasoning using creativity, flexibility, and "out-of-the-box" thinking to understand a problem or situation from an alternative perspective.

Questions

1. How would one define the boundaries of a tourism system?
2. What role do you play as a researcher in defining a system?
3. How can systems research help strengthen sustainability within the tourism industry?

References

Allee, V. (2008) Value network analysis and value conversion of tangible and intangible assets. *Journal of Intellectual Capital* 9(1), 5–24.

Aronsson, L. (1994) Sustainable tourism systems: the example of sustainable rural tourism in Sweden. *Journal of Sustainable Tourism* 2(1–2), 77–92.

Batat, W. and Prentovic, S. (2014) Towards viral systems thinking: a cross-cultural study of sustainable tourism ads. *Kybernetes* 43(3/4), 529–546.

Bonetti, E., Petrillo, C.S. and Simoni, M.M. (2006) Tourism system dynamics: a multi-level destination approach. In: Lazzeretti, L. and Petrillo, C.S. (eds) *Tourism Local Systems and Networking*. Elsevier, Amsterdam, the Netherlands, pp. 111–133.

Bosch, O., Maani, K. and Smith, C. (2007) Systems thinking—language of complexity for scientists and managers. In: Harrison, S., Bosch, A. and Herbohn, J. (eds) *Improving the Triple Bottom Line Returns from Small-Scale Forestry. Proceedings from Improving the Triple Bottom Line Returns from Small-Scale Forestry*. Ormoc, the Philippines, pp. 57–66.

Bricker, K., Black, R. and Cottrell, S. (eds) (2012) *Sustainable Tourism and the Millennium Development Goals: Effecting Positive Change*. Jones and Bartlett Learning, Burlington, Massachusetts.

Buhalis, D. (2000) Marketing the competitive destination of the future. *Tourism Management* 21, 97–116.

Butler, R. (1980) The concept of a tourist area cycle of evolution: implications for management of resources. *Canadian Geographer* 24(1), 5–12.

Cabrera, D., Colosi, L. and Lobdell, C. (2008) Systems thinking. *Evaluation and Program Planning* 31, 299–310.

Camus, S., Hikkerova, L. and Sahut, J. (2012) Systemic analysis and model of sustainable tourism. *International Journal of Business* 17(4), 365–378.

Clayton, A.M.H. and Radcliffe, N.J. (1996) *Sustainability: A Systems Approach*. Earthscan Publications, London. DOI: 10.1108/K-07-2013-0132.

Farrell, B.H. and Twining-Ward, L. (2004) Reconceptualizing tourism. *Annals of Tourism Research* 31(2), 274–295.

Farrell, B. and Twining-Ward, L. (2005) Seven steps towards sustainability: tourism in the context of new knowledge. *Journal of Sustainable Tourism* 13(2), 109–122.

Faulkner, B. and Russell, R. (1997) Chaos and complexity in tourism: in search of a new perspective. *Pacific Tourism Review* 1, 93–102.

Getz, D. (1987) Tourism planning and research traditions: models and futures. Australian Travel Research Workshop, Bunbury, Western Australia.

Global Sustainable Tourism Council (GSTC) (2015) Global Sustainable Tourism Criteria. Available at: http://www.gstcouncil.org/gstc-criteria/sustainable-tourism-gstc-criteria.html (accessed 1 February 2014).

Gunderson, L., Holling, C. and Light, S. (eds) (1995) *Barriers and Bridges to the Renewal of Ecosystems and Institutions*. Columbia University Press, New York.

Haines, S.G. (2000) *The System Thinking Approach to Strategic Planning and Management*. CRC Press, Boca Raton, Florida.

Hayles, N.K. (1991) *Chaos and Order.* University of Chicago Press, Chicago.

Holling, C. (1986) The resilience of terrestrial ecosystems: local surprise and global change. In: Clark, W. and Munn, R. (eds) *Sustainable Development of the Biosphere.* Cambridge University Press, Cambridge, UK, pp. 292–317.

Laws, E., Faulkner, B. and Moscardo, G. (1998) Embracing and managing change in tourism. In: Laws, E., Faulkner, B. and Moscardo, G. (eds) *Embracing and Managing Change in Tourism: International Case Studies.* Routledge, New York, pp. 1–10.

Leiper, N. (1979) The framework of tourism: Towards a definition of tourism, tourist and the tourist industry. *Annals of Tourism Research* 6(4), 390–407.

Levin, S. (1998) Ecosystems and the biosphere as complex adaptive systems. *Ecosystems* 1, 431–436.

Lim, C.C. and Cooper, C. (2009) Beyond sustainability: optimizing island tourism development. *International Journal of Tourism Research* 11, 89–103.

Liu, Z. (2003) Sustainable tourism development: a critique. *Journal of Sustainable Tourism* 11(6), 459–475.

Lu, J. and Nepal, S.K. (2009) Sustainable tourism research: an analysis of papers published in the *Journal of Sustainable Tourism.* *Journal of Sustainable Tourism* 17(1), 5–16.

Maani, K. and Cavana, R. (2007) *Systems Thinking, System Dynamic: Managing Change and Complexity*, 2nd edn. Prentice-Hall, Pearson, New Jersey.

McIntosh, R. and Goeldner, C.J. (1986) *Tourism: Principles, Practices, Philosophies.* Wiley, New York.

McKercher, B. (1999) A chaos approach to tourism. *Tourism Management* 20(4), 425–434.

Meadows, D.H. (2008) *Thinking in Systems: A Primer.* Chelsea Green, White River Junction, Vermont.

Mill, R. and Morrison, A. (1985, 1992) *The Tourist System: An Introductory Text.* Prentice-Hall, Englewood Cliffs, New Jersey.

Miller, G. and Twining-Ward, L. (2005) *Monitoring for a Sustainable Tourism Transition: The Challenge of Developing and Using Indicators.* CAB International, Wallingford, UK.

Murphy, P.E. (1985) *Tourism: A Community Approach.* Methuen, London.

NRC (1999) *Our Common Journey: A Transition toward Sustainability.* National Academy Press, Washington, DC.

Parry, B. and Drost, R. (1995) Is chaos good for your profits? *International Journal of Contemporary Hospitality Management* 7(1), i–iii.

Pearce, D. (1989) *Tourism Development.* Longman Scientific and Technical, Harlow, UK.

Peric, M. and Djurkin, J. (2014) Systems thinking and alternative business model for responsible tourist destination. *Kybernates* 43(3/4), 480–496. DOI: 10.1108/K-07-2013-0132.

Prigogine, I. (1997) *The End of Certainty: Time, Chaos and the New Laws of Nature.* The Free Press, New York.

Rocha, M., Searcy, C. and Karapetrovic, S. (2007) Integrating sustainable development into existing management systems. *Total Quality Management* 18(1–2), 83–92. DOI: 10.1080/14783360601051594.

Ropret, M., Jere Jakulin, T. and Likar, B. (2014) The systems approach to the improvement of innovation in Slovenian tourism. *Kybernetes* 43(3/4), 427–444.

Russell, R. and Faulkner, B. (1999) Movers and shakers: chaos makers in tourism development. *Tourism Management* 20, 411–423.

Russell, R. and Faulkner, B. (2004) Entrepreneurship, chaos and the tourism area lifecycle. *Annals of Tourism Research* 31(3), 556–579.

Senge, P.M. (1992) Systems thinking and organizational learning: acting locally and thinking globally in the organization of the future. *European Journal of Operational Research* 59(1), 137–150.

Testa, M.R. and Sipe, L.J. (2006) A systems approach to service quality: tools for hospitality leaders. *Cornell Hotel and Restaurant Administration Quarterly* 47(1), 36–48.

Waldrop, M. (1992) *Complexity: The Emerging Science at the Edge of Order and Chaos.* Simon & Schuster, New York.

Walker, B. and Salt, D. (2006) *Resilience Thinking: Sustaining Ecosystems and People in a Changing World.* Island Press, Washington, DC.

Walker, P.A., Greiner, R., Mcdonald, D. and Lyne, V. (1999) The tourism futures simulator: a systems thinking approach. *Environmental Modeling and Software* 14, 59–67.

Weaver, D. (2006) *Sustainable Tourism: Theory and Practice.* Elsevier Butterworth-Heinemann, Burlington, Massachusetts.

Weaver, D. (2009) Reflections on sustainable tourism and paradigm change. In: Gössling, S., Hall, C.M. and Weaver D.B. (eds) *Sustainable Tourism Futures: Perspectives on Systems, Restructuring and Innovations.* Routledge, New York, pp. 33–40.

World Commission on Environment and Development (1987) Report of the World Commission on Environment and Development: Our common future. Available at: http://www.un-documents.net/wced-ocf.htm (accessed 21 June 2015).

Zahra, A. and Ryan, C. (2007) From chaos to cohesion—complexity in tourism structures: an analysis of New Zealand's regional tourism organizations. *Tourism Management* 28, 854–862.

M. Hunt and K. Bricker

8 Theoretical Perspectives on Tourism Marketing

STATIA ELLIOT*

School of Hospitality, Food and Tourism Management, University of Guelph, Guelph, Ontario, Canada

The Objectives

The purpose of this chapter is to examine the evolution of marketing theory and its application in tourism research. The objectives are to:

1. Define and describe the four "Ps" of marketing theory.
2. Explain how approaches such as the Theory of Planned Behavior, Image Theory, Persuasion Theory, Image Theory, and Self-Concept Theory, for example, are relevant to theory-driven market research.
3. Explain how theory-driven research is and can be used to inform destination branding and marketing.
4. Provide a critical review of existing tourism marketing research and suggest topics and approaches for further theoretical inquiry.

The Vignette

Place branding the rural landscape has become an almost art-like process to capture the unique essence of place. The Township Trail in Quebec, Canada, unlike many trails that establish in iconic locations (e.g. Pacific Coast Way, Australia), or connect a strong product cluster (e.g. Wine Road, California), represents the type of idyllic rural features that could be found down many country roads: "its 415 kilometres of scenic views, picturesque villages, round barns, factories and schools are signs of a former era" (http://www.bonjourquebec.com/qc-en/chemincantons0.html). Beyond a basic supply of accommodations and restaurants, an inventory of heritage attractions identified 20 historic villages, featuring churches, mills, schools, and other historically significant buildings, and 15 museums or interpretive centers. Heritage themed signs mark the route of regional roads east of Montreal, the closest target market. But for a rural trail to truly succeed, its marketing strategy must not only attract visitors, it must contribute to a community's well-being, quality of life, and sense of pride.

*Corresponding author, e-mail: statia@uoguelph.ca

The Context

Marketing is the activity, set of institutions, and processes for creating, communicating, delivering, and exchanging offerings that have value for customers, clients, partners, and society at large (American Marketing Association, 2013). Tourism marketing, by extension, is a broad field of research and practice, fundamental to practitioners for its operational significance, and to academics for its theoretical richness. While a significant body of empirical work exists, with threads of theory throughout, the science of tourism marketing continues to build from theories in related fields, notably service marketing, communications, and consumer behavior, which at their base, are theories from philosophy, sociology, anthropology, and other social sciences related to human behavior.

A summary of tourism marketing theory represents a mixed and borrowed list, presented in Table 8.1 below. Foundations, such as the concept of the four Ps, come from general marketing practice. Tourist behavior is largely based on theories from consumer psychology and sociology. Much of what is known about the concept of persuasion and the use of promotion in tourism has been discovered through studies in the communications field. Then there are the common tourism marketing activities, such as segmentation and branding, where theory lags behind their practice. This chapter presents the theoretical underpinnings of these key marketing concepts. Inextricably linked to marketing is behavior, for tourism is about consumption. Early theories of behavior and action are touched on to introduce the attitudes-beliefs-behavior model that has influenced much of the tourism marketing literature. Behavioral theories are at the base of satisfaction, trust and loyalty research, and studies of persuasion. Theories relevant to communications and promotions are identified, as well as those relating to other decision areas of pricing, segmentation, and branding, critical to marketing. In most instances, early research from a non-tourism field provides the theoretical base for the tourism research that follows.

The Theory

Theories relevant to tourism marketing reviewed in this chapter are summarized in Table 8.1.

Marketing foundations

Broadly, marketing theory supposes that an organization performs at its best when customer oriented, or customer-centric, meaning the needs and desires of its customers are at the center of all decisions and activities (Kotler *et al.*, 1999). The marketing mix presents four key variables or decision areas, to be managed or mixed, best to achieve customer satisfaction. Over time, others have played with the mix, including Kotler *et al.* (1999), who restated the Ps as Cs, to reflect the customer orientation central to modern marketing: Product became Customer value; Price became Cost; Place became Convenience; and Promotion became Communication. Another widely accepted mix, by Booms and Bitner (1982), expanded the four Ps to seven, adding People, Process, and Physical evidence, to reflect the importance of intangibles in service marketing.

Table 8.1. Summary of theories reviewed.

Marketing subject	Theories and models	Authors
Marketing foundations	The four Ps	Borden, 1964
	The seven Ps	Booms and Bitner, 1982
	Relationship marketing	Gronroos, 1997
	Image theories	Dichter, 1985
Tourist behavior	Relationship cost theory	Gronroos, 1997
	Norm theory	Fishbein and Ajzen, 1975
	Theory of planned behavior	
	Theory of reasoned action	
Persuasion	Elaboration likelihood model	Meyers-Levy and Malaviya,
	Resource matching theory	1999
	Cognitive-response model	
	Dual-process model	
Promotion	Visual rhetoric theory	Scott, 1994
	Picture superiority effect	Babin and Burns, 1997
	Image congruence theory	Graeff, 1996
Pricing	Adaptation-level theory	Petroshius and Monroe, 1987
	Reference price	
	Assimilation-contrast effects	
Segmentation	Personality-type theory	LaBarbera et al., 1998
	Self-concept theory	Elliot and Wattanasuwan, 1998
	Positioning theory	Crompton et al., 1992
Place branding	Branding theory	Morgan and Pritchard, 1998
	Tourism destination image	Ritchie, 1996

The latter mix gained particular acceptance in tourism marketing, given the intangibility and service orientation of the tourism experience (Middleton *et al.*, 2009). Yet, as markets shifted away from mass media, and the importance of integrated marketing and customer relationships grew, new theories and contemporary models developed.

Representing a significant shift from transactions to relations, the concept of customer relationship marketing emerged in the services field in the 1980s, and in the tourism field in the 1990s. The mutual exchange and fulfillment of promises, according to relationship cost theory, suggests that mutually satisfying relations make it possible for customers to avoid unnecessary transaction costs associated with changing suppliers, and for suppliers to avoid the incremental costs of obtaining new customers (Gronroos, 1997). A stream of tourism research has supported the benefits of relationship marketing, focusing on two dimensions: attracting customers and maintaining them. Key elements related to relationship marketing success include trust and loyalty, quality, and satisfaction. These multifaceted concepts are modeled and measured to understand causality, commonly built upon the theory of planned behavior, an extension of the theory of reasoned action (Fishbein and Ajzen, 1975), whereby beliefs influence attitudes, and attitudes influence behavior. Much of the tourism marketing literature relates in some way to understanding the processes of attitude formulation, and/or to the persuasion of behavior.

Customer satisfaction, for example, is a frequently studied and important concept in tourism research. Viewed as a prerequisite for sustainable operations, it has been examined in various hospitality settings, including lodging, restaurants, and destinations

(Neil and Gursoy, 2008). One satisfaction model, based on norm theory, measures tourists' images of a destination as representations of their norms, or reference points, in comparison to their actual experiences at the destination. It is the confirmation or disconfirmation of their expectations that determines satisfaction (Chon, 1989) and reinforces that, in tourism, image matters.

Image theory

In tourism marketing, image permeates much of what is known and practiced about appealing to customers. However, image remains an elusive concept, challenging academics and practitioners to define it, understand it, and manage it. Originating from the Latin word *imitari*, or imitation, a current definition from Webster's Dictionary is that image is "an optically formed representation of form or feature, of someone or something." In short, it is a mental picture. In practice, the concept has germinated a range of definitions. It can be defined narrowly as a visual cue, or broadly as "the total impression an entity makes on the minds of people" (Dichter, 1985). The entity that is the object can also range from a single product or service to a brand or company, person or place. A *gestalt* of the conceptualizations produces a meta-definition of image as the summation of all impressions, perceptions, beliefs, attitudes, ideas, experiences, knowledge, feelings, and emotions an individual holds toward an object.

In the services marketing literature, the study of image first appeared in the mid-1980s. Gronroos (1984) developed a service quality model with image as the central filter, influencing the perceptions and expectations of the consumer. Later tests of the influence of image on service found it to be the primary path to customer loyalty, and the strongest driver of repurchase intentions (Andreassen and Lindestad, 1998). Other studies have examined the influence of specific attributes, such as contact personnel and physical environment, concluding that there are multifaceted cues with the potential to affect both attitudes and behaviors toward the service provider (Nguyen and LeBlanc, 2002). Studies that consider the role of image in distribution find that factors such as personal selling and contact are key to image, and even subtle differences can translate into substantial sales gains or losses (Panitz, 1988).

Image theory in marketing provides some insight to the psychological mechanisms that link image to beliefs, attitudes, and behavior, the factors that moderate these links, the potential for positive and negative influences, and the complexities of image management beyond the first impression. Above all, the importance of image across fields of marketing is manifest, supporting the exploration of image as it relates to tourism marketing.

Persuasion theory

Advertising and a company's visual communication are often considered the principal components of image creation. Two streams of models that explain how advertising affects consumers are cognitive and behavioral. The cognitive approach presents consumer decision-making as a linear, sequential process. These models follow rational steps in an analytical manner, and are most often associated with consumers who are highly involved in the decision process. The cognitive-response model views persuasion as a function of the consumer's cognitive responses (e.g. thoughts, knowledge accessed, views stored in memory) evoked as they elaborate on an advertising message. While data exist to support this model, it does not address how people can sometimes be persuaded without elaboration of a message (Meyers-Levy and Malaviya, 1999).

This limitation prompted the emergence of dual-process models of persuasion, such as the elaboration likelihood model (ELM), that consider two routes to persuasion: central and peripheral. The central route to persuasion is thought to be more systematic, and to produce more enduring judgments. The peripheral, or heuristic, route is considered to be more intuitive and simple, evoked as a result of more readily processed cues with little elaboration. In a study of the effectiveness of destination website design ELM was employed, and found both routes to be effective, in that highly involved people are more inclined to elaborate on information (central route), while those with low involvement are more likely to make decisions based on simple cues (peripheral route), with the design significantly influencing both groups (Tang *et al.*, 2012).

Emerging from the concept of elaboration, or resources applied to an advertising message, the resource-matching theory takes into account the demand for resources imposed by the message itself. This theory holds that the likelihood of persuasion is greater if the levels of cognitive resources required for the supply and demand are comparable, under systematic processing conditions (Meyers-Levy and Malaviya, 1999). The influence of elaboration on persuasion suggests that there are at least two types: item-specific and relational elaboration. Item-specific elaboration, for example, results in thoughts about a particular feature of an advertised product. In contrast, relational elaboration results in thoughts that categorize the product, enabling consumers to relate and compare particular features with other like products.

The experiential basis of persuasion theory holds that judgments do not evolve exclusively from consumer's cognitions about an advertising message, but are also affected by the sensations evoked by the message-processing act itself (e.g. frustration if the message processing is complex). The integration of these theories of persuasion encompass three processing strategies differentiated by the degree of resource allocation (minimal, modest, substantial), as well as by the type of elaboration (item-specific, relational). Meyers-Levy and Malaviya (1999) include a judgment correction stage, recognizing that consumers may alter their initial judgment.

The key implication of persuasion theory for tourism marketers is that messages need not evoke intensive elaboration to persuade, and that message-type effectiveness depends upon mental processing-type. Under heuristic processing conditions, whereby consumers are more likely to be persuaded by simple message cues, print advertisements that feature pictures may stimulate a positive aura about the product. Meyers-Levy and Malaviya (1999) identify three ways that pictures can influence persuasion under systematic processing conditions, whereby consumers are more likely to critically evaluate advertising messages: (i) pictures can substantiate an advertising claim by providing visual testimony; (ii) they can influence the type of elaboration evoked by portraying either a product detail (item-specific elaboration), or a usage occasion (relational elaboration); and (iii) pictures can influence the cognitive demands an advertisement requires. Executional techniques can also influence persuasion, such as the application of full color to evoke positive feelings, and an upward camera angle to evoke a sense of power. The more elements and color in an advertisement, the more cognitively demanding it is.

Meyers-Levy and Malaviya (1999) note that the more familiar a consumer is with a product, and the easier it is to comprehend an advertisement, the greater the persuasive impact of the advertisement. The authors also suggest that their framework can be used to assess media placement effectiveness. For example, advertisements that work best under systematic processing conditions should be placed in uncluttered media to avoid diversion. Advertisements that work best under heuristic processing conditions should consider the heuristic of the media itself, for the positive or negative influence of the media might be inferred on to the product. Similarly, under experiential processing conditions, advertisers should ensure that the media facilitates delivery of their message to avoid negative associations of the process from being assigned to the product.

The theories summarized and integrated by Meyers-Levy and Malaviya (1999) are grounded in the information-processing school of thought, which for the most part holds to the rational approach to decision making of "think before you act." The visual imagery of an advertisement is processed cognitively. Another school of thought is the behavioral, whereby the response to imagery is more automatic, effective, and/or unconscious. Here, the visual imagery of an advertisement, in a classical conditioning manner, acts as a stimulus, or visual association with a product. This approach to theorizing the way visual imagery in advertisements influences consumers has been criticized for its interpretation of images as simple representations of reality, passively absorbed without interpretive activity (Scott, 1994).

Promotion and communication

Another theory of how advertising is processed is the theory of visual rhetoric. Scott (1994:252) criticizes both the information processing and behavioral approaches for "reflecting a bias in Western thinking about pictures that is thousands of years old: the assumption that pictures reflect objects in the real world." Scott (1994) introduced the theory of visual rhetoric, recognizing the sender's intention to influence the consumer through the selection of advertising elements in anticipation of the consumer's response. For Scott (1994:252), "pictures are not merely analogues to visual perception, but symbolic artifacts constructed from the conventions of a particular culture." In her framework, visual imagery must be cognitively processed, versus automatically absorbed. She also criticizes the common methodologies used to study imagery, such as content analysis, whereby pictures are typically counted according to *what* is pictured, instead of more deeply considering *how* an image is pictured, its intent, and its interpretation. The interpretation is what creates the imagery, for imagery is a process, elicited by a picture, or concrete words, or even by instructions to imagine. Visual rhetoric has been used not only to assess destination advertising and place branding, but also to explore the creation of meaning (Campelo *et al.*, 2011).

The consideration of images in symbolic ways is not new, as images in advertisements are frequently used to shape consumers' impressions (Burns *et al.*, 1993). Interest in imagery has grown for a number of reasons. Images are thought to be experiential, multisensory, more closely linked to long-term memory, of greater personal relevance, more robust and richer, resulting in a greater effect on consumer attitudes and intentions than discursive stimuli (Burns *et al.*, 1993). Burns *et al.* (1993) developed a framework that places visual imagery as a mediating factor and individual consumer differences as moderators of advertising. Thus, differences in consumers' processing style and product familiarity will evoke attitude and intention differences.

The vividness dimension of visual imagery can be a strong mediator of consumers' reactions. Studies of the use of pictures and instructions to imagine in print advertisements confirm that visual imagery processing influences attitudinal judgments (Babin and Burns, 1997).

Research supports the picture superiority effect, whereby pictures are found to be more effective than verbal information, presumably because images are more rapidly internalized, and activate visual and verbal processes, known as the dual-coding hypothesis (Babin and Burns, 1997). Also, advertisements with objective pictures can be more effective at influencing attitudes than advertisements with abstract pictures, or without pictures. Interestingly, even instructions to image can stimulate effective imagery. For tourism destination websites, pictures can positively affect mental imagery processing, and evoke strong attitudes, an important element of persuasive communication (Lee and Gretzel, 2012).

Some research of advertising imagery has gone further to attempt to link the use of imagery to advertising strategy. One approach suggests that personality-type preferences for processing information can serve as a classification system for advertising imagery (LaBarbera *et al.*, 1998). The authors base their classification system on the personality-type theory of Carl Jung, who summarized individual differences according to three dimensions: extroversion/introversion, sensing/intuiting, and thinking/feeling. Jung's classification is also the basis of the Myers-Briggs Type Indicator, still the most extensively used personality assessment instrument in use. LaBarbera *et al.* (1998) applied the sensing/intuiting dimension to consumers' evaluations of advertisements, and found significant effects for overall advertising appeal, image appeal, and purchase intentions when visual imagery and personality-type were congruent. Images that were perceived as realistic, concrete, and informative were evaluated more favorably by individuals with sensor-type personalities, and images that were perceived as imaginative, conceptual, and abstract were evaluated more favorably by individuals with intuitive-type personalities.

Also relevant to tourism marketing is the image congruence theory, whereby consumers favor products perceived to be congruent with their self-image (Graeff, 1996). Studies of symbolic purchasing behavior have found the communication of favorable and congruent symbolic images to be effective (Leigh and Gabel, 1992). Advertising has become one of the most potent sources of symbolic meaning in the consumer's world, creating, modifying and transforming cultural meanings, and dialectically, representing cultural meanings taken from the consumer's view (Elliot and Wattanasuwan, 1998). Elliot and Wattanasuwan (1998) view advertising as a mediator of self-symbolism (the inward construction of self-identity) and social-symbolism (the outward construction of the social world), based on a considerable literature that suggests *consumers are what they own*. Self-concept theory holds that people act in ways that maintain and enhance their self-concept, including through the purchase and use of products. The image congruence hypothesis states that consumers favor products perceived to be congruent with their self-image. Graeff (1996) found that consumers who have self-images similar to a brand's image are more persuaded by advertisements encouraging them to think about their own self-image. The implication for tourism marketers is to present symbolic meanings in advertisements that are congruent with a particular target consumer's desired identity. For example, customers whose self-images are congruent with high-end dining are more likely to be satisfied, build trust, and less likely to switch from luxury restaurants (Han and Hyun, 2013).

Pricing theory

Observations of consumer behavior suggest that pricing, too, acts as a cue to image formation, and much research has been conducted to understand its influence. Pricing theories have recognized that the way price influences consumer perceptions depends on the context in which prices are perceived (Petroshius and Monroe, 1987). This adaptation-level theory derives from behavioral theory that an individual's response to stimuli is influenced by how they adapted to past stimuli. In pricing, the adaptation level is set by the individual's reference price—the price they hold from past experience in relation to a product. Another behavioral theory that lends itself to the study of pricing is assimilation-contrast effects. Stimuli close in value to an individual's adaptation level, or reference price, will be assimilated more readily than extreme values, which can produce a contrast effect.

These theories form the basis of studies of price cues and their effect on price perceptions: reference price, lowest price, and highest price. In their study of product-line prices, Petroshius and Monroe (1987) found that not only did an individual product price influence consumer judgment, but so did the range of prices within a product-line, the highest price in the line, and the relative price position of a product within the line. The authors confirmed a positive association between price and perceived quality, yet found that the relationship did not carry through to willingness to purchase. While positive price image may positively affect consumer evaluation, it may or may not affect purchases. In a study of reference pricing in tourism, Nicolau (2011) assessed the influence of reference price on destination choice, and found that tourists take their expectations of prices into account more so for less well-known destinations than for well-known destinations.

Marketing segmentation

Another link to general marketing practice is segmenting. A vast stream of segmentation research exists in the tourism literature establishing the effectiveness of segmentation strategies (Ritchie, 1996). While the most traditional approach has been to segment the travel market by socio-demographic variables such as age and income, other popular criteria include activity and lifestyle (Gonzalez and Bello, 2002), and notably in tourism, studies that use tourism destination image (TDI) as a means of market segmentation. For example, Haahti (1986) considered the relative position of Finland in a 12-country study in which he identified the strengths and weaknesses of each country in the tourist's minds in order to develop perceptual segments of traveler types (e.g. scenery seekers, economy travelers, culture tourists). Based on his findings of each country's unique advantages, he suggested positioning strategies. While TDI studies have frequently considered a country's image in isolation, positioning studies require an expansion of the frame of reference to include more than one destination (Pike and Ryan, 2004).

Ahmed (1991) concludes that an overall image assessment is inadequate to develop tourism positioning strategies, because different segments perceive components of TDI differently. He identifies image strengths in relation to competition, to segment the US market both regionally, and in terms of touring experience in Utah, the destination state. The author concludes that an organic image exists post-travel that is distinct from the induced image of non-visitors. He recommends that image strengths identified regionally and in terms of experience could be the basis of an effective campaign to position the destination.

Leisen (2001) segments the US market of potential visitors to New Mexico based on images held, or perceptions of attributes, finding four distinct segments: sociocultural, natural, recreational, and climate. The segment expressing the most favorable image also stated the highest intent to visit. Conversely, the segment expressing the least favorable image stated the lowest intent to visit. The author recommends allocation of promotional resources to target these segments accordingly—a strategy recommended in early research by Crompton. From segmenting, TDI studies moved toward positioning, defined as "the act of establishing a specific image of services offered and rendered in the minds of consumers in a target market" (Crompton *et al.*, 1992), and place branding.

Place branding

Recently, tourism marketing has turned its attention to destination branding, and the practical implications for marketing strategy. Perhaps this current phase has simply come full circle. One of the first researchers to identify image as a factor in tourism's development, Hunt (1975) was stimulated to consider the influence of image on travelers based on early marketing and consumer research of the influence of brands (Spector, 1961). He reasoned that if consumers were buying brands not only for what the product did for them, but for what the product meant to them, then perhaps it was a destination's image that differentiated it from other places, and not simply the functional resources, which can be quite equal. Thus began the research focus on TDI, which has lasted for four decades. While the link to branding occasionally surfaced, it remained for the most part unstated until the late 1990s. In 1997, the American Marketing Science conference included a special track on "Branding Tourism Destinations." The Track organizer, Gnoth (1998: 759) observed that "although branding has been with marketers for quite some time and, since the late 80s, experienced a renewed interest in academe and the market place, branding tourism destinations is a relatively new development."

While the evolution to brand may seem natural, it has been slowed by the unique challenges that destination branding presents. These challenges are frequently documented. Morgan and Pritchard (1998) identify three unique challenges of destination branding: (i) a lack of control over the total marketing mix; (ii) relatively limited budgets; and (iii) political considerations. Henderson (2000) discusses the difficulties of commodification of a place that is in reality a multifaceted entity, serving a variety of users, constantly evolving, and with a history comprised of layers of meaning. Laws *et al.* (2002) raises issues related to the very nature of the tourism industry, such as seasonality, the resulting short-term planning cycle, and the divergence of aims between public and private sector stakeholders. The basic principles of branding call for cohesive management of all product and service elements, and coordination of the complete marketing mix. In tourism, however, a destination marketing organization most often controls only one of the traditional four "Ps" of the mix, that being "promotion," with limited direct control of "price," "place," or even "product." Attempts to apply branding techniques to destinations tend to focus on the selection of key attributes to promote, and branding is at the symbolic level, rather than the functional or experiential level. Gnoth (1998) believes that the more symbolic experiences are for tourists, the more successful the brand is in the long term. However, the more symbolic the brand attributes, the more difficult they are to communicate as unique, and the more easily they can be copied by competitors in any number of ways (Gnoth, 1998). The challenge of destination branding can be daunting, but it has its advantages. Destination branding can enhance a nation's or other place's economy, national self-image, and identity (Morgan *et al.*, 2002). Laws *et al.* (2002) view the essential advantage of destination branding as the creation of a favorable position for the destination that distinguishes it from competitors. Using product-branding terminology, he calls this the destination brand *personality*, defined as the emotional link between consumer and product.

Perhaps the practice of place branding by destination marketers has out-paced the extent to which it has been studied academically. In a collection of destination-branding case studies, Morgan *et al.* (2002) present a balance between academics who argue its complexities, and practitioners who espouse its virtues. Regardless, the bulk of the destination branding literature has only emerged this century, and central to its inquiry is image. Cai (2002) distinguishes between the formation of a destination image and the branding of it. He defines destination image as "perceptions about a place as reflected by the associations held in tourist memory," and destination branding as "selecting a consistent element mix to identify and distinguish it through positive image building" (Cai, 2002: 722–723). Simply, "image" is a mental construct, and "branding" is a strategy or process. Image is therefore not synonymous with brand, but rather a source of its equity. The process of destination branding has been compared to the process of destination image management (Laws *et al.*, 2002).

Basic consumer behavior theory suggests that consumers make product choices based on brand images. The parallel theory in tourism is that travelers make destination choices based on destination brand. Cai (2002) believes that the link required to move destination image studies to the level of branding is the *brand identity*, defined as "a set of brand associations that the brand strategist aspires to create or maintain" (Aaker and Joachimsthaler, 2000: 40). The process of destination branding begins with the selection of brand elements in order to form strong associations that are reflective of the attributes, affective and attitude components of the destination image in a complex recursive model. The results of a destination branding case study of Old West Country, a marketing consortium in New Mexico, show that cooperative branding across multiple communities builds a stronger destination identity than branding of an individual community (Cai, 2002).

Cooperative marketing is also the focus of a case study by Laws *et al.* (2002) that explores the destination image of five tourist regions in Australia. The authors identify unique brand personalities, such as "relaxed fresh outdoors" for Brisbane, and "exciting, fast paced" for the Gold Coast. To address the complexity of TDI, they view the destination product not as the totality of all possible destination elements, but rather as a packaged selection of elements. Findings support a cooperative marketing approach, based on respondents' needs for a mix of regional information *and* accommodation-specific information.

The experience of New Zealand's 100% Pure brand, launched in 1999, is presented by Morgan *et al.* (2003). Here, the authors focus on the management context, and expand the traditional marketing mix to include two additional "Ps": "politics" and "paucity." Recognizing that branding a country is a politicized activity, they advocate the involvement and cooperation of public and private stakeholders as vital to the creation of a durable destination brand. The authors detail a branding process as follows. The brand is New Zealand; the brand essence is landscape; the brand position is New Pacific Freedom; the brand values are contemporary, spirited, free, sophisticated, and innovative. Key to the process is the input of multiple stakeholders, credited for the resulting and now recognizable tagline, "100% Pure New Zealand," though its effectiveness has been questioned (Jaffe and Nebenzahl, 2006). Multiple brands within a destination may also exist. National brands may need to encompass several regional sub-brands, and supra-brands may require coordination across regions, or countries (Morgan *et al.*, 2002). Corporate image theories hold some relevance for place image, in that the identification of a corporate brand identity with individual sub-brands is somewhat analogous to a country brand with individual sector brands.

Pike and Ryan (2004) analyzed the market positions held by a competitive set of destinations through a comprehensive comparison of cognitive, affective, and conative perceptions, as a means to identify the key features of a multi-attributed destination to differentiate it from its competition in a way meaningful to consumers. They tested their theory by surveying households across New Zealand and assessing the relative importance-performance of five domestic destinations. The cognitive image component was measured by factor analysis of attribute importance items, ranging from infrastructure to weather. Conation was measured by stated intention to visit, and the affective component of image was measured with an affective response grid consisting of four semantic differential scales: pleasant/unpleasant, relaxing/distressing, arousing/sleepy, and exciting/gloomy. The results supported strategies for positioning domestic short-break destinations in New Zealand. By this process, measuring image is seen as a necessary step to destination branding. Conceptual frameworks for destination branding now incorporate brand image, brand equity, and brand associations, to represent the multidimensional nature of place (Im *et al.*, 2012).

The Future

While much attention has been given to marketing in the tourism literature, many basic questions remain unanswered. Marketing is a complex subject, with much to offer the researcher or practitioner who takes the time to look beyond the first impression. To date, the study of tourism marketing has largely built upon borrowed theories from consumer behavior, psychology, and related fields. To further tourism research requires the formulation of more tourism-specific theories, tested in tourism settings, to improve marketing, and advance understanding and prediction. This calls for a clearer conceptualization of image, satisfaction, loyalty, and other key constructs, with greater homogeneity of measures; more sophisticated measurement techniques; and, a solidification of theoretical foundations for this important field of study.

Questions

1. What are the key psychological concepts that link marketing activities and tourist behavior?
2. What does "modern marketing" mean in the context of tourism?
3. How can tourism marketing theory be effectively advanced?

References

Aaker, D.A. and Joachimsthaler, E. (2000) *Brand Leadership*. The Free Press, New York.

Ahmed, Z.U. (1991) The influence of the components of a state's tourist image on product positioning strategy. *Tourism Management* December, 331–340.

American Marketing Association (2013) https://www.ama.org/AboutAMA/Pages/Definition-of-Marketing.aspx (accessed 15 June 2015).

Andreassen, T.W. and Lindestad, B. (1998) Customer loyalty and complex services: the impact of corporate image on quality, customer satisfaction and loyalty for customers with varying degrees of service expertise. *International Journal of Service Industry Management* 9(1), 7–23.

Babin, L.A. and Burns, A.C. (1997) Effects of print Ad pictures and copy containing instructions to imagine on mental imagery that mediates attitudes. *Journal of Advertising* XXVI(3), 33.

Booms, B.H. and Bitner, M.J. (1982) Marketing strategies and organization structures for service firms. In: Donnelly, J.H. and George, W.R. (eds) *Marketing of Services.* American Marketing Association, Chicago, Illinois, pp. 47–51.

Borden, N. (1964) The concept of the marketing mix. *Journal of Advertising Research* 4(2), 2–7.

Burns, A.C., Biswas, A. and Babin, L.A. (1993) The operation of visual imagery as a mediator of advertising effects. *Journal of Advertising* XXII(2), 71–84.

Cai, L.A. (2002) Cooperative branding for rural destinations. *Annals of Tourism Research* 29 (3), 720–742.

Campelo, A., Aitken, R. and Gnoth, J. (2011) Visual rhetoric and ethics in marketing of destinations. *Journal of Travel Research* 50(1), 3–14.

Chon, K. (1989) Understanding recreational travelers' motivation, attitude and satisfaction. *Tourist Review* 44(1), 3–7.

Crompton, J.L., Fakeye, P.C. and Lue, C.-C. (1992) Positioning: the example of the Lower Rio Grande Valley in the winter long stay destination market. *Journal of Travel Research* 31(2), 20–27.

Dichter, E. (1985) What's in an image. *Journal of Consumer Marketing* 2(1), 75–81.

Elliot, R. and Wattanasuwan, K. (1998) Brands as symbolic resources. *International Journal of Advertising* 17(2), 131.

Fishbein, M. and Ajzen, I. (1975) *Belief, Attitude, Intention and Behavior: An Introduction to Theory and Research*. Addison-Wesley, Reading, Massachusetts.

Gnoth, J. (1998) Branding tourism destinations. *Annals of Tourism Research* 25(3), 758–760.

Gonzalez, A.M. and Bello, L. (2002) The construct "Lifestyle" in market segmentation: the behaviour of tourist consumers. *European Journal of Marketing* 36(1/2), 51–85.

Graeff, T.R. (1996) Using promotional messages to manage the effects of brand and self-image on brand evaluations. *Journal of Consumer Marketing* 13(3), 4–18.

Gronroos, C. (1984) A service quality model and its marketing implications. *European Journal of Marketing* 18(4), 36–44.

Gronroos, C. (1997) From marketing mix to relationship marketing—towards a paradigm shift in marketing. *Management Decision* 35(4), 322–339.

Haahti, A. (1986) Finland's competitive position as a destination. *Annals of Tourism Research* 13, 11–35.

Han, H. and Hyun, S. (2013) Image congruence and relationship quality in predicting switching intention. *Journal of Hospitality and Tourism Research* 37(3), 303–329.

Henderson, J.C. (2000) Selling places: the new Asia-Singapore brand. *Journal of Tourism Studies* 11(1), 36–44.

Hunt, J.D. (1975) Image as a factor in tourism development. *Journal of Travel Research* 13(3), 1–7.

Im, H., Kim, S., Elliot, S. and Han, H. (2012) Conceptualizing destination brand equity dimensions from a consumer-based brand equity perspective. *Journal of Travel and Tourism Marketing* 29(5), 385–403.

Jaffe, E.D. and Nebenzahl, I.D. (2006) *National Image and Competitive Advantage: The Theory and Practice of Country-of-Origin Effect*, 2nd edn. Copenhagen Business School Press, Copenhagen.

Kotler, P., Bowen, J. and Makens, J. (1999) *Marketing for Hospitality and Tourism*, 2nd edn. Prentice-Hall, Upper Saddle River, New Jersey.

LaBarbera, P.A., Weingard, P. and Yorkston, E.A. (1998) Matching the message to the mind: advertising imagery and consumer processing styles. *Journal of Advertising Research* September/October, 29–43.

Laws, E., Scott, N. and Parfitt, N. (2002) Synergies in destination image management: a case study and conceptualisation. *International Journal of Tourism Research* 4, 39–55.

Lee, W. and Gretzel, U. (2012) Designing persuasive destination websites: a mental imagery processing perspective. *Tourism Management* 33, 1270–1280.

Leigh, J. and Gabel, T. (1992) Symbolic interactionism: its effects on consumer behavior and implications for marketing strategy. *Journal of Consumer Marketing* 9(1), 27.

Leisen, B. (2001) Image segmentation: the case of a tourism destination. *Journal of Services Marketing* 15(1), 49–66.

Meyers-Levy, J. and Malaviya, P. (1999) Consumers' processing of persuasive advertisements: an integrative framework of persuasion theories. *Journal of Marketing* 63 (Special Issue), 45–60.

Middleton, V.T.C., Fyall, A., Morgan, M. and Ranchhod, A. (2009) *Marketing in Travel and Tourism*, 4th edn. Butterworth-Heinemann, Burlington, Massachusetts.

Morgan, N. and Pritchard, A. (1998) *Tourism Promotion and Power, Creating Images, Creating Identities*. John Wiley, Chichester, UK.

Morgan, N., Pritchard, A. and Pride, R. (eds) (2002) *Destination Branding: Creating the Unique Destination Proposition*. Butterworth-Heinemann, Oxford, UK.

Morgan, N., Pritchard, A. and Piggott, R. (2003) Destination branding and the role of the stakeholders: the case of New Zealand. *Journal of Vacation Marketing* 9(3), 285–299.

Neil, J.D. and Gursoy, D. (2008) A multifaceted analysis of tourism satisfaction. *Journal of Travel Research* 47, 53–62.

Nguyen, N. and LeBlanc, G. (2002) Contact personnel, physical environment and the perceived corporate image of intangible services by new clients. *International Journal of Service Industry Management* 13(3/4), 242–263.

Nicolau, J.L. (2011) Research note: coastal and inland reference prices—a differentiated effect. *Tourism Economics* 17(5), 1140–1151.

Panitz, E. (1988) Distributor image and marketing strategy. *Industrial Marketing Management* 17(4), 315–323.

Petroshius, S.M. and Monroe, K.B. (1987) Effect of product-line pricing characteristics on product evaluations. *Journal of Consumer Research* 13(March), 511–519.

Pike, S. and Ryan, C. (2004) Destination positioning analysis through a comparison of cognitive, affective and conative perceptions. *Journal of Travel Research* 42(4), 333–343.

Ritchie, J.R.B. (1996) Beacons of light in an expanding universe: an assessment of the state-of-the-art in tourism marketing/marketing research. *Journal of Travel and Tourism Marketing* 5(4), 49–84.

Scott, L.M. (1994) Images in advertising: the need for a theory of visual rhetoric. *Journal of Consumer Research* 21(2), 252–273.

Spector, A.J. (1961) Basic dimensions of the corporate image. *Journal of Marketing* 25(6), 47–51.

Tang, L., Jang, S. and Morrison, A. (2012) Dual-route communication of destination websites. *Tourism Management* 33, 38–49.

9 Theoretical Perspectives on Destination Image

ALISHA ALI*

Sheffield Business School, Sheffield Hallam University, Sheffield, UK

The Objectives

1. Identify two main approaches to defining destination image.
2. Describe three theoretical approaches to destination image research.
3. Summarize the methodological challenges associated with destination image research.
4. List at least four areas for future destination image research.

The Vignette

Hannah sipped her local beer and reflected on how good life was as she sat by the seaside with the waves washing upon her feet on a hot February day. She smiled at her friends who were excitedly chattering about their trip so far. They were a group of five close friends and this was their tenth year reunion. Upon graduation from university they pledged to keep in touch and met once a year. On a rotational basis, each year someone from the group would select the destination to visit. This year was Hannah's choice and they were in the Caribbean islands of Trinidad and Tobago for the carnival festivities.

The motivations for Hannah's visit to Trinidad and Tobago stemmed from stories her grandfather told her from his time spent there working in the oil industry and reading books from local writers he had brought back to England with him. While living in London, she had also made a number of friends from Trinidad. She had developed a mental image of sunny islands, warm people, and a rich cultural heritage reflecting its history of colonization, indenture-ship and immigration and felt an emotional attachment to this place, which prompted her intent to visit. On their trip so far the friends had sampled the local cuisine, learnt more about the history and culture of the country, visited many beaches, enjoyed the carnival parties, and made friends with a few locals. Hannah's expectations were matching up to the reality she was experiencing and a few of her friends were thinking that they would return to Trinidad and Tobago for another visit.

From this we can see that people form particular images of a destination which encourages them to visit. During the actual visit these images can be modified, which may lead to repeat visits and through positive word of mouth and word of mouse may encourage visits by others. But how are these images formed and how are they

---

*Corresponding author, e-mail: alisha.ali@shu.ac.uk

measured? Can we identify what image a destination such as Trinidad and Tobago is projecting? What are the information sources that lead to the formation of destination image?

This chapter focuses on a discussion of how destination image has been conceptualized in the tourism literature. Additionally, the chapter presents a definition, use of various measurements, and suggestions for future research.

The Context

Image is a powerful concept in the eyes of the consumer (Ryan and Cave, 2005) as it is the image that the tourist holds, rather than what is the actual image of a destination (Mayo, 1973), that is critical in the tourist decision-making process in choosing a destination to visit (Di Marino, 2008; Molina *et al.*, 2010). Tourists often do not act in a rational manner and their destination choice may be grounded in perceptions initiated by motivations, emotions, interests, and other factors, which lead to the development of a particular image of a destination rather than an unbiased viewpoint (Chon, 1990). This decision making is not only reflected in the initial destination choice, but once the tourist has been to the destination his/her image perceptions can accrue post-visit satisfaction, repeat visits, and positive word of mouth/mouse (Di Marino, 2008; Agapito *et al.*, 2013). Destination image is critically important due to the inherent intangible characteristic of the tourism product. As a tourist cannot touch or taste the tourist product before he/she actually experiences it, images play a more significant role in making tangible an intangible product.

Given the heightened competition by destinations for tourism revenues, it is critical that destinations carve out their marketplace by ensuring that their destination is well differentiated and clearly positioned for its visitors (Echtner and Ritchie, 1993; Molina *et al.*, 2013) through a strong, clear, and tempting image (Calantone *et al.*, 1989), which is aligned to the destination's marketing strategy. Pike and Ryan (2004) observed that destination positioning should fortify the positive images and amend the negative ones and there is evidence that a relationship exists between positive perceptions and favorable intention to purchase, revisit, and recommend (Woodside and Lysonski, 1989; Agapito *et al.*, 2013; Zhang *et al.*, 2014). A destination can only be intelligently marketed when there is a strong understanding of how customers interpret the destination (Stepchenkova and Mills, 2010).

The concept of destination image has received considerable attention in the tourism literature since the early 1970s due to its relationship with marketing, planning, and management of tourism, and being a key attractor of tourists (Gartner, 1989; Chon, 1990; Stepchenkova and Mills, 2010). There have been several meta-analyses of the literature (Echtner and Ritchie, 1991; Gallarza *et al.*, 2002; Pike, 2002; Tasci *et al.*, 2007; Stepchenkova and Mills, 2010) that have succinctly categorized and summarized the existing literature and identified gaps and directions for the future. The destination image research has concentrated on the conceptualization and dimensions, the image formation process, assessment and measurement, image management policies, image and tourist satisfaction, image formation, and the role of residents and destination image and its relationship with variables such as trip purpose, distance, time, and sociodemographic factors (Gallarza *et al.*, 2002; Govers *et al.*, 2007; Stepchenkova and Mills, 2010). However, despite this considerable progress, research in destination image has been accused of suffering from conceptual and theoretical issues (Gallarza *et al.*, 2002; Beerli and Martin, 2004; Tasci *et al.*, 2007). This can be attributed to image formation being a complex process (Gartner, 1989; Gallarza *et al.*, 2002; Beerli and Martin, 2004), which Tasci *et al.* (2007: 194) has identified as "elusive and confusing."

Destination image can be studied from numerous theoretical perspectives such as anthropology, consumer behavior, sociology, social and environmental psychology, geography, semiotics, and marketing due to its implications for human behavior (Gallarza *et al.*, 2002; Stepchenkova and Morrison, 2008). It is not the purpose of this chapter to labor over these various disciplines and the relationship to destination image, rather the focus will be to provide a critical understanding of how destination image has been theorized in the tourism literature.

The concept was introduced to the tourism field through the works of Mayo (1973), Hunt (1975), and Gunn (1972). The first step in understanding the theoretical frameworks surrounding destination image is to understand how it is defined.

Defining destination image

To date, the literature provides no consensus in defining destination image. However, attempts have been made at reaching a resolution on the variety of definitions that currently exist (Echtner and Ritchie, 1993; Gallarza *et al.*, 2002; Martin and Bosque, 2008). While some are not surprised given that each definition is seeking to define a certain aspect of destination image (Tasci *et al.*, 2007), others have moved toward defining constructs, which include "complex, multiple, relativistic, and dynamic" characteristics (Gallarza *et al.*, 2002: 56). Table 9.1 provides a summary of some of the more well-known and cited destination image definitions and it demonstrates the breadth of the dimensions that are used to define this concept.

There are two main approaches to defining destination image. The first interprets how a tourist perceives the elements at the destination. This idea has been supported by Gartner (1986). The second approach considers destination image as being a picture in the minds of the tourists. This has been supported by Crompton (1979) and Reilly (1990). The former approach sees the tourists as having the ability to be evaluative of a destination based on the attributes and activities available, while the latter views it more as a gestalt experience. Researchers therefore conceptualize defining destination image as either effortful or a limited processing by the tourists (Tasci *et al.*, 2007). Focusing on these ideas, in its simplicity, destination image is the general impression of a place formed by the tourist from diverse sources over a period of time either through in-depth or limited processing.

The Theory

When theorizing destination image, some of the key works one should be familiar with are Hunt (1975), Gartner (1989), Chon (1990), Echtner and Ritchie (1991, 1993), Baloglu and McCleary (1999), and Gallarza *et al.* (2002). The three-dimensional continuum suggested by Echtner and Ritchie (1991, 1993), the three-component approach (the cognitive-affective-conative model) proposed by Gartner (1993), and

Table 9.1. Commonly cited destination image definitions (from Gallarza *et al*., 2002; Martin and Bosque, 2008; Tasci *et al*., 2007).

Definition	Source
The sum of beliefs, ideas, and impressions that a person has of a destination	Crompton (1979)
One's perception of attributes or activities available at a destination	Gartner (1986)
Result of the interaction of a person's beliefs, ideas, feelings, expectations, and impressions about a destination	Chon (1990)
The perceptions of individual destination attributes and the holistic impression made by the destination	Echtner and Ritchie (1991)
Image is the mental construct developed by a potential tourist on the basis of a few selected impressions among the flood of total impressions	Fakeye and Crompton (1991)
Destination images are developed by three hierarchically interrelated components: cognitive, affective, and conative	Gartner (1993)
A composite of various products (attractions) and attributes woven into a total impression	MacKay and Fesenmaier (2000)
An individual's mental representation of knowledge, feelings, and global impressions about a destination	Baloglu and McCleary (1999)
Perceptions or impressions of a destination held by tourists with respect to the expected benefit or consumption values	Tapachai and Waryszak (2000)

the image formation process stemming from the work of Gunn (1972) have been the foremost approaches in understanding the theory behind destination image. Each of these are discussed in greater detail below.

The three-dimensional approach

Echtner and Ritchie's (1991, 1993) research was the first effort to marry the destination image literature with primary image components and provide a conceptual framework to operationalize and visualize all the particular elements that form destination image. The psychology, consumer behavior, and image processing literature are considered to be the roots of research into destination image. According to Myers (1968, cited in Baloglu and McCleary, 1999: 871), the "world is a psychological or distorted representation of objective reality residing and existing in the mind of the individual." Image processing can be interpreted as "mental picturing," which incorporates all senses and provides a universal depiction of the information being processed. This is contrasted with "discursive processing," which adopts attributes rather than a holistic representation of the information under consideration (Echtner and Ritchie, 1993). Using MacInnis and Price's (1987) research on consumer behavior and image processing and Martineau's (1958) work on retail store personality, Echtner and Ritchie (1993) argued that the image of a tourist destination is created from the perception of individual attributes such as weather and accommodation, and the more universal views of the destination such as images and mental pictures.

Destination image also includes three overlapping continuums, including attribute-holistic, functional-psychological, and common-unique, which form destination image (Echtner and Ritchie, 1993). The functional-psychological continuum is focused on those aspects of destination image that can be directly measured (functional) to more intangible aspects that cannot be so easily gauged (psychological). The functional-psychological continuum can also be observed within the context of the attribute-holistic continuum. For example, there are a number of attributes considered within a destination, such as services and amenities (functional), or feelings one has about the destination (psychological), such as romantic, chaotic, peaceful, or exciting. Within these varied interpretations, a person may see these holistically, or with a complete mental picture of services or as many separate attributes of service. The common-unique continuum ranges from the perceptions based on more general or typical to more specialized, uniquely identified features of a particular destination. Table 9.2 provides a summary of the three continuums.

The three-component approach

Proposed by Gartner (1993), the three-component approach identifies that destination image is a composite construct which includes cognitive, affective, and conative components. Gartner's (1993) research was largely based on the work of Boulding (1956), who specified that image is about what one knows about an object (cognitive), how one feels about what one knows about the object (affective), and how one acts based on this information (conative). Adopting a tourism perspective, the cognitive component (i.e. rational) refers to a tourist's beliefs, perceptions, and knowledge about a destination (Baloglu and McCleary, 1999; Beerli and Martin, 2004; Stepchenkova and Mills, 2010). The affective component (i.e. emotional) is the tourist's feelings about the destination, which comes into play when a tourist is evaluating potential destinations. These dimensions have support both conceptually and empirically in the literature (Baloglu and Brinberg, 1997; Baloglu and McCleary, 1999; Beerli and Martin, 2004; Li *et al.*, 2010). The third construct is the conative (also known as behavioral) element, which is about how the tourist acts toward a destination (Gartner, 1993).

According to Gartner (1993), these three elements are hierarchically interrelated. This means that as the tourist develops a cognitive image, this leads to the formation of the affective, and then the conative. This model has received significant support in

Table 9.2. Three-continuum approach to destination image (from Echtner and Ritchie, 1993).

Continuum	Description
Attribute-holistic	Perceptions of individual destination attributes and holistic impression
Functional-psychological	Difference between the directly measureable, functional components and the intangible, psychological elements
Common-unique	Generic, common features and unique features, feelings, auras of the destination

A. Ali

the literature (see, e.g. Tasci *et al.*, 2007; Agapito *et al.*, 2013). Research by Baloglu and McCleary (1999), Beerli and Martin (2004), and Li *et al.* (2010) demonstrated that the cognitive and affective components are interconnected, with the affective component being dependent on cognitive dimension. Baloglu and McCleary (1999) found that overall destination image was formed through the tourist cognitive and affective evaluation as well. Molina *et al.* (2013) surmised that the cognitive and affective components determine the overall image of the destination regardless of the context and the characteristics of the tourist. They also found that the importance placed on the attributes of a destination impact the cognitive image, and this varies depending on the amount of direct experience the tourist has had with a destination.

The three-component approach has been associated with research on attitude theory, as destination image can impact a tourist's attitude toward visiting a particular place. Baloglu and McCleary (1999) found that image is primarily an attitudinal construct, whereas White (2004) contends that destination image is used in developing a destination attitude.

In determining which destination to visit, a tourist is presented with a range of options, yet the final selection involves each destination being evaluated for its individual attributes (Gartner, 1993). It is at this point attitudes toward a potential destination play a significant role. The cognitive-affective-conative model aligns well with the tripartite model of attitude structure that gained popularity in the 1960s. This concept identified attitude formation as the interaction between the cognitive, affective, and conative processes of an individual (Fishbein, 1967; Breckler, 1984; Bootzin *et al.*, 1991). "Attitude" has been defined as a "response to an antecedent stimulus or attitude object with the affective, cognitive and conative being the unnoticed responses to the stimulus" (Breckler, 1984: 1191). These attributes parallel Gartner's (1993) description, whereby affect refers to an emotional response, cognition relates to one's belief, thoughts and knowledge, while conative is the behavior that is displayed (Jorgensen and Stedman, 2001; White, 2004).

The image formation process

Tourists gather information from a variety of sources, including, but not limited to, friends, family, Internet, and TV, all of which influence the images they form of a destination. These information sources are also called stimulus factors (Baloglu and McCleary, 1999) or image formation agents (Gartner, 1993). The intangibility of the tourism product means that a tourist is continuously searching for information that assists in stabilizing their image of a destination (Govers *et al.*, 2007). One of the first attempts to reconcile the sources of image formation was Gunn (1972), who presented a travel experience model consisting of the following seven phases:

1. Accumulation of mental images about vacation experiences.
2. Modification of those images by further information.
3. Decision to take a vacation.
4. Travel to the destination.
5. Participation at the destination.
6. Return travel.
7. New accumulation of images based on the experience.

Gunn (1972) argued that it is the first two phases that are critically important in influencing the tourist's decision to visit a destination or not. In phases 1 and 2, a destination image is formed based on secondary information sources while in phase 7, it is the first-hand experience of the tourist that is used to change or confirm the image (Echtner and Ritchie, 1991). The image formed in phase 1 is what Gunn (1972) termed organic, which refers to information about the destination gathered from non-commercial sources and not related to the destination tourism marketing and promotion. This image is the result of the tourist's encounter with information about the destination secured over a period of time informally (i.e. via friends, family, movies, etc.), and this accumulation is primarily an unconscious effort by the individual. In phase 2, the tourist receives information from more commercial sources related to destination marketing and promotion, which becomes more of a conscious accumulation of information. This may lead to modification of the organic image into what Gunn (1972) termed the induced image.

In Gunn's (1972) work this difference in organic versus induced images led researchers to understand that little could be done to influence the organic imagery, however a lot could be done to influence the induced imagery. Yet research also found that non-commercial sources of information actually bear higher credibility (Gursoy and McCleary, 2004). Research has also determined that organic images are significant when it comes to influencing destination image formation overall (Gartner, 1993; Beerli and Martin, 2004; Govers et al., 2007).

Gartner (1993) found that destination image was formed from a variety of information sources from independent sources which lead to a single image. Through alteration of Gunn's (1972) typology, he categorized these as listed below:

- Overt induced—destination advertising and promotions in the mass media through the relevant destination organization or third party agents.
- Covert induced—celebrity, destination report or articles use in destination promotion.
- Autonomous—news, documentaries, movies, or other forms of mass media on the destination.
- Organic—voluntary or involuntary information shared about the destination by friends/relatives or other people.
- Personal experience—where the tourist visits the destination.

The overt, covert, and autonomous induced are considered secondary information sources, while the organic and visit to the destination are considered primary (Beerli and Martin, 2004). Beerli and Martin (2004) found that secondary sources of information were critical in the formation of the destination image and the travel decision-making process. Gartner's (1993) continuum was based on the trustworthiness of the information provided and the market penetration (Gartner and Shen, 1992). For example, in the overt and covert induced sources, the destination market has high market penetration, however, this may not be as reliable as a source. Whereas with autonomous information sources, communicating with friends and relatives, and by way of personal experiences, the information generated tends to have more credibility, but it may have less market penetration. It is a quality versus quantity conundrum. Beerli and Martin (2004) have also identified that personal characteristics have an impact on destination image formation. They found that perceived destination image is formed through a combination of the projected destination image and by the tourist's sociodemographic (age, gender, education) and psychological (needs, motivation, personality) characteristics.

Since the work of earlier researchers, the development of and expanded access to the Internet has dramatically changed the way people communicate with one another, actually seek information, and how information is shared. This of course has had a significant impact on organic sources of information, as well as other types. Tourists now have a wealth of information easily available literally at their fingertips, and information generated by other tourists (known or unknown) who have actually been to the destination, in the form of blogs, photos, wikis, discussion forums, and travel reviews. This has led to wider market penetration of organic sources. The advent of personal sites such as blogs and webpages has been shown to greatly enhance the publicity a destination receives as well (Niininen *et al.*, 2006). Ultimately, this may impact all of the previous models and add to the complexity of expanding research on destination image and marketing.

Measuring destination image

Due to the complex nature of destination image, the construct is considered difficult to measure. There is a debate about the most appropriate methodology(ies) and how to achieve consistency in destination image measurement (Tasci *et al.*, 2007). As we have learned from the literature noted above, destination image has cognitive, affective, and conative aspects, and each of these ideas require different measurement approaches to be able to form a comprehensive formation of destination image by an individual. Measuring these three components in effect poses difficulty for researchers.

The measurement of destination image has either adopted a structured or unstructured approach (Pan and Li, 2011), with preference in the literature toward more quantitative investigations than qualitative ones (Pike, 2002; Tasci *et al.*, 2007). Most of the research on destination image has sought to only measure the cognitive component (Pike, 2002; Stepchenkova and Mills, 2010) through a structured approach. In this approach, the cognitive variables are measured through the formation of a list of destination attributes based on literature surrounding the destination. The cognitive element lends itself better to approaches that can be quantified as it consists of the objective reality of the destination attributes (Echtner and Ritchie, 1991; Tasci *et al.*, 2007). The quantitative approaches have primarily incorporated surveys, where attributes are developed from secondary information sources and are measured and tested through using either one or more of the following: semantic differential scaling, multidimensional scaling, Likert scales, categorical yes/no, and ranking order. The responses from these scaling procedures are then tested through statistical procedures ranging from multivariate analysis (data reduction techniques, dependence analysis and grouping) to bivariate analysis (*t*-tests and correlation analysis) to derive the key components which form the destination image. With this attribute-based approach the generated list of attributes varies widely, based on the context of study (Bigne *et al.*, 2009).

There have been attempts to define a list of collective attributes (Echtner and Ritchie, 1993; Gallarza *et al.*, 2002), but to date there is not a catalogue of universal image items that are validated and applied to different types of destinations (Pan and Li, 2011). Deslandes *et al.* (2006) asserts that a standardized scale instrument is needed to address the challenge of consistent comparisons in measuring destination image and across destinations. Another difficulty with current approaches to destination image attribute development is that this leads to the measurement of individual attributes rather than a holistic image of the entire destination (Tapachai and Waryszak, 2000).

Some studies have measured the affective element only (Baloglu and Brinberg, 1997), while even fewer have attempted to concurrently measure both the cognitive and the affective component (Beerli and Martin, 2004; Pike and Ryan, 2004; Martin and Bosque, 2008; Byon and Zhang, 2010); very few studies have actually focused on the conative elements, or have measured all three elements together. Studies that have sought to measure the cognitive, affective, and conative elements in the literature tend to utilize mixed methods. While the cognitive component has been an objective and quantifiable measurement, the affective and conative elements are typically more subjective as they focus on attitudes, perceptions, and behaviors of individuals (Echtner and Ritchie, 1993; Tapachai and Waryszak, 2000; Tasci *et al.*, 2007). Echtner and Ritchie (1991) in their seminal work argued for more mixed method approaches to allow for the development of a comprehensive list of image attributes. For example, within this approach, quantitative methods could be utilized to identify destination attributes while qualitative techniques would be used to identify the sensory and behavioral components. In capturing the various components of destination image, Echtner and Ritchie (1993: 5) designed three open-ended questions:

- What images or characteristics come to mind when you think of X as a vacation destination? (functional holistic component)
- How would you describe the atmosphere or mood that you would expect to experience while visiting X? (psychological holistic component)
- Please list any distinctive or unique tourist attractions that you can think of in X.

These questions have been adapted for use in subsequent qualitative studies of destination image research utilizing such interviews, focus groups, and pictorial techniques.

Despite the growth in qualitative studies surrounding destination image, they are not used as frequently as quantitative approaches (Stepchenkova and Mills, 2010). The reality is that despite a legacy of research in destination image there is still no standardized approach to analyzing destination image and its components (Stepchenkova and Mills, 2010). "Defining and measuring destination image is still fuzzy in most of the literature" (Tasci *et al.*, 2007: 217). Song *et al.* (2013) noted that a good measure of destination image should possess three qualities:

- The cognitive, affective and conative elements should be measured together to provide a more comprehensive picture of a destination's image.
- It should measure both the common and unique attributes.
- It should empirically display satisfactory levels of psychometric properties.

The Future

Despite the considerable wealth of knowledge developed in destination image research, there is still a wealth of opportunity to solidify the theoretical foundations of the domain. As Gallarza *et al.* (2002) noted, this topic is quite versatile, which makes it an appealing area of research. One area in which destination image research can be advanced is through the use of the Internet. Web 2.0 tools have changed the projection of destination image and tourist search behavior (Camprubi *et al.*, 2013). The Internet is a fertile aspect of destination research both now and into the future. The Internet can be used for both qualitative and quantitative data collection, with questionnaires developed, distributed, and analyzed online; and, qualitatively, continual advances in technology, interviews, and focus groups can be conducted using such mediums as Skype and Google Voice, as well as other meeting space mechanisms (e.g. Go to Meetings). Stepchenkova and Mills (2010) identified a small number of studies that have actually employed the Internet for data collection. They argued that this medium should not be ignored as it greatly influences a vast majority of potential tourists and must be taken into consideration in order to further our understanding of destination image.

With the proliferation of information on the Internet there exists a plethora of material published by destination promoters and businesses, as well as tourists—all contributing to the destination image formation process. For example, most destinations have an information portal which contains images and rich media about the destination, meanwhile tourists are engaging in rich conversations through pictorial formats and textual conversation on sites such as WAYN, Pinterest, Flickr and Trip Advisor. The Internet has become a potent medium where the tourists are able to share their travel experiences while they are occurring and therefore have become critical agents in image formation (Camprubi et al., 2013). The "word of mouth" conduit of communication has taken on new meaning via technology, whereby information is relayed through independent sources in the form of blogs, wikis, and review forums—greatly increasing customer-to-customer communication. This is a new area ripe for research, to help understand the influences of online personal communication and destination image formation. It is also important to understand how this might align or misalign with the images the destinations are attempting to project. With the advent of Web 2.0, people are now considering the opinions of people they may not know personally, yet become a greater source of organic image formation. This presents the researcher with a new body of information to develop further a more comprehensive picture of destination image formation. It also adds even greater complexity to an already challenging measurement issue.

As a result of the Internet, another aspect of understanding destination image is in understanding individual's online information search behavior and relationships to the formation destination's image. Individuals identify with then utilize keywords when they search for information about a destination, and these keywords are based on their existing knowledge and mental construct of a destination (Pan and Li, 2011). Understanding keywords used in an online search may help develop a greater understanding of what images tourists have of a destination.

Additionally, the definition of a destination in the literature is also subject to broad interpretation. Ali and Frew (2012: 56) defined a destination "as a physical space/ geographical area which contains tourism products and services to be consumed by the tourists as part of the experience and which is managed and marketed by destination authorities/organizations." The reality is that a destination can be any distinct geographical area such as a continent, region, country, island, town, community, or attraction (Ritchie and Crouch, 2003; Sainaghi, 2006), or it can be a perceptual concept construed by the tourist which is different from any formal boundary (Buhalis, 2000). It would be useful for researchers to understand how the image of these smaller or self-defined destination entities contribute to the formation of the larger destination image.

Despite attempts to develop a standardized destination image measurement scale (Echtner and Ritchie, 1993; Gallarza et al., 2002; Deslandes et al., 2006), such a scale has not been validated in the literature (Pan and Li, 2011). Having a uniform scale could save time and effort in destination image research (Stepchenkova and Mills, 2010). Because results of destination image studies can and have informed management policies and strategic marketing efforts, it is important that future destination image studies utilize appropriate and relevant destination image measurements (Tasci *et al.*, 2007). Having a standardized measurement scale may help to eliminate some bias within the varying approaches that currently exists. Hence there is tremendous opportunity for work within this research area.

Current research on destination image continues to focus heavily on the cognitive image (Zhang *et al.*, 2014) despite the work of Baloglu and McCleary (1999) and Echtner and Ritchie (1991, 1993), which has identified that destination image is made up of multiple constructs. Contrary to the arguments that constructs should be examined individually (Li *et al.*, 2010), we still know very little about the affective and conative elements of destination image. There is an opportunity to triangulate this information in order to increase our understanding and develop a comprehensive profile of a destination.

Destinations often develop a singular image to share and promote to all potential markets. However, to date there has been little recognition of the fact that tourists originate from different cultural backgrounds and socio-demographics (Therkelsen, 2003; Govers *et al.*, 2007). Further work is needed to understand what influences are most prominent with respect to cultural background and image formation.

A significant amount of destination image research has focused on the first visit intention of an individual. However, research has demonstrated that an individual has the ability to encourage others to visit through a modification process after a visit has taken place. This can lead to re-visitation and positive word of mouth communication. However, more research is necessary to investigate the image of a visitor pre- and post- of their tourism experience. Further, we know very little as to what influenced a change to occur, if there was one, and if so, what were the influences that caused a change. This type of information could be very useful in developing repeat visitation strategies.

This chapter has sought to amalgamate a wealth of information which exists on destination image research. Despite significant advances, given the versatile nature of the concept, new technological advances in communication (Internet, social media, etc.), and lack of formalized approaches to understanding destination image, there are significant opportunities to expand research in this area. Yet researchers interested in destination image must continue to work through the theoretical and methodological challenges that are apparent from previous studies, and find new approaches and perhaps theories to frame the next generation of destination complexity.

Questions

1. What is the importance of destination image to tourism research and how has it been conceptualized in the literature?
2. What theoretical constructs have been used to guide destination image research?
3. How can understanding of destination image help to satisfy the requirements of destination planners and marketers and the needs and wants of the tourists?
4. What steps would you take in developing a strong conceptual framework in which destination image can be studied?

A. Ali

References

Agapito, D., Oom do Valle, P. and Da Costa Mendes, J. (2013) The cognitive-affective-conative model of destination image: a confirmatory analysis. *Journal of Travel & Tourism Marketing* 30(5), 471–481.

Ali, A. and Frew, J.A. (2012) *Information and Communication Technologies for Sustainable Tourism*. Routledge, London.

Baloglu, S. and Brinberg, D. (1997) Affective images of tourism destination. *Journal of Travel Research* 35(4), 11–15.

Baloglu, S. and McCleary, K.W. (1999) A model of destination image formation. *Annals of Tourism Research* 26, 868–897.

Beerli, M. and Martin, D. (2004) Factors influencing destination image. *Annals of Tourism Research* 31 (3), 657–681.

Bigne, E., Sanchez, I. and Sanz, S. (2009) The functional-psychological continuum in the cognitive image of a destination: a confirmatory analysis. *Tourism Management* 30, 715–723.

Bootzin, R., Bower, G., Crocker, J. and Hall, E. (1991) *Psychology Today: an introduction*. McGraw-Hill, New York.

Boulding, K. (1956) *The Image-Knowledge in Life and Society*. University of Michigan Press, Ann Arbor, Michigan.

Breckler, S. (1984) Empirical validation of affect, behavior, and cognition as distinct components of attitude. *Journal of Personality and Social Psychology* 47(6), 1191–1205.

Buhalis, D. (2000) Marketing the competitive destination of the future. *Tourism Management* 21(1), 97–116.

Byon, K. and Zhang, J. (2010) Development of a scale measuring destination image. *Marketing Intelligence & Planning* 28(4), 508–532.

Calantone, R., Benedetto, A., Hakam, A. and Bojanic, D.C. (1989) Multiple multi-national tourism positioning using correspondence analysis. *Journal of Travel Research* 28(2), 25–32.

Camprubi, R., Guia, J. and Comas, J. (2013) The new role of tourists in destination image formation. *Current Issues in Tourism* 16(2), 203–209.

Chon, K. (1990) The role of destination image in tourism: a review and discussion. *Revue du Tourisme* 2, 2–9.

Crompton, J.L. (1979) An assessment of the image of Mexico as a vacation destination and the influence of geographical location upon that image. *Journal of Travel Research* 17, 18–23.

Deslandes, D., Goldsmith, R., Bonn, M. and Joseph, S. (2006) Measuring destination image: do the existing scales work? *Tourism Review International* 10(3), 141–153.

Di Marino, E. (2008) The strategic dimension of destination image: An analysis of the French Riviera image from the Italian tourists' perceptions. PhD thesis. Faculty of Economics, University of Naples "Fredrico II," Italy.

Echtner, C. and Ritchie, J. (1991) The meaning and measurement of destination image. *Journal of Tourism Studies* 2(2), 2–12.

Echtner, C.M. and Ritchie, J. (1993) The measurement of destination image: an empirical assessment. *Journal of Travel Research* 31(4), 3–13.

Fakeye, P. and Crompton, J. (1991) Image differences between prospective, first-time, and repeat visitors to the Lower Rio Grande Valley. *Journal of Travel Research* 30(2), 10–16.

Fishbein, M. (1967) *Readings in Attitude Theory and Measurement*. John Wiley & Sons, New York.

Gallarza, G., Saura, G. and Garcia, C. (2002) Destination image: towards a conceptual framework. *Annals of Tourism Research* 29(1), 56–78.

Gartner, W. (1986) Temporal influence on image change. *Annals of Tourism Research* 13, 635–644.

Gartner, W. (1989) Tourism image: attribute measurement of state tourism products using multi-dimensional scaling techniques. *Journal of Travel Research* 28(2), 16–20.

Gartner, W. (1993) Image formation process. *Journal of Travel & Tourism Marketing* 2, 191–216.

Gartner, W. and Shen, J. (1992) The impact of Tiananmen Square on China's tourism image. *Journal of Travel Research* 30, 47–52.

Govers, R., Go, M. and Kuldeep, K. (2007) Promoting tourism destination image. *Journal of Travel Research* 46, 15–23.

Gunn, C. (1972) *Vacationscape: Designing Tourist Regions*. Bureau of Business Research, University of Texas, Austin, Texas.

Gursoy, D. and McCleary, K. (2004) An integrative model of tourists' information search behavior. *Annals of Tourism Research* 31(2), 353–373.

Hunt, J. (1975) Image as a factor in tourism development. *Journal of Travel Research* 13(3), 1–7.

Jorgensen, S. and Stedman, C. (2001) Sense of place as an attitude: lakeshore owners attitudes towards their properties. *Journal of Environmental Psychology* 21(3), 233–248.

Li, M., Cai, L., Lehto, X. and Huang, J. (2010) A missing link in understanding revisit intention—the role of motivation and image. *Journal of Travel & Tourism Marketing* 27, 335–348.

MacInnis, D. and Price, L. (1987) The role of imagery in information processing: review and extensions. *Journal of Consumer Research* 13(4), 473–491.

MacKay, K. and Fesenmaier, D. (2000) An exploration of cross-cultural destination image assessment. *Journal of Travel Research* 38(4), 417–423.

Martin, H. and Bosque, I. (2008) Exploring the cognitive-affective nature of destination image and the role of psychological factors in its formation. *Tourism Management* 29(2), 263–277.

Martineau, P. (1958) The personality of the retail store. *Journal of Retailing* 52(Fall), 37–46.

Mayo, E. (1973) Regional images and regional travel behavior. In: *The Travel Research Association Fourth Annual Conference Proceedings*, Sun Valley, Idaho, pp. 211–218.

Molina, A., Gomez, M. and Martin-Consuegra, D. (2010) Tourism marketing information and destination image management. *African Journal of Business Management* 4(5), 722–728.

Molina, R., Frias-Jamilena, D. and Castaneda-Garcia, A. (2013) The moderating role of past experience in the formation of a tourist destination's image and in tourists' behavioural intentions. *Current Issues in Tourism* 16(2), 107–127.

Niininen, O., March, R. and Buhalis, D. (2006) Consumer centric tourism marketing. In: Buhalis, D. and Costa, C. (eds) *Tourism Management Dynamics: Trends, Management and Tools*. Butterworth-Heinemann, Amsterdam, pp. 176–186.

Pan, B. and Li, X. (2011) The long tail of destination image and online marketing. *Annals of Tourism Research* 38(1), 132–152.

Pike, S. (2002) Destination image analysis—a review of 142 papers from 1973 to 2000. *Tourism Management* 23, 541–549.

Pike, S. and Ryan, C. (2004) Destination positioning analysis through a comparison of cognitive, affective and conative perceptions. *Journal of Travel Research* 42, 333–342.

Reilly, M.D. (1990) Free elicitation of descriptive adjectives for tourism image assessment. *Journal of Travel Research* 28, 21–26.

Ritchie, J. and Crouch, G. (2003) *The Competitive Destination: A Sustainable Tourism Perspective*. CAB International, Wallingford, UK.

Ryan, C. and Cave, J. (2005) Structuring destination image: a qualitative approach. *Journal of Travel Research* 44, 143–150.

Sainaghi, R. (2006) From contents to processes: versus a dynamic destination management model (DDMM). *Tourism Management* 27(5), 1053–1063.

Song, Z., Su, X. and Li, L. (2013) The indirect effects of destination image on destination loyalty intention through tourist satisfaction and perceived value: the bootstrap approach. *Journal of Travel & Tourism Marketing* 30(4), 386–409.

Stepchenkova, S. and Mills, E. (2010) Destination image: a meta-analysis of 2000–2007 research. *Journal of Hospitality Marketing & Management* 19(6), 575–609.

Stepchenkova, S. and Morrison, M. (2008) Russia's destination image among American pleasure travelers: Revisiting Echtner and Ritchie. *Tourism Management* 29, 548–560.

Tapachai, N. and Waryszak, R. (2000) An examination of the role of beneficial image in tourist destination selection. *Journal of Travel Research* 39(1), 37–44.

Tasci, D., Gartner, C. and Cavusgil, S. (2007) Conceptualization and operationalization of destination image. *Journal of Hospitality & Tourism Research* 31, 194–223.

Therkelsen, A. (2003) Imagining places: Image formation of tourists and its consequences for destination promotion. *Scandinavian Journal of Hospitality & Tourism* 3, 134–150.

White, C. (2004) Destination image: to see or not to see? *International Journal of Contemporary Hospitality Management* 16(5), 309–314.

Woodside, G. and Lysonski, S. (1989) A general model of traveler destination choice. *Journal of Travel Research* 27(4), 8–14.

Zhang, H., Fu, X., Cai, A. and Lu, L. (2014) Destination image and tourist loyalty: a meta analysis. *Tourism Management* 40, 213–223.

10 Theoretical Perspectives in the Study of Community Residents and Tourism

ARA PACHMAYER,* SHENGNAN ZHAO, AND KATHLEEN ANDERECK

School of Community Resources and Development, Arizona State University, Phoenix, Arizona

The Objectives

1. Describe how social exchange theory helps us to understand how resources are exchanged between residents and tourists.
2. Explain how community attachment can affect a community's perception of and acceptance of tourism development.
3. Describe how social representation theory explains how shared values and perspectives influence a community's perspectives and expectations associated with tourism development.
4. Critique the utility of the theory of reasoned action for predicting community support for tourism development and general attitudes about tourism.

The Vignette

Staff in a community economic development office is considering additional tourism to add to the mix of its existing development strategies. While generally positive toward this idea, some of the staff members recognize that tourism comes not only with benefits but it can also result in costs to the community. Tourism most often results in contact between residents and visitors in a number of settings. Without resident support for tourism development and accompanying positive attitudes toward visitors, these resident–tourist encounters have the potential to result in negative experiences for both the tourists and residents. Therefore, an assessment of what residents think about additional tourism and the kinds of tourism development they find acceptable is critical for a community prior to implementation of tourism development and promotion activities.

The Context

The residents' perspective regarding tourism in their community has been a topic of study for many years. This is especially true with respect to the perceived impacts of

*Corresponding author, e-mail: ara@asu.edu

tourism, resident attitudes toward tourism, and the amount of support that residents have for the development of tourism in their communities. As is often the case, much of the early work in this area was atheoretical, but as the research became more sophisticated with the introduction of explanatory relationships and corresponding statistical analysis, theoretical frameworks began to emerge as a foundation for causal models. This chapter will discuss select theories that are commonly used to further our knowledge about residents and how they perceive tourism within their communities.

The Theories

Social exchange theory

Evolving from the works of Homans (1958), Blau (1964), and Emerson (1972), social exchange theory (SET) is a general sociological theory which is concerned with understanding the exchange of resources between individuals and groups in interaction situations (Ap, 1992). It has been frequently used as a theoretical framework in sociology, economics, and social psychology to interpret the social relations that accompany the exchange of resources of any kind between individuals and groups (Ap, 1992). SET was perhaps the first clear theoretical framework to be introduced as a potential foundation for research related to residents and tourism and, in the last 20 years, it has been the most commonly used theory guiding this research stream (Perdue *et al.*, 1990; Ap, 1992; Jurowski *et al.*, 1997; Andereck and Vogt, 2000; Gursoy *et al.*, 2002; Jurowski and Gursoy, 2004; Andereck *et al.*, 2005; Wang and Pfister, 2008).

Tourism is a scenario where resources between hosts and guests are exchanged suggesting the use of SET as a framework for studying such interactions (Sutton, 1967). These encounters can be asymmetrical and unbalanced (Mathieson and Wall, 1982). While they can provide an opportunity for rewarding and satisfying exchange, they may instead stimulate and reinforce impulses for exploitation on the host side resulting in suspicion and resentment on the visitor side (Sutton, 1967). As well, some residents reap the benefits, whereas others may be negatively impacted. The process of tourism-related encounters and/or interaction includes two basic elements: actors and resources. While the former refers to a person or a group that acts as a single unit (Emerson, 1972), the latter can be viewed as any type of resource whether material, social, or psychological. When considering tourism's impact on the local community, "actors" refers to potential hosts who decide to participate in exchange with tourists if the perceived benefits exceed costs, and vice versa (Jurowski *et al.*, 1997).

Based on SET, various models have been developed to examine the variety of relationships between perceived impacts, residents' attitudes and support for tourism development. Generally speaking, perceived impacts or attitudes have been broken down into three categories: economic, environmental, and socio-cultural. The structural relationship between both positive and negative impacts (benefit/cost) and residents' attitudes towards and support for tourism development have been explored in previous research (Ap, 1992; Jurowski *et al.*, 1997; Lindberg and Johnson, 1997; Gursoy *et al.*, 2002). These studies can be categorized into several broad areas of research including: investigation of general attitudes toward tourism; variables that predict attitudes toward tourism; variables that predict support for tourism development; and theory development/model testing. There has been mixed support for SET among these studies.

Multiple studies have employed SET in determining general attitudes toward tourism (Andriotis and Vaughan, 2003; Pérez and Nadal, 2005; Andereck et al., 2005; Vargas-Sanchez et al., 2009). For example, Perez and Nadal's (2005) study investigated how residents felt tourism was impacting their community. The authors performed a cluster analysis, dividing the residents into different groups, finding that residents recognized both the benefits and the costs of tourism. Andriotis and Vaughan (2003) also used cluster analysis to separate residents into three groups to explore resident attitudes toward tourism on the isle of Crete. Unlike other studies, the authors found full support for SET in this instance. The authors state that their study "concludes that those residents who benefit from tourism perceive on average greater social and economic advantages than those who do not receive any benefits" (p. 183). Andereck et al. (2005) also used SET in their study of general attitudes toward tourism. However, only partial support for SET was found in that residents who relied on the positive benefits of tourism did not feel differently from other groups when considering the negative costs of tourism. Vargas-Sanchez et al. (2009) investigated resident general attitudes toward tourism in a town experiencing relatively recent tourism development. Like Andriotis and Vaughan (2003), Vargas-Sanchez et al. also found support for SET. In their study, perceptions of tourism impacted whether or not residents had positive or negative attitudes toward tourism.

Multiple studies have used SET in identifying variables that are most likely to predict resident attitudes toward tourism (Perdue et al., 1987; Gursoy and Rutherford, 2004; Andereck et al., 2005). As mentioned earlier, Andereck et al. (2005) used SET to form the basis of their study and included variables that had potential to predict resident attitudes toward tourism including demographic variables such as age and education, as well as income received from tourism, and personal benefit from tourism. When considering these predictors, the study revealed residents who perceived personal benefit from tourism and received their income from tourism felt that tourism was more positive.

The framework for SET has also been used to determine resident support for tourism development. Using support for tourism development as their dependent variable, Andereck and Vogt (2000) tested the relationship between support for tourism and several variables including community development, negative impacts, and quality of life. While results differed across communities, all variables were found to be significant predictors of support for tourism development when combined in a single model. Sirakaya et al. (2002) also used SET when testing resident support for tourism infrastructure development and support for the hospitality industry in general in two communities in Ghana. Independent variables consisted of residents' attitudes toward tourism and tourists, demographics, community involvement, personal benefit from tourism, and awareness of tourism development in the region. Much like other studies, partial support was found for SET in this instance.

Community attachment

McCool and Martin (1994: 30) define community attachment "as the extent and pattern of social participation and integration into the community, and sentiment or affect toward the community." Essentially, community attachment is an individual's feelings of connection to a community through social ties and integration into the

A. Pachmayer, S. Zhao, and K. Andereck

community. McCool and Martin's definition also references the emotion an individual may have for a community and the specific features of a community, such as access to recreation areas, scenic beauty, or other community amenities (McCool and Martin, 1994; Jennings and Krannich, 2011).

In the field of tourism research, community attachment has been adopted to understand how people's attachment to their community could influence their perception and attitudes towards changes or developments in their community (Um and Crompton, 1987; Lankford and Howard, 1994; McCool and Martin, 1994; Deccio and Baloglu, 2002; Gursoy and Rutherford, 2004; Andereck et al., 2005; Nicholas et al., 2009). This concept has been used as both a theoretical construct (McCool and Martin, 1994; Vargas-Sanchez et al., 2009) and more frequently as a variable in predicting resident attitudes toward tourism (Jurowski et al., 1997; Gursoy and Rutherford, 2004; Andereck et al., 2005; Gursoy et al., 2009; Nicholas et al., 2009). Mixed results have been found when using community attachment to predict resident attitudes toward tourism and support for tourism development.

As a theoretical construct, community attachment figured prominently in two studies in particular. McCool and Martin (1994) considered how community attachment, attitudes toward tourism, and the level of tourism development in a community were related. They measured community attachment by length of residency and by two questions designed to determine an individual's affinity to their community. McCool and Martin found residents with longer tenures in their communities were more attached to the community. In this study community attachment and length of residency had a significant and positive relationship though the relationship was not strong. However, the authors conclude "Our results concerning the relationship between community attachment and attitudes are anything but clear" (McCool and Martin, 1994: 33). While length of residency was positively correlated to community attachment in that the longer people stay in a community the more attachment they will have to their community, results differed when level of tourism development in the community was considered. McCool and Martin (1994) discovered that in the communities with the highest level of tourism development it was the shorter term residents who exhibited higher levels of attachment to the community. By way of explanation the authors suggest the residents with shorter tenures of residency, the newcomers, may have moved to the community specifically due to the tourism resources offered. Due to their intentional choice to move to a community these residents could show enhanced attachment to the community (McCool and Martin, 1994).

Operationalization of the community attachment theory as a function of demographic variables has been an issue and may have impacted results. This fact is mentioned by Andereck et al. (2005), who suggested that the results of their study may have been non-significant due to the way community attachment was measured. Attachment to community is an elusive concept that cannot be easily measured based solely on length of residency in a community or other demographic variables.

Social representation theory

Social representation theory (SRT) suggests that groups of people create order in their world through their system of values and behaviors. Furthermore, these values and behaviors allow for individuals to communicate with each other and across groups (Moscovici, 1984). There are various definitions of social representation, such as "myths, knowledge, images, ideas, and thoughts about a social object or a matter of social interest" (Andriotis and Vaughan, 2003), and "a metasystem which includes values, benefits, and common-sense explanations of how the world operates" (Pearce *et al.*, 1996). In other words, social representation is simply the mechanism that people use to understand the world and to turn the unfamiliar into the familiar (Fredline and Faulkner, 2000). It suggests how social knowledge is created and shared between the individual and the social world (Philogene and Deaux, 2001). The interaction between individuals and their social or cultural world is central to social representation theory and is useful for researchers who study "what communities think tourism is, what they expect it will bring and how they respond to tourism" (Pearce *et al.*, 1996: 31).

Such cognitive process is not simply an analogy, rather, it is a "socially meaningful fusion with a shift in values and feelings" (Moscovici, 1981: 189). This process depicts the bidirectional relationships between social phenomena and individuals. On one hand, social phenomena help to shape the contents of individuals' minds, meanwhile, communication and interaction between individuals facilitates formation of social phenomena. Therefore, SRT assumes that social phenomena do not exist outside of individuals but within interpersonal and mediated communications, and thus is characterized as "constructed and negotiated."

Purkhardt (1993) generalized three major sources of social representations: (i) direct experience; (ii) social interactions; and (iii) the media. Past and direct experience of an event and/or activity serves as the information source and reference to shape people's perceptions and understanding towards the external world. This type of source is probably more influential than other information sources as it is under the direct control of the individual. When direct experience of a particular social phenomenon is lacking, individuals tend to "borrow" social representations from some other sources, such as social interactions with others, including family, friends, cohorts, colleagues, and even strangers. The means of transmission of social representations is on the basis of group membership and peer pressure, which makes people adopt a consistent representation with other group members. Individuals, however, do not necessarily belong to one group and there could be some conflicts existing among their various group memberships. In this case, individuals are probably forced to reconcile contradictory positions among different reference groups. The third source is the media, which influences perceptions through filtering, presenting, and sometimes manipulating the content of stories. In addition, it is able to provide people with perspectives of other groups, offering rich second-hand experiences, which potentially serve as new references for individuals.

Not all groups are uniformly cohesive and homogeneous and Moscovici (1988) suggested that there are three levels of social representations: hegemonic, emancipated, and polemical. Hegemonic representations exist when all the opinions and ideas are stable and homogenously accepted by the whole community; "emancipated" representations are described as less stable and somewhat differently interpreted by various subgroups within one community; and "polemical" representations refers to the large-scale conflicting and opposing outlooks existing in one community. Given that heterogeneous representations could exist within social groups, SRT necessitates identifying the subgroups in an attempt to understand the perceptions and corresponding reactions of each group respectively.

A. Pachmayer, S. Zhao, and K. Andereck

The most commonly used statistical method to make segmentations of nested groups is cluster analysis on the basis of people's attitudes and, more specifically, to what extent people's overall perceptions are positive or negative. Most studies support the assumption that a host community is not homogeneous but comprises a number of subgroups of like-minded individuals. Emancipated and polemical representations were found to be salient across various studies. A continuum of segments has been found, such as "lover, love 'em for a reason, cautious romantic, in-betweener, and hater," by Davis et al. (1988); "lover, selfish, controlled, and hater," by Davis et al. (1988); "ambivalent supporter, haters, realists, lovers, and concerned for a reason," by Fredline and Faulkner (2000); and "embracers and tolerators," by Zhou and Ap (2009). Andriotis and Vaughan used this theory in attempting to identify and clarify resident attitudes toward tourism (Andriotis and Vaughan, 2003) and to provide the framework around which their study was built. Investigating resident attitudes toward tourism and the variables that may predict attitudes, the authors divided the participants into three distinct groups: (i) advocates; (ii) socially and environmentally concerned; and (iii) economic skeptics. They found full support for SRT as results indicated distinct groups within the host community can be identified based on their attitudes toward tourism.

Sociodemographic characteristics of each cluster have also been used to generate a closer look at the identifications of different clusters. No relationship was found between a number of variables and residents' attitudes towards tourism, such as gender and education (Davis et al., 1988; Weaver and Lawton, 2001). On the other hand, other variables yielded multiple results across several studies, indicating unclear patterns in different study contexts, such as age, employment, income level, born in the community, and length of residency (Davis, et al., 1988; Ryan and Montgomery, 1994; Fredline and Faulkner, 2000; Weaver and Lawton, 2001). For example, some studies described haters as significantly older (Fredline and Faulkner, 2000; Weaver and Lawton, 2001), whereas in other studies age was found not to be significantly different across cluster types (Davis et al., 1988; Ryan and Montgomery, 1994). Similarly, Fredline and Faulkner (2000) found that the majority of the realists worked in the tourism industry or tourism-induced industries, and most lovers were less likely to be involved in tourism businesses.

The power of SRT in identifying how individuals respond to tourism development and how they construct and are influenced by shared views has been recognized in the tourism literature. Future research should focus on classifying residents based on their attitudes towards tourism, describing their sociodemographic profiles, and understanding how these attitudes are formed, shaped, and transformed. In other words, the questions of what are the sources of their particular social representations and what are the underlying meaning-making processes needs to be addressed. Such studies can be conducted by applying, for example, longitudinal methods, which can help track the transformation of social representations along with the progress of tourism development over the course of a relatively long period.

Theory of reasoned action

The theory of reasoned action (TRA), originally proposed by Fishbein and Ajzen (1975), assumes that individuals are rational, make use of available information, and evaluate the possible implications of their actions based on the information and beliefs they possess, before deciding to engage or not to engage in a particular activity (Ajzen, 1985). Ajzen and Fishbein (1980) demonstrated a hierarchical model of TRA which describes the structural relationships between behavior, intention, attitude, subjective norms, and beliefs. *Intention*, comprised of all the motivational factors, refers to the subjective probability that individuals will engage in a specific behavior (Ajzen and Fishbein, 1980). *Attitude* towards the behavior is the degree to which performance of the behavior is positively or negatively valued. Although attitude theory categorizes attitude into cognitive, affective, and behavioral components, Fishbein and Ajzen (1975) argued that they were often not distinguishable and the three-component terminology was not necessary. As a result, TRA adopts a unidimensional model of attitude. *Subjective norms* concerning the behavior are the perceived social pressure to engage or not to engage in a behavior. Fishbein and Ajzen (1975) divided the *beliefs* into two conceptually distinct sets, *behavioral belief* and *normative belief*. While behavioral beliefs link the behavior of interest to expected outcomes, normative beliefs refer to the perceived behavioral expectations of such important referent individuals or groups such as spouse, family, friend, teacher, doctor, supervisor, and co-worker. The causal relationships in this theoretical model are as follows: behavior is proposed to be influenced by behavioral intention, and behavioral intention is determined by attitudes and subjective norms, and attitudes and subjective norms are affected by behavioral belief and cognitive belief, respectively.

To date, TRA has been used successfully to analyze various types of behaviors, such as water conservation (Kantola *et al.*, 1982), environmental activism (Fielding *et al.*, 2008), recycling (Taylor and Todd, 1995; Mannetti *et al.*, 2004), and eco-products choice (Hao *et al.*, 2010), and its efficacy has been proven in terms of the relatively high percentage of covariance of behavior and behavior intention that are explained by other antecedents (Armitage *et al.*, 2004). In the research on residents' attitudes towards tourism, most researchers only adopted some part of the TRA model, namely, the attitude–intention relationship, along with SET, to explore whether residents are more likely to support tourism development as long as they believe that the expected benefits of development exceed the cost of the development (Lepp, 2007; Kwon and Vogt, 2009). In Dyer *et al.* (2007), resident perceptions of the impacts of tourism and the effect on their attitudes toward tourism were explored. Using TRA, the authors found a relationship between attitudes toward tourism and support for tourism development. However, the authors suggest that differences in the model could be found if the research were performed in locations with varying levels of tourism development. Employing qualitative methods, Lepp (2007) also used TRA to form a study of resident attitudes toward tourism in a rural village in Uganda. The decision to use qualitative methods was made due to previous research that suggested this method would allow for a more specific description of resident attitudes which would aid in hypothesizing the behaviors of residents where tourism was concerned. Through observations in the community and interviews and conversations with residents, Lepp found 94% of respondents had positive attitudes towards tourism in their community. Lepp (2007) expected to find that the positive attitudes that residents exhibited toward tourism would result in "pro-tourism" behavior (p. 878) and he found that this hypothesis was supported through "indirect evidence" (p. 883). His indirect evidence rested on observations he made, which included a new-found desire by the community to conserve natural tourism resources as well as positive interactions between locals and

A. Pachmayer, S. Zhao, and K. Andereck

tourists. Additionally, the author cites the lack of anti-tourism behavior in the community as further indirect evidence of the community's support for tourism.

Results are inconsistent across various studies. While some studies fully confirm the TRA that residents' attitudes are strongly related to the formation of intention (support) for place marketing activities and tourism products (Kwon and Vogt, 2009), some studies only partially support TRA theory in that only perceived economic benefits and perceived cultural benefits have significant positive direct impact on local residents' support for tourism development (Gursoy and Rutherford, 2004; Dyer et al., 2007). Sometimes, TRA's application as a behavioral or intentional predictor is questioned. The failure of the TRA could be the inappropriate application where general measures of attitude are used to predict specific behaviors (Kaiser et al., 1999).

The Future

A variety of theories have been used in the context of residents' attitudes toward tourism. The earliest research was descriptive in nature with a focus on resident perceptions of impacts and this preoccupation continues to this day. To increase our understanding of the way residents perceive tourism and how we might advocate for tourism as a community development strategy, a more considered approach to research needs to be taken. It is also time to invest in the development of a theory specific to residents' attitudes toward tourism; one that builds on the theories that have been borrowed from other disciplines and the lessons learned about their application in the tourism context. Enough research has been, and is being, conducted on this topic to suggest a causal model that is testable and can guide the further development of research focused on the way residents view tourism in their communities.

Questions

1. Discuss the evolution of the use of theory in the study of resident attitudes toward tourism since the late 1980s.
2. How has theory helped us better understand the way residents think and feel about tourism in their communities?
3. How do you think we could enhance our understanding of residents and their opinions about tourism over the next several years from a theoretical perspective?

References

Ajzen, I. (1985) From intentions to actions: a theory of planned behavior. In: Kuhl, J. and Beckmann, J. (eds) *Action-control: From Cognition to Behavior*. Springer, Heidelberg, Germany, pp. 11–39.

Ajzen, I. and Fishbein, J. (1980) *Understanding Attitudes and Predicting Social Behavior*. Prentice-Hall, Englewood Cliffs, New Jersey.

Andereck, K. and Vogt, C.A. (2000) The relationship between residents' attitudes toward tourism and tourism development options. *Journal of Travel Research* 39(1), 27–36.

Andereck, K., Valentine, K., Knopf, R. and Vogt, C.A. (2005) Residents' perceptions of community tourism impacts. *Annals of Tourism Research* 32(4), 1056–1076.

Andriotis, K. and Vaughan, R. (2003) Urban residents' attitudes toward tourism development: the case of Crete. *Journal of Travel Research* 42(2), 172–185.

Ap, J. (1992) Residents' perceptions on tourism impacts. *Annals of Tourism Research* 19(4), 665–690.

Armitage, C., Sheeran, P., Conner, M. and Arden, M. (2004) Stages of change or changes of stage? Predicting transitions in transtheoretical model stages in relation to healthy food choice. *Journal of Consulting and Clinical Psychology* 72(3), 491–499.

Blau, P.M. (1964) *Exchange and Power in Social Life.* Transaction Publishers, Piscataway, New Jersey.

Davis, D., Allen, J. and Cosenza, R. (1988) Segmenting local residents by their attitudes, interests, and opinions toward tourism. *Journal of Travel Research* 27(2), 2–8.

Deccio, C. and Baloglu, S. (2002) Nonhost community resident reactions to the 2002 winter Olympics: the spillover impacts. *Journal of Travel Research* 41(1), 46–56.

Dyer, P., Gursoy, D., Sharma, B. and Carter, J. (2007) Structural modeling of resident perceptions of tourism and associated development on the sunshine coast, Australia. *Tourism Management* 28(2), 409–422.

Emerson, R. (1972) Exchange theory, Part I: a psychological basis for social exchange. Part II: exchange relations and networks. *Sociological Theories in Progress* 2, 38–87.

Fielding, K., Mcdonald, R. and Louis, W. (2008) Theory of planned behaviour, identity and intentions to engage in environmental activism. *Journal of Environmental Psychology* 28(4), 318–326.

Fishbein, M. and Ajzen, I. (1975) *Belief, Attitude, Intention and Behavior: An Introduction to Theory and Research.* Addison-Wesley, Reading, Massachusetts.

Fredline, E. and Faulkner, B. (2000) Host community reactions: a cluster analysis. *Annals of Tourism Research* 27(3), 763–784.

Gursoy, D. and Rutherford, D.G. (2004) Host attitudes toward tourism: an improved structural model. *Annals of Tourism Research* 31(3), 495–516.

Gursoy, D., Jurowski, C. and Uysal, M. (2002) Resident attitudes: a structural modeling approach. *Annals of Tourism Research* 29(1), 79–105.

Gursoy, D., Chi, C.G. and Dyer, P. (2009) An examination of locals' attitudes. *Annals of Tourism Research* 36(4), 723–726.

Hao, H., Long, P. and Kleckley, J. (2010) Factors predicting homeowners' attitudes toward tourism: A case of a coastal resort community. *Journal of Travel Research* 0047287510385463.

Homans, G.C. (1958) Social behavior as exchange. *American Journal of Sociology* 63(6), 597–606.

Jennings, B.M. and Krannich, R.S. (2011) Bonded to whom? Social interactions in a high-amenity rural setting. *Community Development* 44, 3–22.

Jurowski, C. and Gursoy, D. (2004) Distance effects on residents' attitudes toward tourism. *Annals of Tourism Research* 31(2), 296–312.

Jurowski, C., Uysal, M. and Williams, D. (1997) A theoretical analysis of host community resident. *Journal of Travel Research* 36(2), 3–11.

Kaiser, F.G., Wolfing, S. and Fuhrer, U. (1999) Environmental attitude and ecological behaviour. *Journal of Environmental Psychology* 19(1), 1–19.

Kantola, S., Syme, G. and Campbell, N. (1982) The role of individual differences and external variables in a test of the sufficiency of Fishbein's model to explain behavioral intentions to conserve water. *Journal of Applied Social Psychology* 12(1), 70–83.

Kwon, J. and Vogt, C. (2009) Identifying the role of cognitive, affective, and behavioral components in understanding residents' attitudes toward place marketing. *Journal of Travel Research* 49(4), 423–435.

A. Pachmayer, S. Zhao, and K. Andereck

Lankford, S. and Howard, D. (1994) Developing a tourism impact attitude scale. *Annals of Tourism Research* 21(1), 121–139.

Lepp, A. (2007) Residents' attitudes towards tourism in Bigodi village, Uganda. *Tourism Management* 28(3), 876–885.

Lindberg, K. and Johnson, R.L. (1997) Modeling resident attitudes toward tourism. *Annals of Tourism Research* 24(2), 402–424.

Mannetti, L., Pierro, A. and Livi, S. (2004) Recycling: planned and self-expressive behaviour. *Journal of Environmental Psychology* 24(2), 227–236.

Mathieson, A. and Wall, G. (1982) *Tourism, Economic, Physical and Social Impacts.* Longman, London.

McCool, S. and Martin, S. (1994) Community attachment and attitudes toward tourism development. *Journal of Travel Research* 32(3), 29–34.

Moscovici, S. (1981) On social representations. In: Forgas, J.P. (ed.) *Social Cognition: Perspectives on Every-day Understanding*. Academic Press, London, pp. 181–209.

Moscovici, S. (1984) The phenomenon of social representations. In: Farr, R.M. and Moscovici, S. (eds) *Social Representation*. Cambridge University Press, Cambridge, UK, pp. 3–69.

Moscovici, S. (1988) Notes toward a description of social representations. *European Journal of Social Psychology* 18, 211–250.

Nicholas, L., Thapa, B. and Ko, Y.J. (2009) Residents' perspectives of a world heritage site: the Pitons Management Area, St Lucia. *Annals of Tourism Research* 36(3), 390–412.

Pearce, P.L., Moscardo, G. and Ross, G.F. (1996) *Tourism Community Relationships.* Emerald Group Publishing Limited, Bingley, UK.

Perdue, R.R., Long, P.T. and Allen, L. (1987) Rural resident tourism perceptions and attitudes. *Annals of Tourism Research* 14(3), 420–429.

Perdue, R.R., Long, P.T. and Allen, L. (1990) Resident support for tourism development. *Annals of Tourism Research* 17(4), 586–599.

Perez, E.A. and Nadal, J.R. (2005) Host community perceptions a cluster analysis. *Annals of Tourism Research* 32(4), 925–941.

Philogene, G. and Deaux, K. (2001) Introduction. In: Deaux, K. and Philogene, G. (eds) *Representations of the Social: Bridging Theoretical Traditions*. Blackwell, Oxford, UK, pp. 3–7.

Purkhardt, S. (1993) *Transforming Social Representations: A Social Psychology of Common Sense and Science.* Routledge, New York.

Ryan, C. and Montgomery, D. (1994) The attitudes of Bakewell residents to tourism and issues in community responsive tourism. *Tourism Management* 15(5), 358–369.

Sirakaya, E., Teye, V. and Sonmez, S. (2002) Understanding residents' support for tourism development in the central region of Ghana. *Journal of Travel Research* 41(1), 57–67.

Sutton, W. (1967) Travel and understanding: notes on the social structure of touring. *International Journal of Comparative Sociology* 8(2), 218–223.

Taylor, S. and Todd, P. (1995) An integrated model of waste management behavior: a test of household recycling and composting intentions. *Environment and Behavior* 27(5), 603–630.

Um, S. and Crompton, J. (1987) Measuring resident's attachment levels in a host community. *Journal of Travel Research* 26(1), 27–29.

Vargas-Sanchez, A., Plaza-Mejia, M. and Porras-Bueno, N. (2009) Understanding residents' attitudes toward the development of industrial tourism in a former mining community. *Journal of Travel Research* 47(3), 373–387.

Wang, Y. and Pfister, R. (2008) Residents' attitudes toward tourism and perceived personal benefits in a rural community. *Journal of Travel Research* 47(1), 84–93.

Weaver, D.B. and Lawton, L.J. (2001) Resident perceptions in the urban–rural fringe. *Annals of Tourism Research* 28(2), 439–458.

Zhou, Y. and Ap, J. (2009) Residents' perceptions towards the impacts of the Beijing 2008 Olympic Games. *Journal of Travel Research* 48(1), 78–91.

11 Theoretical Perspectives on Tourism and Sustainable Community Development

CLAUDIA JUROWSKI*

School of Hotel and Restaurant Management, W.A. Franke College of Business, Northern Arizona University, Flagstaff, Arizona

The Objectives

1. To define sustainable community development.
2. Explain why social representation theory helps us to understand how representation, power, and equity of various groups within a community contribute to sustainable community development.
3. Describe the utility of stakeholder theory for examining the relationships between stakeholders and their contributions towards sustainable tourism and community development.
4. Explain how social network theory can be used to guide research concerned with tourism and sustainable community development.
5. Explain how chaos theory and complexity theory can be used to examine the tourism system and its patterns of organization and operation that lead to sustainable or unsustainable communities.
6. Identify future areas of research and areas where theoretical contributions are needed to understand better the relationships between tourism and sustainable community development.

The Vignette

After dinner Joan and Jason were conversing about the future of their children. Their son Mark was going to go to college in September and Marcy would be following in his footsteps the next year. Mark planned to major in business and Marcy was quite artistic. They worried that once the children finished college they would not return to their home town because their prospects for employment were going to be poor with the declining population of the community and the number of businesses that had closed in the last few years.

That same evening the owner of the dry cleaners, Josh, and the owner of the flower shop, Kirsten, were talking on the sidewalk after closing their shops. They were

*Corresponding author, e-mail: claudia.jurowski@nau.edu

concerned about their ability to stay in business. The forest was not producing enough trees to maintain a viable industry because of the failure of the lumber companies to operate in a sustainable manner. As jobs in the lumber industry dwindled local shop owners experienced a downturn in sales. Already the local hardware store, the jeweler, and one of the dress shops had gone out of business.

The town's elected officials were equally concerned about the sustainability of their community. At the council meeting that evening, council members were discussing various economic development options. They first thought that they might be able to attract a furniture-making factory because of the ready supply of lumber but learned that transporting bulky furniture to distribution centers was going to add extraordinary transportation costs resulting in uncompetitive prices. The mayor supported efforts to improve the Internet infrastructure so that computer-based service organizations such as call centers and financial services might locate in their community bringing the jobs needed to encourage residents to stay in the community. Some council members expressed concerns that their town could not compete with island nations like Barbados that offer location incentives and relatively cheap labor. The council members were looking for a way to create a sustainable community that could supply goods and services the residents needed and could create opportunities for all levels of employment so that college graduates could see a bright future in their home community. They wanted a clean industry that would respect the beauty of the natural surroundings in which the community was located. They knew some development plans would result in political disfavor because of the strong affiliations citizens had with environmental preservation and social equity groups. At the same time, they were concerned that a new industry would change the character of the community. Change of course was inevitable, but the citizens wanted to sustain the town's values and the strong sense of community that permeated relationships in the town.

What industry would offer Mark business employment opportunities? What might encourage Marcy to bring her artistic talents to this community? What type of development would improve sales for the florist and the dry cleaner? How can the community preserve its natural beauty and grow economically? What industry would create jobs and respect community values?

The council members agreed that the solution must come from the local people, but what framework would empower the citizens to create a viable industry? What stakeholder structure would allow collaboration among a wide range of actors to deal with the complexities of community development? They identified the networks that connect the varied interests of the community including education, health care, local businesses, distribution firms, social services, and government as a potential starting point. They felt that if they could tap into these networks, the answer to the community's dilemma could be found.

Many communities with a resource-based economy similar to this one have turned to tourism as an industry that could preserve the character of the town while creating economic opportunity and maintaining environmental integrity and social equity. Can tourism be the right industry to promulgate sustainable development in this community?

The Context

The purpose of this chapter is to provide the reader with an understanding of the theories that have been applied to the study of tourism and sustainable community development and to introduce theories applied in other fields of community development that might be adapted to the examination of the role tourism plays in achieving sustainable communities.

Even though the concept of sustainable development has been widely recognized since the publication of *Our Common Future* (Brundtland Commission; WCED, 1987), communities struggle to identify and act in a manner that preserves enough resources for future generations while satisfying the needs of the present generation. While many communities seek to achieve sustainable community development that balances the use of resources to bring about economic opportunities for its citizens while preserving the natural environment and social structures that create value for the citizens, they are challenged to understand, develop, and implement policies and plans. The breadth and value-laden nature of the Brundtland Commission's definition allows for significant interpretation thereby making it difficult to define an accepted model of sustainable development. Even though the literature discusses sustainable development through many diverse and contested lenses, there is fundamentally the recognition of the inability of the earth's resources to satisfy the increasing human demands on the finite natural system and the belief that communities must address the problem if they are to survive (Markey *et al.*, 2010). Sustainable development enables a community to sustain its social and environmental character while providing economic opportunities for its current and future citizens. It incorporates the collective action of community members to generate solutions to community-common problems to improve the quality of life within the community. Each community must decide what its current needs are and what sacrifices the residents of that community are willing to make to achieve sustainability. Consequently, a model that would allow one community to compare its success in achieving sustainability with that of another community cannot be specified (Butler, 1998). Addressing the problem requires communities to identify, plan, implement, and monitor long-term social, economic, and environmental goals, a process that requires significant compromises and trade-offs (Beeton, 2006).

Sustainable community development requires the efforts of a large number of complex systems that must cooperate to create a sustainable system. Tourism further confounds the process of achieving community sustainability since tourism itself is a complex system within a complex system. Equally important to consider is the potential tourism has to either stabilize the ability of a community to meet current and future needs or to create a disturbance that deters sustainable community development.

A significant amount of research has examined the concept of sustainable tourism development (see Hardy *et al.*, 2002 for an overview of sustainable tourism) rather than examining tourism as a component of sustainable community development. Even though numerous theoretical and conceptual frameworks have been proposed (Wight, 1993; Ross and Wall, 1999; Reynolds and Braithwaite, 2001; Walsh *et al.*, 2001; Ward *et al.*, 2002), no universally accepted model of sustainable tourism has evolved (Hardy *et al.*, 2002). This may be largely because of the complexity of the concept and because tourism is not an isolated phenomenon in community development. Furthermore, tourism, as a component of a complex system, has its own set of complexities that further obfuscates the sustainable tourism model.

Tools such as the tourism optimization management model guide residents in setting economic, market opportunity, environmental, experiential, sociocultural, and

---

C. Jurowski

infrastructure development goals, measures, benchmarks, and acceptable ranges. Once these are in place community members can evaluate the role tourism can play in achieving the desired state of the community (Manidis Roberts Consultants, 1997 in Beeton, 2006). For a community to meet both current and future needs it must be able to absorb or safeguard against turbulences and still maintain its core attributes. For example, substituting locally produced goods or services for imported ones supports the community's resilience (Jacobs, 1984), while an extra-community investor may create sufficient turbulence to change the very character of the community. There are many other models and frameworks relating to the concept of sustainable tourism development delineated in the article by Hardy *et al.* (2002). However, tourism is only one of many components in the complex set of actions and conditions that impact sustainable community development and consequently must be studied not as sustainable tourism but instead as a contributor or deterrent to sustainable community development. The theories in this chapter are discussed from the perspective of developing an understanding of the complexity within and among tourism systems that affects the results of a sustainable development program.

Tourism was first viewed in terms of its function in the community rather than as a unique entity by Murphy (1985), who proposed that tourism is part of a larger ecosystem. Murphy's ecological model defines four components (natural resources, residents, industry, and visitors) that must achieve a state of mutual interdependence and co-existence. He emphasizes the importance of public participation and systems planning and the need to balance tourism development requirements with other requisites and priorities of the community. Within the ecosystem, concepts, theories, and analyses integrate human actions and activities, communications, space, and time as components that potentially generate outcomes of specific strategies. Factors that need to be examined include the essential tourism resources, the scale of the planning area, the industrial components needed to develop a viable tourism product, competition, seasonality and weather patterns, external factors (competitive position, state of the economy, the political, economic, social, technological, and legal conditions), and the stage of development (Murphy, 1983). Another set of analysis targets includes the community's natural resources, its planning structure and processes, economic concerns, educational needs, and the level of awareness of tourism's impacts (Byrd *et al.*, 2008). Murphy's perspective is supported by Faulkner and Russell (1997), who caution that tourism is a living system that needs to be treated as a dynamic entity operating according to chaos theory principles that view tourism functioning similar to an ecological community with living systems that can reorganize themselves with non-linear, non-deterministic dynamic characteristics.

The concept of sustainable tourism development lacks a universally accepted theory (Hardy *et al.*, 2002), even though numerous theoretical and conceptual frameworks have been proposed (Wight, 1993; Ross and Wall, 1999; Reynolds and Braithwaite, 2001; Walsh *et al.*, 2001; Ward *et al.*, 2002). Consequently, this chapter discusses tourism as a component of the sustainable development of a community rather than focusing on *sustainable tourism* as the research unit. This perspective concentrates on developing an understanding of the complexity within and among systems that affect the results of a development program. Factors that require examination include the scale, structure, and scope of collaborations, and the challenges of structural development and implementation (Jamal and Stronza, 2009).

The Theory

Social representation and empowerment

Social representation theory proposes that broad-based representation of the various groups within a community is necessary to ensure the sustainable development principle of equitable distribution of benefits to all stakeholders (Moscovici, 1972; Pearce, 1992; Pearce *et al.*, 1996). It provides the basis for support for community-based tourism requiring an understanding of how power is balanced to include the needs of all segments of the society. Theoretically, the balance of power results from proactive management by business and the involvement of the community in the planning process in combination with political forces (Sofield, 2003). Through the strategic planning process businesses, community members, and government officials work to minimize negative impacts and maximize efficient use of resources in an environment of shared and equitable power. The theory examines the dynamic nature of knowledge, values, beliefs, attitudes, and explanations that people create and re-create to achieve community empowerment. Empowerment is critical to sustainable community development because it enables individuals or groups to determine their own affairs and exert control over factors that affect their lives (Scheyvens, 1999; Cole, 2006). Cole (2006: 632) contends, "Social empowerment results from increased community cohesion when members of a community are brought together through a tourism initiative." Tourism, as a component of the sustainable development process, has the potential to strengthen the confidence and identity of a community and to shift the balance between the powerful and the powerless through community participation in the sustainable development process (Swain, 1990; Johnston, 1992; Sofield, 2003). Friedmann (1992) recommends that empowerment be examined from psychological, social, economic, and political perspectives. Studies that examine empowerment and community development through tourism may provide valuable information for community leaders. Questions that need to be answered relate to the distribution of power and decision making among community groups.

The development of theories related to empowerment must include analyses of the barriers to participation such as community residents' lack of knowledge, skills, and resources, as well as inexperience with self-governance (Cole, 2006). Little is known about informed participation even though it has been identified as key to successful sustainable development. However, an assessment tool that measures components of a community's knowledge of sustainable tourism revealed five factors that should be analyzed in the examination of community knowledge: natural resources, planning, economic concerns, educational needs, and awareness of tourism (Byrd *et al.*, 2008). More research is needed to evaluate whether community residents have the capacity to participate in the development process. Equally important is the development of theories related to social capital, its content and development. Social capital incorporates the extent of involvement, engagement, and trust between community members (Beeton, 2006). An understanding of both structural and cognitive aspects may be necessary to achieve a sustainable balance of power. Networks, roles, rules, and precedents are considered structural aspects relating to what people do while cognitive aspects include norms, values, beliefs, and attitudes, and describe what people feel (Beeton, 2006).

For tourism to be a force for sustainability there must be a balance of power among the players so that the social equity, ecological integrity, and economic security components of sustainable development can be achieved. Research into the structural and cognitive aspects of power may provide insight into how tourism contributes to or detracts from sustainable community initiatives.

The focus on sustainable community development has shifted tourism research away from resource- and activity-based theories such as limits to growth and carrying capacity toward community-based theories that aim to promote quality of life and the protection of resources (Saarinen, 2006). A critical component of the focus on sustainable development is community participation because it is the participation of the citizens of the tourism destination that creates legitimacy in the development process. The importance and value of involving those whose well-being is impacted by development in the decision making process, i.e. those who have a stake in the outcome, can be examined based on stakeholder theory that scrutinizes the relationship among all who are impacted by community development programs (Bramwell and Sharman, 1999). It focuses on power and legitimacy and is therefore central to the community-based approach that is more concerned with meeting the needs of the local people than the needs of the industry. See Chapter 3 (this volume) for a discussion of the application of stakeholder theory. The following describes how components of the theory can be used to study the role of tourism in sustainable community development.

Stakeholder theory

Understanding the behavior and actions of stakeholders is critical for devising strategies to deal ethically and effectively with them (De Lopez, 2001). Donaldson and Preston (1995) recommend that research be based on a tri-component theory that includes empirically descriptive factors such as the characteristics or behavior of an organization; instrumental factors that identify connections or lack thereof between stakeholder management and the achievement of objectives, and the normative perspective that interprets the moral and philosophical guidelines that direct the organization's behavior. The basic assumption is that all stakeholders have intrinsic value and that an understanding of the descriptive, instrumental, and normative components will lead to predictability, i.e. if certain things are done correctly, certain results will follow. Such models require that participating stakeholders have the understanding and knowledge of the pertinent concepts and issues (Faulkner, 1998; Farrell and Twining-Ward, 2005). However, even though all citizens are theoretically stakeholders, the extent of participation varies considerably from community to community. An early stakeholder model proposed a typology of citizen participation with three categories: non-participation, degrees of tokenism, and degrees of citizen power (Arnstein, 1969). Only in the third category can the stakeholders directly influence decisions being made. Comparisons of the success of sustainable development in tourism communities based on the level of participation of the citizens may yield critical factors important to community managers.

Stakeholder theory replaces deterministic theories of dominance and subordination in power relations between various stakeholders with in-depth social analysis and empirical research on how power is created through the constant readjustment and modification made by social interactions occurring through tourism

(Wearing *et al.*, 2010). Theories and concepts put forth by Foucault (1980) recommend the study of subtle strategies of normalization by differentiating and distinguishing events and networks and the levels to which they belong in order to determine what connects them and what results from these interactions. Wearing *et al.* (2010) in their study of sustainable tourism development in Papua New Guinea propose a first step in the Foucaultian approach to examining the dynamic process that shapes the ways communities work through networking and collaboration.

Variances in power and salience exist not only among destinations and their actors but also among functions such as development versus marketing (Mitchell *et al.*, 1997). Factors that affect power and legitimacy include the size of the tourism industry as well as the position of stakeholders relative to the center of the networks (Timur and Getz, 2007). Research that examines the size of the tourism industry in relation to the power and position of the stakeholders will contribute to understanding about which factors contribute to sustainability and which are deterrents. Communities also need to know the impact of variances in power and salience of marketing versus development. Comparison of the success of sustainable development programs in communities that focus their resources on marketing versus those that focus on development are critical to understanding how tourism assists or hinders sustainable community development.

The stakeholder framework allows a wider range of actors collaborating with each other to be considered in dealing with the complexities of community development than with traditional development structures. When tourism provides the economic incentive to protect the natural environment such as in the case of ecotourism, the natural environment must be considered the primary and primordial stakeholder. The stakeholder theory of collaboration integrates the relationship between public- and private-sector organizations, the natural environment, and the inhabitants (Eckersley, 2004). A political ecology approach to studying collaboration views the domination of nature as mediated by economic-social systems resulting in benefits to some social classes at the expense of others. The theory proposes that social and environmental justices can be achieved through collaboration but recognizes the differing values and the need for knowledge. Three primary attributes that should be included in research examining the role of ecotourism in sustainable community development are: (i) power; (ii) legitimacy; and (iii) urgency (Mitchell *et al.*, 1997). See Chapter 10 (this volume) for a case study that illuminates the examination of the three components.

Social network theory

Social network theory evolved from computer science network theory, which used graphs to examine the relationship between discrete entities. In social network theory the graphs are represented by the linkages between public and private organizations and individuals. A study of the architecture of social networks reveals how relationship systems are formed, managed, and how they evolve. It can be especially useful for studying tourism destination communities seeking sustainable development because of the structure of the tourism system. Its fragmented nature is comprised of complementary and competing organizations, various sectors, numerous infrastructures, and complicated linkages. Network theory is concerned with the collective nature of organization

C. Jurowski

action, constraint, and coordination. It examines the strength and number of linkages between organizations, identifies nodes and interconnected relationships (Pavlovich, 2003). Tourism research that studies the linkages among tourism business, government entities, in-bound tour operators, destination marketing organizations, suppliers, and marketers of tourism may reveal elements that contribute to sustainable development and other elements that deter progress toward sustainability.

Three core concepts dominate the analysis of social networks: nodes or actors, links, and centrality. Social network analysis examines the structural position of entities, persons, organizations, and events (referred to as nodes or actors) that have the potential to either control others or facilitate exchanges that connect different members and have access to different non-redundant sources of information. The effect of tourism on a community's sustainable development program may be related to the structural position of tourism businesses, tourism leaders, destination marketing organizations, or tourism events such as festivals.

Networking theory proposes that structural position in the networks determines the power of a particular stakeholder giving the advantage to those who are best connected. Analysis of the links reveals relationships between the nodes that can be identified as direct or indirect, salient or insignificant, dense or sparse (Meyer and Rowan, 1977). Studies that examine the interaction of tourism entities with each other and with other community nodes or actors will be valuable in determining the role tourism plays in the sustainable development process.

The third component, centrality, refers to the amount of power obtained through the structure of nodes and linkages and the capacity to access information (Wasserman and Faust, 1994). Theoretically, power is increased in direct proportion to access to or possession of critical resources and information, legitimacy, expertise, and connections to other networks. Studies that examine the centrality of tourism entities may reveal the relative power of tourism in a community to effect sustainable development.

Networks are compared on their density and centrality. Density refers to the overall structure of the networks and the number and strength of ties that link actors, while centrality refers to levels of power (Granovetter, 1985, 1992; Gulati, 1998; Jones *et al.*, 1997 in Pavlovich, 2003). Theoretically, optimal network configuration includes both strong and weak ties because a network with too many strong ties will be stifled by demands for conformity and one with too many weak ties will be ineffective (Pavlovich, 2003). To understand the role of tourism in sustainable community development, studies that compare the structure of the networks, the ties that link the actors, and the power of the various tourism entities in one community to that of another community and compare their relative success in achieving sustainability may provide valuable insight for future community development planning and policy promulgation.

Understanding the complexities of networks is extremely important because the interactions among multiple stakeholders impact the ability of a community to create sustainable development strategies. In their study of the interrelationships of stakeholders, Timur and Getz (2007: 458) concluded: "The interconnectedness of diverse stakeholders representing governmental bodies, business firms, persons or other entities on sustainability dimensions can improve the process of sustainable destination development."

Advocates of networking and collaboration in the sustainable community development course of action point to the key role these processes play in resolving problems (Selin, 1993; Roberts and Simpson, 1999). Both action-oriented networks and policy and planning networks are considered governance networks. The action-oriented networks are those that are self-regulating and led by private actors while the policy and planning networks are led by more formal entities such as public institutions and non-governmental organizations (NGOs) (Erkuş-Öztürk and Eraydin, 2010). Policies are a result of interaction between societal and government participants. A policy network approach can be used to describe, analyze, and explain the interactions by focusing on stakeholders in the policy-making process, their relationships, and the structural context in which the interactions take place. Patterns of relationship can emphasize reputational ties, cooperation, and/or information exchange (Pforr, 2006).

Understanding and explaining networks and the power of nodes, links, and centrality in tourism destinations may be enhanced using the tourism relationship model, which depicts relationships within a tourism system comprised of destination resources, community-based intermediaries (CBIs), and extra-community stakeholders (Shikida et al., 2010). The theory behind the model examines the connection between community resources, including natural, cultural, and human, that are transformed to tourists through intermediaries resulting in a continual adjustment of the relationship between the destination resources and extra-community stakeholders. The model demonstrates the circulation mechanism that begins and ends with community resources. Community-based intermediaries transform the resources for tourism and travel intermediaries who use promotion and sales to enact the transformation through the CBIs, thereby making a contribution to community resources. The model can be used to examine the connection between community and extra-community stakeholders that enables reinvestment and added value as well as to control the volume of tourist flow to achieve long-term sustainability. CBI networks are responsible for preventing excess consumption and preserving the community's resources through controlling the flow mechanisms to achieve a balance between the community and extra-community stakeholders. There is a lack of information on the circulation and balancing mechanisms that impact outcomes. One study of a small Japanese community demonstrated the validity of the tourism relationship model but questions remain as to its applicability to larger communities with more than one entity as a CBI. In addition, questions arise as to the effectiveness of reinvestment in destination resources between non-profit and profit-oriented CBIs (Shikida et al., 2010). Involvement of a broad range of stakeholders with complex relationships limits the ability to predict or control outcomes, but the importance of understanding linkages among social, economic, and ecological systems for progress toward sustainability cannot be understated (Cumming et al., 2005).

Chaos theory

Communities seeking to establish policies and procedures that allow the community to use its current resources for economic and social well-being while conserving and preserving resources to ensure opportunities for future generations to enjoy an equally high quality of life need to understand the ecosystem of their community. The principles of chaos theory offer a foundation for research that reveals otherwise hidden knowledge about factors that affect the community's ability to successfully implement sustainable development plans. The term "chaos" when used in everyday language connotes disorder, but when used in the scientific sense, chaos describes a state in

C. Jurowski

which behavior is sensitive to small changes that eventually lead to new patterns of operation and organization (Byrne, 1998). Chaos theory views tourism functioning similar to an ecological community with living systems that can reorganize themselves with non-linear, non-deterministic dynamic characteristics. It expands upon Murphy's (1985) living ecosystem by explaining how tourism functions and includes turbulence and upheaval as essential elements that promote change. Understanding factors that create patterns of operation and organization that lead to either sustainable or unsustainable communities in relation to the tourism industry will assist communities in determining the role tourism can play in the economic and social development of their community.

Chaos theory and the associated complexity theory (Lewin, 1993) recognize that systems operate in a non-linear and non-deterministic manner resulting in a dynamism that limits predictability (Gleick, 1987 as per Overman, 1996 in McKercher, 1999). Chaos theory proposes that organisms in nature react and adapt to their surroundings to form new and novel patterns. This paradigm views humans and their values as part of nature rather than separate from it. It suggests there is no central control but instead self-governing boundaries and values (Waldrop, 1992). These concepts enlighten tourism research by exposing the way systems function and encourage the recognition that nature and human activity cannot be studied separately or with a deterministic approach because of the integrated nature of the ecosystems. Any attempt to examine tourism's operational entity without recognizing its role in an ecosystem whose activities "radiate out from the core to innumerable parts" will lack the necessary data for sustainable development (Farrell and Twining-Ward, 2005: 117). While predictability is limited, the theory proposes that patterns that appear to be haphazard and random actually incorporate recognizable models that may explain the functioning of the system as a whole (Parry and Drost, 1995). Lewin (1993) explains how order resides within chaos with the concept of the "Strange Attractor," which, in a social sense, is likened to common visions, meanings, strategies, or values that drive people to achieve a common goal (Svyantec and DeShon, 1993). An examination of tourism as a potential strange attractor may provide valuable insight as to the role of tourism in sustainable community development.

While the strange attractor provides stability to the chaotic system and somewhat improves predictability, it does not protect the system from exposure to external stimuli that could negate or degrade the power of the strange attractor and stimulate periods of instability that may be necessary for the system to break apart and reorganize itself to progress toward sustainability (Flower, 1993; McKercher, 1999). External stimuli that could negate or degrade the power of the strange attractor include dramatic natural events and mega external investors that disregard the community's efforts toward sustainable development. Research is needed to determine if there are tourism forces that can disrupt a community's sustainable development program.

Three other characteristics associated with chaotic social interactions are the sensitive dependence on initial conditions effect (often referred to as the butterfly effect), the law of increasing returns, and the "lock-in effect." The butterfly effect explains how a small change can result in large differences to a later state; the law of increasing returns explains how success feeds on success; and the "lock-in effect" explains how historical events impact current processes (McKercher, 1999). The understanding of how tourism contributes to or detracts from sustainable development can be enhanced by an examination of how initial errors in decision making or lack thereof about tourism development can result in unsustainable communities, how the success of one tourism entity results in the success of many others, and how historical events have affected the way tourism has or has not contributed to sustainable community development.

Chaos theory may be particularly useful for research related to tourism destinations because they are comprised of clusters of interrelated stakeholders with complex and dynamic relationships and interactions. Such complexity requires an adaptive systems approach that uses complex systems theory to study the relationships and interactions among multiple stakeholders (Baggio *et al.*, 2010). Researchers may find useful the concept of governance, described in Chapter 3 (this volume), to understand how stakeholders determine, implement, and evaluate rules for their interaction. The concept may be important because differences in governance arrangements are presumed to lead to differences in improvement in a destination's competitiveness (Beaumont and Dredge, 2010). The complex adaptive system approach is a tool to measure the effectiveness of the governance. For example, governance determines the length of time a destination remains in any one of the stages in Butler's model (1980) as well as the end result once a destination reaches the top of the cycle with the choice of rejuvenation, stagnation, or decline.

The network (often referred to as a node or cluster), rather than individual entities, is the unit of analysis in the adaptive system approach. Social contracts characterize the interactions. The governance system determines how the destination adapts to change. However, to date there is no agreement on the identification of the components or the interactive factors of the complex system. Baggio (2008) advocates for a quantitative approach based on the statistical physics theories of universality and scaling (Amarall and Ottino, 2004). Scaling laws provide the idea that a set of relations may help in characterizing the singular behavior of a system and its critical transitions (Baggio *et al.*, 2010: 53). Thus, the existence of common underlying laws or principles may be found in similarities among different phenomena within functional elements of different systems or structures (Wigner, 1960; Gentner, 2002; Krieger, 2005; Baggio *et al.*, 2010). Theories related to tourism's role in sustainable tourism development can be tested using scaling laws to compare communities based on various scales such as population, number of tourist arrivals, ratio of tourists to the population, size of the tourism resource in relation to number of visitors, economic gain per visitor, resident attitudes toward tourism, and numerous other scales that are theorized to be relevant to a community's ability to develop in a sustainable manner. Identification of the components and the interactive factors in the complex system may be critical to communities seeking a means to economic growth that protects its social and environmental character.

McKercher's (1999) chaos model with nine components depicts the path from the traveler to outputs. Each of the nine elements (traveler, destination or internal tourism community, communication vectors, other tourism-related externalities, external tourism agencies, considerations (factors that influence effectiveness of communication), non-tourism-related externalities, rogues or chaos makers, and outputs) is connected to other elements either directly, or by no more than one step. This chaos model demonstrates how a disconcertion in one element changes the state of tourism and acknowledges that considerable transference occurs between and within elements. Researchers can use this model to develop theories about elements of change that may positively or negatively impact sustainable community development plans.

C. Jurowski

Russell and Faulkner (1999) propose that entrepreneurship is a critical element that changes the state of tourism. Referring to the work of Lewis and Green (1998), they posit that the evolution of a tourist destination from one stage to the next can be induced by entrepreneurial behavior and depict the impact of various types of entrepreneurship in various stages. The application of chaos theory to the study of the role of the entrepreneur may reveal new understandings of the process of community development. Because the dynamic entrepreneurial process is sensitive to a multiplicity of tiny changes in any one of the many variables in the chaos model, it provides a rich basis for exploring the role of tourism in sustainable community development (Bygrave, 1993). In fact, it may be the outlier entrepreneurs who create the "butterfly effect" that sparks the change process (Stevenson and Harmeling, 1990). Along with the question of how the entrepreneur impacts the process is the question of what climate or environment is conducive to nurturing entrepreneurs that leads to sustainable versus unsustainable community development. Other questions relate to the qualities of the entrepreneur that lead to responsible community development (see Storey, 1994 for dimensions of entrepreneurial personality).

The complexity generated by chaos-driven systems requires new approaches to research. The complex systems approach recognizes the non-linear interactions and turbulence as normalities critical to understanding patterns in chaos.

Complex systems approach

McDonald (2009) advocates the use of complexity science for the study of sustainable tourism development, because complexity science studies how parts of a system inspire the collective behavior of the system. Tourism can be studied as a part of the collective system that critically impacts a community from three interrelated approaches. One approach is to analyze the extent to which tourist interactions influence patterns of behavior within a community. In the second approach attempts are made to understand how to describe tourism's role in the complex system. Tourism can also be studied from the third approach of examining how patterns of behavior form and evolve.

This type of scientific inquiry technique is important because linear explanations of phenomena are limited in their ability to explain the complexity of tourism phenomena. Consequently, scientific inquiry techniques that provide an alternative paradigm for viewing and understanding tourism are required. In contrast to the Newtonian model that implies an expectation of return to normalcy, the complex system model expects non-linear interactions and periods of turbulence and stability that are never permanent due to the unpredictable outcomes of underlying patterns of behavior (Farrell and Twining-Ward, 2005). The major characteristics of complex systems include the dynamic interaction of large numbers of elements and stakeholders, multiple levels in a hierarchical system, perpetual novelty and self-organization, subjectivity to dramatic changes from relatively minor occurrences, and to the influence of historical happenings (Prigogine and Stengers, 1985; Coveney and Highfield, 1995; Geldof, 1995; Cilliers, 1998; Waldrop, 1992 in McDonald, 2009).

Human activity and values are viewed as part of nature rather than separate from it. The systems model proposed by McDonald (2009: 249) shows the dynamic interactions among the components of the tourism industry, the community, government agencies,

NGOs, and the natural environment in the tourism process. It emphasizes scale as an important feature and depicts multiple levels interacting resulting in self-organization and emergent behaviors that allow the system to evolve.

The complex systems approach is useful for the study of tourism destinations in general and especially for those in protected areas that can be viewed as complex planning domains in which tourism and biodiversity conservation are seen as inter-related and interactive components (Jamal and Jamrozy, 2006; Jamal and Stronza, 2009). The interrelationship and interdependence of a coalition of systems that includes tourism, protected area, ecological, and community systems are components to be examined in the complex systems approach. Questions that need to be answered include how does the tourism system fit with the protected area, ecological and community systems; what are the roles and responsibilities within each system; and what factors impact or change the interactions and outcomes. Additionally, the question of who represents the natural environment or ecological system needs to be answered as well as what are the scales, structure, and forms of tourism collaborations, and what are the key factors that assure sustainability. There are multiple stakeholders within each system that affect and are affected by this nested group of systems and external systems to which these internal systems are connected (Jamal and Jamrozy, 2006). Research that illuminates the interrelationship and interdependence of the systems will assist leaders in developing and implementing sustainable development plans.

Collaborations can be studied in terms of scale, structure, and scope. Scale may be limited to local groups or expanded to include regional and even national goals. Structures can be formal or informal (Eckersley, 2004; Jamal and Stronza, 2009). Brown (1991) identifies four types of structures: (i) inter-organizational; (ii) association of organizations and networks; (iii) inter-sectorial partnerships; and (iv) social movement. Research is needed to understand the role tourism plays within the various structures that impact a community's ability to achieve sustainable development.

Which connections create threats or opportunities for sustainable development? Which have the greatest impact? Are there any strange attractors, locked-in components, or sensitive conditions that could have dramatic effects on sustainable community development plans or activities?

Complex systems theory requires stakeholders to shift their goals from an intra- to an inter-organizational collaboration. According to Gray (1989), such collaboration is characterized by the interdependence of stakeholders, the emergence of solutions through constructively dealing with differences, joint ownership of decisions, and collective responsibility. His framework for analysis includes problem setting, direction setting, and implementation or institutionalizing.

The Future

Tourism's ability to contribute to sustainable development of communities is dependent upon scientific knowledge related to tourism components, processes, or factors that strengthen the ability of the community to set and move toward goals appropriate for the values and resources of the community. It is important to learn more about how community participation in tourism might empower citizens and shift the balance between the powerful and the powerless. Studies related to community participation and empowerment through tourism may answer questions related to the distribution of power and decision making among community groups. Specific components of the problem include the need for triple bottom-line indicators and knowledge of the processes for community long-term goal identification. Theories need to be developed related to the relationship between economic motivations, social equity issues, and environmental concerns.

Future research is needed to understand better how tourism development can be a catalyst or major force for empowering a broad base of community citizens. Questions that need to be answered relate to the distribution of power, circulation and balancing mechanisms, and decision making among community groups. Greater insight is needed to explain how networks and collaboration contribute to sustainable development including an analysis of the importance of self-help networking, organization building and barriers such as residents' knowledge and skills. Studies of scale, form, and structure of collaborative work are required to identify those that provide the greatest likelihood of achieving sustainable development goals. The development of a typology of social representation in community development through tourism may also be valued.

The concept of the stakeholder in tourism as a factor in the sustainable development of a community begs the question of who or what represents the natural environment and how the social aspects of sustainable development are incorporated into the planning process. Empirical studies are needed to observe changes in the importance placed on economic versus environmental and social motivations.

More knowledge is needed related to how power is created and exchanged through social network linkages between complementary and competing organizations in various sectors of the community. Testing of the theory that the optimal network configuration is comprised of both strong and weak ties (Pavlovich, 2003) may provide useful information for achieving sustainable development goals. Additionally, more knowledge is needed concerning governance networks that develop and set policy. How do they work in the case of tourism as a development strategy? Who are their members? How is power exchanged? Further testing of the tourism relationship model can answer questions related to the effectiveness of reinvestment in destination resources.

Adaptive management models have not been fully explored in tourism research. They can reveal important information about levels of pluralism and communication, decision making, and authority, linkages and autonomy, and learning and adaptation in relation to community resilience. In the same way, studies that use the framework of Plummer and Armitage (2007) can evaluate numerous components for appraisal of specific experiences and for cross-site comparisons.

Valuable information can be gleaned from chaos theory research that reveals how tourism-related entities react and adapt to their surroundings to form new patterns. This type of research can review the self-governing boundaries and values that may lead to sustainable development goals. Models uncovered in this type of research may be able to explain the functioning system as a whole (Parry and Drost, 1995). Examination of strange attractors, the sensitive dependence on conditions effect, the law of increasing returns, and the lock-in effect will add to knowledge about patterns of tourism and can reveal how these patterns enhance or detract from sustainable development plans.

The use of complexity science to study tourism within the context of sustainable community development is advocated by McDonald (2009). His model can be used to understand the dynamic interactions in the tourism process among the components of the tourism industry, the community, government agencies, NGOs, and the natural environment. It is especially useful for studies in protected areas where natural area conservation is seen as an interactive component and an important stakeholder. The use of Gray's (1989) complex system model that includes a framework useful for analyzing problems, identifying alternative goals, and implementation may advance knowledge about how tourism impacts sustainable development programs.

Communities similar to the one in the vignette, that are considering the development of tourism as an option to replace the loss of their resource-based economic driver, need information to determine if the development of tourism would move the community toward its own sustainable development goals. Researchers are encouraged to test theories that will help the community determine if tourism would be effective in assisting their efforts to create a sustainable community. Communities need information on frameworks that would empower their citizens to create a viable industry. While there is evidence that tourism has the potential to strengthen the confidence and identity of a community and empower the people, research is needed to identify the relationships, interactions, power structures, knowledge, values, beliefs, and attitudes that lead to successful citizen participation. More research on psychological, social, economic, and political perspectives is needed to understand barriers to citizen participation as well as factors that facilitate citizen participation. Such research into the structural and cognitive aspects of power may provide insight into how tourism contributes to or detracts from sustainable community initiatives.

Communities need information on how the characteristics, interactions, and behavior of the various community and industry organizations impact their ability to implement sustainable development policies. Examinations of the dynamic processes that shape the ways communities work through networking and collaboration are critical to community leaders working on sustainable development plans that integrate public and private sector organizations, the natural environment, and the citizens. Studies that examine the architecture of social networks to reveal how relationship systems are formed, managed, and how they evolve are especially useful for tourism destination communities seeking sustainable development because of the fragmented nature of the tourism industry. An investigation of the proximity of the tourism industry to the central power structure and the interaction of tourism entities with each other and with other community entities will be valuable in determining the role tourism plays in the sustainable development process.

Communities need information about adaptive co-management frameworks that analyze conditions in comparable communities to determine conditions and outcomes that are most or least likely to lead to sustainable community development. The application of chaos theory to the study of a community's ecosystem will assist communities in determining if tourism would be a positive or negative force in the economic and social development of their community. Theoretical foundations are needed to identify and explain elements of change, including entrepreneurship that may positively or negatively impact sustainable community development plans.

Especially important for communities in protected natural areas is information about how the tourism system fits with the protected area, ecological, and community systems. Knowledge is required about roles and responsibilities within each system, factors that impact or change interactions and outcomes, and representation of the natural environment or ecological system.

Town leaders will need an understanding of how to engage the citizens in the sustainable development process, how networks operate, and how power is distributed within the community to engage a broad base of citizens in designing an adaptive management approach to very complex systems. Will the research they need to make educated decisions be available?

Questions

1. How can tourism development be a social resource?
2. Who or what should represent the natural environment in the sustainable development process?
3. What factors affect the power relationships within a community?
4. What are the implications of chaos theory for the operation of individual tourism enterprises?
5. What are the implications of chaos theory for the success of destination initiatives?

References

Amarall, L. and Ottino, J.M. (2004) Complex networks—augmenting the framework for the study of complex systems. *The European Physical Journal* 38, 147–162.

Arnstein, S.R. (1969) A ladder of citizen participation. *Journal of the American Institute of Planners* 35(4), 216–224.

Baggio, R. (2008) Symptoms of complexity in a tourism system. *Tourism Analysis* 13(1), 1–20.

Baggio, R., Scott, N. and Cooper, C. (2010) Improving tourism destination governance: a complexity science approach. *Tourism Review* 65(4), 51–60.

Beaumont, N. and Dredge, D. (2010) Local tourism governance: a comparison of three network approaches. *Journal of Sustainable Tourism* 18(1), 1–22.

Beeton, S. (2006) *Community Development through Tourism*. Landlinks Press, Collingwood, Australia.

Bramwell, B. and Sharman, A. (1999) Collaboration in local tourism policymaking. *Annals of Tourism Research* 26(2), 392–415.

Brown, L.D. (1991) Bridging organizations and sustainable development. *Human Relations* 44(8), 807–831.

Butler, R.W. (1980) The concept of a tourist area cycle of evolution: implications for management of resources. *The Canadian Geographer* 24(1), 5–12.

Butler, R. (1998) Sustainable tourism-looking backwards in order to progress. In: Hall, C.M. and Lew, A. (eds) *Sustainable Tourism: A Geographical Perspective*. Addison Wesley Longman, Harlow, UK, pp. 25–34.

Bygrave, W.D. (1993) Theory building in the entrepreneurship paradigm. *Journal of Business Venturing* 8(255), 280.

Byrd, E.T., Cardenas, D.A. and Greenwood, J.B. (2008) Factors of stakeholder understanding of tourism: The case of Eastern North Carolina. *Tourism and Hospitality Research* 8(3), 192–204.

Byrne, D. (1998) *Complexity Theory and the Social Sciences*. Routledge, London.

Cilliers, P. (1998) *Complexity and Post Modernism. Understanding Complex Systems*. Routledge, London.

Cole, S. (2006) Information and empowerment: the keys to achieving sustainable tourism. *Journal of Sustainable Tourism* 14(6), 629–644.

Coveney, P. and Highfield, R. (1995) *Frontiers of Complexity. The Search for Order in a Chaotic World*. Faber and Faber, London.

Cumming, G., Barnes, G., Perz, S., Schmink, M., Sieving, K., Southworth, J., Binford, M., Holt, R.D., Stickler, C. and Van Holt, T. (2005) An exploratory framework for the empirical measurement of resilience. *Ecosystems* 8(8), 975–987.

De Lopez, T. (2001) Stakeholder management for conservation projects: a case study of Ream National Park, Cambodia. *Environmental Management* 28(1), 47–60.

Donaldson, T. and Preston, L. (1995) The stakeholder theory of the corporation: concepts, evidence, and implications. *The Academy of Management Review* 20(1), 65–91.

Eckersley, R. (2004) *The Green State: Re-thinking Democracy and Sovereignty*. MIT Press, Cambridge, Massachusetts.

Erkus-Öztürk, H. and Eraydin, A. (2010) Environmental governance for sustainable tourism development: Collaborative networks and organisation building in the Antalya tourism region. *Tourism Management* 31(1), 113–124.

Farrell, B. and Twining-Ward, L. (2005) Reconceptualizing tourism. *Annals of Tourism Research* 31(2), 274–295.

Faulkner, B. (1998) Tourism development options in Indonesia and the case of agro-tourism in Central Java. In: Laws, E., Faulkner, B. and Moscardo, G. (eds) *Embracing and Managing Change in Tourism: International Case Studies*. Routledge, New York, pp. 202–221.

Faulkner, B. and Russell, R. (1997) Chaos and complexity in tourism: in search of a new perspective. *Pacific Tourism Review* 1, 93–102.

Flower, J. (1993) The power of chaos. *Healthcare Forum* 36(5), 48–55.

Foucault, M. (1980) *Power/Knowledge: Selected Interviews and Other Writing* 1972–77. Harvester Press, Brighton, UK.

Friedmann, J. (1992) *Empowerment: The Politics of Alternative Development*. Blackwell, Cambridge, UK.

Geldof, G.D. (1995) Adaptive water management: integrated water management on the edge of chaos. *Water Science Technology* 32(1), 7–13.

Gentner, D. (2002) Analogy in scientific discovery: the case of Johannes Kepler. In: Magnani, L. and Nersessian, N.J. (eds) *Model-Based Reasoning: Science, Technology, Values*. Kluwer Academic/Plenum Publishers, New York, pp. 21–39.

Gleick, J. (1987) *Chaos: Making a New Science*. Abacus Books, London.

Granovetter, M. (1985) Economic action and social structure: the problem of embeddedness. *American Journal of Sociology* 91, 481–510.

Granovetter, M. (1992) Problems of explanation in economic sociology. In: Nohria, N. and Eccles, R.G. (eds) *Networks and Organizations: Structure, Form and Action*. Harvard Business School Press, Boston, Massachusetts, pp. 25–56.

Gray, B. (1989) *Collaborating: Finding Common Ground for Multiparty Problems*. Jossey-Bass, San Francisco, California.

Gulati, R. (1998) Alliances and networks. *Strategic Management Journal* 19, 293–317.

Hardy, A., Beeton, R. and Pearson, L. (2002) Sustainable tourism: an overview of the concept and its position in relation to operationalisation of tourism. *Journal of Sustainable Tourism* 10(6), 475–496.

Jacobs, J. (1984) *Cities and the Wealth of Nations: Principles of Economic Life*. Random House, New York.

Jamal, T. and Jamrozy, U. (2006) Collaborative networks and partnerships for integrated destination management. In: Buhalis, D. and Costa, C. (eds) *Tourism Management Dynamics*. Elsevier, Amsterdam, the Netherlands, pp. 164–172.

Jamal, T. and Stronza, A. (2009) Collaboration theory and tourism practice in protected areas: stakeholders, structuring and sustainability. *Journal of Sustainable Tourism* 17(2), 169–189.

Johnston, B. (1992) Anthropology's role in stimulating responsible tourism. *Practicing Anthropology* 14(2), 35–38.

Jones, C., Hesterly, W.S. and Borgatti, S.P. (1997) A general theory of network governance: exchange conditions and social mechanisms. *The Academy of Management Review* 22(4), 911–945.

Krieger, M.H. (2005) A 1940 Letter of André Weil on analogy in mathematics. *Notices of the American Mathematical Society* 52(3), 334–341.

Lewin, R. (1993) *Complexity: Life on the Edge of Chaos*. Phoenix, London.

Lewis, R. and Green, S. (1998) Planning for stability and managing chaos: the case of Alpine ski resorts. In: Laws, E., Faulkner, B. and Moscardo, G. (eds) *Embracing and Managing Change in Tourism: International Case Studies*. Routledge, London, pp. 138–160.

Manidis Roberts Consultants (1997) Developing a tourism optimization management model (TOMM): a model to monitor and manage tourism on Kangaroos Island. South Australian Tourism Commission, South Australia, Adelaide.

Markey, S., Connelly, S. and Roseland, M. (2010) "Back of the Envelope": pragmatic planning for sustainable rural community development. *Planning, Practice & Research* 25(1), 1–23.

McDonald, J.R. (2009) Complexity science: an alternative world view for understanding sustainable tourism development. *Journal of Sustainable Tourism* 17, 455–471.

McKercher, B. (1999) A chaos approach to tourism. *Tourism Management* 20, 425–434.

Meyer, J.W. and Rowan, B. (1977) Institutional organizations: formal structures as myth and ceremony. *American Journal of Sociology* 80, 340–363.

Mitchell, R.K., Agle, B.R. and Wood, D.J. (1997) Toward a theory of stakeholder identification and salience: defining the principles of who and what really counts. *Academy of Management Review* 22(4), 853–886.

Moscovici, S. (1972) Society and theory in social psychology. In: Israel, J. and Tajfel, H. (eds) *The Context of Social Psychology*. Cambridge University Press, Cambridge, UK, pp. 3–69.

Murphy, P.E. (1983) Perceptions and attitudes of decision-making groups in tourism centers. *Journal of Travel Research* 21(3), 8–12.

Murphy, P.E. (1985) *Tourism, a Community Approach*. Methuen, New York.

Overman, E.S. (1996) The new science of administration: chaos and quantum theory. *Public Administration Review* 56(5), 487–491.

Parry, B. and Drost, R. (1995) Is chaos good for your profits? *International Journal of Contemporary Hospitality Management* 7(1), i–iii.

Pavlovich, K. (2003) The evolution and transformation of a tourism destination network: the Waitomo Caves, New Zealand. *Tourism Management* 24, 203–216.

Pearce, P.L. (1992) Alternative tourism: concepts, classifications and questions. In: Smith, V.L and Eadington, W.R. (eds) *Tourism Alternatives: Potentials and Problems in the Development of Tourism*. John Wiley & Sons, New York, pp. 18–40.

Pearce, P.L., Moscardo, G. and Ross, G.F. (1996) *Tourism Community Relationships*. Elsevier Science, Oxford, UK.

Pforr, C. (2006) Tourism policy in the making: an Australian network study. *Annals of Tourism Research* 33(1), 87–108.

Plummer, R. and Armitage, D. (2007) A resilience-based framework for evaluating adaptive co-management: linking ecology, economics and society in a complex world. *Ecological Economics* 61, 62–74.

Prigogine, I. and Stengers, I. (1985) *Order Out of Chaos. Man's New Dialogue with Nature*. Flamingo, London.

Reynolds, P. and Braithwaite, D. (2001) Towards a conceptual framework for wildlife tourism. *Tourism Management* 22, 31–42.

Roberts, L. and Simpson, F. (1999) Developing partnership approaches to tourism in Central and Eastern Europe. *Journal of Sustainable Tourism* 7(3–4), 314–330.

Ross, S. and Wall, G. (1999) Ecotourism: towards congruence between theory and practice. *Tourism Management* 20, 123–132.

Russell, R. and Faulkner, B. (1999) Movers and shakers: chaos makers in tourism development. *Tourism Management* 20, 411–423.

Saarinen, J. (2006) Traditions of sustainability in tourism studies. *Annals of Tourism Research* 33(4), 1121–1140.

Scheyvens, R. (1999) Ecotourism and the empowerment of local communities. *Tourism Management* 20, 245–249.

Selin, S.W. (1993) Collaborative alliances: new interorganizational forms in tourism. *Journal of Travel and Tourism Marketing* 2(2), 217–227.

Shikida, A., Yoda, M., Kino, A. and Morishige, M. (2010) Tourism relationship model and intermediary for sustainable tourism management: case study of the Kiritappu Wetland Trust in Hamanaka, Hokkaido. *Tourism and Hospitality Research* 10(2), 105–115.

Sofield, T. (2003) *Empowerment for Sustainable Tourism Development*. Pergamon, Oxford, UK.

Stevenson, H. and Harmeling, S. (1990) Entrepreneurial management's need for a more "chaotic" theory. *Journal of Business Venturing* 5, 1–14.

Storey, D.J. (1994) *Understanding the Small Business Sector*. Routledge, London.

Svyantek, D.J. and DeShon, R.P. (1993) Organisational attractors: a chaos theory explanation of why cultural change efforts often fail. *Public Administration Quarterly* 17(3), 339–355.

Swain, M. (1990) Commoditizing ethnicity in Southwest China. *Cultural Survival Quarterly* 14(1), 26–9.

Timur, S. and Getz, D. (2007) A network perspective on managing stakeholders for sustainable urban tourism. *International Journal of Contemporary Hospitality Management* 20(4), 445–461.

Waldrop, M.M. (1992) *Complexity. The Emerging Science at the Edge of Order and Chaos*. Penguin Books, London.

Walsh, J., Jamrozy, U. and Burr, S. (2001) Sense of place as a component of sustainable tourism marketing. In: McCooll, S. and Moisey, R.N. (eds) *Tourism, Recreation and Sustainability. Linking Culture and the Environment*. CAB International, Wallingford, UK.

Ward, J., Hughey, K. and Urlich, S. (2002) A framework for managing the biophysical effects of tourism on the natural environment in New Zealand. *Journal of Sustainable Tourism* 10(3), 239–259.

Wasserman, S. and Faust, K. (1994) *Social Network Analysis: Methods and Applications*. Cambridge, New York.

Wearing, S.L., Wearing, M. and McDonald, M. (2010) Understanding local power and interactional processes in sustainable tourism: exploring village-tour operator relations on the Kokoda Track, Papua New Guinea. *Journal of Sustainable Tourism* 18(1), 61–67.

Wight, P. (1993) Sustainable ecotourism: balancing economic, environmental and social goals within an ethical framework. *Journal of Tourism Studies* 4(2), 54–65.

Wigner, E.P. (1960) The unreasonable effectiveness of mathematics in the natural sciences. *Communications in Pure and Applied Mathematics* 13(1), 1–14.

World Commission on Environment and Development (WCED) (1987) *Our Common Future*. Oxford University Press, Oxford, UK.

C. Jurowski

12 Theoretical Perspectives on Identity and Culture

YVETTE REISINGER*

College of Business Administration, Gulf University for Science and Technology, Mishref, Kuwait

The Objectives

The purpose of this chapter is to examine selected cultural theories and to explore their applications in tourism research. The objectives are to:

1. Define cultural theories such as cultural diversity, culture contact, culture shock, acculturation, acculturative stress, cultural adaptation and assimilation.
2. Explain how cultural theories in this chapter help us to research and better understand tourism behavior.
3. Suggest topics and approaches for further theoretical inquiry.

The Vignette

In the last decades people of different nationalities and cultural background have been traveling extensively around the world experiencing distinct lifestyles, cultural traditions, and customs. To illustrate difficulties travelers experience in different cultures one can take an example of a Western visitor to the Middle East. While on a short business trip the visitor planned to spend his time off work on dining, shopping, and sightseeing.

The first day, on the way from the airport to a hotel, the taxi driver demanded from the visitor a significantly higher fare than was shown on the taxi meter. When the visitor refused to pay, the taxi driver swore at him and drove away. In the hotel, there were no tea and coffee facilities and/or a mini-bar. There were no toiletries in the bathroom either. Despite being tired the visitor decided to go to a local shop to buy soap and shampoo. It was late at night and he did not know where to go. When he asked pedestrians about the shop where he could make his purchase he received wrong information; everyone was giving him different directions. Because he was thirsty and hungry he gave up on looking for the shop and decided to dine out in a local restaurant. In the restaurant he did not know what to order: the menu was in Arabic and a waiter did not speak English. The visitor ordered the food recommended by other patrons. He waited for his meal a long time. He did not feel comfortable; everyone around him smoked cigarettes. He could not understand why people smoked in a

*Corresponding author, e-mail: reisinger.y@gust.edu.kw

public area. While he was having his meal the waiter brought the bill that was higher than expected. He asked the waiter to recalculate the bill. He was disappointed with the service. He craved for the comfort of his home.

The second day, the visitor went shopping in a local market. He planned to buy a scarf for his wife. The seller's price was US$45. The visitor noticed that at other stores people bought the same scarf for only US$20. He learned he should bargain and buy the scarf cheaper. The seller agreed to sell the scarf for US$25. Next day the visitor saw the same scarf for US$10 in another local market; he felt cheated and exploited. As a result, he decided not to go for sightseeing next day. He stayed in the hotel room after his work for the next 2 days. Upon coming back home he told his friends he would not go back to the same place, and would not recommend it to his friends.

The Context

This chapter examines the selected cultural theories in the context of the increasing cultural diversity around the world. Cultural diversity offers an opportunity for culture contact that in many cases is characterized by difficulties with understanding and communicating with culturally different "others." The feelings of experiencing culture shock, as one of the major difficulties encountered by individuals in culture contact, are discussed. Strategies to be used to minimize or even eliminate these difficulties, such as acculturation, adaptation, and assimilation are examined.

The Theory

Cultural diversity

The theory of cultural diversity was developed based on the sociological concept of differentiation. Luhmann (1977) claimed that society is a self-differentiating system that creates subsystems to control a complex environment. The more differentiation is available in a society, the better the selection and a response to the environment (Ritzer, 2007). However, differentiation can also cause a problem for the social system and even lead to its breakdown (Ritzer, 2007).

Cultural differentiation is often referred to as cultural diversity and, in particular: (i) a variety of cultures and subcultures in a given society, region, or in the world; (ii) a mosaic of individuals and groups with different cultural backgrounds; (iii) differences in race, ethnicity, nationality, languages; and (iv) a variety of social structures and belief systems. Today, the populations of many developed countries (e.g. Australia, Canada, and the USA) are culturally diverse due in part to individuals immigrating to these countries.

Cultural diversity acknowledges, accepts, and values differences and the various ways that people live and interact in the world. Supporters believe that cultural diversity is beneficial to the society because every culture significantly contributes to its history and economy. For example, the USA have been very successful because of the contributions of many diverse groups to the social, economic, and cultural values of US society. According to UNESCO, cultural diversity is a source of exchange, innovation, creativity, and development; a vector of identity, value, and meanings; and a

Y. Reisinger

means to sustainable development that is capable of humanizing globalization (UNESCO, 2007). Therefore, cultural diversity is vital for the success of a society and long-term human survival. The more culturally diverse is the society, the more successful the society as a whole. However, critics argue that the complexity of cultural diversity can create social, cultural, and economic problems in the social system.

The increasing culturally diverse ethnic populations around the world represent a significant tourism potential (as a tourist market and workforce) with large purchasing power. It is important that future research studies investigate cultural differences among various ethnic groups, especially in their behavior, communication style, experiences, technology use, and leisure and tourism needs. It is important to examine the impacts of cultural diversity on destination marketing and management, and tourism sustainability. Research studies should also explore the appropriate ways to deal with cultural diversity for tourism purposes.

Culture contact

Culture contact refers to contact between culturally different people who behave differently, use different communication styles, and speak different languages. According to Reisinger (2009), cultural differences inhibit cultural contact because they negatively affect mutual attraction and liking. Large cultural dissimilarity among the contact participants can lead to misunderstanding, culture shock, and even hostility and conflict. Misunderstanding occurs because the contact participants are not on the same wavelength; the meanings of their behavior and messages sent during conversations are not the same. Instead of understanding, participants experience frustration, anger, and social barriers. Cultural stereotypes and prejudices develop and cultural tension arises. Culture contact with culturally different "others" creates physical, emotional, and psychological problems that result from the inability to cope with difficulties experienced during this contact in a new culture (Oberg, 1960; Bochner, 1982). Pearce (1982, 1988) analyzed contact between tourists and hosts from different cultures and noted that it can create tension due to cultural differences.

However, according to Moufakkir (2011), cultural dissimilarity can attract people to each other and result in satisfying interaction. In his study of Asian and German tourists' perceptions by Dutch tourism workers, Dutch respondents expressed positive feelings toward Asian tourists, despite cultural distance, and negative feelings toward German tourists, despite cultural proximity. Chan (2006) found Vietnamese working tourists were irritated by the behavior of Chinese tourists visiting Vietnam, despite cultural proximity. In order to reduce the potential difficulties experienced in a culture contact, cultural brokers or mediators, such as tour guides, can be used to mediate and interpret participants' cultural experiences (Ap and Wong, 2001). However, interpretation of cultural experiences might not be popular in authentic tourism because the interpreted experiences are of little assistance in searching for meaning and reflecting on the real world being experienced. The explanations represent the world as the interpretation deems appropriate (Reisinger and Steiner, 2006).

In tourism, culture contact has been examined frequently, especially its nature (Sutton, 1967; DeKadt, 1979; Van der Berghe, 1980; Van Den Berghe and Keyes, 1984; Cohen and Cooper, 1986; Jafari, 1989), types (Sutton, 1967), the spatial, temporal, communicative, and cultural contexts (Festinger and Kelly, 1951; Triandis, 1977;

Bochner, 1982; Gudykunst and Kim, 1997), degree of inter-culturalness (Kim and Gudykunst, 1988; Samovar and Porter, 1991; Reisinger, 2009), and difficulties experienced (Pearce, 1982, 1988; Reisinger, 2009).

As the world becomes more interconnected, future global tourism will be characterized by increasing culture contact. It is important to examine the difficulties experienced in a culture contact and strategies that can be used to minimize or even eliminate these difficulties. Eliminating difficulties in cultural contact will depend upon understanding culturally different "others" and paying more attention to cultural differences in their behavior and identities.

Culture shock

Culture shock is one of the difficulties experienced by individuals in the unfamiliar cultural environment. Culture shock is experienced when individuals feel they are unable to cope with the difficulties faced in a new cultural environment, such as different language spoken, different food or hygiene standards, and different ways of thinking and doing things. The individuals do not know how to behave and react (Reisinger, 2009). Those who experience culture shock often feel disoriented, depressed, rejected, emotionally and intellectually withdrawn, frustrated, helpless, scared, incompetent, angry and lonely, and have a sense of loss.

Distinct stages of culture shock determine how the individual feels and reacts. For example, at the first *honeymoon* stage an individual is excited and optimistic; she or he treats all cultural encounters as a means of learning. At the *hostility* stage an individual becomes annoyed and irritated by foreign customs and rules, and often feels disinterested and even hostile toward the new environment. Those who are not willing to adjust to a new culture are home sick. At the *recovery* stage an individual learns how to cope in the foreign environment and begins to understand new ways of life. At the final *adjustment* stage an individual accepts and enjoys the new cultural environment (Oberg, 1960). Similar patterns of culture shock (initial optimism, subsequent disappointment, adaptation, gradual recovery) were identified by Gullahorn and Gullahorn (1963). Hofstede (1997) also identified different stages of culture shock and feelings of those who travel to a foreign culture. During the *euphoria* phase individuals have pleasant experiences, feel excitement about traveling and seeing new places, whereas during the *culture shock* phase individuals experience difficulties with living in a new cultural environment.

Different types of culture shock were distinguished, such as role shock (Byrnes, 1966), language shock (Smalley, 1963), culture fatigue (Taft, 1977), transition shock (Bennett, 1977), and re-entry (return home) with reverse culture shock and readjustment upon return home (Gullahorn and Gullahorn, 1963; Trifonovitch, 1977). The type of culture shock experienced depends on the difficulties encountered in the foreign environment, ability to adjust, cultural knowledge, motivation, past travel experience, and the length of stay in a foreign country. Some visitors to a new culture may never experience culture shock (e.g. if their stay is short or if they are familiar with the culture visited). Others may experience only the excitement stage, while many may feel confused. Those who visit a large number of foreign cultures in a short time can be in constant culture shock (Taft, 1977) because they are exposed to many new cultural environments and have little opportunity to adapt to each new culture. Also,

Y. Reisinger

those who seek a more direct contact with locals and their culture can experience more culture shock. Those with good cultural knowledge and communication skills can easier cope with culture shock, however they may find it difficult to adjust in a foreign culture if their stay is prolonged. Having friends in a foreign culture, using services of a foreign tour guide, or traveling in a group can help to reduce the impact of culture shock. Further, individuals who go abroad for an extended period of time can experience a reverse culture shock upon returning home. They may feel disoriented, confused, and intimidated by the home environment and not willing to adjust back to their original culture.

Culture shock and reverse shock are extremely important influences on human behavior that offer very useful learning experience. By experiencing both types of shock an individual can gain a better insight into the home and visited culture and become more culturally aware of oneself and others, and sensitive. As a result, the individual can develop a better perspective on life and the world and become more culturally effective.

In tourism, culture shock is one of the most recognized difficulties encountered by travelers in a foreign culture. Tourists experience culture shock when they travel to a foreign country and do not have adequate knowledge of that country. Tourists can experience many types of culture shock and its symptoms, especially when they frequently change destinations. As the world becomes more global and people travel more, it is important to examine various types of culture shock that travelers can encounter in a foreign culture, its stages, and symptoms. It is possible that different types of culture shock can be experienced in different destinations and thus different strategies need to be adopted to reduce the symptoms of culture shock. Also, since the differences *between* cultures are decreasing and the differences *within* cultures are increasing (Reisinger and Crotts, 2010), a question arises whether future culture contacts will lead to more or less culture shock and reverse shock, and what factors will cause both shocks when one travels between cultures versus within cultures.

Acculturation

Acculturation is the outcome of continuous contact between individuals from different cultures that results in changes in the original culture patterns of these individuals (Redfield *et al.*, 1936). Acculturation is "a long-term process in which individuals modify or abandon certain aspects of their original culture as they adopt patterns of the new (adopted) culture" (Park *et al.*, 2003: 142) and incorporate the values of their host culture into their own norms and lifestyles (Sasidharan *et al.*, 2005). As a result, the person becomes more culturally diverse and better understands others.

Berry (1997) distinguished between an individual's acculturation and a group (society) acculturation. An individual's acculturation, also called psychological acculturation, occurs at the individual level and involves the changes to an individual's psychological make-up and physical well-being, whereas a group acculturation occurs at the group level and involves changes to groups' culture, customs, social institutions, food, clothing, and languages (Sam and Berry, 2010). Acculturation varies depending on migration status, length of residency, social affiliations, language preferences and proficiency, cultural identity (Magnini, 2003), and a person's personality and their worldview (Kramer, 1992, 1997, 2003). For example, the outgoing individuals with strong self-esteem and a sense of identity are more resilient to influences of a foreign culture, whereas introvert individuals with low self-confidence and weak sense of identity are more prone to influences of a foreign environment (Kramer, 1992, 1997, 2003).

An individual can be placed along a continuum from low to high acculturation with the dominant host culture (Meridith *et al.*, 2000). When visiting a foreign culture an individual may either follow their own original culture (and be lowly acculturated in the host culture) or new culture patterns (and become highly acculturated to the host culture) (Ryder *et al.*, 2000). Hofstede (1997) explained that individuals acculturate with a new culture when they learn how to deal with a stress caused by a foreign cultural environment. Individuals can either: (i) remain negative toward a new environment and reject it; (ii) consider themselves as being bicultural; or (iii) remain positive toward the new environment and accept it. According to Berry (1997), an individual can: (i) retain or reject their own native culture; or (ii) adopt or reject the dominant host culture. Thomas and Znaniecki (1919) distinguished among three forms of acculturation corresponding to three personality types: Bohemian (one adopts the new culture and abandons original culture), Philistine (one rejects the new culture and follows original culture), and Creative-Type (one adapts to the new culture and preserves original culture).

The acculturation process transforms the individual into an individual being more culturally diverse (bicultural or multicultural), with multiple cultural identities (Ryder *et al.*, 2000). The acculturation process also transforms the host culture into a multicultural society (Mitchell, 2006). There are four major strategies that are used by individuals in the multicultural society: (i) assimilation (individuals adopt the host culture over their original culture); (ii) separation (individuals reject the host culture and preserve their original culture; they resist acculturation); (iii) integration (individuals adopt some aspects of the host culture and hold on to their original culture; they become bicultural); and (iv) marginalization (individuals reject both the culture of origin and the dominant host culture) (Berry, 1980, 2003). Assimilation strategy is used in a melting pot society, which promotes a homogeneous dominant culture where everyone adopts the host culture. A separation strategy is endorsed in a segregationist society, in which people are separated into racial groups. Integrationist strategy is used in a multicultural society, in which multiple cultures are appreciated and integrated. Finally, marginalization strategy is adopted in societies that promote cultural exclusion (Berry, 1980, 2003). In today's global society, minority groups identify themselves as unique groups of people with their own cultural values and norms that form a society described as a salad bowl rather than a melting pot where minority groups fully assimilate with the host culture (Berry, 1997).

The research in the area of acculturation mostly focuses on the changes experienced by the minority groups, such as immigrants, refugees, and indigenous peoples, as a result of their contact with the dominant culture of majority. In tourism, relatively little research has been done on acculturation. The exception is the study by Reisinger and Crotts (2012), who examined the acculturation process of foreign-born US residents. The study results showed that acculturation of the Korean born residents of the USA occurred, as measured by language preferences and Hofstede's (2001) national cultural instruments, but only to a limited extent. The authors concluded that tourism marketers should consider foreign-born residents as a unique market segment that needs to be explored. The children of the immigrant parents and their children's children should also be studied as they can show higher degrees of acculturation, and be more selective of which aspects of their own cultural heritage they will hold on to.

Acculturative stress

The acculturation process is accompanied by acculturation stress. Acculturative stress refers to the psychological and social difficulties experienced as a result of culture contact. Some scholars called acculturative stress a "psychic conflict" that develops from conflicting cultural norms (Redfield *et al.*, 1936: 152). Every culture contact between individuals from different cultures generates stress (Ward, 2001). Acculturative stress is part of culture shock. According to Berry (1980), acculturative stress is a fundamental psychological force in acculturative processes. Acculturative stress represents a significant problem for minority groups (Ausubel, 1960; Berry *et al.*, 1987; Burnam *et al.*, 1987; Hovey, 2000).

In tourism, both tourists and locals experience acculturative stress as a result of culture contact with culturally different others. According to Doxey (1976), although initially locals welcome tourists and are excited about their presence (*euphoria stage*) they become indifferent towards them (*apathy stage*) when the number of newcomers increases, and may experience irritation and even antagonism toward tourists (*irritation or annoyance stage*) when the number of tourists reaches the maximum, and eventually may become hostile toward tourists (*hostility stage*) when cultural rules are being broken and locals blame visitors for crime, violence, or rising prices. Since no related studies on acculturative stress have been done in tourism, it is recommended to examine acculturative stress experienced by tourists and locals as a result of their culture contact.

Cultural adaptation

Cultural adaptation occurs during the process of acculturation. According to the intercultural adaptation theory (IAT) (Gudykunst and Kim, 2003), cultural adaptation is the process through which individuals in cross-cultural situations adjust their behavior to reduce misunderstanding and facilitate positive cultural interactions. According to Ellingsworth (1988), individuals adapt to a new cultural environment when they are motivated to achieve certain goals, and have social status and power. The more people are motivated and the more power they have, the more they adapt, and change their behavior and perceptions of themselves and others.

The cultural adaptation process involves the cultural re-integration and disintegration of the individual (Gudykunst and Kim, 2003). In the process of cultural adaptation an individual must culturally re-integrate in order to behave, think, and feel as locals of a foreign culture. The individual must also culturally disintegrate to unlearn their own original culture and deculturalize. Those who fail to deculturalize and unlearn their original culture can never perceive the world correctly (Gudykunst and Kim, 2003). Many immigrants or migrants are unsuccessful in a foreign culture because they are unwilling to deculturalize and unlearn their original culture, which often leads to cultural conflict and even aggression toward the host culture. Some individuals may have a personality that does not allow for deculturalization, whereas others may have the personality type that allows them to adapt (Gudykunst and Kim, 2003).

According to Gudykunst and Kim (2003), cultural adaptation is an "upward-forward progress" during which an individual abandons their own cultural patterns and conforms to behavioral patterns of the dominant culture. During this process an individual becomes more mature, knowledgeable, integrated, emotionally balanced, psychologically grown up, and developed. Adaptation to the dominant host culture is the only way to fit into a new culture, or otherwise an individual will be regarded incompetent and immature, and "functionally unfit" (Gudykunst and Kim, 2003). During the cultural adaptation process an individual undergoes a personal cultural transformation; s/he becomes an "intercultural person" or "universal person" with "transcultural identity," and is more culturally aware, sensitive, and competent. Personal transformation during the cultural adaptation process is the ultimate solution to intercultural misunderstanding and cultural conflict (Gudykunst and Kim, 2003).

However, according to the dimensional accrual and dissociation (DAD) theory (Kramer, 2000, 2003, 2009), cultural adaptation does not mean "progress" or moving "upward-forward," as suggested by Gudykunst and Kim (2003); individuals do not have to conform and deculturalize to become culturally adapted and competent. The most competent and successful people are those who can innovate and create something new. According to the cultural fusion theory (Kramer, 2000, 2010, 2011), innovation can be achieved through fusion and integration of cultural elements. Individuals should learn and integrate the new cultural patterns to develop and enrich themselves, and form new identities.

Kramer's DAD theory also postulates that cultural differences must be accepted and integrated in the acculturation process because they affect communication styles, meaning, and identity. When cultural differences are not accepted or even eliminated and everyone conforms to another culture, then identity, meaning, and communication cease to exist. According to the co-evolution theory (Kramer, 2009), in intercultural situations both sides have to accept cultural differences and adjust to each other's behavior. Forcing only newcomers to adapt to cultural patterns of locals can make them stressed out and psychologically imbalanced (Festinger, 1957; Festinger and Carlsmith, 1959) and thus lead to resistance to change.

Cultural assimilation

Cultural assimilation is the higher degree of adaptation (Gudykunst and Kim, 1984, 1997, 2003), and is the final goal of acculturation and adaptation. It is a process in which individuals or groups of different cultural background or ethnicity fully assimilate or integrate themselves into a new country by replacing their original home culture with their new culture. The process can be very long and may be never complete because most individuals try to maintain preferences for own cultural values, religion, or language. The study by Reisinger and Crotts (2012) showed that Korean born residents of the US only partially assimilated into US society.

Although it is debatable whether it is desirable for individuals visiting a new culture to fully assimilate, the concept of assimilation must be analyzed for the tourism purpose. This is because foreign-born residents represent a viable tourist market. They not only increase inbound tourism (because they invite friends and relatives to visit the host country) and outbound tourism (because they return to their home country for short visits), but also promote their new country as a tourism destination when traveling back to their home country. In addition, they develop business links with partners in the country of their birth and promote business tourism (Seetaram, 2008). For these reasons, future tourism studies should examine the process of assimilation of newcomers, especially how their socioeconomic status, geographical concentration, residential patterns, language attainment, travel motivation, intermarriage, naturalization, and access to leisure and travel affect the process of their assimilation into a new environment.

The Future

Future studies should examine the acculturation process of both long-term travelers and foreign-born residents and the degree to which they adjust to another culture. Those who stay in a foreign culture for an extended period of time and/or have frequent culture contacts with different "others" may be more acculturated even though they may maintain a strong preference for their native language and values.

Since acculturation is a two-way process that entails a change of tourists (who adopt habits and language patterns of the locals) and a change of locals (who adopt cultural patterns of tourists, especially in popular destinations with a high number of tourists), future studies should focus on acculturation patterns of different international tourist markets and groups of the local community (e.g. hotel managers, restaurateurs, shop assistants). The effects of demographics and psychographics, especially personality and motivation, on the acculturation patterns of tourists and locals need to be explored. Other factors that may show how well tourists adapt to local behavioral patterns and how well locals adapt to tourist behavioral patterns, in specific destinations, must also be studied. These factors include the languages spoken, their proficiency and usage; values placed on maintaining cultural origin versus learning about other cultures; attitudes to intercultural contact and socialization; intercultural interaction patterns; relationships maintained with the country of origin; cultural custom and tradition choices practiced at home (e.g. culinary and dress preferences); and lifestyle of particular cultural groups (e.g. dietary habits, physical activity patterns).

Questions

1. What factors influence the increasing cultural diversity around the world?
2. Should international tourists adapt to cultural traditions and customs of locals at tourism destinations?
3. Should locals of tourism destinations adapt to cultural traditions and customs of international tourists?
4. What factors facilitate international understanding among people from different cultures?
5. Does international tourism contribute to international understanding and peace or increased conflict and violence?
6. What strategies would you apply to facilitate adaptation of newcomers to foreign cultures and reduce their cultural stress?

References

Ap, J. and Wong, K. (2001) Case study on tour guiding: professionalism, issues and problems. *Tourism Management* 22(5), 551–563.

Ausubel, D. (1960) Acculturative stress in modern Maori adolescence. *Child Development* 31(4), 617–631.

Bennett, J. (1977) Transition shock: putting culture shock in perspective. In: Jain, N. (ed.) *International and Intercultural Communication Annual*, Vol. 4. Speech Communication Association, Falls Church, Virginia, pp. 45–52.

Berry, J. (1980) Social and cultural change. In: Triandis, H. and Brislin, R. (eds) *Handbook of Cross-Cultural Psychology: Social Psychology*. Allyn and Bacon, Boston, Massachusetts, pp. 211–279.

Berry, J. (1997) Immigration, acculturation and adaptation. *Applied Psychology: An International Review* 46(1), 5–68.

Berry, J. (2003) Conceptual approaches to acculturation. In: Chun, K., Balls-Organista, P. and Marin, G. (eds) *Acculturation: Advances in Theory, Measurement and Applied Research*. American Psychological Association, Washington, DC, pp. 17–37.

Berry, J., Kim, U., Minde, T. and Mok, D. (1987) Comparative studies of acculturative stress. *International Migration Review* 21, 491–511.

Bochner, S. (1982) *Cultures in Contact: Studies in Cross-Cultural Interaction*. Pergamon Press, New York.

Burnam, M., Hough, R., Karno, M., Escobar, J. and Telles, C. (1987) Acculturation and lifetime prevalence of psychiatric disorders among Mexican Americans in Los Angeles. *Journal of Health and Social Behavior* 28, 89–102.

Byrnes, F. (1966) Role shock: An occupational hazard of American technical assistants abroad. *Annals of the American Academy of Political and Social Science* 368(1), 95–108.

Chan, Y. (2006) Coming of age of the Chinese tourists: the emergence of non-Western tourism and host–guest interactions in Vietnam's border tourism. *Tourist Studies* 6(3), 187–213.

Cohen, E. and Cooper, R. (1986) Language and tourism. *Annals of Tourism Research* 13(4), 533–563.

DeKadt, E. (1979) *Tourism: Passport to Development? Perspectives on the Social and Cultural Effects in Developing Countries*. Oxford University Press, London.

Doxey, G. (1976) A causation theory of visitor-resident irritants, methodology, and research inferences. *6th Annual Conference Proceedings of the Travel and Tourism Research Association: The Impact of Tourism*, San Diego, California, pp. 195–198.

Ellingsworth, H. (1988) A theory of adaptation in intercultural dyads. In: Kim, Y. and Gudykunst, W. (eds) *Theories in Intercultural Communication*. Sage, Newbury Park, California, pp. 259–279.

Festinger, L. (1957) *A Theory of Cognitive Dissonance.* Stanford University Press, California.

Festinger, L. and Carlsmith, J. (1959) Cognitive consequences of forced compliance. *Journal of Abnormal and Social Psychology* 58(2), 203–210.

Festinger, L. and Kelly, H. (1951) *Changing Attitudes through Social Contact*. University of Michigan, Institute for Social Research, Ann Arbor, Michigan.

Gudykunst, W. and Kim, Y. (1984) *Communicating with Strangers. An Approach to Intercultural Communication*. Addison-Wesley, Reading, Massachusetts.

Gudykunst, W. and Kim, Y. (1997) *Communicating with Strangers: An Approach to Intercultural Communication*, 3rd edn. McGraw-Hill, Boston, Massachusetts.

Gudykunst, W. and Kim, Y. (2003) *Communicating with Strangers: An Approach to Intercultural Communication*, 4th edn. McGraw-Hill, New York.

Gullahorn, J. and Gullahorn, J. (1963) An extension of the U-curve hypothesis. *Journal of Social Issues* 19(3), 33–47.

Y. Reisinger

Hofstede, G. (1997) *Cultures and Organizations. Software of the Mind*. McGraw-Hill International, New York.

Hofstede, G. (2001) *Culture's Consequences: Comparing Values, Behaviors, Institutions and Organizations across Nations*, 3rd edn. Sage Publications, Thousand Oaks, California.

Hovey, J. (2000) Acculturative stress, depression, and suicidal ideation in Mexican immigrants. *Culture Diversity and Ethnic Minority Psychology* 6(2), 134–151.

Jafari, J. (1989) Socio-cultural dimensions of tourism: an English language literature review. In: Bystrzanowski, J. (ed.) *Tourism as a Factor of Change: A Socio-Cultural Study*. European Coordination Centre for Research and Documentation in Social Sciences, Vienna, pp. 17–60.

Kim, Y. and Gudykunst, W. (1988) *Theories in Intercultural Communication. International and Intercultural Communication Annual*, Vol. 12. Sage Publications, Newbury Park, California.

Kramer, E. (1992) Consciousness and culture. In: Kramer, E. (ed.) *Consciousness and Culture: An Introduction to the Thought of Jean Gebser*. Greenwood, Westport, Connecticut, pp. 1–60.

Kramer, E. (1997) *Modern/Postmodern: Off the Beaten Path of Antimodernism*. Praeger, Westport, Connecticut.

Kramer, E. (2000) Cultural fusion and the defense of difference. In: Asante, M. and Min, J. (eds) *Socio-cultural Conflict between African and Korean*. University Press of America, New York, pp. 182–223.

Kramer, E. (2003) *The Emerging Monoculture: Assimilation and the Model Minority*. Praeger, Westport, Connecticut.

Kramer, E. (2009) Theoretical reflections on intercultural studies: preface. In: Croucher, S. (ed.) *Looking Beyond the Hijab*. Cresskill, Hampton, New Jersey, pp. ix–xxxix.

Kramer, E. (2010) Immigration. In: Jackson, R. II (ed.) *Encyclopedia of Identity*. Sage, Thousand Oaks, California, pp. 384–389.

Kramer, E. (2011) Preface. In: Croucher, S. and Cronn-Mills D. (eds) *Religious Misperceptions: The Case of Muslims and Christians in France and Britain.* Hampton Press, Cresskill, New Jersey, pp. vii–xxxii.

Luhmann, N. (1977) Differentiation of society. *Canadian Journal of Sociology* 2, 29–53.

Magnini, V. (2003) A look at changing acculturation patterns in the United States and implications for the hospitality industry. *Journal of Human Resources in Hospitality and Tourism* 2(2), 57–74.

Meridith, S., Wenger, N., Liu, H., Harada, N. and Khan, K. (2000) Development of a brief scale to measure acculturation among Japanese Americans. *Journal of Community Psychology* 28(2), 103–113.

Mitchell, J. (2006) Food acceptance and acculturation. *Journal of Foodservice* 17(1), 77–83.

Moufakkir, O. (2011) The role of cultural distance in mediating the host gaze. *Tourist Studies* 11(1), 73–89.

Oberg, K. (1960) Culture shock: adjustment to new cultural environments. *Practical Anthropology* 7, 177–182.

Park, S., Park, H., Skinner, J., Ok, S. and Spindler, A. (2003) Mother's acculturation and eating behaviors of Korean American families in California. *Journal of Nutritional Education Behavior* 35(May–June), 142–147.

Pearce, P. (1982) *The Social Psychology of Tourist Behavior. International Series in Experimental Social Psychology*, Vol. 3. Pergamon Press, New York.

Pearce, P. (1988) *The Ulysses Factor: Evaluating Visitors in Tourist Settings*. Springer-Verlag, New York.

Redfield, R., Linton, R. and Herskovits, M. (1936) Memorandum for the study of acculturation. *American Anthropologist* 38, 149–152.

Reisinger, Y. (2009) *International Tourism: Cultures and Behavior*. Butterworth-Heinemann/Elsevier, Burlington, Massachusetts.

Reisinger, Y. and Crotts, J. (2010) Applying Hofstede's national culture measures in tourism research: illuminating issues of divergence and convergence. *Journal of Travel Research* 49(2), 153–164.

Reisinger, Y. and Crotts, J. (2012) An exploration of the flipside of international marketing: the acculturation of foreign born residents of the US. *Tourism Review* 67(1), 42–50.

Reisinger, Y. and Steiner, C. (2006) Reconceptualising interpretation: the role of tour guides in authentic tourism. *Current Issues in Tourism* 9(6), 481–498.

Ritzer, G. (2007) *Contemporary Sociological Theory and Its Classical Roots. The Basics*, 2nd edn. McGraw-Hill, New York.

Ryder, A., Alden, L. and Paulhus, D. (2000) Is acculturation unidimensional or bidimensional? A head to head comparison in the prediction of personality, self-identity, and adjustment. *Journal of Personality and Social Psychology* 79(1), 49–65.

Sam, D. and Berry, J. (2010) Acculturation: when individuals and groups of different cultural backgrounds meet. *Perspectives on Psychological Science* 5(4), 472–481.

Samovar, L. and Porter, R. (1991) *Communication between Cultures*. Wadsworth Publishing Company, Belmont, California.

Sasidharan, V., Willits, F. and Godbey, G. (2005) Cultural differences in urban recreation patterns: an examination of park usage and activity participation across six population subgroups. *Managing Leisure* 10(1), 19–38.

Seetaram, N. (2008) Where bloody hell are we? Immigration and tourism demand: Evidence from Australia (1992–2006). CAUTHE 2008 Conference, Gold Coast, Australia, 11–14 February.

Smalley, W. (1963) Culture shock, language shock, and the shock of self-discovery. *Practical Anthropology* 10, 49–56.

Sutton, W. (1967) Travel and understanding: notes on the social structure of touring. *International Journal of Comparative Sociology* 8(2), 218–223.

Taft, R. (1977) Coping with unfamiliar cultures. In: Warren, N. (ed.) *Studies in Cross-Cultural Psychology 1*. Academic Press, London, pp. 121–151.

Thomas, W. and Znaniecki, F. (1919) *The Polish Peasant in Europe and America, Monograph of an Immigrant Group.* University of Chicago Press, Chicago, Illinois.

Triandis, H. (1977) *Interpersonal Behavior*. Brooks/Cole Publishing Company, Monterey, California.

Trifonovitch, G. (1977) Culture learning/culture teaching. *Educational Perspectives* 16(4), 18–22.

UNESCO (2007) Universal Declaration on Cultural Diversity. Available at: http://www.unesco.org/shs/most (accessed 13 December 2013).

Van den Berghe, P. (1980) Tourism as ethic relations: a case study of Cuzco, Peru. *Ethnic and Racial Studies* 3(4), 375–392.

Van den Berghe, P. and Keyes, C. (1984) Introduction: tourism and re-created ethnicity. *Annals of Tourism Research* 11(3), 343–352.

Ward, C. (2001) The A, B, Cs of acculturation. In: Matsumoto, D. (ed.) *The Handbook of Culture and Psychology*. Oxford University Press, Oxford, UK, pp. 411–445.

13 Theoretical Perspectives on Place Perceptions

Laurlyn K. Harmon*

*Department of Recreation Management & Therapeutic Recreation
University of Wisconsin—La Crosse, La Crosse, Wisconsin*

Objectives

1. Understand the historical development of studying place-related constructs.
2. Explain how place perceptions can relate to personal identity development.
3. Describe the evolution and associated challenges of measuring place.
4. Identify and explain potential antecedents and outcomes relevant to the study of place.
5. Develop and explain possible applications of place-related research to tourism models and practice.

The Vignette

Four friends embark on a lifetime adventure—a trip to the Fijian Islands. Two women, one from the Midwestern USA and one from southern Germany, and two men, one from the north-eastern USA and one from Taiwan, originally traveling together as part of a university international study program in Australia, decide to continue their travels in Fiji after their study program. As tourists, they take two day-trips with Rivers Fiji—one down the Luva River in an inflatable kayak, and one down the Upper Navua in a whitewater raft. Both trips combine the adventure of whitewater with floating opportunities allowing our four tourists to enjoy the cultural, historical, and natural heritage of the island nation. They explore waterfalls from the river and hiking trails, engage in a traditional village kava ceremony with tribal leaders, and negotiate challenging river stretches framed, in some cases, by 40-m-plus high volcanic walls. Throughout their adventure, they come to experience and make meaning of Fiji in a variety of ways, each one within his or her own frame of reference. As a result of these place interactions as well as their social interactions, each visitor develops a sense of the place that is Fiji and, ultimately, becomes in some way connected to Fiji. But, what is that connection? How do we measure it? And, what can it mean in terms of subsequent attitudes and behaviors about and toward tourist destinations such as Fiji?

*Corresponding author, e-mail: lharmon@uwlax.edu

And, what about the native Fijians? Unique to the Fijian society, they embrace a concept called "vanua." Fijians use the term "vanua" to describe the meaning of place. In this instance, however:

> [Vanua] does not mean only land and the area one is identified with, and the vegetation, animal life, and other objects on it, but also includes the social and cultural system—the people, their traditions and customs, beliefs and values, and the various other institutions established for the sake of achieving harmony, solidarity, and prosperity within a particular social context.
>
> Ravuvu (1983: 70)

How does tourism impact their perception of vanua? How might understanding vanua influence tourism planning efforts? And, how might these differing perspectives drive multiple behaviors, attitudes, and future interactions with tourists?

This chapter will focus on the discussion of how place perspectives have been studied as well as the variety of theoretical frameworks that have been applied in tourism research. Additionally, examples are presented of how place-based research has been applied and suggestions for future application and research.

The Context

Tourism places are spaces we have imbued with meaning such that they become more than just a geographical location. They become special, unique, we identify with them, and we may even become attached to places. Space evolves into place when our understanding of it is influenced by our past experiences, memories, connections to individuals or events, and our identity (e.g. Cuba and Hummon, 1993). When traveling, individuals can become connected to or influenced by places representing particular moments in history (e.g. the Vietnam Veterans Memorial Wall in Washington, DC), places which elicit certain moods or emotions, or places in which significant events occur (Manzo, 2003). Other factors may also influence our perceptions of a place such as its physical characteristics (Eisenhauer et al., 2000), its similarity to other familiar places, and the activities in which we engage while visiting that place (Bricker and Kerstetter, 2000). Place connections can also be a function of our interactions with particular people in those places such as family or friends (Eisenhauer et al., 2000).

Place, then, is the space within which the tourism experience frequently occurs. Understanding how we develop our sense of place and place connections from a tourism perspective allows us to not only develop a richer understanding of the tourist experience, but also to identify and perhaps even manage experience outcomes. Place-based research attempts to understand both the nature of our connection to places as well as a variety of variables which may lead to place connections, i.e. antecedents, and behaviors or attitudes we may expect as a result of being connected to a particular place, i.e. outcomes. The first step in understanding place is to provide a historical context and to identify the variety of theoretical frameworks within which we have studied and come to understand place perceptions, connections, and outcomes. This endeavor will not be exhaustive since place has been studied under a wide variety of epistemologies (Devine-Wright and Clayton, 2010).

L.K. Harmon

However, key theories will be highlighted, with a focus on those that may have the most relevant application to tourism.

The Theory

A variety of approaches have been used to study place connections. In this chapter, a brief historical evolution of these theories and examples of applications with a focus on those most frequently observed is given.

- Attention restoration theory (Hartig *et al.*, 2001).
- Attitude theory (Jorgensen and Stedman, 2001).
- Identity development theory (Proshansky *et al.*, 1983; Twigger-Ross and Uzzell, 1996).
- Meaning theory (Casakin and Kreitler, 2008).
- Place attachment construct (Williams and Vaske, 2003).
- Rootedness (Relph, 1976).
- Sense of place (Shamai, 1991; Kyle and Chick, 2007).
- Self-regulation theory (Korpela, 1989).
- Social judgment theory (Kyle *et al.*, 2003).
- Specialization theory (Bricker and Kerstetter, 2000).
- Topophilia (Tuan, 1974).

Origins of place research

The study of place perceptions first appeared in the 1970s (Tuan, 1974). Literally translated as love of place, Tuan used the term *topophilia* to describe the emotional connections individuals feel toward particular places. Soon after, Relph's (1976) work examining the meaning of place and the construct of rootedness from a human geographical perspective contributed to the foundations for a burgeoning line of research. Identifying both the tangible and abstract boundaries of space, Relph posited place was a space in which the individual's lived experience was framed. In other words, it was through the experiential relationship to a space that one developed place meaning and connections to that place via the construct of rootedness. In other research, McAndrew (1998) predicted and measured rootedness among college students relative to their homes as a combination of a "desire to change," i.e. the degree to which an individual was desirous of living elsewhere, and "home/family satisfaction," i.e. the degree to which an individual was connected to family members, friends, and their actual home. Williams (1998) further suggested rootedness is our connection with a place as it becomes entwined with our identity and that it frequently elicits a sense of security.

As research developed, findings on how rootedness affected behaviors toward place ranged from Hay's (1998a) suggestion that it contributed to a more bioregional land management approach to Kyle and Chick's (2007) more recent observations that family and generational ties were the predominant contributors to a sense of place among those tenting at a Pennsylvania agricultural fair. The core tenet to psychological rootedness remains consistent and is an outcome of a lengthy relationship or interaction with a particular environment.

Place and self

How place perceptions might play a role in identity development became an important avenue of research in the 1980s and continues to be critical to our current understanding of the person–place relationship. Building on Mead's (1934) theory of the self, which suggests perception is in terms of action, i.e. to perceive a place is to perceive how that place functions in our life, Proshansky *et al.* (1983) were among the first to explore an identity component of the person–place relationship. Using social roles and social attribution theory to understand how self-identity develops, they found it was necessary for an individual to have an environmental past, i.e. experience with the physical setting, in order to develop a set of cognitions relative to that place which either contributed or detracted from a person's conception of self. Described as place identity, this construct's functions included two primary components: (i) recognition, i.e. the environmental past against which any physical setting can be judged; and (ii) meaning, i.e. how people should behave in the place. Using a phenomenological approach, Rowles (1983) further substantiated the importance of personal meaning, or identity, in attachment to place among young and older individuals living in the Appalachians. Specifically, he observed that older adults who internalized and incorporated their local community characteristics as part of their identity were able to negotiate physical pathways in their familiar environment, which in non-familiar territory would have been too physically difficult or challenging to negotiate. More recently, Bricker and Kerstetter (2000) found whitewater rafters who exhibited higher levels of activity specialization were also more like to express higher levels of place identity to the South Fork of the American River than those who were less specialized. Kyle *et al.* (2003) found place identity magnified attitudes toward fee programs and increased support for spending.

Measuring place

An exploration of a possible place attachment construct was a logical next step in the research process and, in 1992, Williams *et al.* provided foundational methodological efforts focused on measuring the constructs of place attachment. Specifically, they examined two subscales: place identity and place dependence. Place identity was conceived as the symbolic importance of environment to one's self-identity while place dependence addressed how necessary place was to an individual's ability to reach his or her recreation goal.

In leisure and tourism research, place attachment has been conceptualized in a multitude of ways, though most definitions include, at minimum, the dimensions of place identity and place dependence. In 2003, Willams and Vaske (2003) examined the psychometric properties of place attachment. Their study included four samples of individuals: 65 Colorado State University students, 380 University of Illinois students, 2005 Shenandoah National Park visitors, and 369 Mt Rogers National Recreation Area visitors. Within each sample, confirmatory factor analysis (CFA) results led the authors to accept the two-dimensional solution, which was further supported by convergent validity among the four samples.

However, some scholars have suggested place attachment is a unidimensional construct (e.g. Stedman, 2003), though it was measured using statements similar to those measuring place identity and place dependence. Yet others conceive of a broader construct, sense of place, which is comprised of place attachment, place identity, and place dependence (Cross *et al.*, 2011). Additional studies have been conducted examining dimensions such as social bonding (Kyle *et al.*, 2005) and place bonding (Hammitt *et al.*, 2004). More recently, there have been attempts to distinguish between various types of place attachment, such as Scannell and Gifford's (2010) findings differentiating natural place attachment from civic (or social-symbolic) place attachment. Brehm *et al.*'s (2013) findings regarding the contributions of place meaning in predicting environmental concern about a place further suggested that knowing how a person values a place in terms of impact perceptions and as a scenic family getaway, i.e. place meaning, is as helpful in terms of understanding behavior as place attachment. The value in these distinctions may be in our ability to more specifically predict outcomes such as the potential for tourists to engage in pro-environmental behaviors.

Understanding the potential variation in scale relative to place attachment is also an important consideration in measuring place. Scale in place attachment refers to the size of the locale and may vary from a small room (either indoors or outdoors) to an entire park, or even a country. The acknowledgement of place size as a potential variation in the construct of place attachment is something that is rarely addressed in the literature. Where it has been, it has been primarily in the definition of place. Derr (2002), for example, found that children have a very different understanding of scale than adults and have expressed attachment to places that are described as intimate and allow them to develop a sense of place through creative place-structuring such as building forts. Adults, however, express connections toward places of varying scales. Hidalgo and Hernandez (2001), for instance, found that among different place scales such as house, neighborhood, and city, Spanish residents were least attached to their neighborhoods but more attached to home or the larger city within which they lived. Lewicka (2010) confirmed this relationship and further indicated attachment was strongest in attractive cities, but place scale differences dropped in rural areas and small towns. She suggests this finding "may throw light on the possible cognitive mechanisms of place attachment, and thus confirm Tuan's intuition that the better geographically and cognitively defined space, the more meaning it may acquire and the higher chance that it will become a target of attachment" (Lewicka, 2011: 213). This information is particularly valuable to tourism destinations wishing to inspire attachment among visitors.

Place features

As place research has developed, so has an interest in the characteristics of places that elicit connections (see Fig. 13.1). This preference for particular setting characteristics (see also Kaplan *et al.*, 1998) has been helpful in understanding the nature of our attraction to particular destinations. For example, Fishwick and Vining (1992) found that for college students, the factors that most contributed to their choice of locale and their overall sense of place were: (i) setting; (ii) landscape; (iii) ritual; (iv) routine; and (v) past experience. Water, specifically, was a significant predictor of sense of place, which confirms a wide range of anecdotal and economic indicators for this phenomenon, e.g. higher rental rates for water-side and -view rental units. Other physical features that have been found to relate positively to place attachment include

Fig. 13.1. Cultural artifacts such as statuary and place specific colors such as those seen at Schönbrunn Palace in Vienna, Austria contribute to creating a sense of place and can enhance place attachment. (Photo: Laurlyn K. Harmon)

presence of green areas, cleanliness or well-maintained spaces, and aesthetically appealing spaces (Fornara *et al.*, 2009).

Landscape preference type can also be mediated by our past experiences, as in the case of individuals who have few experiences of wilderness and who prefer landscapes that appear somewhat manicured or human managed (Kaplan *et al.*, 1998). Conversely, individuals with more frequent previous wilderness-type experiences tend to express a preference for landscapes with fewer observable human impacts, e.g. backcountry locales.

Understanding group differences of place connections

Understanding the relationship between various tourism constructs and place connections and how these relationships may affect tourist behavior is a burgeoning area of research. When segmenting visitors by motivations to visit, for example, it appears each group expresses differing levels of attachment to places. The recreation experience preference (REP) scale, confirmed by Manfredo *et al.* (1996) to assess motivations has been used to some extent to explore the impact of place on the tourist experience. Warzecha and Lime (2001), in their study of river recreationists, used a measure of functional attachment, which included items structurally similar to place dependence and items identified as emotional/symbolic attachment that were similar to previous place identity measures (see Willams and Vaske, 2003). They found Green River users were generally more functionally and emotionally attached to their location than Colorado River users. However, among both groups of respondents, individuals who preferred recreation experiences of autonomy/leadership, solitude seeking, and introspection for their trip also expressed higher levels of place attachment. Anderson and Fulton (2008), in an extension of this study, found visitors' attachments to waterfowl production areas (WPAs) in Minnesota were partially mediated by their REP motives. Specifically, preferences for autonomy/leadership or teaching/leading others mediated the relationship between hunting participation and place dependence. Among wildlife watchers, the relationship between activity participation and place dependence was mediated by their preference for learning and creativity, while the place identity relationship was partially mediated by their preference for watchable wildlife/educational activity participation. Similarly, among clusters of visitors to Daintree and Cape Tribulation in Australia, those who were motivated to visit based on an expressed interest in appreciating nature with others, scored higher on natural values such as place meaning, while those who were motivated to visit primarily to escape and relax in a natural environment, scored higher on aesthetics as the primary contributor to place meaning (Young, 1999).

Understanding the extent of place connections can also be examined by applying established theoretical visitor typologies such as those posited in specialization theory. Bricker and Kerstetter (2000), for instance, segmented whitewater rafters by specialization levels, conceptualized as activity-specific behaviors ranging from the general to the particular and found rafters who were highly specialized were also more likely to place importance on place identity and lifestyle than those who were low specialists, while specialization did not predict place dependence.

Differentiating visitors or non-locals from residents of a host community has also been helpful in understanding place attachment. Bonaiuto *et al.* (2002) found residents of areas near proposed Italian National Parks to be less supportive of park development due to the potential for disrupting their current lifestyle, while visitors were generally supportive of the parks. Research has also indicated that long-time residents rate natural features such as wildlife, woods, and other environmental amenities lower than short-term residents (Walker and Ryan, 2008) and visitors (Stedman, 2006). Understanding local perceptions for landscape characteristics can provide the focus for identifying support for future tourism development as well as how that development should proceed. For example, framing the conversation to acknowledge important place aspects for the host community are as important as responding to differing desires and interests of the potential tourist.

Another interesting line of research has recently evolved using the lifespan model to explore multiple senses of place dimensions. Specifically, while both adults and adolescents have been found to express preferences for quality of activities as well as community belonging, adults' preferences discriminated on emotional bonding and behavioral commitment to a place, while adolescents' preferences discriminated on their perceptions of the opportunities offered in that place (Pretty *et al.*, 2002). See further discussion in Antecedents, below.

And while not grounded in a particular theoretical framework, Mitchell *et al.* (1993) found when segmenting visitors into attachment-oriented and use-oriented, attachment-oriented visitors were more likely to exhibit high levels of site investment and show a strong desire to share their affections toward the place with others than were their use-oriented counterparts. These various subgroupings reveal unique characteristics that can offer guidance to organizations attempting to reinforce or minimize place connections among visitors.

Antecedents

Potential predictors of the human–place bond range greatly and results have been inconsistent. Vorkinn and Riese (2001), for example, found among Norway residents that use intensity, use history, and recreation activities in which individuals engaged explained 40–60% of the variance in their expressed levels of place attachment. However, when participation in park ranger interpretive programs was explored as a possible initiator of place attachment, no differences were found among visitors to Isle Royale National Park (Harmon *et al.*, 2005; Fig. 13.2). Interestingly, even though Elderhostel members were more likely to participate in the educative programs than non-group visitors to the park, both groups exhibited similar levels of place identity and place dependence. It is possible in this scenario that the interpretive programs served as a surrogate method for interaction with the park, i.e. it allowed them to experience the unique features of the park without having to actually hike through the park (which is somewhat physically challenging). Thus, the overall quantity of total interactions, i.e. environmental past as conceived by Proshansky *et al.* (1983) may have been similar for both Elderhostel and non-Elderhostel groups, and was equally likely to predict place attachment upon trip completion.

Fig. 13.2. Elderhostel program visitors participating in an interpretive program at the Edison Fishery in Isle Royale National Park. (Photo: Laurlyn K. Harmon)

This brings us to the extent of environmental past, or length of time spent in a particular place as a potential predictor of place attachment. Time spent in a place has been explored at great length with varying results. In some cases length of stay was found to positively correlate to various place attachment measures (e.g. Moore and Graefe, 1994; Harmon *et al.*, 2005), while in others there was no relationship (e.g. Williams *et al.*, 1992). These studies have been within the context of tourism and recreation visits to particular destinations. However, when examining life history of participants, particularly within the context of local spaces, older individuals have consistently demonstrated either a stronger or more complex level of place attachment than younger individuals (e.g. Hay, 1998b; Hidalgo and Hernandez, 2001). This supports the notion that place relationships develop and transform over time (Manzo, 2005).

Outcomes

Our connections with places have the power to drive our behaviors both toward and within the place. One category of behaviors we are interested in exploring is sustainability-related or pro-environmental behaviors. As pressure on our natural resources increases worldwide, our ability to understand what might facilitate sustainable actions among tourists while visiting a place, as well as understanding what might encourage post-visit actions, is increasingly relevant. Multiple findings offer insights into the relationship between place constructs and sustainable behaviors.

Individuals with higher place attachment have, generally, been more likely to express pro-environmental attitudes toward a particular place (Williams *et al.*, 1995). Using sense of place to predict empathy, visitors who expressed higher levels of empathy toward Elk Island National Park in Alberta, Canada, for example, were more likely to engage in future pro-environmental behaviors such as volunteering, paying higher fees to prevent poaching, and telling others to act responsibly (Walker and Chapman, 2003). Among youth (14–17 years) who worked in a Colorado natural resource-based work program, those who expressed higher levels of place dependency and place identity were also more likely to engage in environmentally responsible behaviors (ERBs) (Vaske and Kobrin, 2001). However, the relationship was secondary among those examined, in that place dependence significantly predicted place identity which predicted engagement in ERBs once students completed their work program. When examining overall environmental attitudes, Vorkinn and Riese (2001) found place attachment, as measured by Williams *et al.*'s (1992) scale, explained as much variation in attitude, approximately 17%, as did demographic characteristics. Similarly, Cross *et al.* (2011) found that conservation ethics positively correlated with a sense of place. Thus, developing place connections among visitors clearly has the potential to influence environmental attitudes as well as behaviors.

Additional place-related measures have further facilitated our understanding of human actions in tourism locales. Among southwest Virginia residents, individuals who expressed higher levels of community attachment (Shamai, 1991), another human–place bonding measure, were generally more supportive of tourism development (Williams *et al.*, 1995). However, old-timers (as defined by the authors) were less favorable toward development options than newcomers, suggesting a moderating effect of time spent in the location. Additionally, individuals have been to found to be more willing to substitute alternative recreation areas when they were less attached to a particular locale (Williams *et al.*, 1992).

Applications of place theory

While there is no specific place attachment theory as yet agreed upon among researchers, there are a multitude of paradigms within which place is studied. In each case, the goal is to understand the meaning behind the behaviors, attitudes, beliefs, or connections being examined. A primary purpose of using place to examine tourism behavior lies in its contribution to understanding emotional, symbolic, and intangible measures of our ties to places.

Understanding place connections can help us understand how likely people are to engage in protective behaviors toward places. For example, displacement, or the threat of displacement, can trigger place protective behaviors such as resistance to tourism development (Gu and Ryan, 2008). Individuals expressing strong place connections may also be more supportive of conserving property, as in the case of highly attached Colorado and Wyoming agricultural landowners who expressed high levels of support for putting part of portions of their properties into conservation land easements. Property owners may be more likely to engage in maintenance behaviors toward their property, as in the case of lakeshore residents in northern Wisconsin (Stedman, 2002). Further, we can explore relationships between host communities and visitors as done in the context of a Norwegian National Park (Kaltenborn and Williams, 2002) where both locals and visitors who expressed higher levels of place attachment also exhibited an increased propensity to protect nature, wilderness, and cultural qualities.

When individuals identify places as special, they are also more likely to express strongly polarized views, whether positive or negative, about future management actions relative to that place (Smaldone *et al.*, 2005). Assessing place attachment allows us to identify individuals who may be less likely to support tourism and use related development; however, there has been some conflicting information. For example, while Kaltenborn and Williams (2002) found higher expressed place attachment predicted less support for tourism development in a national park, Kyle *et al.* (2004) considered a slightly different approach. Specifically, when differentiating visitors based on the separate dimensions of place identity and place dependence, Appalachian Trail hikers who expressed higher levels of place identity toward the Appalachian Trail were more likely to perceive that social and environmental trail conditions were problematic (e.g. crowding, trail development) than did trail hikers who expressed lower levels of place identity. Conversely, hikers who expressed stronger place dependency were not as likely as hikers expressing less place dependency to identify those same conditions as problematic.

Understanding place meaning can also provide foundations for determinations of properties which may be appropriate to protect from historical or culturally significant perspectives (Cresswell and Hoskins, 2010). Attachment-oriented individuals tend to have high site investment and a strong desire to share their affection of place with others (Mitchell *et al.*, 1993). Additionally, highly attached individuals are less likely to be willing to substitute that place for a similar one than are individuals expressing less attachment (Williams *et al.*, 1992).

We can also foster desired tourism experiences by evoking place features. For example, "when the aim is to increase the individual's responsiveness to the particular atmosphere characteristic of certain place, it would be desirable to make that person aware of the sensory qualities of the place, such as its color, morphology, sound, etc. or to focus on the emotions experienced and evoked by that place" (Casakin and Kreitler, 2008).

The applications identified here are not exhaustive by any means. Scholars over the globe in the areas of anthropology, geography, social psychology, and many other disciplines continue to explore the meaning of the human–place relationship, how it is conceptualized and measured, and the range of potential applications. In addition, it is time to come together to form a coherent theory of place as is suggested by Lewicka's (2011) recent review of place research. As we proceed in this endeavor, it will behoove us to reach out to multiple disciplines in order to build on the foundation of existing place-based research.

The Future

As we consider the variety of outcomes potentially related to understanding place perspectives as well as the variety of strategies that have been used to examine them, it is necessary to consider what might be worthy of future research. As with some of the other chapters in this text, and as noted throughout the research on place, an increased focus on developing a place-specific theory to contextualize and understand research on tourism places/destinations and the person–place relationship would be quite useful. Although the construct of place attachment appears relatively well tested, theory specific to place attachment or sense of place has yet to be fully articulated within the literature. Thus, it is important to continue supporting the call for theoretical development addressing the human–place relationship.

Another avenue of exploration may be to expand on the diversity of participants in place-based research. Studies to date have addressed multiple regional contexts including perspectives from individuals who are Hispanic (Derr, 2002), Swedish (Gustafson, 2001), Norwegian (Vorkinn and Riese, 2001; Kaltenborn and Bjerke, 2002), Finnish (Korpela and Hartig, 1997), Hindi (Mazumdar and Mazumdar, 1993), Australian (Young, 1999; Pretty *et al.*, 2002), Canadian (Shamai, 1991; Steel, 2000; Walker and Chapman, 2003), English (Twigger-Ross and Uzzell, 1996), from New Zealand (Hay, 1998a) and Wales (Garrod, 2008), China (Gu and Ryan, 2008), and Canada (Scannell and Gifford, 2010). However, there appear to be limited findings relative to individuals who identify as black or African American, individuals with a variety of physical and/or cognitive abilities, or individuals from traditionally marginalized groups (which would be identified based on particular regional majority/minority relationships).

Similarly, while scholars have addressed the concept of place meaning making from multiple cultures, i.e. indigenous and historically entrenched groups of people identifying as unique societies (Gupta and Ferguson, 1997), it has been suggested that place attachment is still frequently considered from a North American perspective with associated values and constructs imposed upon much of the research in this area. Expanding our research to consider local meanings within the context of regional and global meanings, not simply as conceptually opposing forces, can provide a richer understanding of place-related constructs and contribute to theoretical development.

A third intriguing avenue may be that of taking a geocentric position in the study of place perspectives. Thinking of places as entities, how might we continue to apply human relationship theories such as Bowlby's (1977) attachment theory to the human–place bond? For example, likening the loss of a place to that of losing an individual, we might examine how or if grieving over lost places can be beneficial in allowing us to move on and establish new relationships with new places. Lonely individuals may form a relationship, of sorts, with desolate landscape forms, which could become places in which individuals can find solace (see Casey, 1993).

An additional, and relatively new, area of suggested research is related to Chapter 14 (this volume) and involves exploring the environmental past construct first discussed by Proshansky *et al.* (1983). While their initial understanding of environmental past, i.e. our interactions with a place, drew primarily from direct experiences with a place, contemporary technological advances have advanced to such a degree that we can now interact virtually with places in ways we previously could not. We have a plethora of tools allowing us virtual access to places through modes such as internet virtual trips, real-time social media audio, text and video, and real-time communication tools, e.g. Skype. A great example of the role virtual access may take in place attachment is seen in the public's recent engagement with the ice caves in Apostle Islands National Lakeshore (Fig. 13.3). In 2014, the caves were accessible across frozen Lake Superior in Wisconsin, USA, for the first time in 5 years. Real-time social media posts inspired visitors from as far away as Australia, China, and Japan (Meador, 2014). Visitor and nearby resident Facebook comments from 2015, the second consecutive year in which the caves were accessible, indicate potential place identity development among individuals posting responses and potential likelihood to be supportive of the newly instituted special event fee of US$5 per person for access. While this is merely anecdotal evidence, it is certainly a potential avenue for more systematic analysis.

Finally, exploration of place characteristics which reflect our own self-characteristics as a way to further examine identity development may be another productive area of research within the tourism realm. As part of our self-identity, we have both transient and stable characteristics. We make a variety of behavioral choices based not only on our own characteristics, but in terms of how we wish to present ourselves to others. How, then, might this influence our tourism destination and activity choices?

Questions

1. How do you believe place perceptions are relevant to the tourism industry: the tourist; the tourism provider; and the host community?
2. What has been the most challenging aspect of place research?
3. How can understanding the human–place bond improve our ability to enhance the satisfaction of the tourist experience?
4. What would be the next steps that might most effectively contribute to developing a solid conceptual framework within which to study tourism place perceptions?

Fig. 13.3. The Lake Superior Ice Caves drew almost 150,000 tourists in 2014, approximately 15 times the average annual visitation to the Apostle Islands National Lakeshore, the park unit within which the caves reside. (Photo: Laurlyn K. Harmon)

L.K. Harmon

References

Anderson, D.H. and Fulton, D.C. (2008) Experience preferences as mediators of the wildlife related recreation participation: place attachment relationship. *Human Dimensions of Wildlife* 13, 73–88.

Bonaiuto, M., Carrus, G., Martorella, H. and Bonnes, M. (2002) Local identity processes and environmental attitudes in land use changes: the case of natural protected areas. *Journal of Economic Psychology* 23, 631–653.

Bowlby, J. (1977) The making and breaking of affectional bonds. *The British Journal of Psychiatry* 130, 201–210.

Brehm, J.M., Eisenhauer, B.W. and Stedman, R.C. (2013) Environmental concern: examining the role of place meaning and place attachment. *Society and Natural Resources* 26, 522–538.

Bricker, K.S. and Kerstetter, D.L. (2000) Level of specialization and place attachment: an exploratory study of whitewater rafters. *Leisure Sciences* 22, 233–257.

Casakin, H.P. and Kreitler, S. (2008) Place attachment as a function of meaning assignment. *Open Environmental Sciences* 2, 80–87.

Casey, E.S. (1993) *Getting Back into Place: Toward a Renewed Understanding of the Place-World.* Indiana University Press, Bloomington, Indiana.

Cresswell, T. and Hoskins, G. (2010) Place, persistence, and practice: evaluating historical significance at Angel Island, San Francisco, and Maxwell Street, Chicago. *Annals of the Association of American Geographers* 98(2), 392–413.

Cross, J.E., Keske, C.M., Lacy, M.G., Hoag, D.L.K. and Bastian, C.T. (2011) Adoption of conservation easements among agricultural landowners in Colorado and Wyoming: the role of economic dependence and sense of place. *Landscape and Urban Planning* 101, 75–83.

Cuba, L. and Hummon, D. (1993) A place to call home: identification with dwelling, community, and region. *Sociological Quarterly* 34(1), 111–131.

Derr, V. (2002) Children's sense of place in northern New Mexico. *Journal of Environmental Psychology* 22, 125–137.

Devine-Wright, P. and Clayton, S. (2010) Introduction to the special issue: place, identity and environmental behavior. *Journal of Environmental Psychology* 30(3), 267–270.

Eisenhauer, B., Krannich, R. and Blahna, D. (2000) Attachments to special places on public lands: an analysis of activities, reasons for attachments and community connections. *Society and Natural Resources* 13(5), 421–441.

Fishwick, L. and Vining, J. (1992) Toward a phenomenology of recreation place. *Journal of Environmental Psychology* 12(1), 57–63.

Fornara, F., Bonaiuto, M. and Bonnes, M. (2009) Cross-validation of abbreviated perceived residential environment quality (PREQ) and neighborhood attachment (NA) indicators. *Environment and Behavior* 42, 171–196.

Garrod, B. (2008) Exploring place perception: a photo-based analysis. *Annals of Tourism Research* 35(2), 381–401.

Gu, H. and Ryan, C. (2008) Place attachment, identity and community impacts of tourism: the case of a Beijing hutong. *Tourism Management* 29, 637–647.

Gupta, A. and Ferguson, J. (1997) Beyond "culture": space, identity and the politics of difference. In: Gupta, A. and Ferguson, J. (eds) *Culture, Power, Place: Ethnography at the End of an Era.* Duke University Press, Duke, North Carolina, pp. 1–33.

Gustafson, P. (2001) Meanings of place: everyday experience and theoretical conceptualizations. *Journal of Environmental Psychology* 21, 5–16.

Hammitt, W.E., Backlund, E.A. and Bixler, R.D. (2004) Past use history and place bonding among avid trout anglers. Paper presented at the Northeastern Recreation Research Symposium, Bolton's Landing, New York.

Harmon, L.K., Zinn, H.C. and Gleason, M. (2005) Place identity, place dependence, and place-based affect: examining their relationship to participation in educational and interpretive programs at Isle Royale National Park. In: Harmon, D. (ed.) *People, Places, and Parks: Proceedings of the 2005 George Wright Society Conference on Parks, Protected Areas, and Cultural Sites*. The George Wright Society, Hancock, Michigan, pp. 149–156.

Hartig, T., Kaiser, F.G. and Bowler, P.A. (2001) Psychological restoration in nature as a positive motivation for ecological behavior. *Environment and Behavior* 33(4), 590–607.

Hay, R. (1998a) A rooted sense of place in cross-cultural perspective. *Canadian Geographer* 42(3), 245–266.

Hay, R. (1998b) Sense of place in developmental context. *Journal of Environmental Psychology* 18, 5–29.

Hidalgo, M.C. and Hernandez, B. (2001) Place attachment: conceptual and empirical questions. *Journal of Environmental Psychology* 21, 273–281.

Jorgensen, B.S. and Stedman, R.C. (2001) Sense of place as an attitude: lakeshore owners' attitudes toward their properties. *Journal of Environmental Psychology* 21, 233–248.

Kaltenborn, B.P. and Bjerke, T. (2002) Associations between landscape preferences and place attachment: a study in Roros, Southern Norway. *Landscape Research* 27(4), 381–396.

Kaltenborn, B.P. and Williams, D.R. (2002) The meaning of place: attachments to Femundsmarka National Park, Norway, among tourists and locals. *Norwegian Journal of Geography* 56(3), 189–198.

Kaplan, R., Kaplan, S. and Ryan, R.L. (1998) With people in mind: design and management of everyday nature. Island Press, Washington, DC, 239 pp.

Korpela, K.M. (1989) Place identity as a product of environmental self-regulation. *Journal of Environmental Psychology* 9(3), 241–256.

Korpela, K. and Hartig, T. (1997) Restorative qualities of favorite places. *Journal of Environmental Psychology* 16, 221–233.

Kyle, G. and Chick, G. (2007) The social construction of a sense of place. *Leisure Sciences* 29, 209–225.

Kyle, G.T., Absher, J.D. and Graefe, A.R. (2003) The moderating role of place attachment on the relationship between attitudes toward fees and spending preferences. *Leisure Sciences* 25(1), 33–50.

Kyle, G., Graefe, A., Manning, R. and Bacon, J. (2004) Effects of place attachment on users' perceptions of social and environmental conditions in a natural setting. *Journal of Environmental Psychology* 24(2), 213–225.

Kyle, G., Graefe, A. and Manning, R. (2005) Testing the dimensionality of place attachment in recreation settings. *Environment & Behavior* 37, 153–177.

Lewicka, M. (2010) What makes neighborhood different from home and city? Effects of place scale on place attachment. *Journal of Environmental Psychology* 30, 35–51.

Lewicka, M. (2011) Place attachment: how far have we come in the last 40 years? *Journal of Environmental Psychology* 31, 207–230.

Manfredo, M.J., Driver, B.L. and Tarrant, M.A. (1996) Measuring leisure motivation: a meta-analysis of the recreation experience preference scales. *Journal of Leisure Research* 28(3), 188–213.

Manzo, L.C. (2003) Beyond house and haven: toward a revisioning of emotional relationships with places. *Journal of Environmental Psychology* 23, 47–61.

Manzo, L.C. (2005) For better or worse: exploring multiple dimensions of place meaning. *Journal of Environmental Psychology* 25, 67–86.

Mazumdar, S. and Mazumdar, S. (1993) Sacred space and place attachment. *Journal of Environmental Psychology* 13(3), 231–242.

McAndrew, F.T. (1998) The measurement of "rootedness" and the prediction of attachment to home-towns in college students. *Journal of Environmental Psychology* 18, 409–417.

Mead, G.H. (1934) *Mind, Self, and Society: From the standpoint of a social behaviorist*, Vol. 1. The University of Chicago Press, Chicago, Illinois.

Meador, R. (2014) As "ice caves" go viral, hordes of visitors swarm to the Apostle Islands. *The Minnesota Post*, 3 March. Available at: https://www.minnpost.com/earth-journal/2014/03/ice-caves-go-viral-hordes-visitors-swarm-apostle-islands (accessed 1 October 2014).

Mitchell, M.Y., Force, J.E., Carroll, M.S. and McLaughlin, W.J. (1993) Forest places of the heart: incorporating special spaces into public management. *Journal of Forestry* 91(4), 32–37.

Moore, R. and Graefe, A. (1994) Attachments to recreation settings: the case of rail-trail users. *Leisure Sciences* 16, 17–31.

Pretty, G.H., Chipuer, H.M. and Bramston, P. (2002) Sense of place amongst adolescents and adults in two rural Australian towns: the discriminating features of place attachment, sense of community and place dependence in relation to place identity. *Journal of Environmental Psychology* 23, 273–287.

Proshansky, H.M., Fabian, A.K. and Kaminoff, R. (1983) Place identity: physical world socialization of the self. *Journal of Environmental Psychology* 3, 57–83.

Ravuvu, A. (1983) *Vaka i Taukei: The Fijian Way of Life*. University of the South Pacific, Suva, Fiji.

Relph, E.C. (1976) *Place and Placelessness*. Pion, London.

Rowles, G.D. (1983) Place and personal identity in old age: observations from Appalachia. *Journal of Environmental Psychology* 3(4), 299–313.

Scannell, L. and Gifford, R. (2010) The relations between natural and civic place attachment and pro-environmental behavior. *Journal of Environmental Psychology* 30(3), 289–297.

Shamai, S. (1991) Sense of place: an empirical measurement. *Geoforum* 22(3), 347–358.

Smaldone, D., Harris, C.C., Sanyal, N. and Lind, D. (2005) Place attachment and management of critical issues in Grand Teton National Park. *Journal of Park and Recreation Administration* 23(1), 90–114.

Stedman, R.C. (2002) Toward a social psychology of place: predicting behavior from place-based cognitions, attitude, and identity. *Environment and Behavior* 34(5), 561–581.

Stedman, R.C. (2003) Is it really just a social construction? The contribution of the physical environment to sense of place. *Society and Natural Resources* 16, 671–685.

Stedman, R.C. (2006) Understanding place attachment among second home owners. *American Behavioral Science* 50, 187–205.

Steel, G.D. (2000) Polar bonds: environmental relations in the polar regions. *Environment and Behavior* 32(6), 796–816.

Tuan, Y.F. (1974) *Topophilia: a study of environmental perception, attitudes, and values*. Prentice Hall, Englewood Cliffs, New Jersey, 260 pp.

Twigger-Ross, C.I. and Uzzell, D.I. (1996) Place and identity processes. *Journal of Environmental Psychology* 16, 205–220.

Vaske, J. and Kobrin, K. (2001) Place attachment and environmentally responsible behavior. *The Journal of Environmental Education* 32(4), 16–21.

Vorkinn, M. and Riese, H. (2001) Environmental concern in a local context: the significance of place attachment. *Environment and Behavior* 33(2), 249–263.

Walker, A.J. and Ryan, R.L. (2008) Place attachment and landscape preservation in rural New England: a Maine case study. *Landscape and Urban Planning* 86(2), 141–152.

Walker, G.J. and Chapman, R. (2003) Thinking like a park: the effects of sense of place, perspective taking and empathy on pro-environmental intentions. *Journal of Park and Recreation Administration* 21(4), 71–86.

Warzecha, C.A and Lime, D.W. (2001) Place attachment in Canyonlands National Park: visitors' assessment of setting attributes on the Colorado and Green Rivers. *Journal of Park and Recreation Administration* 19(1), 59–78.

Williams, A. (1998) Therapeutic landscapes in holistic medicine. *Social Science & Medicine* 46(9), 1193–1203.

Willams, D.R. and Vaske, J.J. (2003) The measurement of place attachment: validity and generalizability of a psychometric approach. *Forest Science* 49(6), 830–840.

Williams, D.R., Patterson, M.E., Roggenbuck, J.W. and Watson, A.E. (1992) Beyond the commodity metaphor: examining the emotional and symbolic attachment to place. *Leisure Sciences* 14, 29–46.

Williams, D.R., McDonald, C.D., Riden, C.M. and Uysal, M. (1995) Community attachment, regional identity and resident attitudes toward tourism. In: *Proceedings of the 26th Annual Travel and Tourism Research Association Conference Proceedings*. Travel and Tourism Research Association, Wheat Ridge, Colorado, pp. 424–428.

Young, M. (1999) The relationship between tourist motivations and the interpretation of place meanings. *Tourism Geographies* 1(4), 387–405.

L.K. Harmon

14 Theoretical Perspectives on Environmental Attitudes and Travel Choices

CLAUDIA JUROWSKI[1]* AND ROSEMARY BLACK[2]

[1]*School of Hotel and Restaurant Management, Northern Arizona University, Flagstaff, Arizona;* [2]*School of Environmental Sciences, Charles Sturt University, Albury, New South Wales, Australia*

The Objectives

The purpose of this chapter is to examine select theories relevant to understanding, predicting, and explaining the relationship between environmental attitudes and traveler's decision making and behaviors. The objectives are to:

1. Define attitude theories and models such as: value-belief-norm theory, the new ecological paradigm, and the elaboration likelihood model (ELM).
2. Define behavioral theories and models such as: the theory of planned behavior, transaction cost theory, green consumerism, the responsible environmental behavior model, and the green purchase perception matrix.
3. Explain how theories and models help us to research and understand better the relationships between environmental attitudes, decision making, and environmental behaviors among travelers.
4. Provide a set of recommendations to further theoretical inquiry in this area of research.

The Vignette

Babette and Ward, who consider themselves green consumers, are discussing where they are going on vacation this year. Both are concerned about how their choice will affect the environment and are strong proponents of nature conservation. They consider themselves environmentalists and demonstrate their values by volunteering with local conservation groups. They feel it is their responsibility to help protect the natural environment for future generations. Babette and Ward do not always buy environmentally friendly products but are willing to pay more for products that are less harmful to the environment when they are conveniently available. Babette read about the Punta Cana Resort, a complex in the Dominican Republic, in her sustainable living magazine. She thinks the resort would be a good choice for their vacation because it is operated

*Corresponding author, e-mail: claudia.jurowski@nau.edu

in an environmentally friendly manner and supports a nature reserve and a coastal preservation organization. She thinks their tourism dollars would be contributing to the preservation of a fragile natural environment. Ward agrees the resort is environmentally responsible but is concerned about the carbon footprint of the flight to the Dominican Republic from Arizona. As an alternative he suggests Shadowcliff Lodge in Colorado describing it as an ecofriendly mountain sanctuary designed to connect its visitors with the natural environment. The resort offers nature and wildlife lectures, interpretive hikes, programs by national park rangers, and volunteer restoration activities. Babette agrees this is a better choice because of the smaller carbon footprint, but feels like she would like more relaxation and luxury on her vacation. They decide to continue searching for an ecofriendly resort closer to home with the pampering Babette is seeking and where their tourism dollars will contribute to nature preservation and conservation. They realize that it is unlikely that they will find a destination that meets all their criteria and that they may have to consider some trade-offs.

The Context

Concern has been raised about the direct and indirect impacts of increasing tourism on the natural environment (Dwyer et al., 2010; Gössling and Schumacher, 2010). An estimated 5% of the global carbon dioxide emissions and 14% of the total greenhouse gas emissions can be attributed to the travel industry (UNWTO, 2009). This significant contribution to global warming is likely to disquiet those who value environmental sustainability. Yet, the travel choices of environmentalists who may be more thoughtful about the types of travel products and services they purchase are complex and not easily explained (Jackson, 2005; Barr and Prillwitz, 2012; do Paço et al., 2013). For example, one study found that those with pro-environmental attitudes are more likely to select mobility styles that reduce their carbon footprint for daily travel, but are no more likely to choose sustainable transport for holiday travel than those less concerned about climate change (Barr and Prillwitz, 2012).

According to Budeanu (2007), many surveys indicate most tourists are unaware of environmental and social problems associated with tourism yet have positive attitudes to reducing these impacts. Much of the tourism research related to environmental issues focuses on environmental attitudes (Juvan and Dolnicar, 2014). Many studies demonstrate a low association between stated pro-environmental tourism intentions and reported behavior (McKercher et al., 2010; Barr and Prillwitz, 2012; Juvan and Dolnicar, 2014). Other studies suggest that in the context of tourism people rarely make the link between their own actions and environmental problems (Dawson et al., 2010). For example, Chafe (2007) found that while tourists may have high eco-social concerns these may not translate into purchase decisions that reflect their concerns, and evidence suggests the majority of tourists are reluctant to modify their behavior to meet sustainability goals (Yan et al., 2008; McKercher et al., 2010; Juvan and Dolincar, 2014). Choices consumers make are moderated not only by their concern for the environment but also by social, cognitive, situational, and cultural factors (Jackson, 2005; do Paço et al., 2013). There is clear evidence of consumer trade-offs and practicalities such as price or availability in consumer choices, even when the consumer is aware of and concerned about the impact the purchase might have on the environment (Diekman and Preisendörfer, 2003; Barr and Prillwitz, 2012).

C. Jurowski and R. Black

It is important for the travel industry to understand factors that affect the decisions of travelers who may or may not be increasing demand for "green" tourism destinations, attractions and services. Currently, the tourism industry is responding to the growing "green" consumerism by adopting strategies and approaches that include environmentally sensitive construction and design of buildings (Mehta *et al.*, 2002; Singh and Houdre, 2010), sustainable operational standards (Mihalic, 2013), carbon offsetting schemes (Scott *et al.*, 2012), and sustainable tourism or ecotourism products (Jaafar and Maideen, 2012; Ogonowska and Torre, 2012). However, the concept of green consumerism is not well understood and additional theoretical research is needed to investigate the influence of environmentalism on travel choices.

While tourism businesses need to understand components of travel products and services that might result in favorable and unfavorable travel choices, addressing environmental concerns extends beyond the realm of business. Appropriate government policy development is dependent on an understanding of travelers' motivations, attributes, behaviors, and barriers. In one case theoretically based knowledge helped the UK's Department for Environment, Food and Rural Affairs (DEFRA) design a social marketing campaign aimed at changing behavior for seven "sustainable lifestyles" segments (see Barr and Prillwitz, 2012). Theoretical approaches that include collaborations between government, industry, and the consumers are needed to successfully plan and design tourism activities that are sensitive to environmental concerns while maintaining consumer willingness to purchase (McKercher and Prideaux, 2011).

Ecotourism research suggests that while tourists may have high eco-social concerns these may not translate into purchasing decisions (Chafe, 2007). There is evidence that the majority of tourists are reluctant to modify their behavior to meet sustainability goals especially with regard to holiday travel (CERM, 2000; Yan *et al.*, 2008; Barr and Prillwitz, 2012). Choices consumers make are moderated not only by their concern for the environment but also by social, cognitive, situational, and cultural factors, which may result in cognitive dissonance in relation to choices that impact the environment (Jackson, 2005; Dickinson and Dickinson, 2006; Barr *et al.*, 2010; do Paço *et al.*, 2013). Theories that explain consumer trade-offs and practicalities such as price or availability when the consumer is aware of and concerned about the impact the purchase may have on the environment are needed to resolve dilemmas faced by governments and the tourism industry (Diekman and Preisendörfer, 2003). Destination and tourism industry managers need information that defines how travelers will interpret and react to policies and practices that affect the environment.

This chapter presents some selected theories, models, and concepts developed and applied in a range of disciplines that focus on attitudes and behaviors that may have applicability in the tourism discipline to improve our understanding of the influence of environmentalism on travel choices. The chapter is designed to encourage the continual development of theories that explain travel choices in relation to traveler's environmental impact and offer avenues for further research to explore this topic.

The Theory

The following section describes theories and models related to attitudes and behaviors drawn from a wide range of academic fields. The first group of theories explores attitudes, while the second section focuses on behavior theories in relation to environmentalism.

Attitude theories

Attitudes are considered to be an enduring set of beliefs about an object that prompts them to behave in particular ways toward the object, reflects a value orientation and determine how facts are interpreted. In the case of environmental attitudes they are commonly understood to be comprised of both cognitive and affective components incorporating beliefs, emotions, and behavioral intentions regarding environmentally related activities or issues (Schultz *et al.*, 2004; Ballantyne and Packer, 2005). The strength and direction of environmental attitudes are related to beliefs about the consequences of behavior toward the environment and the importance given to the consequences of that behavior (Manfredo *et al.*, 2004, 2014; Schultz *et al.*, 2004; Ballantyne and Packer, 2005).

Much has been written about environmental attitudes in the environmental psychology, consumer behavior, and tourism disciplines (Kim *et al.*, 2011). Positive attitudes toward the environment have been differentiated in three ways, as either: (i) an eco-centric attitude that values the natural environment for its own sake; (ii) as a type of anthropocentric altruism in which environmental degradation poses a threat to the individual; and (iii) as an expression of self-interest or concern about harm to oneself or as a function of a deeper cause such as religious beliefs (Stern, 1992; Stern *et al.*, 1993).

In the tourism research literature, environmental attitudes have been conceptualized and the term "attitude" has sometimes been used interchangeably with concerns, values, and world view (Kim *et al.*, 2011). Four theoretical constructs of attitude that can be applied to travel choices will be discussed in this section: the value-belief-norm theory (VBN), the new ecological paradigm (NEP), the relationship between antecedents and outcomes of attitudes and behaviors model, and the elaboration likelihood model (ELM).

Value-belief-norm theory

Since the 1990s concern about human's impact on the environment has become an increasingly important political and social issue (Mainieri *et al.*, 1997; Ogonowska and Torre, 2012). While technological advancements and innovations such as alternative energy sources have been developed to reduce people's negative impacts on the environment, less focus has been given to addressing consumption behavior and lifestyles. Questions as to how to encourage environmentally friendly behavior have largely focused on attitudes about people's relationship with the environment based on the belief that those with the strongest attitudes might be the most likely to participate in activities considered "green," including purchasing green travel products and services.

One of the theories proposed to understand environmental attitudes is VBN, depicted in Fig. 14.1. VBN suggests that values create beliefs and beliefs impact attitude toward behavior, which affects intentions and finally results in behavior. It is an

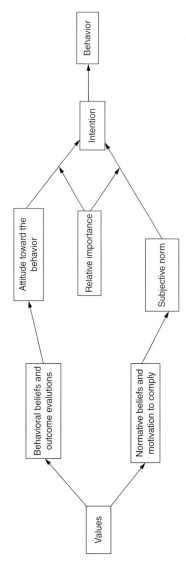

Fig. 14.1. Value-belief-norm theory applied to environmental attitudes.

extension of Ajzen and Fishbein's (1997) theory of reasoned action (TRA) that is discussed later in this chapter. VBN, commonly applied in psychology research, proposes that environmental behavior stems from personal norms activated by the belief that what is valued by the individual is under threat along with the belief that actions initiated by them can help lessen the threat and restore that which is valued (Chan, 1999; Chan and Lau, 2000). This theory was employed by Stern and colleagues in 1999 (Stern *et al.*, 1999) specifically in the context of trying to explain public support for the environmental movement. As such they focused on four behavior types: (i) activism; (ii) non-activist public sphere; (iii) private sphere behaviors; and (iv) behaviors in organizations. They based their model on Schwartz's norm-activation theory, by "generalizing" and broadening out his theory.

Stern *et al.* (1999) suggest that all environmental movements, discourses, and behaviors are underpinned by the same beliefs and values; that is, human action has the potential for adversely affecting the biophysical environment. Changes in the biophysical environment can harm things people care about, and steps should be taken to avoid at least some harmful actions. Stern *et al.* (1999) begin by assuming that behavior is determined by the person's values, beliefs, and personal norms, and that norms are important because normative claims on individuals and social organizations encourage action on the movement's principles for reasons other than self-interest (Stern *et al.*, 1999). Norms are considered to be a function of normative beliefs created by pressure to comply and/or a desire to accommodate a person's salient referents (Ajzen and Driver, 1992). Therefore, people's personal norms are an important factor in determining behavior, because social movements aim for social change and therefore, by definition, cannot be based on existing social norms. They propose that social movements reshape personal norms to create feelings of obligation and in the context of environmental movements personal norms are most likely based on altruistic values.

New ecological paradigm

Various scales and methods have been used to measure environmental attitudes. One commonly applied scale is the NEP scale developed by Dunlap and Van Liere (1978) and revised by Dunlap and others (Dunlap *et al.*, 2000). The 14 statements of the revised NEP scale, listed in Table 14.1, measure beliefs about the relationship between humans and the natural environment by asking respondents the extent to which they agree or disagree with the statements using a Likert-type scale. The NEP contrasts respondents' anthropocentric and eco-centric world views. The anthropocentric view believes that humans have a right to exploit the natural environment, while the eco-centric view values the ecosystem for its own sake. This widely applied scale has high construct validity but does not measure specific attitudes toward specific behaviors. The findings of empirical studies that used this scale have been inconsistent in making the connection between attitudes and behaviors (Kim *et al.*, 2011).

Several reasons have been postulated as to why studies do not always show a direct correlation between pro-environmental attitudes and behaviors. First, different methods have been adopted to define and measure environmental attitudes. Second, studies have attempted to demonstrate a relationship between general attitudes and specific behaviors (Arcury, 1990; Alwitt and Berger, 1993; Fransson and Garling, 1999; Kim *et al.*, 2011). In general, the attitude–behavior concept has been amalgamated to the point of creating misunderstandings about the link between the two factors.

Table 14.1. New ecological paradigm statements (from Dunlap *et al.*, 2000).

Eco-centric point of view statements	Anthropocentric point of view statements
We are approaching the limit of the number of people the earth can support	Humans have the right to modify the natural environment to suit their needs
When humans interfere with nature it often produces disastrous consequences	Human ingenuity will insure that we do not make the earth unlivable
Humans are severely abusing the environment	The earth has plenty of natural resources if we just learn how to develop them
Plants and animals have as much right as humans to exist	The so-called "ecological crisis" facing humankind has been greatly exaggerated
Despite our special abilities humans are still subject to the laws of nature	Humans were meant to rule over the rest of nature
The earth is like a spaceship with very limited room and resources	Humans will eventually learn enough about how nature works to be able to control it
The balance of nature is very delicate and easily upset	
If things continue on their present course, we will soon experience a major ecological catastrophe	

A moderate or weak relationship between attitude and behavior is often the result of using a single measure of environmental attitude. When attitude is disaggregated into its various components, the relationship becomes stronger (Schwartz, 1992; Vining and Ebreo, 1992; Grob, 1995; Thogersen and Olander, 2002; Fraj-Andres and Martinez-Salinas, 2007). For example, the examination of the relationship between environmental attitudes related to specific behaviors and behavioral intention toward local environmental issues concluded that more valuable information results from studies that examine specific attitudes toward specific behaviors (Kim *et al.*, 2011). This scale has been applied in the field of recreation (see for example, Thapa, 2010).

Antecedents of attitudes

Some researchers have disaggregated the measurement of attitude by examining the antecedents and components of attitude. For example, Maloney and Ward (1973) proposed a tri-component attitude model outlining the relationships between environmental knowledge, the degree of emotionality (affect), and the level of verbal and actual commitment to ecological issues. Based on the tri-component attitude model, Chan (1999) tested a structural model that proposed that knowledge impacts emotions, which in turn affect verbal commitment, which has a strong relationship to actual commitment. In a similar vein, in a study of Spanish consumers, attitudes were segmented into cognitive, emotional, and intentional components (Fraj-Andres and Martinez-Salinas, 2007). This study, along with a study of recreational scuba divers (Thapa *et al.*, 2006), confirmed the moderating effect of environmental knowledge on the relationship between attitudes and behavior. A further component was added by Chan and Lau (2000), who expanded the model to include the impact of the cultural value of living in harmony with nature as an antecedent to intention to engage in green purchases, which led to actual green purchases.

A group of European marketing researchers examined the antecedents of pro-environmental attitudes and related the antecedents to behavior (Leonidou *et al.*, 2010). They concluded that attitudes are positively influenced by cultural, political, and ethical sources such as the degree of collectivism, long-term orientation, political involvement, deontology, and law obedience, but found no connection between liberalism and pro-environment attitudes. The do Paço *et al.* (2013) study confirmed the existence of significant differences in environmental concerns of respondents of four countries with different realities in terms of economic development, social context, and cultural issues. Leonidou *et al.*'s conceptual model (2010) illustrated in Fig. 14.2 proposes that cultural, political, and ethical factors affect both inward and outward environmental attitudes that affect behavior and eventually satisfaction.

Elaboration Likelihood Model

The question of the antecedents of attitudes implies a need for an understanding of the process of forming or changing attitudes. The ELM depicted in Fig. 14.3 proposes a continuum that ranges from low to high elaboration related to the development of knowledge that changes attitudes (Petty and Cacioppo, 1996).

Studies that have applied this theory have revealed two main routes through which people can be persuaded through communication, i.e. the central and peripheral routes. The amount of mental effort a person gives to processing and thinking about a message determines which route is used. The central route requires an individual to invest a lot of mental effort (a process called "elaboration"). They draw upon prior experience and knowledge to evaluate the relevant arguments presented in the communication. For this to happen the person must be motivated and able to process the information presented. The result of elaboration is an attitude that is well integrated with the person's beliefs. Studies have found that attitudes changed through this route are accessible, persistent over time, predictive of behavior, and resistant to change (Petty and Cacioppo, 1996).

In contrast, the peripheral route involves much less mental effort. This process is a form of short-cutting that individuals use when they are not motivated or capable of thinking carefully about a message. In this case, they use some small non-message aspects of communication to decide if they are in favor or not in favor of it. Typical peripheral cues can be the credibility of the source (such as a celebrity endorsement), how they feel after receiving the message, and the number of arguments offered. In all these cases the individual arrives at a quick and easy attitude with little effort. Attitude impact though the peripheral route is weaker, less enduring, and less predictive of future behavior than the central route. However, both routes involve persuasion. This model has been applied in the fields of tourism, environmental interpretation, and recreation (see for example, Manfredo and Bright, 1991; Petty *et al.*, 1997; Ham *et al.*, 2008).

Behavior theories

The numerous and diverse factors that affect attitudes suggest that, theoretically, attitudes should be considered in context along with other variables that may be influencing behavior. The importance given to understanding the relationship between environmental

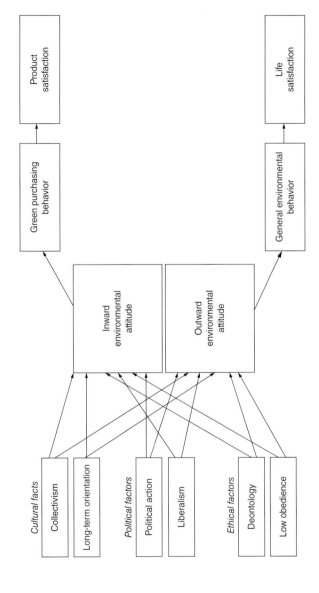

Fig. 14.2. Antecedents and outcomes of consumer environmentally friendly attitudes and behavior (from Leonidou *et al.*, 2010).

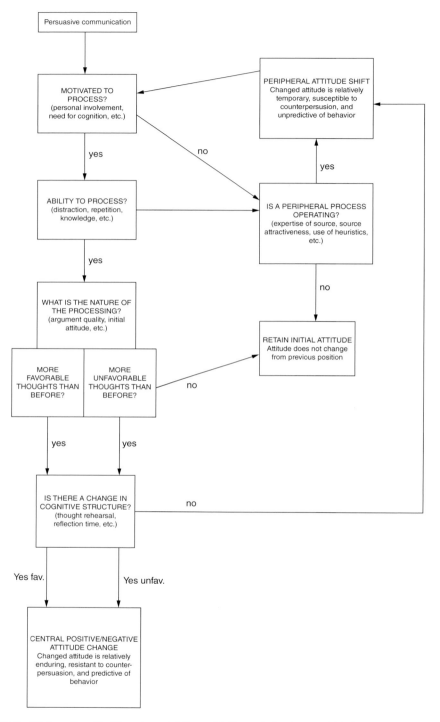

Fig. 14.3. Elaboration likelihood model (from Petty and Cacioppo, 1996).

C. Jurowski and R. Black

attitudes and behavior is based on the belief that tourists have an interest in the tourist destination and have the ability to influence the management of a destination. Theoretically, consumers with pro-environmental attitudes may be willing to pay more or sacrifice convenience for the sake of preserving and/or protecting the ecological integrity of the tourism destination. In contrast, the theory of selfish altruism suggests that consumers will only act in this way if they receive some personal benefit (Miller, 2003), which may partially explain the inconsistent results in studies that examine the correlation between environmental attitudes and behavior (for a meta-analysis of environmental attitude and behavior studies see Hines *et al.*, 1987). The degree to which consumers are willing to make sacrifices is related to the cost the consumer is required to pay. To a certain extent, environmental behavior is governed by the economic "law of demand." When costs are low and there is little inconvenience, those with pro-environmental attitudes are more likely to behave in an environmentally friendly manner. However, as costs and inconvenience rise, the strength of the effects of environmental concern on environmental behavior diminishes (Diekman and Preisendörfer, 2003). Attitudinal factors play a minor role when the investment is large (Stern, 1992), but decrease with increasing costs. The attitude-behavior-condition (A-B-C) model is limited in high-cost situations and rational-choice theory is limited in low-cost situations. The A-B-C model proposes that attitudes and behaviors are affected by external conditions to the point where attitude theories lose predictive value as external conditions strengthen (Guagnano *et al.*, 1995).

Pro-environmental behavior can be described as behavior exhibited by an individual who engages in actions to minimize any negative impact on the natural and built environs (Kollmuss and Agyeman, 2002). Many studies have tried to demonstrate relationships between pro-environmental behavior and both knowledge about and concern for the natural environment (see Hines *et al.*, 1987; Lee *et al.*, 2013). Some studies have found a positive correlation between environmental concern and pro-environmental behavior (see Mainieri *et al.*, 1997) but others found only weak relationships between attitude and behavior (see Diekman and Preisendörfer, 2003). In an early meta-analysis of environmental attitudes and behaviors, Hines *et al.* (1987) noted stronger correlations between attitudes toward a specific (rather than general) environmental behavior and the frequency of that behavior than between general environmental concern and related environmental behavior.

Efforts to promote pro-environmental behavior have been examined in a range of contexts, including tourism and recreation (see Noe *et al.*, 1993; Uysal *et al.*, 1994; Thapa, 2010; Ballantyne *et al.*, 2011). Disciplines outside tourism and recreation including environmental psychology, environmental education, planning and management, geography, and consumer behavior, for example, have examined the relationship between pro-environmental behavior and environmental attitudes, knowledge, and concerns (see Uysal *et al.*, 1994; Ballantyne and Packer, 2005; Barr and Prillwitz, 2012; Ogonowska and Torre, 2012; do Paço *et al.*, 2013; Lee *et al.*, 2013). Even though some studies have found a positive correlation between environmental concern and pro-environmental behavior (see Mainieri *et al.*, 1997), others have found only weak relationships between attitude and behavior (see Diekman and Preisendörfer, 2003). Review studies on environmental attitudes and behaviors (Hines *et al.*, 1987; Lee *et al.*, 2013) have noted stronger correlations between attitudes toward a specific (rather than general) environmental behavior and the frequency of that behavior than between general environmental concern and related environmental behavior.

The reasons why individuals do or do not behave in a pro-environmentally responsible way are very complex, requiring examination from different theoretical perspectives (see e.g. Vining and Ebreo, 1992). Early work on green consumer behavior explored demographic factors but these factors were found to be inconclusive and inconsistent (Noe *et al.*, 1993; Uysal *et al.*, 1994). Fransson and Garling (1999) suggest that factors that affect behavior appear to be knowledge, internal locus of control (positive control beliefs), personal responsibility, and perceived threats to personal health. Other authors such as Steg and Vlek (2009) have identified factors such as status, comfort, effort, and behavioral opportunities as contributors to pro-environmental behavior.

In addition to this range of variables that influence pro-environmental behavior, the influence of situational or contextual factors, or barriers or constraining factors such as income, infrastructure, and habit also need to be considered (Chan and Lau, 2000; Jackson, 2005; Leonidou *et al.*, 2010; do Paço *et al.*, 2013). Stern (2000) suggests that a persons' pro-environmental predisposition can be affected by others' behavior, the actor's attitude, and the context. In the case of tourism, the context can be internal barriers such as lack of knowledge and ability to understand the consequences of individual's behavior, habits, and external barriers such as financial resources (Budeanu, 2007).

Some behavior theories and concepts critical to understanding the relationship between environmentalism and travel choices are presented in the next section. The theory of planned behavior (TPB) and TRA and transaction cost theories (TCT) explain some aspects of travel choices. Other components are explored in the concept of green consumerism with a model of responsible environmental behavior and a green purchase matrix.

Theory of Reasoned Action

Changing environmental behavior is challenging for many reasons because of the complexity of interrelationships between behaviors and motives, delayed benefits against immediate gain, and the lack of personal relevance because environmental problems are often framed on a global scale. As previously mentioned, one of the paradoxes of environmental psychology is that some individuals may hold pro-environmental attitudes but often engage in environmentally unfriendly behaviors (Shipworth, 2000), often referred to as the "value–action gap" (Kempton *et al.*, 1995). Research demonstrates that behavior cannot be predicted on knowledge and/or attitudes alone (Brandon and Lewis, 1999; McKenzie-Mohr, 2000; Shipworth, 2000; Stern, 2000; Nordlund and Garvill, 2002; Abrahamse *et al.*, 2005), although where specific rather than general attitudes and behaviors have been explored there is a stronger correlation (Burton *et al.*, 2006: 684). The range of internal (individual, psychological, and social) and external (institutional, economic, social, and cultural) factors limiting people from making behavior choices that are consistent with their environmental attitudes and values is extensive (Kollmuss and Agyeman, 2002).

TRA, developed by Fishbein and Ajzen (1975), proposes that the most important determinant of a person's behavior is behavioral intent (Ajzen, 1971), which reflects the willingness to perform a certain act and is determined by individual attitudes and subjective norms. Attitude is a strong determinant of behavior. TRA (Fig. 14.4) proposes

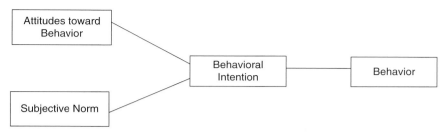

Fig. 14.4. Theory of reasoned action (from Fishbein and Ajzen, 1975, *Belief, Attitude, Intention, and Behavior: An Introduction to Theory and Research*. Reading, Massachusetts; Addison-Wesley Pub. Co., Don Mills, Ontario).

that behavior is driven by intentions that are derived from a person's attitude toward the behavior based on beliefs about outcomes and their evaluation of those outcomes along with the subjective norms that originate from what others believe is right and one's motivations to do what others believe is correct.

The Theory of Planned Behavior

TPB (Ajzen and Fishbein, 1980) is an extension of TRA (Ajzen and Fishbein, 1980; Ajzen, 1985) with the addition of one major predictor—perceived behavioral control. The theory has been useful and has been applied to analyze people's motives and is of relevance in addressing environmental behavior (Ajzen, 1985, 1991; Ajzen and Madden, 1986). The theory (see Fig. 14.5) postulates three conceptual determinants of intentions: attitudes, subjective norms, and perceived behavioral control. The antecedent of attitude is behavioral beliefs, the antecedent of subjective norm is normative beliefs, and the antecedent of behavioral control is control beliefs. The theory assumes that behavioral intention is the best predictor of future behavior and this intention is determined by three components: (i) an individual's attitude towards the behavior (a person's global evaluation of performing the behavior); (ii) the subjective norm, the perceived social pressure to perform the behavior; and (iii) perceived behavioral control, the person's conviction about whether the required skills and resources to perform the behavior are at their disposal. For a more detailed explanation of the theory and its limitations see Ajzen (1985) and Staats (2003).

TPB suggests people have the capacity to influence how others behave in a given situation by influencing three categories of beliefs they have about the desired behavior. The three sets of beliefs are behavioral, normative, and control beliefs. As a general rule, the more favorable the attitude and subjective norm, the greater the perceived control, the stronger should be the person's intention to perform the behavior in question. Given a sufficient degree of actual control over the behavior, people are expected to carry out their intentions when the opportunity arises. Intention is assumed to be the immediate antecedent of behavior. Perceived control can serve as a proxy for actual control and contribute to the prediction of the behavior in question.

TPB is a well-accepted framework that has and can be applied to a range of settings including tourism, where managers or organizations want to use communication

---

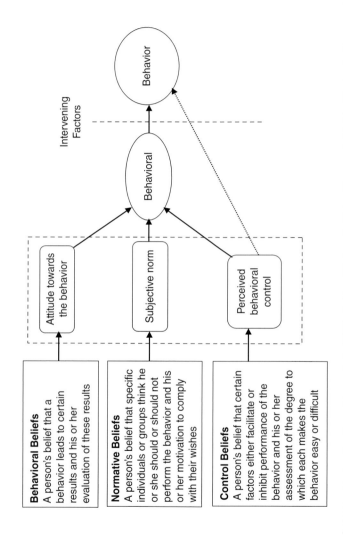

Fig. 14.5. Theory of planned behavior (from Ham *et al.*, 2008, *Asking Visitors to Help: Research Guide Strategic Communication for Protected Area Management*. CRC for Sustainable Tourism Pty Ltd, Gold Coast, Australia, p. 2).

C. Jurowski and R. Black

to persuade people to behave in particular ways. TPB has been successfully applied in a wide range of behavioral situations (for an overview see Ajzen, 1991) including changing travel mode (Bamberg and Schmidt, 1999) and adoption of "green consumerism" (Sparks and Shepherd, 1992). In tourism the theory has been used to explain destination choices (Lam and Hsu, 2006), recreational boater behavior (Jett *et al.*, 2013), tourist segmentation (Carr, 2002), and satisfaction with holiday experiences (Bigne *et al.*, 2005). More recent studies have added additional constructs to TPB. For example, Han and Kim (2010) examined the effect of service quality on attitudes that led to repeat visitation by green hotel consumers. Jett *et al.* (2013) applied the theory to examine the importance of specific attitudes on self-reported compliance of laws associated with boater speed.

The value of the theory has been demonstrated in a number of studies and meta-analyses (e.g. Sparks and Shepherd, 1992; Boldero, 1995; Taylor and Todd, 1995; Armitage and Conner, 2001). For example, social norms and others' pro-environmental behavior significantly influence the individual's pro-environmental behavior (Oskamp *et al.*, 1991; Tucker, 1999; McKenzie-Mohr and Smith, 2000). That is, behavior is likely to be modified when individuals are aware of an existing social norm and more importantly if they accept this norm (Fishbein and Ajzen, 1975). Other psychological variables related to pro-environmental behaviors have also been independently explored, for example altruistic influences (Hopper and Nielsen, 1991), intrinsic motivations (De Young, 2000), self-efficacy (Chan, 1999), and social norms (Oskamp *et al.*, 1991). It is now recognized that an individual's choice to participate in pro-environmental behaviors is a consequence, in some part, of a shared interest in "the other" and not just based on self-interest (Kalinowski *et al.*, 2006). Other theories relevant to the discussion on environmentalism and travel choices focus on consumer behavior in terms of price and quality trade-offs, for example the transaction cost theory (TCT).

Transaction cost theory

TCT posits green purchase behavior is considered in terms of price/quality trade-offs (e.g. Crosby *et al.*, 1981; Sriram and Forman, 1993) and the "price" includes a number of factors: the cost of the risk consumers take when purchasing, the cost of the time and effort required to research and seek out the item, and the psychological costs of rational deliberation (Verplanken and Faes, 1999; Peattie, 2001b; Jackson, 2005). Examining the full range of costs to the consumer along with the affective nature of decisions may provide insight into the disconnect between environmental concern and pro-environmental consumer behavior. Further, the question of cost must recognize the limits of rational choice, the role of defensive denial, and the impact of affective elements. However, further work is needed to address the relationship between willingness to pay higher costs and consumer concern and/or greater knowledge and the impact of the cost of "green" products on consumers.

Clearly, fostering green consumer behavior change, as with other environmental behaviors, is a challenge because of the complexity of interrelationships between behaviors, motives, attitudes, delayed benefits against immediate gain, and perception of environmental problems. Often environmental problems are perceived to be global in nature and out of the realm of the individual's sphere of influence. In the case of green consumers, increased environmental knowledge may reduce the consumers' confidence in the suitability of a product and raise their concern to the complex nature of the environmental issues. Information provided to consumers may be complex, inconsistent, and contradictory from a range of different credible or non-credible sources. Furthermore, the variety of approaches used to attract the green consumer, including green product reformulations, green advertising and public relations activity and green labeling, may not be effective. Evidence suggests that consumers are easily confused by environmental claims and labels and tend to be highly skeptical (Mintel, 1991; Einsmann, 1992; Siminitiras *et al.*, 1993). In the tourism industry mainly informative tools such as eco-labels and awareness campaigns have been used to influence tourists' choices and behavior in a pro-environmental manner (Font and Tribe, 2001; Budeanu, 2007). Economic instruments (taxes, fees) and regulatory measures have been used to a limited extent to achieve the same outcome (see Budeanu, 2007 for a discussion of these tools).

Green consumerism

The term green consumer has been used in many contexts with an underlying assumption of environmentally responsible or sustainable purchase choices and environmentally or socially sensitive behaviors (Gilg *et al.*, 2004; Han *et al.*, 2010). Green consumers have been segmented according to their activism, green knowledge, and green practices (Miller, 2003), and by the intensity of their environmental concern and behavior (Diekman and Preisendörfer, 2003).

The most pro-environmental consumers are assumed to be those with the highest degree of environmental conscious orientation, the strongest concern about the natural environment, and the greatest likelihood of being influenced and informed by environmental concerns when making purchase decisions (Peattie, 2001b; Ham and Han, 2013). As discussed in relation to TCT, while many consumers make green purchases at some time, most green purchases include a trade-off. Even the most committed consumers may be faced with temporal or spatial dimensions that compromise their purchase preferences (Staats, 2003). Understanding why individuals do or do not behave in an environmentally responsible way is "dauntingly complex, both in its variety and in the causal influences on it" (Stern, 2000: 421).

A meta-analysis of environmental behavior by Hines *et al.* (1987) revealed a relationship between environmental behavior and knowledge of issues, knowledge of action strategies, locus of control, attitudes, verbal commitment, and an individual's sense of responsibility (Hines *et al.*, 1987). The authors of the meta-analysis proposed a model of responsible environmental behavior (Fig. 14.6). The model proposes that attitudes, locus of control, and one's sense of personal responsibility make up the personality factors that influence intention to act in an environmentally responsible manner and that this intention is also influenced by one's own abilities (skills), knowledge of what one can do, and understanding of the issues related to environmentalism. The intention to act then influences responsible behavior along with other situational factors.

However, as the research suggests, fostering green consumer behavior change, as with other environmental behaviors, is a challenge because of the complexity of interrelationships between behaviors, motives, perceived benefits, knowledge, and perceptions. Work by Fransson and Garling (1999) proposes that factors that affect behavior

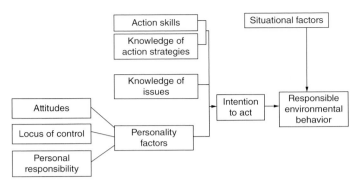

Fig. 14.6. Model of responsible environmental behavior (from Hines *et al.*, 1997).

appear to be knowledge, internal locus of control (positive control beliefs), personal responsibility, and perceived threats to personal health. Other researchers have identified factors such as status, comfort, effort, and behavioral opportunities (Steg and Vlek, 2009). In the case of tourism, internal barriers include lack of knowledge of the consequences of individual's behavior and lack of skill to affect change while external barriers encompass insufficient financial resources or green supply alternatives (Budeanu, 2007). Stern (2000) suggests that a person's environmental predisposition should be examined from the perspective of the behavior, the actor, and the context. Another perspective which may be especially useful in the field of tourism research recommends an analysis of what is being purchased or the travel choice (i.e. the service or good the consumer is purchasing) instead of the consumer's environmentalism (Peattie, 2001a). This type of approach requires the identification of factors that make a product "green" and a categorization of green products.

Green purchase perception matrix

Peattie's (2001a) green purchase perception matrix (Fig. 14.7) may be useful in classifying travel choices. The model proposes that two key variables affect the likelihood of any purchaser being influenced by environmentalism when considering a purchase: the degree of compromise involved and the degree of confidence in the environmental benefits of a particular choice. The model proposes that willingness to compromise and accept trade-offs (sacrificing quality or cost or reduced comfort) will be influenced by environmental awareness and concern, socio-demographic factors, and psychological factors. For consumers to behave in a pro-environmental manner they must be confident that the environmental issue is real and that purchasing the product will make a difference. Studies have demonstrated a significant correlation between perceived consumer effectiveness (PCE), which represents an individual's belief in their ability to exert an influence as a consumer when coupled with environmental concern, and ecologically conscious consumer behavior (Peattie, 2001a; Gilg *et al.*, 2004; Yahya *et al.*, 2013).

   This model brings together the four needs of green consumers—the need for information, the need for control, the need to make a difference, and the need to maintain current lifestyles (Ottman, 1992). The matrix can be applied to tourism products

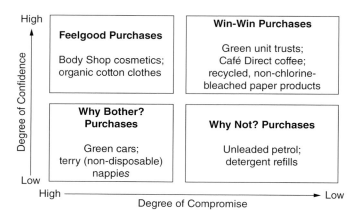

Fig. 14.7. Green purchase perception matrix (from Peattie, 2001a).

to identify the relationship between purchases based on the degree of confidence in the ability of a product to "make a difference," and the degree of compromise required. Tourism products that evoke a high degree of confidence that the purchase will have a positive effect on the environment and require a high degree of compromise are classified as "feel good purchases." In contrast "why not?" purchases are those that require minimal compromise but low confidence that they will actually make a difference. Products that require little effort but achieve significant perceived positive results are "win-win" purchases. Purchases that require significant effort but provide a lower level of technical performance or significantly higher costs are "why bother?" purchases. The focus on classifying purchases rather than the level of consumers' environmentalism may be more effective for understanding the trade-offs consumers are willing to make.

As demonstrated in TCT, trade-offs are important in green consumption because if the perceived cost outweighs the perceived benefit the consumer will not engage in a pro-environmental choice even if they have pro-environmental attitudes. A study of tour operators found that while 50% of them are willing to pay a higher price for an eco-labeled motor coach, other factors such as price, reputation for safety and service, and previous partnerships hold much more importance in their selection of a transporter (Anderson *et al.*, 2013).

The Future

Studies undertaken across a number of disciplines exploring environmental attitudes and behaviors and the relevant theories discussed in this chapter provide a solid platform for future research on environmentalism and travel choices. More research is needed to gain a better understanding of how attitudes, values, beliefs, personalities, lifestyles, and other factors influence travel choices, as well as a better understanding of barriers that prevent tourists from behaving in a pro-environmental manner (Budeanu, 2007).

Research findings from such studies can assist in designing more effective policies and the acceptance of sustainable tourism products that complement tourists' willingness to engage in environmentally responsible behavior. In particular, more research is needed on environmental holiday behaviors in general, on the relationship between everyday behaviors and holiday behavior, and on holistically changing lifestyles (Barr *et al.*, 2010). In particular further work is needed to explore why pro-environmental behavior in one life segment does not predict pro-environmental behavior in other life segments such as travel choices (Stern, 2000).

Studies are also needed to investigate tourists' environmental behavior and factors that predict their pro-environmental behavior, as well as additional research on the dynamics between tourist motivations and environmental values. Future studies may consider building on past studies that did not include the concept of self-identity as an added predictor to TPB (Sparks and Shepherd, 1992; Conner and Armitage, 1998; Staats, 2003).

In terms of methods, many challenges exist for researchers seeking to understand how attitudes affect tourist behavior. Specifically, methodologies and valid and reliable tools are needed to understand how general attitudes impact specific behaviors (Mainieri *et al.*, 1997). Also in the realm of methodologies, behavior studies rely on self-reported behaviors and caution is needed to interpret the results as many studies report low correlations between self-reported and observed behavior especially when the behaviors involve consumers' willingness to pay more for a socially desirable concept like environmentalism (Steg and Vlek, 2009).

Steg and Vlek (2009) suggest that to accurately assess environmental behavior valid behavioral measures are needed to decide which groups of individuals should be targeted and note that behavior change should be monitored over time especially if there has been an intervention to determine if behavior change over time persists. They propose there are shortcomings in many studies of environmental behavior measures because they assume that people make reasoned choices when many decisions are not rational. They recommend prioritization of targeted behaviors with a selection of those with the most negative environmental impact taking into consideration the feasibility and acceptability of behavioral changes. This approach needs valid and reliable measures of self-reported behavior. Generally, there is a lack of systematic research on the range of application of different theoretical perspectives for environmental behavior research, i.e. perceived cost and benefit, moral and normative concerns and effect.

Further research is needed to evaluate systematically the effects of interventions to prompt and change pro-environmental behavior (Steg and Vlek, 2009) as most evaluation studies have focused on informational strategies, and the workings and effectiveness of structural strategies have been studied far less (see Dwyer *et al.*, 1993; Schultz *et al.*, 1995 for reviews; Abrahamse *et al.*, 2005), which is problematic as structural strategies are more effective in promoting pro-environmental behavior. In the context of tourism, Budeanu (2007) suggests more research is required on the effectiveness of tools to change behavior such as informative tools, economic and regulatory measures.

An interdisciplinary research approach is needed to effectively address the global environmental issues of resource use because these issues are not just psychological problems, they are also ecological, technological, and socio-cultural problems (Schoot Uiterkamp and Vlek, 2007). Further work is also needed to assess systematically the merits of various theories and the conditions under which a particular theory is most successful in explaining environmental attitudes and behavior. A theory-driven approach to understanding environmental attitudes and behavior will provide a sound basis for understanding and managing global environmental issues (following Lewin, 1951: 169): "Nothing is as practical as a good theory."

The Questions

1. What factors would you include in designing a study to identify variables that influence tourists' pro-environmental behavior and attitudes?

2. How would you design a study to test if daily pro-environmental behaviors spill over into the holiday context?

3. How can theories of broad environmental behaviors be used to explain tourists' behaviors?

4. How could a research project be designed to consider multiple motivations?

References

Abrahamse, W., Steg, L., Vlek, C. and Rothengatter, T. (2005) A review of intervention studies aimed at household energy conservation. *Journal of Environmental Psychology* 25(3), 273–291.

Ajzen, I. (1971) Attitudinal vs. normative messages: an investigation of the differential effects of persuasive communications on behavior. *Sociometry* 34, 2663–2680.

Ajzen, I. (1985) From intentions to actions: a theory of planned behavior. In: Kuhl, J. and Beckman, J. (eds) *Action-Control: From Cognition to Behavior*. Springer, Heidelberg, pp. 11–39.

Ajzen, I. (1991) The theory of planned behavior. *Organizational Behavior and Human Decision Processes* 50, 179–211.

Ajzen, I. and Driver, B.L. (1992) Application of the theory of planned behavior to leisure choice. *Journal of Leisure Research* 24(3), 207–224.

Ajzen, I. and Fishbein, M. (1980) *Understanding Attitudes and Predicting Social Behavior*. Prentice Hall, Englewood Cliffs, New Jersey.

Ajzen, I. and Fishbein, M. (1997) Attitude-behavior relations: a theoretical analysis and review of empirical research. *Psychological Bulletin* 84, 888–918.

Ajzen, I. and Madden, T.J. (1986) Prediction of goal-directed behavior: a structured review. *Psychology and Health* 15, 173–189.

Alwitt, L.F. and Berger, I.E. (1993) Understanding the link between environmental attitudes and consumer product usage: measuring the moderating role of attitude strength. *Advances in Consumer Research* 20, 189–194.

Anderson, L., Mastrangelo, C., Chase, L., Kestenbaum, D. and Kolodinsky, J. (2013) Eco-labeling motorcoach operators in the North American travel tour industry: analysing the role of tour operators. *Journal of Sustainable Tourism* 21(5), 750–764.

Arcury, T.A. (1990) Environmental attitude and environmental knowledge. *Human Organization* 49(4), 300–304.

Armitage, C.J. and Conner, M. (2001) Efficacy of the theory of planned behavior: a meta-analytic review. *British Journal of Social Psychology* 40, 471–499.

Ballantyne, R. and Packer, J. (2005) Promoting environmentally sustainable attitudes and behavior through free-choice learning experiences: what is the state of the game? *Environmental Education Research* 11(3), 281–295.

Ballantyne, R., Packer, J. and Falk, J. (2011) Visitors' learning for environmental sustainability: Testing short-and long-term impacts of wildlife tourism experiences using structural equation modelling. *Tourism Management* 32(6), 1243–1252.

Bamberg, S. and Schmidt, P. (1999) Regulating transport: behavioural changes in the field. *Journal of Consumer Policy* 22(4), 479–501.

Barr, S. and Prillwitz, J. (2012) Green traveller? Exploring the spatial context of sustainable mobility styles. *Applied Geography* 32, 798–809.

Barr, S., Shaw, G., Coles, T. and Prillwitz, J. (2010) A holiday is a holiday: practicing sustainability, home and away. *Journal of Transport Geography* 18, 474–481.

Bigne, J.E., Andreu, L. and Gnoth, J. (2005) The theme park experience: an analysis of pleasure, arousal and satisfaction. *Tourism Management* 26, 833–844.

Boldero, J. (1995) The prediction of household recycling of newspapers: the role of attitudes, intentions and situational factors. *Journal of Applied Social Psychology* 25, 440–462.

Brandon, G. and Lewis, A. (1999) Reducing household energy consumptions: a qualitative and quantitative field study. *Journal of Environmental Psychology* 19(1), 75–85.

Budeanu, A. (2007) Sustainable tourist behavior—a discussion of opportunities for change. *International Journal of Consumer Studies* 31, 499–508.

Burton, L., Weston, D. and Kowalski, R. (2006) *Psychology*, 2nd edn. Wiley, Milton, Queensland, Australia.

Carr, N. (2002) The tourism-leisure behavioral continuum. *Annals of Tourism Research* 29, 972–986.

Chafe, Z. (2007) Consumer demand for quality in ecotourism. In: Black, R. and Crabtree, A. (eds) *Quality Assurance and Certification in Ecotourism*. CAB International, Wallingford, UK, pp. 164–195.

Chan, R.Y.K. (1999) Environmental attitudes and behavior of consumers in China: survey findings and implications. *Journal of International Consumer Marketing* 11(4), 25–52.

Chan, R.Y.K. and Lau, L.B.Y. (2000) Antecedents of green purchases: a survey in China. *Journal of Consumer Marketing* 17(4), 338–357.

Conner, M. and Armitage, C. (1998) Extending the theory of planned behavior: a review and avenues for further research. *Journal of Applied Social Psychology* 28(15), 1429–1464.

Consultancy and Research in Environmental Management (CERM) (2000) *Feasibility and Market Study for a European Eco-Label for Tourist Attractions (FEMATOUR)*. CREM, Amsterdam.

Crosby, L.A., Gill, J.D. and Taylor, J.R. (1981) Consumer/voter behavior in the passage of the Michigan container law. *Journal of Marketing* 9(4), 19–32.

Dawson, J., Stewart, E., Lemelin, H. and Scott, D. (2010) The carbon cost of polar bear viewing tourism in Churchill, Canada. *Journal of Sustainable Tourism* 18(3), 1–19.

De Young, R. (2000) Expanding and evaluating motives for environmentally responsible behavior. *Journal of Social Issues* 56(3), 509–526.

Dickinson, J.E. and Dickinson, J.A. (2006) Local transport and social representations: challenging the assumptions for sustainable tourism. *Journal of Sustainable Tourism* 14, 192–208.

Diekman, A. and Preisendörfer, P. (2003) Green and greenback: the behavioral effects of environmental attitudes in low-cost and high-cost situations. *Rationality and Society* 15(4), 441–472.

do Paço, A., Alves, H., Shiel, C. and Filho, W.L. (2013) A multi-country level analysis of the environmental attitudes and behaviors among young consumers. *Journal of Environmental Planning and Management* 56(10), 1532–1548.

Dunlap, R.E. and Van Liere, K.D. (1978) The new environmental paradigm: a proposed instrument and preliminary results. *The Journal of Environmental Education* 9, 10–19.

Dunlap, R.E., Van Liere, K.D., Mertig, A.G. and Emmet Jones, R. (2000) Measuring endorsement of the new ecological paradigm: a revised NEP scale. *Journal of Social Issues* 56, 425–442.

Dwyer, W.O., Leeming, F.C., Cobern, M.K., Porter, B.E. and Jackson, J.M. (1993) Critical review of behavioral intentions to preserve the environment: research since 1980. *Environment and Behavior* 25, 275–321.

Dwyer, L., Forsyth, P., Spurr, R. and Hoque, S. (2010) Estimating the carbon footprint of Australian tourism. *Journal of Sustainable Tourism* 18(3), 355–376.

Einsmann, H. (1992) The environment: an entrepreneurial approach. *Long Range Planning* 25(4), 22–24.

Fishbein, M. and Ajzen, I. (1975) *Belief, Attitude, Intention and Behavior: an introduction to theory and research.* Addison-Wesley, Reading, Massachusetts.

Font, X. and Tribe, J. (2001) Promoting green tourism: the future of environmental awards. *International Journal of Tourism Research* 3(1), 9–21.

Fraj-Andres, E. and Martinez-Salinas, E. (2007) Impact of environmental knowledge on ecological consumer behavior: an empirical analysis. *Journal of International Consumer Marketing* 19(3), 73–102.

Fransson, M. and Garling, T. (1999) Environmental concern: conceptual definitions, measurement methods and research findings. *Journal of Environmental Psychology* 19, 369–382.

Gilg, A., Barr, S. and Ford, N. (2004) Green consumption or sustainable lifestyles? Identifying the sustainable consumer. *Futures* 37(6), 481–504.

Gössling, S. and Schumacher, K.P. (2010) Implementing carbon neutral destination policies: issues from the Seychelles. *Journal of Sustainable Tourism* 18(3), 377–391.

Grob, A. (1995) A structural model of environmental attitudes and behavior. *Journal of Environmental Psychology* 15, 209–220.

Guagnano, G.A., Stern, P.C. and Dietz, T. (1995) Influences on attitude-behavior relationships. A natural experiment with curbside recycling. *Environment and Behavior* 27, 699–718.

Ham, S. and Han, H. (2013) Role of perceived fit with hotels' green practices in the formation of customer loyalty: impact of environmental concerns. *Asia Pacific Journal of Tourism Research* 18(7), 731–748.

Ham, S.H., Weiler, B., Hughes, M., Brown, T., Curtis, J. and Poll, M. (2008) *Asking Visitors to Help: Research Guide Strategic Communication for Protected Area Management.* CRC for Sustainable Tourism Pty Ltd, Gold Coast, Australia, p. 2

Han, H. and Kim, Y. (2010) An investigation of green customers' decision formation: developing an extended model of the theory of planned behavior. *International Journal of Hospitality Management* 29, 659–668.

Han, H., Hsu, L.T.J. and Sheu, C. (2010) Application of the theory of planned behavior to green hotel choice: testing the effect of environmental friendly activities. *Journal of Environmental Psychology* 26, 227–235.

Hines, J.M., Hungerford, H.R. and Tomera, A.N. (1987) Analysis and synthesis of research on responsible behavior: a meta analysis. *Journal of Environmental Education* 18, 1–8.

Hopper, J.R. and Nielsen, J. (1991) Recycling as altruistic behavior: normative and behavioral strategies to expand participation in a community recycling program. *Environment and Behavior* 23(2), 195–220.

Jaafar, M. and Maideen, S.A. (2012) Ecotourism-related products and activities, and the economic sustainability of small and medium island chalets. *Tourism Management* 33(3), 683–691.

Jackson, T. (2005) *Motivating Sustainable Consumption: A Review of Evidence on Consumer Behavior and Behavioral Change.* Poly Studies Institute, London. Report to the Sustainable Development Research Network.

Jett, J., Thapa, B. and Swett, R. (2013) Boater speed compliance in manatee zones: examining a proposed predictive model. *Society & Natural Resources: An International Journal* 26(1), 95–104.

Juvan, E. and Dolnicar, S. (2014) Can tourists easily choose a low carbon footprint vacation? *Journal of Sustainable Tourism* 22, 175–194.

Kalinowski, C., Gary, L. and Johnson, B. (2006) Recycling as a reflection of balanced self-interest: a test of the Metaeconomics Approach. *Environment and Behavior* 38(3), 333–355.

C. Jurowski and R. Black

Kempton, W., Boster, J.S. and Hartley, J.A. (1995) *Environmental Values in American Culture*. MIT Press, Cambridge, Massachusetts.

Kim, A.K., Airey, D. and Szivas, E. (2011) The multiple assessment of interpretation effectiveness: promoting visitors' environmental attitudes and behavior. *Journal of Travel Research* 50, 321–334.

Kollmuss, A. and Agyeman, J. (2002) Mind the gap: why do people act environmentally and what are the barriers to pro-environmental behavior. *Environmental Education Research* 8(3), 240–260.

Lam, T. and Hsu, C.H.C. (2006) Predicting behavioral intention of choosing a travel destination. *Tourism Management* 27, 589–599.

Lee, T.H., Jan, F.H. and Yang, C.C. (2013) Environmentally responsible behavior of nature-based tourists: a review. *International Journal of Development and Sustainability* 2(1), 1–16.

Leonidou, L.C., Leonidou, C.N. and Kvasova, O. (2010) Antecedents and outcomes of consumer environmentally friendly attitudes and behavior. *Journal of Marketing Management* 26(13–14), 1319–1344.

Lewin, K. (1951) *Field Theory in Social Science: Selected Theoretical Papers*. Harper & Brothers, New York.

Mainieri, T., Barnett, E.G., Valdero, T.R., Unipan, J.B. and Oskamp, S. (1997) Green buying: the influence of environmental concern on consumer behavior. *Journal of Social Psychology* 137(2), 189–204.

Maloney, M.P. and Ward, M.P. (1973) Ecology: let's hear from the people. An objective scale for the measurement of ecological attitudes and knowledge. *American Psychologist* 28, 583–586.

Manfredo, M.J. and Bright, A.D. (1991) A model for assessing the effects of communication on recreationists. *Journal of Leisure Research* 23(1), 1–20.

Manfredo, M.J., Teel, T.L. and Bright, A.D. (2004) Application of the concepts of values and attitudes in human dimensions of natural resources research. In: Manfredo, M.J., Vaske, J.J., Bruyere, B.L., Field, D.R. and Brown, P.J. (eds) *Society and Natural Resources: A Summary of Knowledge*. Modern Litho, Jefferson, Michigan, pp. 305–314.

Manfredo, M.J., Rechkemmer, A. and Vaske, J.J. (2014) *Understanding Society and Natural Resources: Forging New Strands of Integration Across The Social Sciences*. Springer Press, New York.

McKenzie-Mohr, D. (2000) Fostering sustainable behavior through community-based social marketing. *American Psychologist* 55(5), 531–538.

McKenzie-Mohr, D. and Smith, W. (1999) *Fostering Sustainable Development: An introduction to community-based social marketing*. New Society Publishers, Gabriola Island, Canada.

McKercher, B. and Prideaux, B. (2011) Are tourism impacts low on personal environmental agendas? *Journal of Sustainable Tourism* 19(3), 325–345.

McKercher, B., Prideaux, B., Cheung, C. and Law, R. (2010) Achieving voluntary reductions in the carbon footprint of tourism and climate change. *Journal of Sustainable Tourism* 18(3), 297–317.

Mehta, H., Baez, A. and O'Loughlin, P. (2002) *International Ecolodge Guidelines*. The International Ecotourism Society, Washington, DC.

Mihalic, T. (2013) A green tourism barometer in the time of economic crisis—the concept and case of Slovenia. *Tourism in South East Europe* 2, 1–17.

Miller, G. (2003) Consumerism in sustainable tourism: a survey of UK consumers. *Journal of Sustainable Tourism* 11(1), 17–39.

Mintel (1991) *The Second Green Consumer Report*. Mintel, London.

Noe, F.P., Jurowski, C., Uysal, M. and Fessenmaier, D.R. (1993) Effects of user and trip characteristics on responses to communication messages. *Communication & Channel Systems in Tourism Marketing* 2/3, 147–169.

Nordlund, A.M. and Garvill, J. (2002) Value structures behind proenvironmental behavior. *Environment and Behavior* 34(6), 740–756.

Ogonowska, M. and Torre, D. (2012) Sustainable tourism and the emergence of new environmental norms. *European Journal of Tourism Research* 6(2), 141–153.

Oskamp, S., Harrington, M.J., Edwards, T.C., Sherwood, D.L., Okuda, S.M. and Swanson, D.C. (1991) Factors influencing household recycling behavior. *Environment and Behavior* 23, 494–519.

Ottman, I. (1992) Industry's response to green consumerism. *Journal of Business Strategy* 3(10), 3–10.

Peattie, K. (2001a) Towards sustainability: the third age of green marketing. *The Marketing Review* 2, 129–146.

Peattie, K. (2001b) Golden goose or wild goose? The hunt for the green consumer. *Business Strategy and the Environment* 10, 18–19.

Petty, R.E. and Cacioppo, J.T. (1996) *Attitudes and Persuasion: Classic and Contemporary Approaches*. Wm. C. Brown, Dubuque, Iowa.

Petty, R.E., Wegener, D.T. and Fabrigar, L.R. (1997) Attitudes and attitude change. *Annual Review of Psychology* 48, 609.

Schoot Uiterkamp, A. and Vlek, C. (2007) Practice and outcomes of multidisciplinary research for environmental sustainability. *Journal of Social Issues* 63(1), 175–197.

Schultz, P.W., Oskamp, S. and Mainieri, T. (1995) Who recycles and when? A review of personal and situational factors. *Journal of Environmental Psychology* 15, 105–121.

Schultz, P.W., Shriver, C., Tabanico, J.J. and Khazian, A.M. (2004) Implicit connections with nature. *Journal of Environmental Psychology* 24, 31–42.

Schwartz, S.H. (1992) Universals in the content and structure of values: theoretical advances and empirical test in 20 countries. *Advances in Experimental Social Psychology* 10, 221–270.

Scott, D., Hall, M. and Gössling, S. (2012) *Tourism and Climate Change: Impacts, Adaptation and Mitigation*. Routledge, New York.

Shipworth, M. (2000) *Motivating Home Energy Action — A Handbook of What Works*. Australian Greenhouse Office. Available at: http://www.greenhouse.gov.au/local/motivating/index.html (accessed 8 November 2006).

Siminitiras, A., Schlegelmilch, B.B. and Diamantopoulos, A. (1993) Greening the marketing mix: a review of the literature and an agenda for future research. In: Chias, J. and Sureda, J. (eds) *Proceedings of the 1993 EMAC Conference*. Marketing for the New Europe, Barcelona, pp. 1355–1381.

Singh, A.J. and Houdre, H. (eds) (2010) *Hotel Sustainable Development: Principles and Best Practices*. American Hotel and Lodging Educational Institute, Lansing, Michigan.

Sparks, P. and Shepherd, R. (1992) Self-identity and the theory of planned behavior: assessing the role of identification with "green consumerism." *Social Psychology Quarterly* 55, 388–399.

Sririam, V. and Forman, A.M. (1993) The relative importance of products' environmental attributes: a cross cultural comparison. *International Marketing Review* 10(3), 51–70.

Staats, H. (2003) Understanding pro-environmental attitudes and behavior: an analysis and review of research based on the theory of planned behavior. In: Bonnes, M., Lee, T. and Bonaiuto, M. (eds) *Psychological Theories for Environmental Issues*. Ashgate Publishing Ltd, Aldershot, UK, pp. 171–201.

Steg, L. and Vlek, C. (2009) Encouraging pro-environmental behavior: an integrative review and research agenda. *Journal of Environmental Psychology* 29, 309–317.

Stern, P.C. (1992) Psychological dimensions of global environmental change. *Annual Review of Psychology* 43, 269–302.

Stern, P.C. (2000) Toward a coherent theory of environmentally significant behavior. *Journal of Social Issues* 56, 407–424.

Stern, P.C., Dietz, T. and Kalof, L. (1993) Value orientations, gender and environmental concerns. *Environment and Behavior* 24, 332–348.

C. Jurowski and R. Black

Stern, P.C., Dietz, T., Abel, T., Guagnano, G.A. and Kalof, L. (1999) A value-belief-norm theory of support for social movements: the case of environmentalism. *Human Ecology Review* 6, 81–97.

Taylor, S. and Todd, P. (1995) An integrated model of waste management behavior: a test of household recycling and composting intentions. *Environment and Behavior* 27, 603–630.

Thapa, B. (2010) The mediation effect of outdoor recreation participation on environmental attitude-behavior correspondence. *Journal of Environmental Education* 41(3), 133–150.

Thapa, B., Graefe, A.R. and Meyer, L.A. (2006) Specialization and marine based environmental behaviors among SCUBA divers. *Journal of Leisure Research* 38(4), 601.

Thogersen, J. and Olander, F. (2002) Human values and the emergence of a sustainable consumption pattern: a panel study. *Journal of Economic Psychology* 23, 605–630.

Tucker, P. (1999) Normative influences in household waste recycling. *Journal of Environmental Planning and Management* 42(1), 63–83.

United Nations World Tourism Organization (UNWTO) (2009) *From Davos to Copenhagen and Beyond: Advancing Tourism's Response to Climate Change*. United Nations World Tourism Organization. Available at: http://www.unwto.org/pdf/FromDavos_to%Copenhagen_beyond_UNWTOPaper_ElectronicVersion.pdf (accessed 1 October 2014).

Uysal, M., Jurowski, C., Noe, F.P. and McDonald, C.D. (1994) Environmental attitude by trip and visitor characteristics: US Virgin Island National Park. *Tourism Management* 15(4), 284–295.

Verplanken, B. and Faes, S. (1999) Good intentions, bad habits and effects of forming implementation intentions on healthy eating. *European Journal of Social Psychology* 29, 591–604.

Vining, J. and Ebreo, A. (1992) What makes a recycler? A comparison of recyclers and non-recyclers. *Environment and Behavior* 22(1), 55–73.

Yahya, W.K., Hashim, N.H., Mohamad, S.A. and Ramly, Z. (2013) The relationship between perceived consumer effectiveness, environmental concern and ecologically conscious consumer behavior. *Annual International Conference on Enterprise Marketing & Globalization*, Singapore, pp. 93–98. DOI: 10.5176/2251-1970_BizStrategy13.11.

Yan, J., Barkmann, J., Zschiergner, A.K. and Marggraf, R. (2008) The sceptics' challenge for sustainable tourism in the Southwest China biodiversity hotspot: a choice experiment approach. *Journal of China Tourism Research* 4(1), 3–21.

15 Theory and the Future of Tourism Research

HOLLY DONOHOE[1]* AND KELLY S. BRICKER[2]

[1]Eric Friedheim Tourism Institute, Department of Tourism, Recreation and Sport Management, University of Florida, Gainesville, Florida; [2]Department of Parks, Recreation, and Tourism, College of Health, University of Utah, Salt Lake City, Utah

Introduction

The purpose of this book was to provide scholars in tourism with a text to explore a range of theoretical perspectives and concepts, as well as the creative use of theory and conceptual frameworks and constructs to expand our understanding of the complexities of tourism research. As you may recall, this book began with several questions that were posted to a tourism list serve and these questions sparked an unresolved discussion about tourism and its theoretical underpinnings. We sincerely hope this text contributes to the ongoing discussion and we trust that it provides some clarity, and ignites curiosity for graduate students and scholars who are working through the theoretical underpinnings of their own research. By extension, it is our ambition that this book will reveal new opportunities for expanding how we pursue research in tourism and related fields. As the previous chapters identified, there is a multitude of issues relative to tourism and equally a multitude of ways to go about researching them. The implications for research in tourism and application to the field are discussed in this chapter.

The Utility of Theory

Several chapters reflected on the utility of theory in understanding tourism. Several references were made to the fact that theory provides a guide to action. Theory has been utilized to deliver guidance on inclusion when it comes to strengthening stakeholder and community development processes. Theory and conceptual frameworks have also been used to help understand the complexities of locations. For example, some theories are congruent with current issues and problems faced in society, and offer support in framing issues within locales. Stakeholder theory, for example, provides a framework to assist researchers in contemplating all actors within sustainability, as well as public processes for planning and sustainable development of tourism.

Because sustainability embraces economic, social-cultural, and environmental considerations and benefits, several theories were identified that address the need for several ideas, such as: inter-organizational cooperation, bringing together diverse stakeholders,

---

*Corresponding author, e-mail: hdonohoe@hhp.ufl.edu

integrating planning and management frameworks that fit with issues relative to poverty alleviation, biodiversity conservation, and social and environmental justice concepts. However, it was also noted that there is not a theory per se that specifically addresses sustainability in its entirety.

In summary, we use theory to establish ways of thinking or lenses for interpretation of what is happening or the issues in the world around us. Theory creates a place to land, a place to build questions and concepts, a place from which to focus for further systematic inquiry.

The Application of Theory

Tourism is an applied area or field of study; as a result, there are scores of examples and actual application of theory is quite diverse. Through several chapters we learned that the development of tourism should be integrated into overall tourism planning efforts on all scales (i.e. nationally, regionally, state, community, business).

Many of the theories involved with tourism planning and management have recognized that a top-down decision-making model is no longer appropriate when considering tourism development. Theories such as stakeholder theory and systems theory have proven useful for identifying tourism stakeholders, understanding the complex relationships and power dynamics that may or may not exist between them, identifying their commonalities and differences, examining where conflict and consensus take place, and the processes and outcomes of planning and management activities. Further, from an applied perspective, indicators for gauging success are needed as part of a community development framework.

Many authors within this text have suggested that it is important to expand beyond the typical uses of theory and that tourism is well positioned to do so by pulling from other disciplines because of its extensive links to economic, social-cultural, and environmental issues within society. Authors also suggest that applications of new and extant theories such as innovation theory provide an opportunity to address innovation in the context of destinations, sustainability, product development, stakeholder and actor networks, and visitor behavior. In fact, there may also be complementary theories as well. Some have suggested utilizing a systems thinking approach to innovation within sustainability for example. By doing so, there is the opportunity to expand beyond the context of a business and move the boundaries of spatial influences into a larger context. For instance, some authors have suggested utilizing innovation theory at the destination level, to help understand the success and challenges of diverse destinations. This expands its application from a business-centric view to a larger understanding on how destinations develop, etc.

Another use of innovation theory could be in the application of understanding sustainability from the localized business level to destination or country level. This would potentially help address why and perhaps how sustainability and sustainable tourism practices take root in one locale and not in others. With all of the challenges facing the planet, and given that tourism is one of the largest economic development sectors, there is an opportunity to tie tourism to many social, environmental, and economic aspects of society in terms of development and management.

The results of this text give the impression that there are many opportunities to expand our understanding of the tourism product and its influence on guests mediated through guides or in essence "the frontlines" of many tourism products. Applied research beyond ecotourism and adventure tourism can have significant application for how the industry manages tourism, sustainability, cultural issues, and impacts. Since employment is such a crucial aspect in tourism and the tourism product, there are many opportunities to explore the extent of staff development, and the extent to which guides are recruited, trained, and empowered to deal with variations in role expectations and performance. When we consider the important role guides have, not only in ensuring a positive tourism experience, but also with respect to poverty alleviation through employment, safety, education, and destination image, guides or liaisons that translate the tourism experience are understudied and have important contributions for the industry. Further, tourists' experiential expectations are diverse and in a constant state of change, and we know little about the impacts of these changes on guides regarding trends, new and emerging markets, and crisis management (natural and sociopolitical related).

Research Gaps: Considering the Future of Tourism Scholarship

To summarize the gaps and future directions of research in tourism would require a volume so large it would take the next millennium to complete. However, through our research and the presentation of the many ideas contained within these chapters, there is much to ponder as we move forward as scholars. These ideas are briefly summarized below.

Stakeholders, residents, and community

Through an exploration of several chapters we have learned that there continues to be inequality between stakeholders within communities while local business owners struggle to maintain a voice in the decision-making process. Yet research has shown the unique relationships between perceived success in tourism development and community engagement. Some have suggested a need to develop a typology of social representation within community development through tourism, to ensure representativeness and empowerment success.

Within this realm of community development, it is important to learn more about how community participation in tourism might empower all citizens and shift the balance between the powerful and the powerless. Expanded studies that explore empowerment through tourism may assist in our understanding of the effect of the distribution of power and decision making among community groups. It appears that understanding the distribution of power within the community could greatly benefit from the application of new and extant theories that could help us understand the interrelationships that exist among the stakeholders or sectors within and beyond the tourism domain.

Power differentiation was mentioned in several chapters. Since tourism is often at odds with other forms of development, especially extractive or environmentally disruptive forms, an area that appears to be missing in tourism-related literature is how power is created and exchanged through social network linkages, especially between both complementary and competing organizations within diverse sectors within a community.

H. Donohoe and K.S. Bricker

Further, as part of the quadruple bottom line, where governance and policy or institutional notions are addressed, theory-driven research is needed to develop a knowledge base on governance networks that develop and set policy. While stakeholder theory does provide a framework for understanding power relations, theories borrowed from development, business, sociology, and/or politics may help to shape new research and shed new light on power, development, social networks, and tourism.

To increase our understanding of the way residents perceive tourism and how we might advocate for tourism as a community development strategy, researchers have called for a causal model that is testable and can guide the further development of research. Again, perhaps there is a theory that can be borrowed or adapted from another discipline that could assist us in better understanding the causal relationships associated with tourism as a community development strategy. Concomitantly, inductive research should be encouraged in this area and all areas of tourism research so as to facilitate the development of new theories, models, conceptual frameworks and constructs that are reflective of the truly unique subject of inquiry that is tourism.

Tour guiding

Tour guiding is an area of tourism research that holds many opportunities for understanding the positive outcomes for visitors, guides, and other stakeholders involved. While there has been significant work in understanding the role of guides within the ecotourism and adventure tourism sectors, there is an opportunity to expand understanding of the role tour guides have in other sectors within the industry. Researchers have identified gaps with respect to intercultural communication and linguistics theories to tour guiding experiences but there remain many areas of inquiry that would benefit from a theory-driven approach. For example, leadership theory has been suggested and would seem like a natural fit for research concerned with tour guides, but it has not yet been empirically tested and its utility for research of this kind has not yet been established.

Tourism marketing

Because of the experiential, as well as complex nature of the tourism product, marketing researchers are calling for tourism-specific theories that incorporate constructs such as destination image, tourist satisfaction, and loyalty with greater homogeneity of measures and more sophisticated measures.

Travel is being shared at unprecedented rates, not only pictures, but video as well, which is consistently having an impact on how a destination is perceived. From blogs to wikis to Trip Advisor, how potential travelers search for and access information has widened and become very complex. Word of mouth has taken on an entirely new meaning; no longer is it just friends and family, individuals are seeking out the opinions of strangers and fellow travelers through communications portals such as Trip Advisor, Expedia, and online blogs as potentially "trusted" sources of information. Clearly this is an evolving area of research that could certainly benefit from incorporating theory from other disciplines—particularly communications theories that could help us better understand the drivers, motivations, outcomes, and challenges associated with marketing in this (new) electronic landscape.

Sustainability in tourism

Sustainability appears to be a foundational aspect for successful tourism development, marketing and communications, economic growth, environmental conservation, and community development. Yet there continues to be a need for research that addresses indicators in social-cultural justice concepts, economic viability, and conservation of biodiversity ideas—known as the "triple bottom line" for long-term destination planning and management success. While there are theories such as political ecology, eco-feminism, and others that have provided a framework for critical inquiry related to sustainable development and management, their specific application in sustainable tourism research has been sparse.

Systems thinking and resiliency theoretical approaches may be one way to begin addressing these complex ideas. For example, while several studies address the importance of economic, social-cultural, environmental, and political/institutional elements, it is not clear what the sphere of influence each has on the other. Nor is it clear what the relationships between and among these constructs is. Some have suggested that chaos theory provides a conceptual lens from which to study how tourism-related entities adapt to their surroundings to form new relationships and partnerships. There may be complementary uses within future research that addresses the relationship(s) between stakeholder theory, tourism success, and sustainability. There also appears to be a need for tools and techniques for actually measuring this success, including benefits to the environment, socio-cultural or economic aspects to development and management of tourism. The complex systems approach is useful in the study of tourism destinations, and some acknowledge this especially for those destinations in and/or near protected areas. Increasing the interplay between ecosystem services and sustainable tourism development adds to the complexity. Certainly there is room here to improve upon what we know and how we know it with regards to the sustainable development of tourism. If sustainability is to be the paradigm under which tourism should be developed into the future, then future research should also be driven by new and extant theories that challenge the current ways of knowing and doing tourism today and into the unforeseeable tomorrow.

Destination place and behavior

While the research concerned with place perspectives has developed over the last few decades, it lacks in areas concerned with the diversity of participants and marginalized populations. This is especially relevant with respect to those who identify as black or African American, Indigenous, Aboriginal or Native, lesbian, gay, bisexual, and transgender (LGBT), and others from traditionally marginalized groups. Furthermore, researchers suggest that place attachment has been conceptualized from a privileged and hegemonic North American perspective that overlooks, submerses, ignores, and/or overlooks other perspectives on destination and place in the tourism context. A call to action has been issued in the scientific literature for scholars and practitioners to consider local place meanings within the context of regional or global meanings, which can enrich understandings of place-related constructs. There is an emerging theoretical and methodological literature that is shaping research concerned with the "other" within the tourism domain but there is much to be learned, borrowed, and adapted from other disciplinary domains that are attempting to be more inclusive of the voices of the other; disciplines such as anthropology, sociology, and political science.

Theory-driven research is also needed to understand better how processes of change impact spaces, places, and destinations. Research that addresses what happens when significant and/or acute change occurs, or when places are lost beyond recognition through development, natural disasters, or other causes, could certainly benefit from the application of Bowlby's attachment theory (1977) for example, to understand recovery, and how individuals establish new relationships with places. Another area is the impact of technology and how it changes all aspects of the tourism exchange from the ways in which people are connecting with destinations to the ways in which they are experiencing them. Technological advances can and do provide real-time connections to places around the globe. This is happening in National Parks, wildlife viewing sites in protected areas, UNESCO World Heritage Sites, historic attractions, amusement parks, and many other places and destinations around the world. Interactions with place are changing and these new types of interactions provide viable areas for research that could certainly benefit from one or more of the theoretical perspectives mentioned in this book.

Methods and approaches

In terms of methods, many challenges exist for researchers seeking to understand how attitudes affect tourist behavior. Specifically, methodologies and valid and reliable tools are needed to understand how general attitudes impact specific behaviors, how individuals interact with the internet in developing destination image, the role of social media in marketing and image development, etc.

A consistent theme through all areas of the text includes a need for interdisciplinary approaches to complex issues. This may include combining theories, or moving towards comprehensive constructs that account for systematic impacts of social, environmental, and economic considerations.

Final Thoughts

Tourism research spans social science and natural science, and tourism is intertwined in almost every aspect of the social, economic, natural, and cultural environment. Arising from Rio+20 came a call to action for one of the largest economic drivers today—tourism. As such, tourism has the opportunity to positively influence the world, directly and indirectly, as the number of travelers continues to increase annually. Yet there are many challenges and questions that research can address to facilitate and/or contribute to responsible economic development, socio-cultural justice, and biological diversity. From climate change to technology, to environmental conservation and land use, to social capital development and equality, there are elements of advancing societies that will change how tourism is planned and managed in the future. Scholars might view this as an opportunity or run in the opposite direction—these problems bring an increased complexity into addressing vital questions through research. Yet it is our belief that research can actively enhance and support how we go about the business of tourism in all of its iterations. The challenge rests with you. We see the only limits to this task being one's creativity, discipline, reflexivity, and perseverance.

We challenge scholars to consider what lies before us and to engage in the theoretical debate that is critical to advancing tourism as a scholastic pursuit and a global industry. Rather than the one-off article here and there, we should engage in and value longitudinal and deeply qualitative work that contributes to the development of tourism theory. Equally, we should value studies that empirically test new theories and/or those borrowed from other disciplines so that we can establish their value for tourism inquiry. These key tasks are echoed and emphasized throughout the pages of this book and, as such, they are strongly reinforced here for our readers. After all, each one of us has a shot to make a difference, to move an industry forward in new, exciting, and sustainable ways, and to have an impact on the complexity, challenges, uncertainty, conflict, and connectivity that is embedded in the academic pursuit of knowledge and the management of tourism around the world. By attempting to demystify the theoretical context in which tourism research and practice takes place, we hope that you will go forward with your own work with some new insights, ideas, and understandings, so that you too can make a difference.

H. Donohoe and K.S. Bricker

Appendix   Additional Theories Applied in the Context of Tourism

PRESENTED BY LAURA BECERRA, KELLY S. BRICKER
AND NORMA NICKERSON

This appendix briefly reviews additional theories that have been applied in the context of tourism and associated citations. While not intended to be a comprehensive or exhaustive list, it may be useful when considering other theories used to explain a diverse set of topics in tourism research. By sharing these theories, in addition to igniting ideas surrounding various topics in tourism, we also hope it inspires new applications of theories and expanding tourism scholarship and innovation in tourism studies.

World Systems or Dependency Theory

World systems theory is a socioeconomic and political theory that seeks to explain the unequal development opportunities and resulting disparities between developed and developing nations. According to world systems theory scholar, Immanuel Wallerstein, developed nations are at the core of the current economic system while developing nations are the periphery or outskirts of it. Nations in the core perpetuate the unbalanced interactions between themselves and the outskirts. Furthermore, interactions are perpetuated because such a system functions to provide for those industrialized nations in the core, which hold economic as well as political control (Wallerstein, 1974).

This theory has been employed in the field of tourism as a means to evaluate and critique the impacts of mass tourism on developing nations and to examine the unequal distribution of economic benefits derived from tourism. This theory has also been used to compare and contrast mass and ecotourism impacts on developing nations and has critiqued failing ecotourism projects. In addition, the world systems theory advocates for ecotourism projects that are better planned and offer more equitable distribution of economic benefits.

References and further reading

Khan, M. (1997) Tourism development and dependency theory: mass tourism vs. ecotourism. *Annals of Tourism Research* 24(4), 988–991.
Lacher, J. and Nepal, S. (2010) Dependency and development in northern Thailand. *Annals of Tourism Research* 37(4), 947–968.
Steiner, C. (1997) Tourism, poverty reduction and political economy: Egyptian perspectives on tourism's economic benefits in a semi-rentier state. *Tourism Planning & Development* 3(3), 161–177.
Wallerstein, I. (1974) *The Modern World-System I. Capitalist Agriculture and the Origins of the European World-Economy in the Sixteenth Century*. Academic Press, New York.

Social Disruption or Social Disorganization Theory

Social disruption theory is a sociological theory that aims to explain rapid sociological changes and the impacts of these changes on communities. The social disruption theory states that communities experiencing rapid growth typically enter a period of generalized crisis and loss of traditional routines and attitudes. Social disruption theory also asserts that rapid community change resulting from population increase leads to an array of social problems indicative of overall community disorganization (Greider *et al.*, 1991).

Social disruption theory is used in the tourism field to better understand changes that are generated from tourism and their influence on communities (i.e. boomtowns, rural communities). Tourism communities seem to provide excellent settings to examine some postulations of social disruption theory because some kinds of tourism communities experience relatively rapid growth accompanied by intensive development and rapid social change over a relatively short period of time. Social disruption theory is also used to explain a community's ability to adjust to an initial change and or its potential to overcome the initial challenges (i.e. crime, uneven distribution of economic resources).

References and further reading

Greider, T., Krannich, R.S. and Berry, E.H. (1991) Local identity, solidarity, and trust in changing rural communities. *Sociological Focus* 24(4), 263–282.
England, J.L. and Albrecht, S.L. (1984) Boomtowns and social disruption. *Rural Sociology* 49(2), 230–246.
Park, M. and Stokowski, P. (2009) Social disruption and crime in rural communities: comparisons across three levels of tourism growth. *Tourism Management* 30(6), 905–915.
Rose, D. and Clear, T. (2006) Incarceration, social capital, and crime implications for social disorganization theory. *Criminology* 36(3), 441–480.

Growth Machine Theory

Growth machine theory is a socioeconomic theory, which seeks to identify the variables that promote or hinder economic development. Growth machine theory is often used to expand on urban (planning) theory discussions. The growth machine theory focuses on the factions and coalitions that emerge in support of urban growth. The theory argues that cities and other urban spaces are not void of specific interests, including economic, sentimental, and psychological interests that have the potential to influence politics and reshape spaces and the economic development that occurs within them (Molotch, 1976).

In tourism, growth machine theory has been used to better understand tourism stakeholders. Moreover, growth machine theory has been employed to expose the differences in development attitudes among residents and elites (locals or tourists). Growth machine theory demonstrates that social actions (manipulation, power, influence) are prevalent in shaping economic development projects and in the kinds of expected economic benefits derived from such projects. In tourism projects this theory has been used to examine land development conflicts as well as assess the differing attitudes and perceptions of tourism projects.

References and further reading

Harrill, R. (2004) Planning residents' attitudes toward tourism development: a literature review with implications for tourism. *Journal of Planning Literature* 18, 251–265.

Harrill, R., Uysal, M., Cardon, P.W., Vong, F. and Dioko, L. (2011) Resident attitudes towards gaming and tourism development in Macao: Growth machine theory as a context for identifying supporters and opponents. *International Journal of Tourism Research* 13(1), 41–53.

Molotch, H. (1976) The city as a growth machine: toward a political economy of place. *The American Journal of Sociology* 82(2), 309–332.

Means–End (Chain) Theory

Means–end (chain) theory is a marketing theory and is based on a model of consumers' cognitive structures, depicting the way in which concrete product characteristics are linked to valued end states desired by consumers. Specifically, it focuses on the linkages among the attributes that exist in products (the means), the consequences for the consumer provided by the attributes, and the personal values (the ends) the consequences reinforce (Gutman, 1982). Means–end theory has been widely used in marketing to identify values-based motivations behind consumption.

Means–end theory has enabled tourism researchers to better understand tourist behavior by examining the relationship between personal values and service attributes (McIntosh and Thyne, 2005). The objective of this theory in tourism research is to provide an effective way of targeting services, means of communications, and the general promotion of services in order to attain higher levels of tourist satisfaction. Thus, this theory advocates for incorporating individual psychological perspectives in tourism marketing and services.

References and further reading

Gutman, J. (1982) A means-end chain model based on consumer categorization processes. *Journal of Marketing* 46, 60–72.

McDonald, S., Thyne, M. and McMorland, L.-A. (2008) Means-end theory in tourism research. *Annals of Tourism Research* 35(2), 596–599.

McIntosh, A. and Thyne, M. (2005) Understanding tourist behavior using means–end chain theory. *Annals of Tourism Research* 32, 259–262.

Reynolds, T. and Gutman, J. (1988) Laddering theory, method, analysis and interpretation. *Journal of Advertising Research*, February/March, 11–31.

Cited often

Reynolds, T. and Olson, J. (2001) *Understanding Consumer Decision Making: The Means–End Approach to Marketing and Advertising Strategy*. Lawrence Erlbaum Associates, New Jersey.

Central Place Theory

Central place theory is a geographic theory that seeks to explain patterns of (economic) development and settlement. Central place theory is concerned with the size, number, functional characteristics, and spacing of settlements, which are nodal points for distribution of goods and services to surrounding market areas (Malczewski, 2009). This theory is heavily employed in urban geography to explain the growth and development of cities (and their services, amenities and population levels). This theory also discusses how a particular area/region may become successful in the economic activities it is able to generate. It is widely used to explain the success of cities but also has been used to explain the uniqueness of remote areas and their success in tourism. Central place theory also enables (development, economic and land-use) planners to predict economically successful areas/regions.

In tourism, central place theory has been used as a basis for understanding the features of a host location and its potential economic outcomes and impacts. Central place theory offers a means for understanding why some destinations are better suited to tourism development than others. The central place theory also states that areas rich in natural amenities yet lacking in infrastructure may receive an inequitable share of the regional economic change brought on by development. Central place theory can also assist in determining the potential that a destination has to develop a certain type of tourism and advocates for experts to evaluate the area's resources as well as those of its competitors. The tourism literature has also indicated the employment of central place theory in sport tourism development (and infrastructure development).

References and further reading

Daniels, M. (2006) Central place theory and sport tourism impacts. *Annals of Tourism Research* 34(2), 332–347.
Hinch, T. and Higham, E. (2002) Sport tourism: a framework for research. *International Journal of Tourism Research* 3(1), 45–59.
Malczewski, J. (2009) Central place theory. *International Encyclopedia of Human Geography*, 26–30.

Collaboration Theory

Collaboration theory has been widely employed in the fields of business, (public) policy, and organizational administration, however its definition has been elusive and thus malleable to these various disciplines. Gajda (2004) recognizes the lack of common understanding for this term and proposed a set of principles to better understand the role and meaning of collaboration theory. The principles she outlines are: (i) collaboration is an imperative; (ii) collaboration is known by many names; (iii) collaboration is a journey and not a destination; (iv) with collaboration the personal is as important as the procedural; and (v) collaboration develops in stages. Collaboration theory seeks to understand a process undertaken by various stakeholders with the same (or similar) goal. The disciplines aforementioned have employed collaboration theory and techniques in marketing (business), consensus building (policy), and decision making (organizations). Thus, this theory seeks to explain the processes that occur in order to achieve a common goal.

In tourism, collaboration theory is employed to conduct stakeholder analyses. This theory is also used in tourism planning and development. Assessing tourism projects from the perspective of collaboration has enabled many projects (in protected areas in particular) to become co-managed, achieving a clearer long-term vision for tourism in a given area and increasing access to the decision-making process. Collaboration theory has been highly regarded the field of tourism as a livelihood strategy in developing countries as a means to increase community participation and decision-making capabilities. Collaboration theory critics regard collaboration theory principles as essential goals to strive for, but state that due to the lack of clarity of this theory, it is impractical and often ineffective.

References and further reading

Gajda, R. (2004) Utilizing collaboration theory to evaluate alliances. *American Journal of Evaluation* 25(1), 65–77.

Jamal, T. and Stronza, A. (2009) Collaboration theory and tourism practice in protected areas: stakeholders, structuring and sustainability. *Journal of Sustainable Tourism* 17(2), 169–189.

Selin, S. and Chavez, D. (1995) Developing a collaborative model for environmental planning and management. *Environmental Management* 19(2), 189–195.

Self Determination Theory

Self determination theory (SDT) is a psychological theory that explores people's motivations as a means to predict human behavior in a social context. The basic premise of SDT is that people are active organisms, with innate tendencies toward psychological growth and development, seeking to master ongoing challenges and maintain an optimal level of stimulation. SDT specifies three innate and universal psychological needs: competence, autonomy (self-determination) and relatedness, and the ongoing satisfaction of these needs are crucial for self-determination.

SDT has been instrumental in tourism marketing and service development. In marketing, this theory has enabled a more targeted and specified approach to various tourism destinations and services, particularly eco- and adventure tourism. In service development, SDT has enabled tourism practitioners to define more readily insights regarding what tourists are looking for (experience). As a result, practitioners can develop sites, activities and services that cater to the motivational and experiential needs of tourists. To a lesser degree, SDT has also been employed to understand the role of host communities and the motivations that encourage or dissuade them from becoming engaged (directly or indirectly) in the tourism industry.

Further reading

Deci, E.L. and Ryan, R.M. (1991) A motivational approach to self: integration in personality. In: Dienstbier R. (ed.) *Nebraska Symposium on Motivation*, Vol. 38, *Perspectives on Motivation*. University of Nebraska Press, Lincoln, Nebraska, pp. 237–288.

White, C. and Thompson, M. (2009) Self-determination theory and the wine club attribute formation process. *Annals of Tourism Research* 36(4), 561–586.

Group/Grid Theory

Group/grid theory is an anthropological theory that aims to explain social relations, positions, and behavior. This theory evaluates the role and influence of the individual to larger groups and vice versa. The concept of "group" in this theory explains the extent to which people are restricted in thought and action by their commitment to a social unit larger than the individual (Gross and Rayner, 1985). High group is classified through strong communal affiliation. Low group, conversely, is represented by individualistic tendencies. The concept of "grid" is referred to as a complementary bundle of constraints on social interaction or the degree to which an individual is constrained by the external (group). These dimensions enable researchers to assess the role, function and behavioral aspects of individuals as shaped by, or as a reaction to, social rules.

Group/grid theory has been extensively employed in the social sciences (to predict political trends, in response to social rules and resulting policies, to compare different demographics, etc.). This theory has also been employed in business and marketing (due to its predictability in trends). In tourism, this theory has been used in the services industry as well as in tourism marketing. More recently, this theory has also been employed in evaluating travel patterns (return visits, destinations, migration as a result of tourism industry). This theory has also been used in tourism to assess the globalized nature of tourism and the impacts of these on national, regional, or cultural identity.

References and further reading

Duval, T. (2006) Grid/Group theory and its applicability to tourism and migration. *Tourism Geographies* 8(1), 1–14.
Gross, L. and Rayner, S. (1985) *Measuring Culture: A Paradigm for the Analysis of Social Organization*. Columbia University Press, New York.

Actor-Network Theory

Actor-network theory (ANT) is a sociological theory that examines the mechanics of power through the construction and maintenance of networks (both human and non-human). The primary focus of ANT is on the relationships between non-humans and humans, and natural and social spheres. Additionally, this theory is concerned with the processes by which scientific disputes become closed, ideas accepted, and tools and methods adopted. This theory rejects distinctions between science and technology. Instead it explores and follows the strategies actors use to mobilize allies, as well as resources, which ultimately results in the construction of heterogeneous networks. Actors become involved in networks through the process of translation. Translation is an ongoing process as it is never permanent and may fail in some circumstances. Thus, ANT focuses on processes that are ever changing and uses the reconfiguration of relationships to explain these changes while offering diverse perspectives on a given issue.

ANT has been employed widely in social sciences because it relies on a large number of concepts including actors, networks, intermediaries, and the elements of translation. As a result, ANT is a suited theoretical approach for multidisciplinary fields including tourism. ANT has been employed in tourism to understand the concept of tourism in new ways; as a hybrid collective in perpetual movement; as a series of networks that shape and guide its own process, and with the essential components of actors, non-human entities, and interactions. Van de Duim (2007) coined the term "tourismscapes," which consist of relations between people and things dispersed in time-space-specific patterns. Thus, tourism spaces are constructed and guided by the series of relationships and networks that occur within a given space. ANT has also been used to understand better the relationships of tourism stakeholders and their role and influence in managing tourism. Moreover, ANT provides a powerful way of revealing stakeholder differences and understanding how these differences affect scientific practices and overall project success.

References and further reading

Paget, E., Dimanche, F. and Mounet, J. (2010) A tourism innovation case: An actor-network approach. *Annals of Tourism Research* 37(3), 828–847.

Rodger, K., More, S. and Newsome, D. (2009) Wildlife tourism, science and actor network theory. *Annals of Tourism Research* 36(4), 645–666.

Van der Duim, R. (2007) Tourismscapes and actor-network perspective. *Annals of Tourism Research* 34(4), 961–976.

The Contact Hypothesis

The contact hypothesis is a way to predict the social behavior of different groups with seemingly little in common (i.e. religion, nationality, gender, race, ethnicity, social standing). The contact hypothesis assumes that different groups with limited or no contact are more likely to have prejudiced opinions and conduct in a discriminatory way toward each other. Thus, the contact hypothesis proposes that interaction/contact between members of different groups reduces intergroup prejudice, and the more contact between groups, the greater the reduction of stereotyping and of discrimination.

The contact hypothesis has been used in a wide range of fields including psychology, race relations, ethnic studies, and behavioral studies. In tourism, the contact hypothesis has been used to evaluate tourists' attitudes (toward a destination, host community, or other tourists) and potential attitude changes over time. This hypothesis has also been used to assess the values and perceptions of travelers and hosts, and examine changes over time through multiple trips to the same destination. This hypothesis has been employed in evaluating international travel, ethnic experiences in travel, and to compare and contrast different groups within a similar tourism experience. Risk and risk perceptions have also been studied in conjunction with this hypothesis.

Further reading

Anastasopoulos, P. (1992) Tourism and attitude change: Greek tourists visiting Turkey. *Annals of Tourism Research* 19(4), 629–642.

Forbes, H. (1997) *Ethnic Conflict: Commerce, Culture and the Contact Hypothesis*. Yale University Press, Boston, Massachusetts.

Pizam, A., Uriely, N. and Reichel, A. (2000) The intensity of tourist–host social relationship and its effect on satisfaction and changes of attitudes: the case of working tourists in Israel. *Tourism Management* 21(4), 395–406.

Path-Goal Theory of Leadership

Path-goal theory seeks to explain varying leadership styles. Path-goal theory states that leaders have to engage in different types of leadership behavior based on the demands of a particular situation so that they can choose the best paths to guide their subordinates toward reaching organizational goals. According to the path-goal theory of leader, there are four leadership styles: directive, achievement-oriented, participative, and supportive. These four styles or concepts can be used to analyze leadership and evaluate its effectiveness in particular situations. This theory has been employed to evaluate the roles of leaders and subordinates in organizations and businesses, and their impact on the overall success of the organizations.

In tourism this theory has been employed predominantly in hospitality research. This theory has been used to evaluate managerial staff, study employee retention, employee perceptions and preferences, and in general service quality studies. This theory has also been employed to generate management/organizational structures. The application of this theory in the hospitality field is vast and extremely applicable for tourism practitioners seeking to become more successful or create better management/working practices.

Further reading

Deery, M. and Jago, L. (2001) Hotel management style: a study of employee perceptions and preferences. *International Journal of Hospitality Management* 20(4), 325–338.

House, R. (1971) A path-goal theory of leader effectiveness. *Administrative Science Quarterly* 16, 321–338.

Ladkin, A. (1999) Hotel general managers: a review of prominent research themes. *International Journal of Tourism Research* 1, 167–193.

Testa, M. (2004) Cultural similarity and service leadership: a look at the cruise industry. *Managing Service Quality* 14(5), 402–413.

Maslow's Hierarchy of Needs Theory

Maslow's hierarchy of needs is a psychological theory that seeks to explain people's needs and motivations. According to this theory, as basic needs are fulfilled people can then begin to think about other needs, thus following a hierarchical model. The hierarchical model outlined in this theory is as follows: fulfillment of basic physiological needs (food, water, shelter), fulfillment of safety (security, insurance), fulfillment of sense of belonging (social demands, love, affection), fulfillment of prestige, self-respect and increased status, and finally self-actualization and sense of complete fulfillment and enjoyment. This theory has been employed in various social science disciplines including sociology, political science, as well as in marketing and business. This theory has been widely employed due to its predictability and applicability at the various hierarchical levels.

In tourism, this theory has been used in a variety of ways, including in evaluating tourism patterns and trends. The hierarchy of needs has also been used to explain tourist's motivations to become engaged in risky behavior (specialists versus generalists) and in the popularization of adventure tourism. Tourism practitioners have been able to draw from this theory to better understand consumer demands and in turn provide the experiences that tourists/consumers expect (destination image, available activities, experiences). This theory has also been instrumental in tourism marketing and outreach by highlighting the potential fulfillment that can be achieved as the hierarchical ladder is climbed (through tourism opportunities).

Further reading

Chon, H. (1991) Tourism destination image modification process: marketing implications. *Tourism Management* 12(1), 68–72.

Gibson, H. and Yianakis, A. (2002) Tourists roles: needs and lifecourse. *Annals of Tourism Research* 29(2), 358–383.

Weber, K. (2001) Outdoor adventure tourism: a review of research approaches. *Annals of Tourism Research* 28(2), 360–377.

Marketing (Communication) Theory

Marketing theory is a business or capital exchange theory that seeks to motivate people to make money exchanges for a particular product. Marketing theory focuses on price, product, place, and promotion. Marketing theory strategies have changed over time from a product-driven approach (i.e. mass tourism) to a more targeted sales approach (demand- or sale-driven approach, i.e. ecotourism, wildlife tourism). The current and most prevalent tourism marketing technique focuses on the needs and desires of consumers. This is critical for tourism promoters to understand in order to be more efficient and effective in promoting tourism destinations and businesses. Technology has enabled this theory to continue to change and has encouraged a more targeted approach.

Marketing theory has been widely employed in the tourism field. This theory has been used to assess competition (of services and destinations), expand and define the role of stakeholders and their impact on destination image, predict tourism business' risks, and generate alternatives to make current strategies more effective. Since marketing theory focuses and targets trends, it can easily be applied in the planning process of tourism projects. Marketing theory, therefore, can enable tourism planners to predict who their consumers will be, how many and what some targeted strategies might look like.

Further reading

Baker, K., Hozier, G. and Roger, R. (1994) Marketing research theory and methodology and the tourism industry: a nontechnical discussion. *Journal of Travel Research* 32(3), 3–9.

Buttle, F. (1996) *Relationship Marketing: Theory and Practice*. Chapman, London.

Co-alignment Model

The co-alignment model is a business model that has been employed in the tourism field, particularly in the hospitality industry to evaluate the performance of the service/hospitality industry. The model acknowledges that the hospitality industry is not an isolated industry and seeks to evaluate its performance and understand its strategies considering the broader market and socio-environmental landscape that shape it. In assuming a more holistic position, the co-alignment model focuses on the relationship between the environment, strategy choice, firm structure, and firm performance. According to Olsen and Roper (1998: 113), the co-alignment takes place:

> If the firm is able to identify the opportunities that exist in the forces driving change, invest in competitive methods that take advantage of these opportunities, and allocate resources to those that create the greatest value, the financial results desired by owners and investors have a much better chance of being achieved.

Thus, the model presents a guideline for success in the hospitality industry. The co-alignment model can also be used to compare and contrast firms' performance.

By analyzing the relationship between environment, strategy choice, firm structure, and firm performance, the co-alignment model is able to better understand hospitality firms, their strategies and their predictions for the future. Additionally, this model can be used to distil major differences in the strategies and approaches of different firms. Also, it can be used to analyze success and develop strategies to achieve that success. As a result, this model has been extensively used in the hotel/service/hospitality industry.

References and further reading

Harrington, R. (2005) The how and who of strategy making: models and appropriateness for firms in hospitality and tourism industries. *Journal of Hospitality & Tourism Research* 29(3), 372–395.
Olsen, M.D. and Roper, A. (1998) Research in strategic management in the hospitality industry. *International Journal of Hospitality Management* 17(2), 111–124.
Prakash, K., Chathoth, P. and Olsen, M. (2005) Testing and developing the environment risk construct in hospitality strategy research. *Journal of Hospitality & Tourism Research* 29(3), 312–340.

Intimacy Theory

Intimacy theory is a socio-psychological theory that aims to explain different facets of intimacy (how and why people seek to become intimate, and how intimacy is retained). Intimacy theory argues that four types of intimacy exist: physical intimacy (actual contact), verbal intimacy (exchange of words and communication), spiritual intimacy (sharing values and beliefs), and intellectual intimacy (sharing reflection and disclosures of knowledge). This theory is prevalent in tourism due to the concept and reality of place. In tourism situations, intimacies within a place are created by interaction with those local to that place, and that intimacy and meanings associated with a place emerge from the nature of the interaction between those who visit the place; particularly when those people possess meaningful relationships between them. Additionally, the meaning of place recaptures memories of shared behaviors that reinforce personal intimacies.

In tourism, high level of intimacy can be expressed though frequent/return visits (childhood memories) or through a deep connection with locals or insiders. The two instances will make a place/destination both memorable and intimate. Authenticity and unique experiences from the perspective of the tourist also enhance his/her level of intimacy with a place or experience. This theory has been employed in conjunction with the concepts of "place attachment," "place meaning," and "place identity" in the tourism literature.

Further reading

Piorkowski, K. and Cardone, S. (2000) *Too Close for Comfort: Exploring the Risks of Intimacy*. Perseus Publishing, Boulder, Colorado.

Trauer, B. and Ryan, C. (2006) Destination image, romance and place experience – an application of intimacy theory in tourism. *Tourism Management* 21, 481–491.

Vela, M. (2009) Rural-cultural excursion conceptualization: a local tourism-marketing model based on tourist destination image measurement. *Tourism Management* 30(3), 419–428.

Complex Systems Theory

Complex systems theory (CST) is a sociological theory that is largely rooted in ecology, predominantly in the field of ecosystem services and functioning. CST provides a more holistic perspective to understand and analyze complex problems. CST recognizes the importance of networks, relationships, and systems. CST acknowledges that systems are dynamic and non-linear, and as a result advocates against simple solutions to complex problems and predictions. CST draws upon understandings of ecosystem functioning (exploitation and conservation) and the dimensions of release and reorganization (the adaptive cycle metaphor); focusing on the property of ecosystem resilience which draws attention to the amount of disturbance a system can absorb while retaining functions and structure; and re-conceptualizing hierarchical features as panarchies which are both nested and connected. CST can be understood in the metaphor of an organism—a living system, which can change and adapt based on feedback. CST states that everything is interconnected and that a part of the whole cannot be understood in isolation.

CST has been extensively used in the tourism discipline. CST has been used to understand the relationship between conservation, development, and tourism. CST advocates that tourism cannot be analyzed in isolation, but that it is embedded in larger system and the networks and flows of these must be understood as a whole first, and then analyze its components. CST has also been used to better understand tourists' travel patterns by recognizing the myriad of values, ideals, and choices that come into play in choosing a destination/activity in which to participate. CST has been employed in tourism planning research, encouraging long-term strategic planning, equilibrium and stability. In addition, Dredge (2006) has shown that CST may be effective for understanding the interrelationships and structures between various actors (stakeholders) in the tourism arena, including government, tourism service providers, and civil society.

References and further reading

Dredge, D. (2006) Networks, conflict and collaborative communities. *Journal of Sustainable Tourism* 14(6), 562–581.

Plummer, R. and Fennell, D. (2009) Managing protected areas for sustainable tourism: prospects for adaptive co-management. *Journal of Sustainable Tourism* 17(2), 149–168.

Tourism Area Life Cycle Model

Butler's 1980 tourism area life cycle (TALC) model aims to explain how and why tourism destinations come to be, how they persist, become successful or fail. Butler's model states that a destination begins relatively unknown and visitors initially come in small numbers restricted by lack of access, facilities, or knowledge (exploration phase). As more people discover the destination, the word spreads about its attractions and the amenities are increased and improved (development phase). Tourist arrivals then begin to grow rapidly toward a preconceived carrying capacity (social and environmental limits) (stagnation phase). The model also states that these three phases occur rapidly but the phase post-stagnation is not always clear. It is possible that a destination may enter a new phase (rejuvenation phase) where technology, infrastructure or knowledge will improve and the carrying capacity will increase. However, if a destination is not properly managed or is competing with another similar destination, tourism development could fail (decline phase).

TALC has been extensively used to better plan and develop tourism projects and understand better how to improve the condition of existing tourism destination areas. TALC has also been used to re-define the kind of development and tourism sought in particular destination areas and has been used to assess economic trends in tourism. TALC has also served as a warning and encouraged innovation in tourism and improved quality service in the tourism field. In addition to serving as a guide for destination areas, TALC has also served as a guide for tourism industries including hospitality and advertising.

Further reading

Lozano, J., Gomez, C. and Rey-Maquiera, J. (2008) The TALC hypothesis and economic growth theory. *Tourism Economics* 14(4), 727–749.

Zhong, L., Deng, Y. and Xiang, B. (2008) Tourism development and the tourism are a life-cycle model: a study of Zhangjiajie National Forest Park, China. *Tourism Management* 29(5), 841–856.

Resistance Theory

Resistance theory is a sociological theory that focuses on understanding social thresholds. This theory is used to explain an individual or group tolerance, adaptability, flexibility, and change. Resistance theory states that there is a wide spectrum of resistance, from fully closed (most resistant) to fully open (least resistant). This theory has also been used to better understand group cohesion and group mentality as well as group responses and decision-making processes.

Resistance theory has been employed in tourism in a variety of ways, including in assessing group dynamics (tourist groups as well as tourism industry workers), and in evaluating how communities adapt to new tourism enterprises or innovations. However, this theory has been most prevalent evaluating how host communities respond to the tourist gaze (see Tourists' Gaze (Concept)). The spectrum of this theory has been used to evaluate the authenticity of host communities, and how strong their resistance is to behave in a way that is expected by the tourist versus to conduct themselves in a genuine behavior regardless of tourists and their preconceived notions. The concept of authenticity can therefore be quantified and qualified under this theory. Resistance theory in tourism has been most prevalent in assessing the impact of tourism and tourists on indigenous, remote groups or groups belonging to a different religion or religious minority. Resistance theory aims to provide a solid foundation to understand better the complex relationship between hosts and tourists.

Further reading

Chhabra, D. (2009) How they see us: perceived effects of tourist gaze on the old order Amish. *Journal of Travel Research* 49(1), 93–105.

Tourists' Gaze (Concept)

The tourists' gaze is a socio-geographical concept developed by John Urry in the late 1980s and early 1990s, which seeks to explain the complex relationship between hosts and tourists. The tourists' gaze concept seeks to highlight the relations of power and behavioral mechanisms that are set forth in tourists. Urry defines the tourist gaze as a practice of the consumption that is extraordinary to tourists. Tourists' extraordinary consumption may be manifested in a festival, ritual, or simply in consuming the events of the hosts' daily lives. The tourists' gaze, therefore, enables tourists to collect and reflect on these novel experiences and perhaps formulate ideas or notions of new gazes they would like to experience. However, the tourists' gaze is essential in explaining the power imbalances between the hosts and tourists. The tourists' gaze is also crucial in highlighting the differences between the extraordinary and the ordinary. Therefore, for hosts, their actions are simply ordinary, thus in addition to being viewed or consumed they are not able to collect new and novel experiences.

The tourists' gaze has been a central concept in tourism studies, especially in evaluating the relationship between tourism and globalization. The tourists' gaze, it is argued, no longer occurs while on-site and is not simply shaped by the social and physical landscape of the moment, but it has the potential to be previously constructed through media, internet, film, etc. These new modes of communication have therefore changed and enhanced the tourists' gaze and how it might impact both tourists and hosts.

Further reading

Maoz, D. (2006) The mutual gaze. *Annals of Tourism Research* 33(1), 221–239.

Recreation Experience Preference Model

The recreation experience preference (REP) scale is a model based on motivation theory. Motivation theory has been instrumental in tourism and leisure studies by identifying what motivates people to engage in travel and/or leisure activities. The experiential model states that recreation should not be viewed merely as an activity but rather, it should be conceptualized as a psycho-physiological experience that is self-rewarding, occurs during non-obligated free time, and is the result of free choice. REP scales, developed by Beverly Driver in the 1960s, are a way to measure the dimensions of people's recreation experience.

The REP scales suggest that a critical motivation for engaging in new experiences (in the outdoors) is attaining certain psychological and physical goals. Therefore an experience was considered a "bundle" of psychological outcomes desired from a recreation engagement. The experience (not the motivation) holds the explanation of why people engage in recreation, gives guidance in understanding what people want from recreation, and offers insight into how it might benefit them.

REP has improved the understanding of what "product" recreationists seek and, as a result, has been extensively used in wildland and tourism planning and management in an effort to avoid conflict and provide a desired product for all. In tourism, REP has been used in marketing as well as in the hospitality industry. It has also been instrumental in the development of alternative forms of tourism (eco-, adventure tourism, volun-tourism, etc.). In marketing, REP has been employed to rebrand destinations and activities. Generally, REP has been used to provide a more comprehensive understanding of the needs and desires of tourists and has motivated the tourism industry to offer a tourism experience.

Further reading

Manfredo, M., Driver, B. and Tarrant, M. (1996) Measuring leisure motivation: A meta-analysis of the recreation experience preference scales. *Journal of Leisure Research* 28(3), 188–213.

Travel Career Ladder Model

Pearce's travel career ladder (TCL) model, developed in the 1980s, is based upon Maslow's hierarchy of needs. The TCL model illustrates the trajectory of psychological maturation towards a goal of self-actualization. TCL specifies that there are five different hierarchical steps affecting tourist behavior, which include: a concern with biological needs (including relaxation), safety and security needs (or levels of stimulation), relationship development and extension needs, special interest and self-development needs, and fulfillment or deep involvement needs (formally defined as self-actualization).

TCL has been equated with the trajectory in a career. Like a career, people start at different levels and are likely to change their levels during their lifecycle. The TCL model also shows that needs change with experiences acquired. Like in a career where more experience leads to more responsibility and higher expectations, in tourism, more experience also leads tourists to desire new satisfaction goals. Therefore the TCL model demonstrates the dynamic nature of motivations and satisfactions. The model also focuses on the personal and intuitive nature of the motivational forces that exist and discusses the relationship between experience, motivation, and satisfaction.

In tourism, this model has been instrumental to assess tourism motivation, purchase decisions, measures of self-concept, holiday satisfaction, changing needs while on holiday, adaptive holiday behaviors, and suboptimal decisions due to constrained choice. This model has been extremely useful for tourism promoters and operators since it has enabled them to acknowledge tourists' expectations so they might be able to satisfy their needs.

This model has been criticized for its simplicity and the fact that it does not fully recognize that steps in the hierarchical ladder might be skipped and that outmost fulfillment has the potential to be achieved lower in the ladder. Despite these critiques, TCL continues to serve as an instrumental model in the tourism field and continues to be extremely relevant in predicting future tourism trends.

Further reading

Ryan, C. (1998) The travel ladder: an appraisal. *Annals of Tourism Research* 25(4), 936–957.

Grounded Theory

Grounded theory is an approach to research that is based on system theory and differs from traditional research approaches. Grounded theory is most accurately described as a research method in which the theory is developed from the data, rather than the other way around. That makes this an inductive approach, meaning that it moves from the specific to the more general. Grounded theory focuses on social patterns and behaviors and draws generalizations, theoretical underpinnings, and hypotheses based on those patterns. In observing patterns, grounded theory also recognizes the systems and networks in place that shape and guide the patterns. As a result, grounded theory also is able to transcend a particular setting, time, or place and broaden to a more abstract system of interrelated concepts. Grounded theory, which is itself a process, is an organized set of principles and methodology.

Grounded theory has been used extensively in the disciplines of sociology, anthropology, and geography. To a lesser degree it has also been used in socioeconomic tourism studies. Additionally, due to the large emphasis on observation, it has also been used for other tourism studies, including travel pace, travel destination and in assessing the relationship between hosts and tourists. However, it should be mentioned that grounded theory better serves tourism as a research approach and process for analysis rather than as a theoretical underpinning.

Further reading

Lumsdon, L. and McGrath, P. (2011) Developing a conceptual framework for slow travel: a grounded theory approach. *Journal of Sustainable Tourism* 19(3), 265–279.
Stillman, S. (2006) Grounded theory and grounded action: rooted in systems theory. *World Futures* 62(7), 498–504.

Modernization (Economic) Theory

The modernization theory is one of many economic (growth) theories and has had most prevalence in the disciplines of economics and sociology. According to modernization theory, economic development is an endogenous process, and all societies have the potential to achieve it. The theory identifies different societies at different points of the traditional–modern development continuum, placed according to indices such as GNP, per capita income, acceptance of "modern values," social differentiation, or political integration, but all are following the evolutionary path to a common goal, modernization. Modernization theory also recognizes that there are stages of economic advancement that must be fulfilled in order to achieve modernity. The trajectory toward development starts with a traditional society and then moves towards a society focused on mass consumption. Modernization theory argues that the economic benefits then are able to trickle down and spread economic growth.

Modernization theory has been employed in tourism to critique tourism economic development. Many critics argue that tourism development follows modernization theory underpinnings, which, they claim, are merely looking at the economic aspect and neglect the social and environmental components. Critics also argue that a firm end goal (of becoming modernized) is unrealistic since the characteristics of each community are different and thus the results are likely to change. Modernity theory has been used to challenge the way that (eco/sustainable) tourism is discussed and advocates for new ways of understanding concepts of "growth" and "equity" that stay true to the principles of ecotourism.

Further reading

Sharpley, R. (2000) Tourism and sustainable development: exploring the theoretical divide. *Journal of Sustainable Tourism* 8(1), 1–19.

New Environmental/Ecological Paradigm

The new environmental paradigm (NEP) is a scale that measures pro-environmental orientation. The NEP scale was designed by sociologists Dunlap *et al.* (2002) in the late 1970s in an effort to obtain a research instrument that could measure the social concerns of the time, predominantly the state and health of the environment, and the relationship of people and the environment. Since the 1970s, the NEP scale has been revised (and is commonly known as the New Ecological Paradigm) to provide a wider range of facets of an ecological worldview and offer a balanced set of pro- and anti-NEP items. Since its development, the scale has been used in many other studies, both replicating as well as modifying the scale. Many of the studies conducted since then have questioned whether in fact a paradigmatic shift is occurring or has occurred. However, most researchers agree that the scale developed by Dunlap *et al.* (2002) is considered one valid measure of environmental attitude.

NEP has been extensively used in the field of politics, particularly in environmental policy issues. This measurement tool enables politicians and policy-makers to have a better understanding of the attitudes, ethics, and values of their constituents.

As a result, NEP has been used to predict trends and outcomes. In tourism NEP has served as a tool to indicate whether tourists prefer "green" or "sustainable" tourism enterprises/projects. NEP has served as an instrument to evaluate trends and attitudes in the hospitality industry, marketing, and in assessing destination choices.

Reference

Dunlap, R., Van Liere, K., Mertig, A. and Jones, R. (2002) New trends in measuring environmental attitudes: measuring endorsement of the new ecological paradigm: a revised NEP scale. *Journal of Social Issues* 56(3), 425–442.

Attribution Theory

Attribution theory is a socio-psychological theory concerned with how individuals interpret events and how this relates to their thinking and behavior. Attribution theory assumes that people try to determine why people do what they do. Attributions are classified along three causal dimensions: locus of control, stability, and controllability. The locus of control dimension has two poles: internal versus external locus of control. The stability dimension captures whether causes change over time or not. For instance, ability can be classified as a stable, internal cause, and effort classified as unstable and internal. Controllability contrasts causes a person can control, such as skill/efficacy, from causes out of a person's control, such as aptitude, mood, others' actions, and luck. Attribution theory is closely associated with the concept of motivation.

Attribution theory has been used in the education field to better understand leadership and achievement skills. This theory has also been used to better understand the organizational structures of business, schools, hospitals, hotels, etc. in tourism. This theory has been used in the hospitality field and has also been extensively used in tourism planning. It has enabled tourism planners to better understand tourist's motivations, expectations, and satisfaction, and thus provide a better product or experience.

Further reading

Gnoth, J. (1997) Tourism motivation and expectation formation. *Annals of Tourism Research* 24(2), 283–304.
Weiner, B. (2010) Attribution theory. In: *Corsini Encyclopedia of Psychology*. John Wiley & Sons, Hoboken, New Jersey.

Regulation Theory

Regulation theory is a political economy theory that seeks to explain the relationship between capitalism and social institutions. According to regulation theory, this relationship is critical to understand the processes of capitalist growth, crisis, and re-production. As a result, this theory focuses the process of accumulation and the ensemble of institutional forms and practices, which together comprise the mode of social regulation.

These institutional forms and practices guide and stabilize the accumulation process and create a temporary resolution to the crisis tendencies, which are seen to be endemic in the accumulation process. The mode of regulation is neither predetermined nor inevitable, as structural forms result from social struggles and conflict. The mode of regulation is the means of institutionalizing these struggles between competing interests leading to the bounds that reproduce and legitimate the balance between production and consumption within a particular regime of accumulation. This places emphasis on the relationships between the main social actors in these processes, including the local and national state, which act as mediators.

This theory has been employed in the field of politics and has been instrumental in explaining decision making, group consensus building, and development and economic growth. It has also been employed to explain new political trends and predict outcomes. This theory has been used to evaluate the role of social institutions and capital institutions (governments versus corporations). This theory has been widely discussed in critiques of globalization and in sustainable development (and sustainable tourism) research. Recently (2000s), this theory has been used to explain the relationship between nature and capital (natural capital) and policy.

Further reading

Bridge, G. (2000) The social regulation of resources access and environmental impact: production, nature and contradiction in the US copper industry. *Geoforum* 31, 237–256.

Appendix: Additional Theories Applied in the Context of Tourism

Index

Index for 'Demystifying Theories in Tourism Research'
